BLACK CULTURE

READING AND WRITING BLACK

BLACK CULTURE

READING AND WRITING BLACK

GLORIA M. SIMMONS
Loop College

HELENE D. HUTCHINSON
Kendall College

Under the direction of HENRY E. SIMMONS
Indiana University, Northwest

New York Chicago San Francisco
Atlanta Dallas Montreal Toronto

HOLT
RINEHART
AND WINSTON, INC.

To Our Children

Goddess *Rob*

Giselle *Laura*

Cover photograph

Reprinted from *African Image* by Sam *Haskins*. Copyright © 1967 by
Samuel Haskins. Published by Grosset & Dunlap, Inc.

Photographs in the Ideology montage, pages 228-229,
are used courtesy of the following: Ted Streshinsky/
Photo Researchers, Inc. (Bobby Seale); *The News,* New
York's Picture Newspaper (Marcus Garvey); Photo Re-
searchers, Inc. (Malcolm X and Jesse Jackson); Chester
Higgins, Jr. (LeRoi Jones); Wide World Photos (Stokely
Carmichael); Tomi Ungerer (Black Power/White Power
poster).

INTRODUCTION

South African scholar Ezekiel Mphalele has bemoaned the fact that many Black writers have dressed up Africa and the Afro-American scene in their finest gowns before bringing them out to meet the public. His statement against a monolithic "Black is beautiful" theme is well founded, and major steps must be taken to correct this picture by the new generation of Black artists.

America has never been beautiful in the broadest sense, nor has any other country entirely portrayed the love-thy-neighbor philosophy throughout its history where minority groups are concerned. However, the ugliness that is part of the American scene permeates the entire society and leans its weight upon the shoulders of Black Americans to such a degree that the whole spectrum of Black existence is touched daily by it. Thus, while an anthology of Black culture may have its many highlights of beauty, it must (like this one) show also the sordid and macabre moments as well.

To begin, few aspects of Black life anywhere escape the African past. The rebellion in the minds of teenage Blacks today differs little from that violent desire for freedom expressed by Cinque, Chaka or Toussaint L'Ouverture. The sharp language of Atlanta, Vine City or Pittsburgh's Hill District is simply a variation of the gut music which Africans and West Indians have been expressing for years in a multitude of ways. All form part of the beauty of Blackness.

The Black man has provided the "strange fruit" for the white man's lynching trees down through the years. Our women have borne their children, knowing in the agonies of childbirth that the tender skull might be smashed against a post by some good citizen expressing his manhood during a visit by the mob to the Black reservation. We have taken up guns to protect our young and our women, and we have killed with a passion that only oppressed people can enjoy.

But we have loved as well in our own way. We have thrilled to that symphony of motion as a proud Black woman strides down 47th St., King Drive or 125th St. bearing all of the traces of her Senegalese background with head held high. We have sung out our love in the patriotic efforts of Peter Salem, William Carney, Dorie Miller and the Buffalo Soldiers fighting for a dream we have yet to realize. And we have blasted out the tune of *determined love* as a last resort from the flaming rooftops of Haiti, Charleston, Newark, and Cleveland's Hough District. But it has not been felt or heard by most.

Consequently, any literary discussion of Black culture must include our different message of love in all of its variations. In the world of the poet, the word "nigger" must be beautiful as well as degrading; endearing—and deadly. The antics of some "Uncle Toms" must be shown as anti-Black, but other "Uncle Toms" (like Brer Rabbit) must be lauded for their abilities to make fools of oppressing white men as a survival technique.

The "dozens" we play and the spirituals we sing are, as one, part of the basis for an understanding of Black life, and as literary forms, are as legitimate as Shakespeare's works. This is true because Black writers most often use their pens to relate experiences rather than ideals. There is neither a "Black style" nor an homogeneous school of thought which spells out the central themes of our lives without the inclusion of the oral, the audial, the visual and the written juxtaposed to compliment each other.

Some slaves *did* shuffle their feet and wear assinine grins; some Blacks *do* spend most of their daylight hours singing of heavenly pie-in-the-sky; and some bourgeoise Negroes *do* run as fast as they can to get to the suburbs away from all that reminds them of the past. However, other slaves chopped off the masters' heads while wearing that assinine grin; and some used spirituals to pass messages of rebellion along ("One of these days, it won't be long, you'll look for me and I'll be gone"); and the new Black revolution has thousands of Brooks Brothers-wearing proponents taking an active part in all phases. And all are part of Black culture.

In pride and shame and love and hatred and sadness and ugliness and bountious beauty which is our very own, we walk through life realizing that there is no Black poetry or prose or art of any kind which does not carry in its bosom the songs of our struggle. There is no song we sing which is not, at once joyous and sad. The classicism of Countee Cullen, the dialect of Paul Laurence Dunbar and the raucus realism of James Baldwin expose our souls to ourselves—and on rare occasions to that larger world which is most often too blind to see and too proud to care.

But our beauty concepts might bruise the senses of some who have not lived our lives. Our realism might shock the minds of those whose lives take on cocoon-like qualities. We, for instance, do not erase the "cullud boy" from our culture, for he deserves a place on the blackboard of our school of life just as does the bourgeois Negro who has forgotten what his mama did for a living to put him through school. We sit Nat Turner, "Sambo", H. Rap Brown, Gwendolyn Brooks, Martin Luther King, Jr., Malcolm X, Roy Wilkins and Marcus Garvey in the same pews of our lives and all contribute to the collection. The Wrights, Toomers, Hughes, Lees and Dunbars march side-by-side to tell our story while Ray Charles sings the melody.

Black *is* beautiful, but there is nothing beautiful about being Black and ignorant of your culture or your heritage! And white can be beautiful too, *if* after reading this collection, the white man has felt himself choking on the rancid sowbelly fed to slaves in the hole of a slave ship, or experienced the nausea produced by the stench from an outdoor privy marked "colored only." Somewhere down the line, suffering creates a commonality which is hard to overcome.

This is Black culture. To paraphrase the Rev. Jesse Jackson, Blacks are tired of being the ingredients scorched at the bottom of America's legendary melting pot, and unless that pot is stirred up enough to allow us to become part of the whole stew, we just might turn the whole damn pot over! This is the determined love and dedication, that whole self which we call the Black world which the editors capture so beautifully in this book. To read it may scar the tender soul, but the Black man, and those who understand, are more likely to lift every voice and sing "I am somebody"!

HENRY E. SIMMONS, CHAIRMAN
Afro-American Studies Department
Indiana University, Northwest

CONTENTS

Introduction v
List of Illustrations xvii

THE BEAUTY OF BLACK

ON BLACKNESS

Color *Langston Hughes 3*
what color is black? *Barbara Mahone McBain 3*
Evolution of a Word *Geraldine Morris 4*
Blue Black *Blake Modisane 4*
My Blackness Is the Beauty of This Land *Lance Jeffers 5*
Evil Is No Black Thing *Sarah Webster Fabio 6*
The Night Is Beautiful *Langston Hughes 7*
Black *Senora Richardson 8*
The Beauty of the Rose *Henry E. Simmons 8*

THINGS BLACK AND BEAUTIFUL

For Langston Hughes *Conrad Kent Rivers 12*
We Wear the Mask *Paul Laurence Dunbar 14*
What Is Black? *Mary O'Neill 15*
Alan Paton Will Die *Johnie Scott 16*
Personally *James Kilgore 17*

ix

BLACK WOMAN

The Black Finger	*Angeline W. Grimke*	*19*
Black Woman	*Leopold-Sedar Senghor*	*20*
To a Black Dancer	*David Diop*	*22*
A Song of Praise	*Countee Cullen*	*24*
Sugar Woman	*Sterling Plumpp*	*24*
The Black Woman	*Paul Nathaniel Johnson—Ahmadin*	*26*
The Black Madonna	*Harun Kofi Wangara*	
	(Harold G. Lawrence)	*27*
Flowers of Darkness	*Frank Marshall Davis*	*28*
For Our Women	*Larry Neal*	*30*
Karintha	*Jean Toomer*	*31*

BLACK MAN

But He Was Cool or he even stopped for green lights	*don l. lee*	*34*
The Smoke King	*W. E. B. DuBois*	*35*
to all sisters	*sonia sanchez*	*35*
Sonnet to a Negro in Harlem	*Helene Johnson*	*36*
I, Too	*Langston Hughes*	*36*
Black	*Lori Lunford*	*37*
About Man	*Johari Amini (Jewel C. Latimore)*	*37*

MAN AND WOMAN

A Necessary Poem	*Nayo (barbara malcom)*	*39*
Beautiful, Black and Beloved	*Margaret Burroughs*	*40*
From Soul Madness	*Val Ferdinand*	*40*
To All Black Women, From All Black Men	*Eldridge Cleaver*	*41*
A Black Ritual	*Robert MacBeth*	*46*
We	*Bernard Gunther*	*49*

LANGUAGE OF SOUL

A LANGUAGE OF MY OWN

Meet Josh   *Josh Fleming 52*
Language Behavior in the Black Community   *Thomas Kochman 53*
Words in Testament of My Nigger Son   *Robert H. DeCoy 56*
The First Dictionary of Nigrite Words   *Robert H. DeCoy 58*
A Chant for Children   *Frank Horne 66*
Incident   *Countee Cullen 66*

JIVE

Harlem Jive   *Dan Burley 67*
Test Your Knowledge of Harlem Jive Talk,
Idioms, Folk Expressions   *Dan Burley 70*
Rhymed Jive   *Dan Burley 72*
"The Barefoot Boy"—A Parody in Harlem Jive   *Dan Burley 73*
Willie Cool Digs the Scene   *Dan Burley 73*

SOUL

Saturday Night   *Langston Hughes 76*
Soul   *Barbara Simmons 77*
The Language of Soul   *Claude Brown 78*

BLACK POWER IS BLACK LANGUAGE

Black Power Is Black Language   *Geneva Smitherman 85*

LANGUAGE AS REVOLUTION

Black Art   *LeRoi Jones 94*
The Undaunted Pursuit of Fury   *Time 95*

PSYCHE OF THE WHITE

THE PSYCHOLOGICAL PERSPECTIVE

How It Looks to Blacks *Time 103*

White Hang-Up *Time 104*

The White American Psyche—
Exploration of Racism *Lloyd T. Delany 106*

THE SEXUAL IMPLICATIONS OF RACISM

The Sexualization of Racism *Calvin C. Hernton 115*

On Being Crazy *W. E. B. DuBois 118*

RACISM AS EXPLOITATION

When in Rome *Mari Evans 122*

Son in the Afternoon *John A. Williams 124*

For a Lady I Know *Countee Cullen 129*

WHITE MILITANTS

The White Race and Its Heroes *Eldridge Cleaver 131*

THE LOVE IT OR LEAVE IT SYNDROME

From Day of Absence *Douglas Turner Ward 136*

MULTIPLE CHOICE

Massa Sussman's First Annual Social
Awareness and Polarized Society Rent-a-Honkie
Multiple Choice Quiz *Vic Sussman 138*

VIOLATED SELF

THE ORDEAL OF BOBBY SEALE

How Blacks View Gagging of Seale   *L. F. Palmer, Jr. 147*
Then They Came for Me   *Robert A. Wilson 149*
"7" Judge Has a Sunnier Side   *Mike Royco 149*

OTHER LYNCHINGS

From "Colors"   *Countee Cullen 151*
i saw them lynch   *carol freeman 152*
Blood-Burning Moon   *Jean Toomer 153*
Between the World and Me   *Richard Wright 159*

CHRIST IS BLACK

Christ in Alabama   *Langston Hughes 163*
The Boy Who Painted Christ Black   *John Hendrik Clarke 163*

THE NEGATIVE ROLE

Status Symbol   *Mari Evans 168*
Brass Spittoons   *Langston Hughes 169*
"You Want a Job, Boy?"   *Eddie Polk 169*
The Hands of the Blacks   *Luis Bernado Honwana 170*

SELF-HATE

Black Bourgeoisie   *LeRoi Jones 171*
Leroy   *LeRoi Jones 173*
Wake-Up Niggers   *Don Lee 174*
Portrait of a White Nigger   *Carolyn Rodgers 174*
Is You Is . . .?   *Ruwa Chiri 175*
Consequence   *David Reese Moody 176*
Because of the King of France   *Adrienne Cornell 177*
The Negro   *Bernard Pearson 181*

LOST IDENTITY

Lost Identity   *Eugene Perkins 183*
Black Jam for Dr. Negro   *Mari Evans 183*
Listen, America, Ebony Middle-Class is Talking   *Jeanne Taylor 184*
A Man of the Middle Class   *Gwendolyn Brooks 184*
Middle-Class Negroes and the Negro Masses   *Whitney M. Young, Jr. 186*

RAGE

SONGS OF HATE

The So-Called White Society's Plight and Racism   *193*
Militant   *Langston Hughes 194*
Warning   *Langston Hughes 194*
Whiteeyes on Black Thighs   *Ted Joans 195*
Let's Get Violent   *Ted Joans 195*
From a Black Perspective   *Don Lee 195*
A Folk Fabel (For My People)   *Johari Amini (Jewel C. Latimore) 197*
for unborn malcolms   *sonia sanchez 199*
A Dance for Militant Dilettantes   *Al Young 199*

TO DIE IS TO BE A MAN

If We Must Die   *Claude McKay 200*
state/meant   *LeRoi Jones 201*
And We Own the Night   *Jimmy Garrett 202*

EXPLODING GHETTO

Dream Deferred   *Langston Hughes 211*
Riot Sale or Dollar Psyche Fake Out   *Ben Caldwell 212*
Black Phoenix   *Blossom Powe 214*
Burn, Baby, Burn   *Marvin E. Jackmon 215*
On Riots   *Cy Leslie 215*

THE WHY OF VIOLENCE

Numbers   *Geraldine Morris 217*
Letter to a Black Boy   *Bob Teague 218*
May Be Fair . . . But It Sho' Is Hard   *Ghetto Scenes 219*
The Wonder Is There Have Been So Few Riots   *Kenneth Clark 221*
Will There Be Another Riot in Watts?   *Harry Dolan 225*

IDEOLOGY

SEPARATION

On Separation   Malcolm X 230
Integration   Richard J. Margolis 232
Garvey   Tom Dent 233
Organize!   Marcus Garvey 234
Yacub's History   Malcolm X 235
On Education   Booker T. Washington 237
Booker T. and W. E. B.   Dudley Randall 239

INTEGRATION

On Integration   James Farmer 240
On the Death of William Edward Burghardt Du Bois
by African Moonlight and Forgotten Shores   Conrad Kent Rivers 242
From The Talented Tenth   W. E. B. Du Bois 243
The Struggle for the Liberation of the
Black Laboring Masses   A. Philip Randolph 245

VIOLENCE YES OR NO

From Negroes with Guns   Robert F. Williams 247
Black People!   LeRoi Jones 249
Breaking Out   Dick Gregory 249
Hypnotism   Ben Caldwell 251
Nonviolence and the Montgomery Boycott   Martin Luther King, Jr. 252
From "I Have a Dream"   Martin Luther King, Jr. 255
From Beyond Racism   Whitney Young 257
Jesse Jackson   Time 258

COALITION YES OR NO

Malcolm   Sonia Sanchez 260
The Ballot or the Bullet   Malcolm X 261
Black Manifesto   National Black Economic Development
Conference 264
Carmichael Resigns   Robert C. Maynard 266
An Open Letter to Stokely Carmichael   Eldridge Cleaver 268
Black Power and Coalition Politics   Bayard Rustin 270
Letter to a Black Boy   Bob Teague 273

BLACK HERITAGE

SONGS OF THE BELOVED HOMELAND

From "Heritage" — Countee Cullen 278
The Africa Thing — Adam David Miller 279
Outcast — Claude McKay 281
Who Am I? — Jack Shepherd 281

THE AFRICAN PAST

We Delighted, My Friend — Leopold Sedar-Senghor 284
Black America's African Heritage — Jack Shepherd 286
The Talking Drums — Kojo Gyinaye Kyei 287
Blackman's God — Francis Ernest Kobina Parkes 288
Ghana — Basil Davidson 289
The Art of Ife W. Nigeria — Geoffrey Parrinder 292
The Oba of Benin — Bini 294
The Yoruba of S. W. Nigeria — 294
The God of War — Yoruba poem 295
The King of Sedo — Senegal folktale 296

MIDDLE PASSAGE

The Interesting Narrative of the Life of
Olaudah Equiano — Olaudah Equiano 299

THEY CHOSE FREEDOM

Dark Symphony — Melvin Tolson 302
Middle Passage — Robert Hayden 304
Frederick Douglass — Robert Hayden 310
From The Life of Frederick Douglass — 311
Why Blacks Pay Honor to Douglass — L. F. Palmer, Jr. 312
Remembering Nat Turner — Sterling A. Brown 315
Runagate Runagate — Robert Hayden 317
The Rescue of Charles Nalle, Fugitive Slave — Earl Conrad 320

STOLEN HERITAGE

From Lost and Found: Africa and Negro Past — Charles E. Silberman 326
I Thank God I'm Free at Last — spiritual 330

LIST OF ILLUSTRATIONS

THE BEAUTY OF BLACK

Opening Design by Omar Lama 1
Sea Scene, photograph by Cedric Wright 6
Black Masks, Bay Lemmon 8
Black Rose, photograph by Hope H. Wurmfeld 9
Black Swan, photograph by Hope H. Wurmfeld 13
Woodcarving, photographed by Samuel Haskins 14
Starry Sky 15
Black Bird, photograph by Hope H. Wurmfeld 16
Fig Tree, photograph by Samuel Haskins 17
Black Woman, photograph by Pete Turner 18
Black Woman, photograph by Hugh Bell 20
Zulu Dancer, photograph by Samuel Haskins 21
Domba Drummer, photograph by Samuel Haskins 23
Black Woman, photograph by Hugh Bell 25
Girl Painting her Face, photograph by Constance Stuart 26
Black Woman, photograph by Kalamu ya Salaam (val ferdinand) 29
Black Woman, photograph by Hugh Bell 31
Black Man, photograph by Hugh Bell 33
Black Man, photograph by Homer Page 33
Man and Woman, drawing by Omar Lama 38
Kathleen and Eldridge Cleaver 42

LANGUAGE OF SOUL

Chuck Berry, photograph by Jim Marshall 50
White Spook 56
Tiger 65
Black Contemporaries 75
Armed Panther 84
H. Rap Brown 92
Don L. Lee 96
Nikki Giovanni 97
LeRoi Jones 98

PSYCHE OF THE WHITE

At the Time of the Louisville Flood, Margaret Bourke White 100
White Spook 102
Chicago Suburb—September 1966, photograph by Benedict J. Fernandez 106
Old Woman 112
Cartoon by Brad Holland 114
Black Woman, photograph by Hugh Bell 117
Land of the Free, 1967, Dana Chandler 121
Black is . . . , Turner Brown 123
Lithograph by John Lennon 129
Uncle Sam, Fred Pusterla 130
Pentagon—October 1967, photograph by Benedict J. Fernandez 133
Union Square, New York City—May 1964, photograph by Benedict J. Fernandez 135

VIOLATED SELF

Slave Chains 144
Bobby Seale Chained and Gagged 146
Am I Not a Man and Brother? 148
Lynching by Hanging 150
Lynching by Burning 159
Christ Painted Black, photograph by James H. Karales 161
Black Hands 171
Pianist, photograph by W. Eugene Smith 177
Detail from Heironymus Bosch, Black King 181
Photograph by W. Eugene Smith 182
Margin design, Keith Ferdinand 185

RAGE

Black Woman Screaming, photograph by Hugh Bell 191
Black Woman Screaming, photograph by Hugh Bell 192
A Folk Fabel, drawing by Jeff Donaldson 196
Revolutionary, drawing by Aaron Puri Pitts 201
Drawing by Richard Lebenson 202
Newark—July 1967, photograph by Benedict J. Fernandez 210
Ghetto Family 216

IDEOLOGY

Ideology montage 228
Marcus Garvey 233
Black Power, White Power, poster by Tomi Ungerer 248
Dr. Martin Luther King, Wood engraving by Stefan Martin, from a drawing by Ben Shahn 254
Whitney Young 257
Jesse Jackson 259
Malcolm X, drawing by Omar Lama 261
Stokely Carmichael 266

BLACK HERITAGE

Sunrise at Olduvai Gorge, Tanzania, photograph by Joel Baldwin 278
A Vervet in a Reclinata Palm Tree, photograph by Emil Schulthess 280
Dianna and Apollo, sculpture by Jack Jordan 285
Wrist Guard for Hausa Archer, photograph by Joel Baldwin 286
Terra Cotta Head, photograph by Joel Baldwin 291
Benin Relief 293
Devotee of the Thunder God Shango, Yoruba carving 295
Slaves 299
Boston Massacre 303
Slaves in the Hold of a Ship 309
Frederick Douglass 311
Nat Turner in Secret Conference 315
Harriet Tubman 319
Harriet Tubman Armed 323
Memorial to an Important Woman, sculpture photographed by Samuel Haskins 325
Mt. Kenya, photograph by Samuel Haskins 328

BLACK CULTURE

READING AND WRITING BLACK

THE
BEAUTY
OF BLACK

Drawing by Omar Lama.

on
blackness

Color

Langston Hughes

Wear it
Like a banner
For the proud—
Not like a shroud.
Wear it
Like a song
Soaring high—
Not moan or cry.

what color is black?

Barbara Mahone McBain

black is the color of
my little brother's mind
the grey streaks
in my mother's hair
black is the color of
my yellow cousin's smile
the scars upon my
neighbor's wrinkled face.
the color of
the blood we lose
the color of our eyes
is black.
our love of self
of others
brothers sisters
people of a thousand
shades of black
all one.
black is the color of
the feeling that we share
the love we must express
the color of our strength
is black.

Evolution of a Word
Geraldine Morris

black
   insult
      whispered
         behind door
            in alley

black
   bleached
      brown
         called
            colored

black
   pseudo-
      middle class
         Negro

black
   chanted
      from window
         on roof top

black
   shouted
      by children
         in classroom

black
   scribbled
      on building
         and sidewalk

black
   pounding
      out rhythm
         of heartbeats

black
   echoed
      by lips
         spelling
           PRIDE

By permission of Geraldine Morris.

Blue Black
Blake Modisane

God!
glad I'm black;
pitch-forking devil black:
black, black, black;
black absolute of life complete.
greedfully grabbing life's living
stupor drunkenness,
happiness
depth of hurt,
anger of sorrows:
synthesis of joy, sadness,
composite child of life.
pulsating,
brash;
hatred coarse,
joy smooth,
stupid
solomon wise;
sallow
coconut-tree tall.
confused;
sure
diverse continent
   cape mild,
acrid scorching sahara,
temperate mediterranean.
sun-total black;
the one that is I,
the one, no-one,
that is us all.

From *Poems from Black Africa*, edited by Langston Hughes. Copyright © 1963 by Langston Hughes. Reprinted by permission of Indiana University Press.

My Blackness Is the Beauty of This Land

Lance Jeffers

My blackness is the beauty of this land,
my blackness,
tender and strong, wounded and wise,
my blackness:
I, drawling black grandmother, smile muscular and sweet,
unstraightened white hair soon to grow in earth,
work thickened hand thoughtful and gentle on grandson's head
my heart is bloody-razored by a million memories' thrall:

>remembering the crook-necked cracker who spat
>>on my naked body,
>remembering the splintering of my son's spirit
>>because he remembered to be proud
>remembering the tragic eyes in my daughter's
>>dark face when she learned her color's
>>meaning,

and my own dark rage a rusty knife with teeth to gnaw
>my bowels,
my agony ripped loose by anguished shouts in Sunday's
>humble church,
my agony rainbowed to ecstasy when my feet oversoared
>Montgomery's slime,
ah, this hurt, this hate, this ecstasy before I die,
and all my love a strong cathedral!
My blackness is the beauty of this land!

Lay this against my whiteness, this land!
Lay me, young Brutus stamping hard on the cat's tail,
gutting the Indian, gouging the nigger,
booting Little Rock's Minniejean Brown in the buttocks and
>>boast,
>my sharp white teeth derision-bared as I the conqueror
>crush!
Skyscraper-I, white hands burying God's human clouds
>>beneath
>the dust!
Skyscraper-I, slim blond young Empire
>thrusting up my loveless bayonet to rape the sky,
then shrink all my long body with filth and in the gutter lie
as lie I will to perfume this armpit garbage.

While I here standing black beside
wrench tears from which the lies would suck the salt
to make me more American than America . . .
But yet my love and yet my hate shall civilize this land,
this land's salvation.

Reprinted by permission of International Publishers from *The New Black Poetry*, edited by Clarence Major.

Evil Is No Black Thing

Sarah Webster Fabio

1.
Ahab's gaily clad fisherfriends,
questing under the blue skies after
the albino prize find the green sea
cold and dark at its deep center,
but calm—unperturbed by the fates
of men and whales.

Rowing shoreward, with wet and
    empty
hands, their sun-rich smiles fuzz
with bafflement as the frothing
surf buckles underneath and their
sea-scarred craft is dashed to pieces
near the shore: glancing backward,
the spiralling waves are white-capped.

2.
Evil is no black thing: black
the rain clouds attending a storm
but the fury of it neither begins
nor ends there. Weeping tear-clear
rain, trying to contain the hoarse
blue-throated thunder and the fierce
quick-silver tongue of lightning, bands
of clouds wring their hands.

Once I saw dark clouds in Texas
stand by idly while a Northeaster
screamed its icy puffs, ringtailing
raindrops, rolling them into baseballs
of hail, then descending upon the
tin-roofed houses, unrelentingly
battering them down.

From a volume of poems, *A Mirror: A Soul*, Success Publishing Co., San Francisco, 1969. Reprinted by permission of Sarah Webster Fabio.

6

3.

And the night is blackest where
gay throated cuckoos sing among the
dense firs of the Black Forest, where
terrible flurries of snow are blinding
bright: somewhere, concealed here
    deeply,
lies a high-walled town, whitewashed.

Seen at sunset, only the gaping ditch
and overhanging, crooked tree are
    painted
pitch to match the night: but I've seen
a dying beam of light reach through
the barred windows of a shower
    chamber,
illuminating its blood-scratched walls.

4.

Evil is no black thing: black
may be the undertaker's hearse
and so many of the civil trappings
of death, but not its essence:
the riderless horse, the armbands
and veils of mourning, the grave shine
darkly; but these are the rituals
of the living.

One day I found its meaning as I
rushed breathless through a wind-
    parched
field, stumbling unaware: suddenly
    there
it was, laying at my feet, hidden
beneath towering golden rods,
a criss-crossed pile of
sun-bleached bones.

THE NIGHT IS
BEAUTIFUL
SO THE FACES
OF MY PEOPLE
THE STARS ARE
BEAUTIFUL
SO THE EYES
OF MY PEOPLE
BEAUTIFUL
ALSO IS THE
SUN
BEAUTIFUL
ALSO THE
SOULS OF MY
PEOPLE ...
LANGSTON
HUGHES

Black

Senora Richardson

Black, black like night
Velvet black, soft caressing
Waiting to wrap you in
Its web of darkness
Hard black, stone black
Onyx, flashing smooth
Pounding beating hard
Black Rocks
Evil black, mysterious
Cunning darkness to
Catch you, unaware, alone
My black, lonely black.
Soft black tears fall from
My eyes to wash the pain
Of Blackness.

The Beauty of the Rose

Henry E. Simmons

Bay Lemmon/BLKARTSOUTH

Black is being beautiful and knowing it! Those who imitate another culture, fearing that they will be rejected because their hair is not "straight" enough, their lips not thin enough, and their skin too dark, can lay no claim to ever having touched the souls of Black folks for they are steering away from the central theme of their heritage—the beauty of being Black. Those are the Blacks who have been so enraptured with the forests of white society that they have failed to see the beauty of their own proud tree of life.

Being Black is not only beautiful, it is sometimes more beautiful than all else. Like a rare black rose which suddenly blossoms in a dreary, uniform garden of petunias, or like a majestic vine spreading its leaves around a shack until that structure becomes an "ivy covered cottage," the Black man's awareness of himself has converted him from a follower to a leader. Externally he has a beauty which needs no processing or bleaching to be improved. Internally, he has a beauty which needs only recognition to blossom forward like the rose to brighten the garden of his own existence. And just as the sons of Africa once spent all of their dreams upon a society which rejected their kinky hair, their lips that were not thin enough, and their skin that was not white enough, they now relax in the splendor of seeing non-Blacks squandering their fortunes on afro wigs and African garb in imitation of Black beauty. They watch suntan manufacturers grow rich turning white folks black, and they view the resulting peeling process and blistering with contempt.

But the beauty of being Black includes the mental growth which now lets the Black man see that it is not important that he is "different" from non-Blacks, but only important that he is *like* his brothers all over the world, whose lives are based not only upon a common sorrow and pain, but more importantly upon the commonality of a deep, abiding beauty so ingrained that many Blacks have yet to discover it. It is being both a negritudinist and a Pan-Africanist and knowing that it has to be that way.

The beauty of Black is not in slavery but in the survival of it. It was sitting in the shack in the slave quarters at night laughing at the many ways "Mr. Charlie" had been tricked that day. It is the waiter who grins while he takes the white man's tip and then rushes to the post office to mail the

Photo by Hope H. Wurmfeld from *Black Is Beautiful* by Ann McGovern, photograph © 1969 by Hope H. Wurmfeld. Reprinted by permission of Scholastic Magazines, Inc.

money to his son who is away in college studying to be a civil rights lawyer. It is scrubbing a floor with dignity during the day and learning karate with determination at night. And, it is hearing B. B. King sing the blues and knowing what the words mean.

But more importantly, it is finding a Chaka to wrap your dreams around while ignorant whites wander through life thinking you are talking about a candy bar instead of a beautifully violent Black man. It is rooting for the rioters instead of Willie Mays but finding a way to get the job done the next time without the fire and looting. It is waving to a man you have never seen before because the two of you are the only Blacks in an all white town in Mississippi or Maine.

It is suddenly realizing that Black women are more beautiful to you than the women who caused thousands of your ancestors to keep a date with "judge Lynch." It is eating watermelon at a picnic without looking over your shoulder to see if anyone is looking. And, it is walking with pride within a society which has rejected you for years but cannot do so any longer because you won't let it.

This is the beauty of the mind. To love yourself, to walk in pride and to dream your own dreams, and to know that you are no longer alone on a hostile sea. The Garveys, Kings, Youngs, Carmichaels, Newtons and H. Rap Browns have laid a mantle of Blackness upon the shoulders of the people which, like the rose, has a tenderness and a virile strength to complement the beauty which it gives to the world. And Black people wear it with pride —amen.

for Langston Hughes

Conrad Kent Rivers

For all things black and beautiful,
The brown faces you loved so well and long,
The endless roads leading back to Harlem.

For all things black and beautiful
The seeking and the labor always waiting and coming
Until you began to dream of Nubian queens
And black kings shifting the dust of eternity
Before the white man brought his shame and God.
For all things black and beautiful
It took a lot of stones from little white boys
To produce the poem and quench the first desire to taste
Their nectar and the black wine of black empires
Flowing through your black bursting bewildered body.

For all things black and beautiful
And your Indian grandmother weaving tragic tales
Until the sea consumed you and the world had you loved
In ports and places few of your black brothers knew.

For all things black and beautiful
And the strange house in Taos and your white old man
Under a yellow Mexican sun dying black and moaning
Those weary blues until you came home to Harlem seeking
A way and worship and luster in the jive and the jazz
Once chained to the bottom of slave ships and whipped
In the public squares of our most democratic colorful cities.

For all things black and beautiful
The white savior and the black Christ dreaming dreams
While a black brother hangs from an oak without branches.

For all things black and beautiful
And big black Bessie doing her solo thrice times
Until Louie saves her by blasting his golden horn
And the whites shout and the blacks dance and night cries
Coming with her bullets in our bodies and death in our brains
But we cry out and finance our misery until our guts
Belong to the holy holy company and they laugh and eat well
While we die young and strong though tired of time payments.

For all things black and beautiful
Your poetry's a monument to our violated homes without hope

12

As we go weeping behind your box wanting to hear your tunes.
But if our poet is dead and Simple no longer sips divinity
Then we have not heard it in the breeze that blows our music
And our song into the vespers and the dens of white America
When our very faces are not wanted somehow we do exist there.

For all things black and beautiful
The music you heard in the hallways and hid in the room
The street woman you loved and saved with a sober ballad
The urban holocaust that swept you through the ghetto-ghetto land
The barbeque and sweet potatoes too many nights you went without
The sounds you heard in your head like dripping meal from cornbread
The dishwater like blood on your hands and filth on your heart
The Renaissance and Du Bois and Roberson and Carl and Arna and Zora
All gone like a Russian moon passes through the night of Benin.

For all things black and beautiful
And Mali rising again and Timbuctu spreading culture across the land
And Yardbird smoking and cleansing this roomy world of dry ashes
Until Sweet Sue understands the beauty of her black sunset silk skin
And the glory of her carmelite brown brighter than a blue red sun
Echoing the ancient truths of her own black culture and being.

For all things black and beautiful seen through your eyes:
Willie Mays doing his ballet in centerfield and Lady Day praying
And Harlem The Black Mother weeping and my own wet eyes, Langston
Feeling the darkness and the decline of the kingdom and glory of all
Things you made so black and beautiful in your fashion and way.
Africa is in your grave and may all the elements find peace with you.

Photo by Hope H. Wurmfeld from *Black Is Beautiful* by Ann McGovern, photograph © 1969 by Hope H. Wurmfeld. Reprinted by permission of Scholastic Magazines, Inc.

One Arab historian reported long ago: "The vanquished always seek to imitate their victors in their dress, insignia, belief and other customs and usages. This is because men are always inclined to attribute perfection to those who have defeated and subjugated them. . . . Should this belief persist long, it will change into a profound conviction and it will lead to the adoption of all the tenets of the victors and the imitation of all their characteristics." The ugly duckling was truly an ugly duck, and he was a naturally beautiful swan.

From the essay "Natural Black Beauty" by Joe Goncalves (San Francisco, Calif: *The Journal of Black Poetry*).

We Wear the Mask

Paul Laurence Dunbar

We wear the mask that grins and lies,
It hides our cheeks and shades
   our eyes,—
This debt we pay to human guile;
With torn and bleeding hearts
   we smile,
And mouth with myriad subtleties.

Why should the world be overwise,
In counting all our tears and sighs?
Nay, let them only see us while
   We wear the mask.

We smile, but, O great Christ, our cries
To Thee from tortured souls arise.
We sing, but oh, the clay is vile
Beneath our feet, and long the mile;
But let the world dream otherwise,
   We wear the mask.

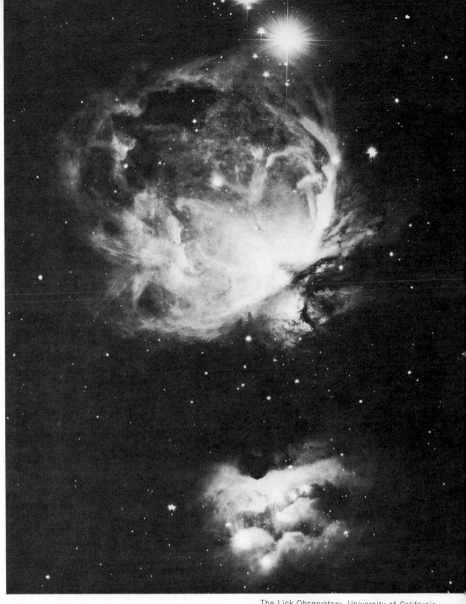

The Lick Observatory, University of California.

What Is Black?

Mary O'Neill

Black is beauty in its deepest form,
The darkest cloud in a thunderstorm.
Think of what starlight and lamplight
   would lack
Diamonds and fireflies if they couldn't
   lean against Black. . . .

15

Alan Paton Will Die

Johnie Scott

Hidden away, nestled
   in a corner of the sadness,
mourns a black bird.

Fire has come
   to the woods, and
of all the kings,
   only animals died.

Fire has come
   to the streets
of the *other* world,
   and only fire died.

Should the forests
   see a sun kissing
a beloved country,
   perhaps they would die.

Streets covered
   by the darkness of
a shattered dream's wrath
   safe no more for walking.

Street burned over
   by the anger of a dying father
safe no more from the disbelieving son
   screaming a tear-glazed blindness.

Perhaps the world
   will solve itself
and be blown to pieces.

Perhaps the world
   will grow fearful,
listening to the lonely
   mourning of the *black* bird.

Reprinted by permission of The World Publishing Company from *From the Ashes: Voices of Watts* edited by Budd Schulberg. An NAL book. Copyright © 1967 by The New American Library, Inc.

Photo by Hope H. Wurmfeld from *Black Is Beautiful* by Ann McGovern, photograph © 1969 by Hope H. Wurmfeld. Reprinted by permission of Scholastic Magazines, Inc.

Personally

James Kilgore

On being asked by a Black freshman college student: "Did the white man give the Negro religion to keep the Negro enslaved?"

In dark woods,
Sinking in the quicksand of slavery,
I reached up,
Frantically,
Among the dark branches,
Clutching for a vine of hope;
In the painful dark,
I found an ancient branch,
Pulled up,
Held on.

Reprinted from *Phylon*, XXX, Fourth Quarter, Winter 1969, p. 420 by permission of *Phylon*, The Atlanta University Review of Race and Culture.

BLACK WOMAN

The Black Finger

Angeline W. Grimke

I have just seen a beautiful thing
        Slim and still,
Against a gold, gold sky,
        A straight cypress,
        Sensitive,
        Exquisite,
A black finger
Pointing upwards.
Why, beautiful, still finger are you
    black?
And why are you pointing upwards?

Black Woman

Léopold-Sédar Senghor

Naked woman, black woman
Clad in your color that is life, in your form that is beauty!
I have grown up in your shade, the sweetness of your hands
  bound my eyes.
And now in the heart of summer and noon, I discover you,
  promised earth, from the tower of your sun-scorched
  neck
And your beauty smites me to the full of my heart like the
  flash of an eagle.

Naked woman, dark woman!
Firm-fleshed ripe fruit, dark raptures of black wine, mouth
  making lyric my mouth
Savanna of sheer horizons, savanna quivering to the East
  wind's fervent caresses
Carved tom-tom, taut tom-tom snarling under the Victor's
  fingers
Your grave, contralto voice is the spiritual of the Beloved.

Naked woman, dark woman!
Oil sweet and smooth on the athlete's flanks,
On the flanks of the princes of Mali
Heaven-leashed gazelle, pearls are stars on the night of your
  skin
Delights of the spirit at play, red gold reflections on your
  shimmering skin.
In the shade of your hair, my anguish lightens with the nearing
  suns of your eyes.

Naked woman, black woman!
I sing your passing beauty, form that I fix in the eternal
Before jealous destiny burns you to ashes to nourish the roots
  of life.

Photograph by Hugh Bell.

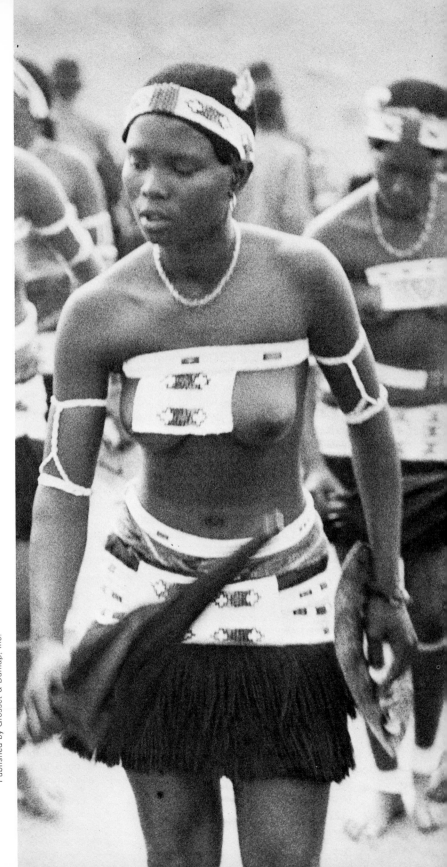

The poem *A une danseuse noire* ("To a Black Dancer") appears in David Diop's anthology Coups de Pilon, published by *Presence Africaine*, Paris (1956). Reprinted by permission.

To a Black Dancer

David Diop

Black woman my warm clamor of Africa
My land of mystery and my fruit of reason
You are the dance in the naked joy of your smile
Through the offering of your breasts and your secret powers
You are the dance by the golden legends of wedding nights
In the new times and the age-old rhythms
Black woman manifold triumph of dreams and of stars
Docile mistress in the embrace of the *kora*
You are the dance by vertigo
By the magic of loins recreating the world
You are the dance
And the myths flame around me
Around me the wigs of the learned
In bonfires of joy in the heaven of your steps.
You are the dance
And false gods burn under your vertical flame
You are the dance of the initiate
Sacrificing his folly under the Guardian-Tree
You are the idea of the All and the voice of the Ancient
Hurled solemn to assault delusions
You are the Word which explodes
In miraculous showers of light on the shores of oblivion.

Domba drummer. The Domba dance takes place mornings and evenings. The single file dance of girls (sometimes boys and girls) holding closely to the dancer in front is done to the accompaniment of ngoma and mirumba drums.

A Song of Praise

Countee Cullen

(For one who praised his lady's being
fair.)

You have not heard my love's dark
    throat,
        Slow-fluting like a reed,
Release the perfect golden note
        She caged there for my need.

Her walk is like the replica
        Of some barbaric dance
Wherein the soul of Africa
        Is winged with arrogance.

And yet so light she steps across
        The ways her sure feet pass,
She does not dent the smoothest moss
        Or bend the thinnest grass.

My love is dark as yours is fair,
        Yet lovelier I hold her
Than listless maids with pallid hair,
        And blood that's thin and colder.

You-proud-and-to-be-pitied one,
        Gaze on her and despair;
Then seal your lips until the sun
        Discovers one as fair.

Sugar Woman

Sterling Plumpp

She was black
And we called her sugar.

In the dense briars
Of life's uncertainties
A pie.

We called her love.

Our sight strengthened
By soft beauty. Our
Manhood moulded in
Her ways.

We called her queen,
(beautiful black queen)
sugar . . . .
           and mother.

Photograph by Constance Stuart, Black Star.

The Black Woman

Paul Nathaniel Johnson—Ahmadin

I am a black woman.
A daughter of Ethiopia.
Men of all races have admired me
Throughout the ages.
The white, the red, the yellow, the brown.
All men swoon under the spell of my magic love
Like did Ulysses' men under the witchery
Of Circe the daughter of the Sun.

I am black and beautiful,
Gentle and fair,
And the mystery of the world.
Bel boweth down
And Nebo stoopeth at my feet.
I conquer all men.

My brothers were Princes in Egypt,
My sisters were Queens on the Nile,
My little sisters were fairies on the
        banks of Swanee River.
Why do the world of men lust after me?
Ah! because I am pure.
I am unmixed.
I am a black woman.

Black Madonna

Harun Kofi Wangara
(Harold G. Lawrence)

You were beautiful when
Your apparition formed
From Tanga mud and Rift;
Rocks of Rhodesia, Kush, Ethiopia,
Sahara sands and Maya mounds,
And Grottes des Enfants
Preserved your image.

You modeled
At the Pharaoh's throne;
Mother of Horus—
Mother of Krishna—
Mother of All!
In dark Virginity.

You, lost for a while
In cadence with the crescent star,
Continued in obscure worship of
    the North
Among many who never knew your
    birth
Yet still adored you.

DaVinci, and Angelo, wiped you white
Releasing floods of forgotten nights;
But you remained beautiful still
In the dim deeds of masters who
    made you mistress;
And bred by pale pleasure,
Your sons denied you.

Free winds winding South,
To storm Bahia and Haiti
Took root in
Shiloh—Bombay—and Ghana;
Bandung announced your return.

Now again we sense your
Sensitive beauty, smiling, Black,
Turban crowned, robed, straight back,
Very Black—and Brown and Beige too,
Singing strong songs of *Negritude*
Through Kaffir lips your vibrant Blues.

Flowers of Darkness

Frank Marshall Davis

Slowly the night blooms, unfurling
Flowers of darkness, covering
The trellised sky, becoming
A bouquet of blackness
Unending
Touched with sprigs
Of pale and budding stars

Soft the night smell
Among April trees
Soft and richly rare
Yet commonplace
Perfume on a cosmic scale

I turn to you Mandy Lou
I see the flowering night
Cameo condensed
Into the lone black rose
Of your face

The young woman-smell
Of your poppy body
Rises to my brain as opium
Yet silently motionless
I sit with twitching fingers
Yea, even reverently
Sit I
With you and the blossoming night
For what flower, plucked,
Lingers long?

Used by permission of Frank Marshall Davis.

For Our Women

Larry Neal

Out of the Earth, this love
moved rivers
sang joy songs, these women wrapped
in the magic of birth;
deep rivers formed your innocence—
knew no evil
knew beyond what knowing
has come to mean
wordlessly knew.

Black women, timeless, are sun
   breaths
are crying mothers
are snatched rhythms
are blues rivers and food uncooked,
lonely villages beside quiet streams,
are exploding suns green yellow
   moons,
the story of the snake and the turtle.
lonely roads.
night-rider. see-see rider. easy men
who got lost returning to you,
blues in our mothers' voices
warning us.
blues people bursting out.
Like it is, I tell it,
and there are towns that
hang lonely in some man's
memory and you are there
and not there.

blackened in the soil of earth-time,
southern towns that release
their secrets to you
and then retreat, returning later
to rape.
you are there and not there.
Looming magic out of endless
   dreams—
our continuousness.

I see you announce their doom,
and the breath of your life
sustains us
sustains us as the sea screams out;
the female in the middle passage,
you endured.
we endured through you.
us endured. endured.

In the soul of my art, I embrace
the world that is you
as we giant step across our earth;
the sea again
again the sea unites us
as we couple with the land
and the stars of our ancestors
ancestor stars.
black universe. sky.
embrace.

Photograph by Hugh Bell.

Karintha

Jean Toomer

Her skin is like dusk on the eastern horizon,
O cant you see it, O cant you see it,
Her skin is like dusk on the eastern horizon
. . . When the sun goes down.

Men had always wanted her, this Karintha, even as a child, Karintha carrying beauty, perfect as dusk when the sun goes down. Old men rode her hobby-horse upon their knees. Young men danced with her at frolics when they should have been dancing with their grown-up girls. God grant us youth, secretly prayed the old men. The young fellows counted the time to pass before she would be old enough to mate with them. This interest of the male, who wishes to ripen a growing thing too soon, could mean no good to her.

Karintha, at twelve, was a wild flash that told the other folks just what it was to live. At sunset, when there was no wind, and the pine-smoke from over by the sawmill hugged the earth, and you couldnt see more than a few feet in front, her sudden darting past you was a bit of vivid color, like a black bird that flashes in light. With the other children one could hear, some distance off, their feet flopping in the two-inch dust. Karintha's running was a whir. It had the sound of the red dust that sometimes makes a spiral in the road. At dusk, during the hush just after the sawmill had closed down, and before any of the women had started their supper-getting-ready songs, her voice, high-pitched, shrill, would put one's ears to itching. But no one ever thought to make her stop because of it. She stoned the cows, and beat her dog, and fought the other children . . . Even the preacher, who caught her at mischief, told himself that she was as innocently lovely as a November cotton flower. Already, rumors were out about her. Homes in Georgia are most often built on the two-room plan. In one, you cook and eat, in the other you sleep, and there love goes on. Karintha had seen or heard, perhaps she had felt her parents loving. One could but imitate one's parents, for to follow them was the way of God. She played "home" with a small boy who was not afraid to do her bidding. That started the whole thing. Old men could no longer ride her hobby-horse upon their knees. But young men counted faster.

> Her skin is like dusk,
> O cant you see it,
> Her skin is like dusk,
> When the sun goes down.

Karintha is a woman. She who carries beauty, perfect as dusk when the sun goes down. She has been married many times. Old men remind her that a few years back they rode her hobby-horse upon their knees. Karintha smiles, and indulges them when she is in the mood for it. She has contempt for them. Karintha is a woman. Young men run still to make her money. Young men go to the big cities and run on the road. Young men go away to college. They all want to bring her money. These are the young men who thought that all they had to do was to count time. But Karintha is a woman, and she has had a child. A child fell out of her womb onto a bed of pine needles in the forest. Pine-needles are smooth and sweet. They are elastic to the feet of rabbits . . . A sawmill was nearby. Its pyramidal sawdust pile smouldered. It is a year before one completely burns. Meanwhile, the smoke curls up and hangs in odd wraiths about the trees, curls up, and spreads itself out over the valley . . . Weeks after Karintha returned home the smoke was so heavy you tasted it in water. Someone made a song:

> Smoke is on the hills.
> Rise up. Smoke is on the hills, O rise
> And take my soul to Jesus.

Karintha is a woman. Men do not know that the soul of her was a growing thing ripened too soon. They will bring their money; they will die not having found it out . . . Karintha at twenty, carrying beauty, perfect as dusk when the sun goes down. Karintha . . .

> Her skin is like dusk on the eastern horizon,
> O cant you see it, O cant you see it,
> Her skin is like dusk on the eastern horizon
> . . . When the sun goes down
> Goes down.

Photograph by Hugh Bell.

BLACK
MAN

But He Was Cool
or he even stopped for green lights

don l. lee

super-cool
ultrablack
a tan/purple
had a beautiful shade.

he had a double-natural
that wd put the sisters to shame.
his dashikis were tailor made
& his beads were imported sea shells
    (from some blk/country i never heard of)
he was triple-hip.

his tikis were hand carved
out of ivory
& came express from the motherland.
he would greet u in swahili
& say good-by in yoruba.

wooooooooooooooooo—jim he bees so cool & ill tel li gent
      cool-cool is so cool he was un-cooled by other nigger's cool
      cool-cool ultracool was bop-cool/ice box cool so cool cold cool
      his wine didn't have to be cooled him was air conditioned cool
      cool-cool/real cool made me cool—now ain't that cool
      cool-cool so cool him nick-named refrigerator.
cool-cool so cold
he didn't even know,
after detroit, newark, chicago &c.,
we had to hip
         cool-cool/super-cool/real-cool
  that
to be black
is
to be
very-hot.

The Smoke King

W. E. B. DuBois

Reprinted by permission of Mrs. Shirley Graham DuBois.

I am the smoke king,
I am black.
I am swinging in the sky.
I am ringing worlds on high:
I am the thought of the throbbing mills,
I am the soul toil kills, . . .

I am the smoke king,
I am black.

I am darkening with song,
I am harkening to wrong;
I will be black as blackness can,
The blacker the mantle the mightier
   the man,
My purpl'ing midnights no day dawn
   may ban.

I am carving God in night,
I am painting hell in white.
I am the smoke king,
I am black.

Photograph by Homer Page.

to all sisters

sonia sanchez

hurt.
      u worried abt a
  little hurting.
         man
hurt ain't the bag u
  shd be in.
       loving is
the bag. man.
         there ain't
no MAN like a
      black man.
he puts it where it is
and makes u
      turn in/side out.

Reprinted from *Black Fire,* edited by LeRoi Jones and Larry Neal, Wm. Morrow & Co., Inc., New York, N.Y., 1968. Used with permission of Sonia Sanchez and Ronald Hobbs Literary Agency.

Sonnet to a Negro in Harlem

Helene Johnson

You are disdainful and magnificent—
Your perfect body and your pompous
    gait,
Your dark eyes flashing solemnly
    with hate,
Small wonder that you are
    incompetent
To imitate those whom you so
    despise—
Your shoulders towering high above
    the throng,
Your head thrown back in rich,
    barbaric song,
Palm trees and mangoes stretched
    before your eyes.
Let others toil and sweat for
    labor's sake
And wring from grasping hands their
    meed of gold.
Why urge ahead your supercilious
    feet?
Scorn will efface each footprint that
    you make.
I love your laughter arrogant and bold.
You are too splendid for this city
    street.

I, Too

Langston Hughes

I, too, sing America

I am the darker brother.
They send me to eat in the kitchen
When company comes,
But I laugh,
And eat well,
And grow strong.

Tomorrow,
I'll be at the table
When company comes.
Nobody'll dare
Say to me,
"Eat in the kitchen,"
Then.

Besides,
They'll see how beautiful I am
And be ashamed—

I, too, am America.

Black

Lori Lunford

Black——
Blacker than ten thousand
    nights without a single
    star's brilliance to guide
    the weary wanderers.

Strong—
Stronger than the forces of a
    gigantic magnet that draws
    all metal into its huge and
    gaping jaws.

Gleaming——
Gleaming with the sweat of
    over a hundred years of
    hard labor heaped upon
    him by the "other man."

Wonderful——
More wonderful than a whole
    year to live independent
    as a flowing river with its
    foaming bubbles and
    magnificent falls.

Free——
Free because the shackles and
    bonds of the "other man"
    cannot hold down this zest
    for life.

Loved——
Loved because he is strong,
    gleaming, wonderful and
    free.

Beautiful——
Beautiful because he is Black.

Used by permission of Lori Lunford.

About Man

johari amini
(jewel c. latimore)

A Man
black
in
strength virility hardness

demigod
he
loves
    —the thrust
        ejaculated extensions of
        black
        life
        black
        soul
love creating black
life

his love is survival
        life essence of
        humanity
        progenating humanness
within the black pulsating
        fundus throbbing
        dark receptive warmth
        existing for
        implantation

From *Images in Black,* Third World Press, Chicago, 1967.
Reprinted by permission of johari amini (jewel c. latimore.)

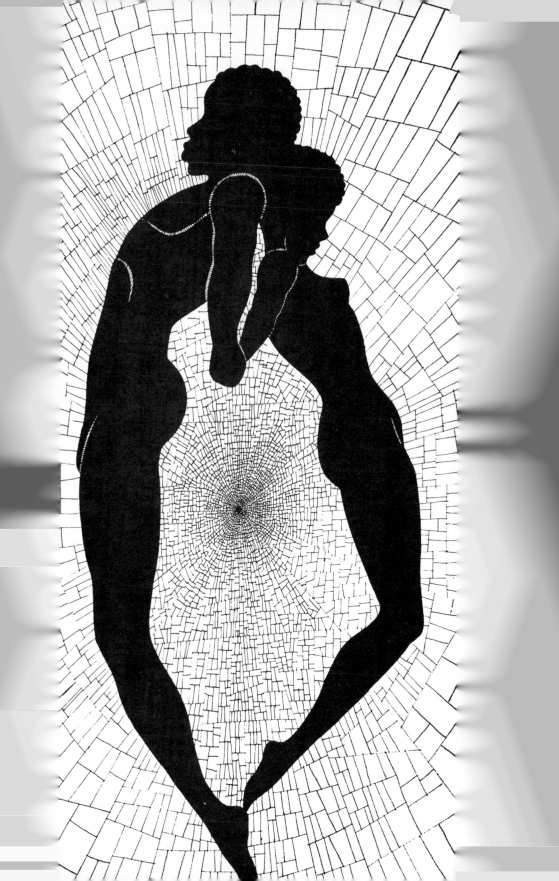

MAN and WOMAN

A Necessary Poem

Nayo (barbara malcom)

Out of necessity
came me
black and ready to defend/defeat/
    dethrone
and from the same pattern came he

and out of necessity
we talked
and dug the coversing of black to
    black

and out of necessity
we touched
gently, yeah just touched
        finger tips and eye lids and
                                lips

and out of necessity
we fucked
and released all that had been withheld
                        in negro fucks

and out of necessity
we spent time together
to talk and touch and fuck
and fill empty spaces
and hours and days
turned to weeks and months
and of necessity we somehow ate
and slept and read and worked
and talked and touched and fucked

and out of necessity
I watched the days of my monthly
    cycle
and suspected it wasn't coming
and it all became quite natural
talking and touching and fucking
and watching

and out of necessity
we got a pad
and a gun
and a kitchen sink
and an understanding
of what to do when cops come

and out of necessity
I wondered if he'd love me
when I'm old and grey
and he wondered why
I needed to deal with that at all

and in the midst of the necessities
of living and loving
we are learning to be
    necessary

Barbara X/BLKARTSOUTH. Reprinted by permission.

Omar Lama.

Beautiful, Black and Beloved

Margaret Burroughs

Hear me, Heed me, my beautiful black
and beloved.
Wherever you are and whatever your
station.
Be you blue collar, or white collar, or
no collar.
Listen.

Black Jesuses in steel mills and stock
yards
Black geniuses sorting and carrying
mail
Black madonnas residing heavenwise
Black runners to the corner pub
Young black scrawlers on ghetto
walls
Listen.

All of you beautiful, and black
beloved;
I want to talk to you, about you, and
me and us
About our black selves, a glory
people.

I wish to speak of image, of black
image
I wish to speak of beauty, of black
beauty
To show you how beautiful our black
people are
I want to smash your mirror reflecting
alien vision
An image not akin to you, which
causes you to reject
Your own very best and beautiful self.

I want to make you proud of your
satin ebony skin
And the wiry crispness of your strong
black hair
Or the rounded flaring of your nostrils
Or the expressive fullness of your lips

Or the large dark pools that are your
eyes
And the lithesome grace of your
athletic bodies.

I want you to be aware of the gifts of
black folk
To this the new world and the entire
world
Of how you beautiful and black
beloved
Gave profound meaning to the word
religion
Enriched a barren land with music
and rhythm
Set unmatched model for generosity,
kindness
Discipline, endurance, hope and
self control
Courage, bravery and compassion.

I want you to know these things about
yourselves
About us, to truly know them and
believe them
To spread this word to all black
sisters and brothers
To counter the hateful racist
propaganda,
With these truths to imbue your black
generations.

And above all my beautiful black and
beloved
To cleave together in unity all as part
of a whole
And to love each other and work
together
So that our black people may become
As DuBois the sage says, our own
very best selves.

Reprinted by permission of Margaret T. G. Burroughs, Director, The Du Sable Museum of African American History, Chicago 53, Illinois, from *What Shall I Tell My Children Who Are Black?*

from Soul Madness

Val Ferdinand

3

The trouble w/h blk women
is nigger men
Nigger men (cock hound
Freaks who will chase a
Piece of pussy all nite
And not stand up once
In the daytime to a whiteman
The trouble w/h blk women
Is they need men
More men than negroes are
The trouble w/h blk women
Is there ain't enough blk men
To go around
What chall gon do abt that men

Kalamu ya Salaam (val ferdinand)/BLKARTSOUTH.

To All Black Women, From All Black Men

Eldridge Cleaver

Queen-Mother-Daughter of Africa
Sister of My Soul
Black Bride of My Passion
My Eternal Love

I greet you, my Queen, not in the obsequious whine of a cringing Slave to which you have become accustomed, neither do I greet you in the new voice, the unctuous supplications of the sleek Black Bourgeoise, nor the bullying bellow of the rude Free Slave—but in my own voice do I greet you, the voice of the Black Man. And although I greet you *anew,* my greeting is now *new,* but as old as the Sun, Moon, and Stars. And rather than mark a new beginning, my greeting signifies only my Return.

I have Returned from the dead. I speak to you now from the Here And Now. **I was dead for four hundred years.** For four hundred years you have been a woman alone, bereft of her man, a manless woman. For four hundred years I was neither your man nor my own man. The white man stood between us, over us, around us. The white man was your man and my man. Do not pass lightly over this truth, my Queen, for even though the fact of it has burned into the marrow of our bones and diluted our blood,

we must bring it to the surface of the mind, into the realm of knowing, glue our gaze upon it and stare at it as at a coiled serpent in a baby's playpen or the fresh flowers on a mother's grave. It is to be pondered and realized in the heart, for the heel of the white man's boot is our point of departure, our point of Resolve and Return—the bloodstained pivot of our future. (But I would ask you to recall, that before we could come up from slavery, we had to be pulled down from our throne.)

42

Photo Researchers, Inc., New York City.

Across the naked abyss of negated masculinity, of four hundred years minus my Balls, we face each other today, my Queen. I feel a deep, terrifying hurt, the pain of humiliation of the vanquished warrior. The shame of the fleet-footed sprinter who stumbles at the start of the race. I feel unjustified. I can't bear to look into your eyes. Don't you know (surely you must have noticed by now: four hundred years!) that for four hundred years I have been unable to look squarely into your eyes? I tremble inside each time you look at me. I can feel . . . in the ray of your eye, from a deep hiding place, a long-kept secret you harbor. That is the unadorned truth. Not that I would have felt justified, under the circumstances, in taking such liberties with you, but I want you to know that I feared to look into your eyes because I knew I would find reflected there a merciless Indictment of my impotence and a compelling challenge to redeem my conquered manhood.

My Queen, it is hard for me to tell you what is in my heart for you today—what is in the heart of all my black brothers for you and all your black sisters—and I fear I will fail unless you reach out to me, tune in on me with the antenna of your love, the sacred love in ultimate degree which you were unable to give me because I, being dead, was unworthy to receive it; that perfect, radical love of black on which our Fathers thrived. Let me drink from the river of your love at its source, let the lines of force of your love seize my soul by its core and heal the wound of my Castration, let my convex exile end its haunted Odyssey in your concave essence which receives that it may give. Flower of Africa, it is only through the liberating power of your *re*-love that my manhood can be redeemed. For it is in your eyes, before you, that my need is to be justified. Only, only, only you and only you can condemn or set me free.

Be convinced, Sable Sister, that the past is no forbidden vista upon which we dare not look, out of a phantom fear of being, as the wife of Lot, turned into pillars of salt. Rather the past is an omniscient mirror: we gaze and see reflected there ourselves and each other—what we used to be, what we are today, how we got this way, and what we are becoming. To decline to look into the Mirror of Then, my heart, is to refuse to view the face of Now.

I have died the ninth death of the cat, have seen Satan face to face and turned my back on God, have dined in the Swine's Trough, and descended to the uttermost echelon of the Pit, have entered the Den and seized my Balls from the teeth of a roaring lion!

Black Beauty, in impotent silence I listened, as if to a symphony of sorrows, to your screams for help, anguished pleas of terror that echo still throughout the Universe and through the mind, a million scattered screams across the painful years that merged into a single sound of pain to haunt and bleed the soul, a white-hot sound to char the brain and blow the fuse of thought, a sound of fangs and teeth sharp to eat the heart, a sound of moving fire, a sound of frozen heat, a sound of licking flames, a fiery-fiery sound, a sound of fire to burn the steel out of my Balls, a sound of Blue fire, a Bluesy sound, the sound of dying, the sound of my woman in pain, *the sound of my woman's pain,* THE SOUND OF MY WOMAN CALLING ME, ME, I HEARD HER CALL FOR HELP, I HEARD THAT MOURNFUL SOUND BUT HUNG MY HEAD AND FAILED TO HEED IT, I HEARD MY WOMAN'S CRY, I HEARD MY WOMAN'S SCREAM, I HEARD MY WOMAN BEG THE BEAST FOR MERCY, I HEARD HER BEG FOR ME, I HEARD MY WOMAN BEG THE BEAST FOR MERCY FOR ME, I HEARD MY WOMAN DIE, I HEARD THE SOUND OF HER DEATH,

A SNAPPING SOUND, A BREAKING SOUND, A SOUND THAT SOUNDED FINAL, THE LAST SOUND, THE ULTIMATE SOUND, THE SOUND OF DEATH, ME, I HEARD, I HEAR IT EVERY DAY, I HEAR HER NOW . . . I HEAR YOU NOW . . . I HEAR YOU. . . . I heard you then . . . your scream came like a searing bolt of lightning that blazed a white streak down my black back. In a cowardly stupor, with a palpitating heart and quivering knees, I watched the Slaver's lash of death slash through the opposing air and bite with teeth of fire into your delicate flesh, the black and tender flesh of African Motherhood, forcing the startled Life untimely from your torn and outraged womb, the sacred womb that cradled primal man, the womb that incubated Ethiopia and populated Nubia and gave forth Pharaohs unto Egypt, the womb that painted the Congo black and mothered Zulu, the womb of Mero, the womb of the Nile, of the Niger, the womb of Songhay, of Mali, of Ghana, the womb that felt the might of Chaka before he saw the Sun, the Holy Womb, the womb that knew the future form of Jomo Kenyatta, the womb of Mau Mau, the womb of the blacks, the womb that nurtured Toussaint L'Ouverture, that warmed Nat Turner, and Gabriel Prosser, and Denmark Vesey, the black womb that surrendered up in tears that nameless and endless chain of Africa's Cream, the Black Cream of the Earth, that nameless and endless black chain that sank in heavy groans into oblivion in the great abyss, the womb that received and nourished and held firm the seed and gave back Sojourner Truth, and Sister Tubman, and Rosa Parks, and Bird, and Richard Wright, and your other works of art who wore and wear such names as Marcus Garvey and DuBois and Kwame Nkrumah and Paul Robeson and Malcolm X and Robert Williams, and the one you bore in pain and called Elijah Muhammad, but most of all that nameless one they tore out of your womb in a flood of murdered blood that splashed upon and seeped into the mud. And Patrice Lumumba, and Emmett Till, and Mack Parker.

O, My Soul! I became a sniveling craven, a funky punk, a vile, groveling bootlicker, with my will to oppose petrified by a cosmic fear of the Slavemaster. Instead of inciting the Slaves to rebellion with eloquent oratory, I soothed their hurt and eloquently sang the Blues! Instead of hurling my life with contempt into the face of my Tormentor, *I shed your precious blood!* When Nat Turner sought to free me from my Fear, my Fear delivered him up unto the Butcher—a martyred monument to my Emasculation. My spirit was unwilling and my flesh was weak. Ah, eternal ignominy!

I, the Black Eunuch, divested of my Balls, walked the earth with my mind locked in Cold Storage. I would kill a black man or woman quicker than I'd smash a fly, while for the white man I would pick a thousand pounds of cotton a day. What profit is there in the blind, frenzied efforts of the (Guilty!) Black Eunuchs (Justifiers!) who hide their wounds and scorn the truth to mitigate their culpability through the pallid sophistry of postulating a Universal Democracy of Cowards, pointing out that in history no one can hide, that if not at one time then surely at another the iron heel of the Conqueror has ground into the mud the Balls of Everyman? Memories of yesterday will not assuage the torrents of blood that flow today from my crotch. Yes, History could pass for a scarlet text, its jot and tittle graven red in human blood. More armies than shown in the books have planted flags on foreign soil leaving Castration in their wake. But no Slave should die a natural death. There is a point where Caution ends and Cowardice begins. Give me a bullet through the brain from the gun of the beleaguered oppressor on the night of seige. Why is there dancing and singing in the Slave Quarters? A Slave who dies of natural causes cannot balance two dead flies in the Scales of Eternity. Such a one deserves rather to be pitied than mourned.

Black woman, without asking how, just say that we survived our forced march and travail through the Valley of Slavery, Suffering, and Death— there, that Valley there beneath us hidden by that drifting mist. Ah, what sights and sounds and pain lie beneath that mist! And we had thought that our hard climb out of that cruel valley led to some cool, green and peaceful, sunlit place—but it's all jungle here, a wild and savage wilderness that's overrun with ruins.

But put on your crown, my Queen, and we will build a New City on these ruins.

A Black Ritual

Robert MacBeth

A large, cleared space, in the center of which is a large, eight-sided platform. Upon the octagon is an altar. It is lit so that one sees only shape, no color. On the edges of the octagon are thirteen Black people dressed in billowing black hooded robes that fall to the floor. The seven men and six women wander about, move with each other, humming.

Witnesses to the ritual sit around the octagon in a half circle.

The supplicants stop and connect themselves one to another by bumping, by locking limbs, by brushing, by coming up to each other, barely touching and then moving away. Music is playing which allows them to find themselves in connection with one another.

All male voices begin humming a pulsing beat. The female voices respond to the men's, in frightened, hysterical murmers bouncing up and up until they bounce away in space and only the male voices remain.

> *The true self is the self with*
> *others.*
> *The true Black self is the self*
> *with others.*
> *The true Black self is*
> *the Black self with the tribe ...*
> *etc.*

The beginning of the ritual is formed.

One male takes the center space in the octagon. The others peel themselves off of the group, the men go diagonally to the right, up and to the right of the lead male. The females go diagonally from the left, down and out.

The humming becomes very level, very clear. The only sound is the humming. Then the lead male begins to chant. He is echoed by the group, echoing one word at a time, so that the sound is a pealing kind of disturbance, the words flicking from the lips.

DEVILS, WHITE DEVILS. WHITE BLUE-EYED DEVILS. DEVILS, WHITE DEVILS. WHITE BLUE-EYED DEVILS, etc.

The words are not chanted clearly. They are spoken in a strange tone. The tone changes and becomes a crescendo of sound, now more frantic, more screaming. As the sounds avalanche it is impossible to distinguish the individual words or voices, and they combine into a mass of sound made up of the words, moans, screams and Black voices.

The voices reach a pinnacle and a gong begins. It helps to bring the sounds out by pacing them.

Strange, soft light is now apparent. Lighter toned bells peal. The voices change. The bells chime in harmonic tones.

Black is the color.
BLACK IS THE COLOR.
Black is the color, etc.

The lead male turns toward the altar, moves up the stairs that lead up above the octagon. The altar is very clearly lit.

The lead male moves up to the altar, turns around and opens himself to let out the Black gods that must be a part of the ritual. He brings the spirits up out of his loins, coughs them up out of his heart, routs them from his soul, screams them out of his brain as the others bow, hands folded, watching his bringing forth of the Black gods into the ritual.

He moves to the violence of the experience. A light comes on, a beam of strange light, blue against the yellows and oranges of the octagon. A clear stream of blue light piercingly illuminates the altar. A giant Black head hangs above the altar. A giant Black face. A peaceful-violent face, a peacefully vindictive Black face.

A black-covered table, holding implements of silver stands on the altar. Strange signs are crocheted onto the table's covering. And thin lines streak up behind the Black head and fan out. Thin lines stretching out to endless space behind and around the head.

The Black gods have entered the ritual.

The lead male turns, raises his hands and speaks.

Let us pray.

He then turns back around and kneels at the altar. The sounds become rhythmic—congo drums, some piano, little bells, rattlers and humming are heard as the others sway at the altar. Some cry out in strange, spiritual pain.

Two large, white columns of hanging cloth are positioned so that they can be seen by everyone. Two slide projectors flash a series of pictures on the columns. Pictures of the devil in many of his guises—Mississippi State Patrolman, whiteman on the street, white people screaming at Black children in Arkansas, Byron de la Beckwith, whitemen with signs saying KILL THE NIGGERS, WHITE POWER, BLUE POWER.

Pictures flash on; the supplicants respond. Pictures of whitemen with dogs, and a Black woman leaps up from the group and screams. Other supplicants respond to other pictures. There are 25 to 30 pictures that are repeated over and over. The movements of the supplicants, the sounds they make and the pictures all move faster and faster. The pictures represent things the supplicants pray for strength to withstand: Elizabeth Taylor, Marlon Brando, Lucie Bird, Jackie Kennedy Onassis, etc.

One of the male supplicants comes up off the floor disrobed. He runs out onto the middle of the floor. The pictures are flashing faster, and he tries to stop one with all his force.

Finally, he stops one, and it is a person—Johnson, a white policeman, a red-neck farmer, anyone of those honkies.

He has the picture and begins to deliver a speech clarifying his soul's intent to withstand the beast, to withstand the devil and to finally overcome him.

> *Black gods and spirits of my fallen fathers; make my Black arms strong, my back straight and my Black bursting heart mighty . . . MIGHTY . . . to withstand and conquer this monster.*

> *Oh, Black gods and spirits of my race, my tribe. Enter my mind and soul to make me righteous . . . A Black righteous man who is worthy to join in struggle with his brothers and sisters in the revolution that is upon us.*

He pauses, almost totally torn from the strain. The females weave together for a moment, then out of their midst is thrown a female, disrobed, just like her man.

She speaks of her soul's intent to support her man in the whole struggle.

She speaks, then she kneels by him, her head lower than his head. Her attitude is one of request.

> *Beautiful Black and righteous brother / husband / father / warrior. Black and righteous god of my universe who I stand beside, who I bear Him Black warriors and young sisters.*

> *I, a Blackwoman, stand beside you and behind you, Blackman. I am your support and comfort in the struggle. I humble myself to you as only a queen can for her king, her god, her righteous Blackman.*

When the woman's speech is completed the man stands, lifts her and begins to walk toward the altar. She walks a step or so behind him, her head slightly bowed; they come to the altar and kneel, making their ritual signs.

The lead male acknowledges them; descends the stairs and kisses them both.

END OF RITUAL

there's no
you or me
theres
just we
            e
              e
                e
                  e
                    e
                      e
                        e
                          e
                            e
                              e
                                e
                                  e
                                    e
                                      e
                                        e
                                          e

LANGUAGE

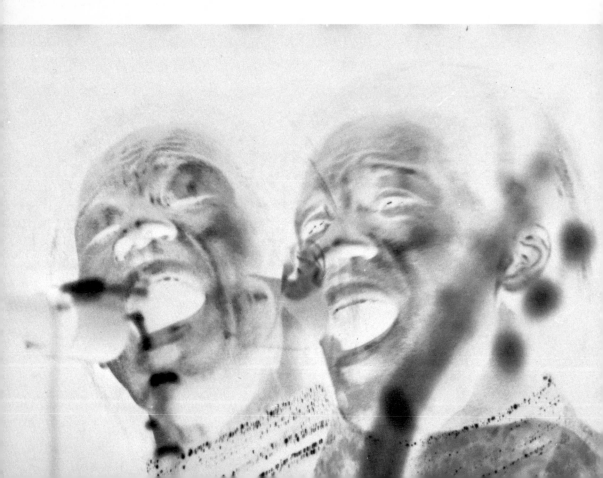

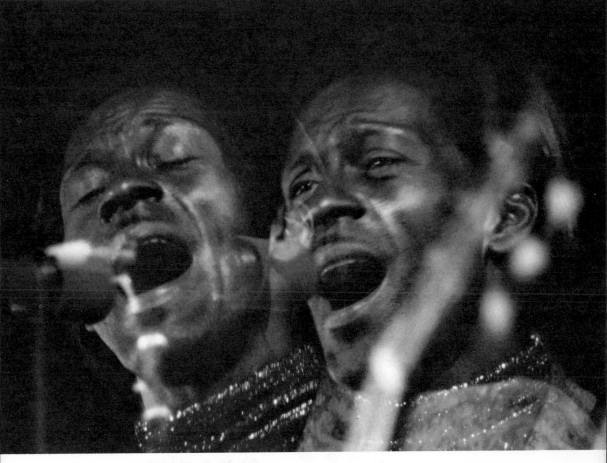

Photograph by Jim Marshall.

OF SOUL

You might don't like the way I write—
well, I sorry about that. That the way
I feel.

Josh Fleming

a language of my own

Meet Josh

Josh Fleming

Meet Josh
Chicago boy
Nineteen
Drive down Pulaski
Never see him
Chi Town drowns so many
Meet Josh
His secret smile . . . .

Excerpt from a paper read at the Illinois Speech Association on November 8, 1968. Used by permission of Thomas Kochman. Originally published in *Synergist,* Northeastern Illinois State College, Winter 1969.

Language Behavior in the Black Community

Thomas Kochman

. . . In Black English, there appear several words and expressions that refer to talking: *rapping, shucking, jiving, running it down, gripping, copping a plea, signifying* and *sounding.* In addition, there is the term *toast* to denote an accomplished oral art form performed by your best Black male speakers. Each of these terms identifies a form of verbal behavior that is generally recognized and often employed by Black street people. This is especially true of the men. Often, they are the models whom boys growing up try to emulate and imitate daily outside of the classroom. In the time remaining I shall discuss two types of verbal behavior in greater detail while abstracting certain features of the other types as they shed light on an overall Black cultural perspective. For a more complete account I refer you to the magazine *Trans-Action* which will publish the study in an, as yet unannounced, forthcoming issue.

Shucking and *Jiving,* S ing and J ing, etc., are terms that refer to one form of language behavior practiced by Blacks when interacting with authority figures and to another when practiced by Blacks interacting with each other on the peer group level.

With authority figures, *shucking* has been used to stay out of trouble, that is, assume a guise or posture that would appease or satisfy "whitey". In an extreme form it became role playing, such as *tomming,* which, before whites in the South, integrated both verbal and non-verbal behavior into a total performance. In less extreme cases, in the North, the pose and overall verbal accompaniment nevertheless became a convenient coping mechanism to avoid the psychological and physical brutalization that invariably followed a Black vs. authority figure confrontation, and could be assumed whenever the situation demanded it.

Just as Jews developed the verbal technique of answering a question with a question:
"How are you feeling today?"
"So how should I feel?"
to avoid the punishment that was invariably inflicted on them whichever way they answered such a question, so Blacks developed comparable survival techniques.

For many of today's Blacks, self-assertion has displaced accommodation, and the form of shucking that accompanied the accommodationist role. Nevertheless, for many Blacks, the behavior pattern that was such an invaluable aid in "staying out of trouble" was found to be equally invaluable in "getting out of trouble" or avoiding punishment when you were apprehended. What follows are some examples from seventh grade children from an inner city school in Chicago. The children were asked to "talk their way out of" a troublesome situation. Examples of the situation and their impromptu responses follow:

Situation:

You're cursing at this old man and your mother comes walking down the stairs. She hears you.

Response to "talk your way out of this,";

"I'd tell her that I was studying a scene in school for a play."

Situation:

What if you were in a store and were stealing something and the manager caught you.

Responses:

"I would tell him that I was used to putting things in my pocket and then going to pay for them and show the cashier."

"I'd tell him that some of my friends was outside and they wanted some candy so I was going to put it in my pocket to see if it would fit before I bought it."

"I would start stuttering. Then I would say "Oh, Oh, I forgot. Here the money is.""

Situation:

You are at the beach and they've got posted signs all over the beach and floating on the water and you go past the mark!" How do you talk your way out of this to the lifeguard?

Responses:

"I'd tell him that I was having so much fun in the water that I didn't pay attention to the sign."

"I'd say that I was swimming under water and when I came back up I was behind the sign."

Rapping, while used synonymously to mean ordinary conversation, is distinctively a fluent and lively way of talking which is always characterized by a high degree of personal style. The form and style of rapping are determined by and large, by the audience. To one's peer group, rapping may be descriptive of an interesting narration or explanation. Malcom X's *MESSAGE TO THE GRASS ROOTS* is an excellent example of this.

Rapping to a woman is the means through which the male obtains ego satisfaction as well as the mechanism through which he hopes to become intimate with her. To accomplish this his rap is often especially lively, colorful and persuasive.

To a *lame,* i.e., sucker, rapping may be used to *whup a game,* i.e., direct the course of a transaction so as to obtain goods and services from the individual. Here again the verbal component is highly developed in its persuasive power.

In all of the forms of language behavior mentioned above, the element of contest prevails and is an important feature of the confrontation between the speaker and his audience. In the three forms of rapping for example, the speaker was seeking to service his ego, as well as obtain goods and services in two of the three instances. In *shucking* and *jiving* he was attempting to avoid difficulty or seeking to mitigate punishment. In other instances he *grips* when he is confronted with superior power, and even though he is right, has to back down. In still other confrontations he may have to *cop a plea,* which is 'to beg and plead for mercy' involving a total loss of face. With *signifying* he provokes a person by implication or by direct taunt. With *sounding* he alternately insults the person, his family and his home and is in turn insulted. By *running it down* he conveys information, generally in the form of a narrative or explanation; this is the only behavior form in which the element of contest is absent.

Since contest is an ever present part of the confrontation the degree to which the speaker exercises control determines his success. Therefore the prestige norms of language use are those which help to manipulate people and control situations. Specifically these are the rich verbal and non- verbal devices, such as intelligence, personality, style, glibness, smoothness, charm, appearance, etc.

There are other aspects of the communication situation which one can discuss further; but of which time permits just a summary: for example . . . setting, seems to have a negligible influence on the form of Black speech behavior used which is in contrast to the influence setting has on verbal behavior in the mainstream culture. Also, the relative absence of status on the street causes street people to develop verbal ability to a high degree since they can establish control over people and situations only with help of the persuasive and projective powers that words can give. People who have status on the street have often acquired it with the use of words. Note that verbal ability is often inversely correlated with status in mainstream culture i.e., we rely on status to get things done rather than on persuasion. The salesman, who has no status from which he can direct you to buy something, relies more heavily on the art of persuasion than your boss.

To conclude, it ought to be clear to educators that we have missed utilizing the cultural resources that were at our disposal, either because we were unaware that they existed, or felt that they were without value. The time has come to find out what the norms and values of the culturally different are and find some way of incorporating them into the educational process.

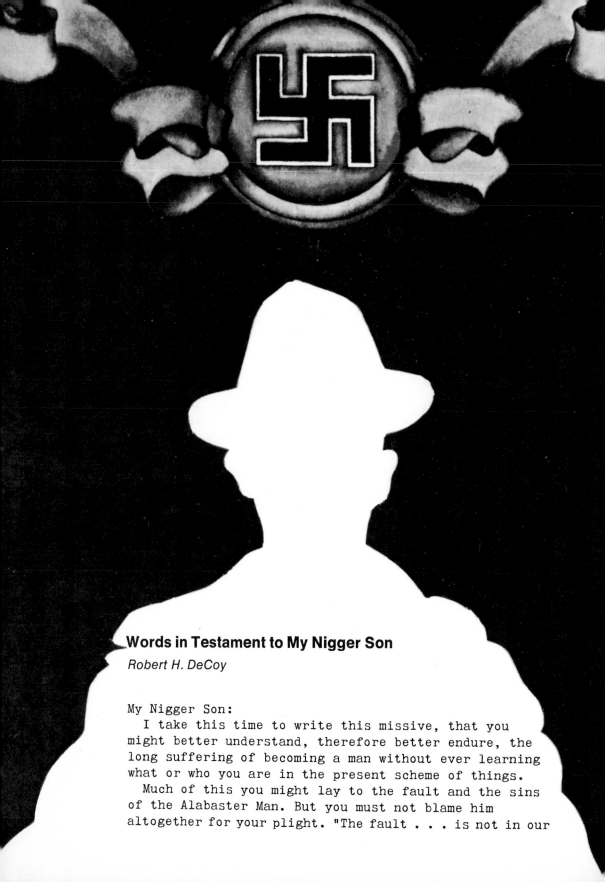

Words in Testament to My Nigger Son

Robert H. DeCoy

My Nigger Son:
   I take this time to write this missive, that you
might better understand, therefore better endure, the
long suffering of becoming a man without ever learning
what or who you are in the present scheme of things.
   Much of this you might lay to the fault and the sins
of the Alabaster Man. But you must not blame him
altogether for your plight. "The fault . . . is not in our

stars, but in ourselves, that we are underlings." The most grievous fault lay in language. Words. His order of words which was never meant to include your kind or the likes of you. His language and philosophy began with a word —and there is where it ends. How can you, my Nigger Son, find your identity, articulate your experiences, in an order of words? Language. Which was created and conceived by a people who did not even know of your black existence or Earthly presence? . . .

How . . . my Nigger Son, can you ever hope to express what you are, who you are, or your experiences with God, in a language so limited, conceived by a people who are quite helpless in explaining themselves?

When we were brought forth, my Nigger Son, depicted as "Beasts of Burden" in his World, upon this Continent, there were still no words invented to describe you. God had given the Alabaster Peer the words, 1. White. 2. God-like. 3. Captor. 4. Master. 5. Christian. 6. Benefactor. 7. Rulers. 8. Caucasians. 9. Patriot.

None of the above words were conceived for you, my Nigger Son, but in equal contrast none of the following words can be applied as a description of him: As you can read and see, each, by corresponding number, is in direct antithesis to what has been reserved for the Alabaster kind: 1. *Black.* 2. *Godless.* 3. *Captive.* 4. *Slave.* 5. *Heathen.* 6. *Beggar.* 7. *Servant.* 8. *Colored.* 9. *Negro. Nigger.*

My Son, you have a choice of being of the latter two, Negro or Nigger, though there are those Bastards amongst us who would say, "It is simply a matter of your conduct and behavior in the presence of white folks." This does quite often distinguish which title the Alabaster Ones will bestow upon you. Note however, there are no contrasting, or counterparts, of such words to describe them. Negro or Nigger? The first is the closest that their language can afford to come, in acknowledging your resemblance to Being—that is, Human. The latter word, "Nigger," is bestowed only upon you to better delineate your differences, as distinctively apart, from the Alabaster Peers. Whatever these two sounds, words, imply, my Son, remember, you have a choice of being either. For "Negro" will never become a reality.

Your Being as a Nigger is closer to your inherent Black nature.

There are no redeeming factors in being accepted as "Negro," for this word was manufactured to describe those Niggers who would waste their existence in the hopeless void of eventually dying as Christian Caucasians.

The Alabaster man invented the word, "Negro," to imply that he could make a Nigger "Grow," that is become a race which even his own God saw no reason to Create. Should the Negro ever become a reality, then, my Nigger Son, the Alabasters will have proved themselves Creators of Human Beings, equal to the very God Whom they are sworn to perpetuate.

eeny meeny miney

WORDS IN TESTAMENT TO MY NIGGER SON

My Dear Nigger Son—In Hope:

I have spoken of their words, which do not apply to you. It behooves me now that I should give you some words which are, or will become, vital to your peculiar existence.

Whereas, at first, words that I give you might evoke humor or jest, remember this is simply because the first words that you learned were theirs. These which I leave you are in direct contrast, for they are Black Words. The ones you have been taught are White. But remember the ones that I list are yours alone. It is part of the heritage that I leave you and your children.

I beseech you, my Nigrite Son, study them well and their meanings. Just as you have attended and tried to find your meanings in the sounds of the Alabaster tongue. You can add to this list as you grow older and begin to discover more of what you really are. I have only commenced the Dictionary for you.

Remember that in words lie many secrets. It is possible that the Secret of God lies in words and the arrangement of words.

Try using the words that I leave you here, learn well their definitions. You will find that as you master them as well as their meanings, they will not only become precious to you, but you will develop a sense of comfort and spiritual security the likes of which you have never known before.

To the extent that you reject these words and their definition is the very marked degree to which you have already been brainwashed. I abjure you to accept this fact. If you do not, I simply lose you to the speed and power of the Alabaster process of which now I write to impede or destroy completely.

THE FIRST DICTIONARY OF NIGRITE WORDS
(A Nigger is a Nigger, by any name)

A GRAY, n.—A Nigrite name reserved for police or law enforcement officers. pl.—The Grays.

AL-A-BAS-TER PEERS, n.—Pertaining to that aspect of Caucasian Power Structure Administrators, Philosophers, Government Officials, Social Organizers and Theologians who exemplify and dictate what Niggers live up to, emulate and worship. Syn.—"Mr. Charlie," "Miss Anne," "The Great White Father," "The Man," "The People," "White Boss."

BLACK-KIND, n.—Pertaining to persons with sufficient Nigger ancestry to be classified as Niggers or Afro-Americans or Negroes. A Nigrite descendant of American slaves, inhabitants of the North and South American continents.

ıoe catch a nigger b

58

BLUE-BOY, n.—Synonym for a Nigger male.

CAN-NI-BAL, n.—Pertaining to a male or female who practices Cannibalism. Syn.—Gouper, Cocksucker, Gash-eater, Joint-copper, Dick-licker, Pussy-eater.

CAN-NI-BAL-ISM, n.—Pertaining to the male or female practice of giving and receiving sexual gratification by applying the mouth and tongue to the genital areas of a partner in love making. Syn.—Gouping, Cock- and Cunt-sucking, Gash-eating, Joint-copping, Dick-licking, Pussy-eating.

COLD, n.—Unreceptive; unfeeling; a shitty attitude, action or reaction of a person or situation.

COM-MON-BRED OUT-CASTS, n.—Pertaining to the underprivileged Nigger Americans. Group Three of the Nigger-American Social Order. See: "History."

CON-NIG-GER-AT-ING, v., adj.—The process of expressing love and concern in relationships with Nigrites or Niggers.

CON-NIG-GER-A-TION, n.—The act of Connigerating.

CON-NIG-GER-ITE, n., adj.—Caucasian or Nigger who is sincere in love and relationships with the Nigrite. Syn.—Conniggerator; f.—Conniggerine; m.—Connigger.

COOL, n., v.—In control, wise, aloof, detached. A state of being in admirable possession of one's wits and emotions.

CRE-OLE, n.—Now a word of American controversy. Originally, a description of the offspring and extension of French or Spanish admixture with a native Black or Nigger. The corrupted and altered American meaning of "Creole" would have it as an offspring and extension of French and Spanish admixture, descendants of Louisiana settlers.
Note: This belies the literal description of "Creole" as still recognized in the West Indies and Spanish America: "An extension of a native of any color but not of indigenous blood." Since the presence of Nigrite or Nigger "blood" carries "stigma" or racial classification of Negro in America, the meaning has been altered in English-speaking dictionaries and encyclopedias of today and has "Creole" allude to white ancestry exclusively.

CRE-OLES, n., pl.—Pertaining to Group One of the Nigger-American Social Order. See: "History."

CRUIS-ING, v.—The practice of extending overt or subtle invitation for intimacy with a member of the opposite or same sex; devious suggestion or promise of intimacy from a faggot, lesbian or prostitute; an exchange of flirtations and willingness for copulation between a Caucasian and a Nigrite. Conjug.: Cruise, cruising, cruised. Syn.: Flagging, Making, Hitting.

DIG, v.—To comprehend, understand well, be wise to. Conjug.: Dig, Dug, Dugged.

the toe if he hollers l

DOWN-HOME, n., adv.—Distinctly pertaining to the Southern part of the United States; to describe a native of any area below the Mason-Dixon Line. Also, adj.—Used to describe something as being satisfying, wonderful or comfortable for Niggers.

FOR-EIGN, n., adj.—Pertaining to unnatural sex practices. Syn.: Way-out.

FOR-EIGN-ER, n.—A male or female who specializes in and favors unnatural sex acts. Syn.: Stranger: f.—dike (or dyke), butch, lez, Lesbian; m.—fag, faggot, fairy, queen (or quean).

GRAY-BOY, n.—A Nigrite name for a Caucasian male. Syn.: Whitey.

HOK-A-GENE, n., adj.—An Oriental, Japanese, Chinese, East Indian who loves, marries, lives with or cohabits with a Nigrite or Nigger.

IN-TE-GRAT-ING, v.—The process of Integration. Ant.: Segregating.

IN-TE-GRA-TION, n.—A Negro aim of being accepted and assimilated into a white or Caucasian community through the process of beseechment, protests and legislation; a process employed by the Black-kind to disappear into a Caucasian society, despite admitted physical, mental and spiritual differences among peoples.

IN-TE-GRA-TION-IST, n.—A Caucasian or a Black-kind who champions and supports the causes and ends of Integration as the ultimate ideal. One who believes in Integration.

JO-DY, n.—A Nigger cocksman who specializes in seducing the wives, daughters and mothers of Caucasians. "Jody" is a contraction of "Joe-the-Grinder" ("Sweet spot finder"), whose balls weighed forty-four pounds, whose penis was gigantic. His occupation was woodchopping for Southern white women during the absence of the husband. As the legend would have it, "Jody" was the original Nigger-in-the-woodpile, who was discovered by a white husband one day, after having seduced both the wife and daughter. He was killed and went to Hell. "There, he grabbed the devil and screwed him so well that Satan sent him back to roam the earth forever, since Heaven certainly wouldn't have him." Today, he comes and injects his spirit and prowess into selected Nigrite males to fulfill the purposes that he lived and died for.

KIN-KIND, n., adj.—One whom a Nigger feels is just and kindly to a Nigrite or Nigger. Ant.: Kolkind.

KOL-KIND, n., adj.—One who is unfeeling toward or hates a Nigrite. Generally used in description of a Caucasian who is harsh and unjust to a Nigrite. Ant.: Kinkind.

KUD-A-MAK-ER, n., adj.—One of Mexican or Spanish descent who loves marries or cohabits with a Nigrite or Nigger.

t him go eeny meeny

MU-THA-FUC-KA, n., adj., adv.—The Nigger's only actual contribution to the American-Caucasian language. Originally conceived to describe the white man's crimes against slave mothers. A term which described the Nigger who unconsciously and unknowingly committed the crime of Oedipus. (See Webster's Dictionary or read the extant drama by Sophocles, *Oedipus Rex*.) Originally, a derogatory term. Presently used as a term of either admiration or disgust, depending on the moment and the emotional or intellectual point of view when written or vocalized. pl.—Muthafuckas. v. Conjug.: Muthafuck, muthafucking, muthafucked. Considered in extremely bad taste by Caucasians and the Niggeroos.

NEG-RO, n., adj.—A vulgar but accepted description of the Nigrite or Nigger. Referring to an American Nigger of decency and status. A white-Nigger. Or a brainwashed Black who would be a Caucasian if possible. A Nigger who desires to be and would believe himself a social factor in the modern American complex. pl.—Negroes. Syn.: Afro-American, Colored person.

NI-GER-I-A, n.—One of the original Nigger settlements of Africa, identified now as a republic on behalf of Caucasian-Christian commercial and industrial interests.

NI-GER-I-AN, n., adj.—Pertaining to Nigeria; a native of Nigeria.

NIG-GER, n., adj.—Same as Nigrite; used by American Caucasians and so-called Negroes to refer to a person of low degree or class.

NIG-GER-AM-ER, n.—A Nigrite pimp who specializes solely in white prostitutes; a Nigger who lives with or sells the services and bodies of white females or white males; a Nigger who sleeps exclusively with white females or white males. Syn.: Bull, Buck, Boar.

NIG-GER-ANCE, n.—Ignorance of Niggerology, Niggerism and Niggermantics; pretense of not understanding the meanings of Niggerlastics, professing not to be a Nigger; embracing the doctrines of Black Nationalists, Zen Buddhists, Orthodox Jews, Yogis, Black Muslims, or others alien to the distinction of Nigger or Nigrite.

NIG-GER-ATE, n.—One who hates Niggers; usually the Caucasian but also some among colored people. v.—The act of hating Niggers.

NIG-GER-A-TOR, n.—A Caucasian who despises, hates, rejects the aspirations and efforts of a Nigrite. A Nigger who despises himself and hates those who resemble him in features and/or color.

NIG-GER-AY, n.—A Caucasian with a sincere desire to live and be as, or among, the Nigrites, one who loves and professes love for a Niggerene or Niggeron. pl.—Niggeraes.

NIG-GER-OON-IE, n.—A Nigger or Nigrite female who is "passing for white."

miney moe catch a n

NIG-GER-OT, n.—A form of propaganda prepared and delivered to Niggers or a contingent of the Nigrite community; a form of questionable or insincere praise bestowed upon a Nigrite or a group of Niggers; drawing a historical parallel between Nigger problems and the problems of the Jews; seeing oneself not as a Nigger, but simply as a human being. Syn.: Bullshit, bull corn, hog wash.

NIG-GER-PHILE, n.—One who worships Blackness exclusively; one who loves Niggers.

NIG-GER-PHIL-I-A, n.—The exclusive love or worship of Blackness and Niggers.

NIG-GER-PHOB-I-A, n.—Intense hate and/or fear of the Nigger or Nigrite; fear of Nigger qualities.

NIG-GER PRO-GRESS-IVES, n. pl.—Pertaining to the intellectual or educated aspects of a Nigger-American Social Order. Group Two of the Nigger-American Social Order. See: "History."

NIG-GER-SOME, n., adj.—Appealing, attractive to Nigrite tastes, as color, "soul-food," dress, language and philosophy.

NIG-GER-TINE, n.—A white female hustler, whore, prostitute who favors a Nigrite or Nigger as her pimp.

NIG-GER-U, n.—A Nigger who despises himself and others like him in physical appearance and color. One who aspires to be a Caucasian. One who embraces the title, Negro. A mispronunciation of the original is Negro pl.—Niggeroos.

NIG-GER-UPPE, n.—A Nigger who is a tool for whites; one who quotes white words as authority; those who serve as peacemaker, negotiator between the white power structure and the Nigrite aspects of a community; one who quotes white man's philosophy and justifies it, pleading for Nigger understanding of a Caucasian cause; one who believes and would have others believe that the Caucasian is as bad off as the Nigger physically, mentally and spiritually; a well-meaning Nigrite in the Caucasian cause; one who carries the Caucasian version of a message or sermon to make it applicable to the Nigrite. Syn.: Uncle Tom, Uncle Mose, Elder Whitehead, Deacon Jones, Aunt Lucy, Aunt Sally, Mammy Lou.

NIG-GER-ENE, n.—A female American Nigger.

NIG-GER-ET-TA, n.—The female counterpart of a Niggeramer, who sleeps and copulates exclusively with Caucasians, slighting the males of her own race. Syn.: Pig, Sow, Cow.

NIG-GER-FI-CA-TION, n.—Process of thinking or being Black, physically, mentally, spiritually. (Rare today.) Generally discouraged among colored peoples, especially in America; a process popular among Caucasians;

gger by the toe if he

commercially exploited with powders, creams, lotions, electrical sun lamps, and practices of open air nudity in order to become darkened. v. Conjug.: Niggerfy, Niggerfying, Niggerfied.

NIG-GER-I-LINE, n., adj.—Pertaining to pure Black qualities, as Analine Black.

NIG-GER-I-SCENT, n., v.—The process of becoming Black as to taste, smell, appearance.

NIG-GER-ISM. n.—Pertaining to the philosophy of Niggers or Nigrites. Quotations and utterances particular to Niggers. pl.—Niggerisms.

NIG-GER-IS-TIC, n.—A Nigger who embraces and worships the doctrines of a Judeo-Christian Deity. A Nigger Preacher, Priest, Nun, Church Official of Christianity. pl.—Niggeristics. Also adj.—Pertaining to Negroes and Negroism.

NIG-GER-ITE, adj.—Pertaining to the characteristics of Blackness and Niggers.

NIG-GER-LAS-TIC, n., adj.—Knowledgeable, sincere, earnest in understanding of relationships, problems and philosophies of Niggers.

NIG-GER-MAN-TIC, n.—A Nigger who is obsessed with love and dedication for African History and Culture. pl.—Niggermantics.

NIG-GER-OFF, n., adj.—A place of business, establishment or facility which discourages, does not admit, insults the attendance or presence of a Nigger.

NIG-GER-OL-O-GIST, n.—One who has mastered the science or study of Niggers or Nigrites.

NIG-GER-OL-O-GY, n.—The study or the science of being Niggers.

NIG-GER-ON, n.—A male American Nigger.

NIG-GER-OON, n.—A Nigger or Nigrite male who is "passing for white."

NIG-GER-WIT, n., adj.—Pertaining to a deceitful Caucasian who prides himself on his personal good will and understanding of the Nigrites that he meets and claims to know; also, shrewd aspects of a Nigger.

NIG-GRI-GARD, n.—Awareness, pride in Niggerness. v.—Niggrigarding.

NIG-GRI-TUDE, n.—The condition of being Black, v.—Niggrituding.

NIG-RITE, n., adj.—A Black descendant born and bred in the United States. pl.—Nigrites. Syn.: Nigger.

NIG-RI-TI-AN, n.—Pertaining to a district or territory of Middle Africa. Also, a pure-blood African Nigger.

SHIT-TY, adj.—Pertaining to an unpleasant reception, attitude and/or treatment of one person to another.

SPOOK, n.—A common nickname for a Nigrite or Nigger. Originally a Nigger word referring to white people.

hollers let him go

UN-ASS, v.—To surrender or give up something; to remove one's presence from a scene or place. Conjug.: Unass, unassing, unassed.

WIPED OUT, n.—A state of being exhausted, unconscious or unaware because of indulgence in liquor, drugs or sex. Syn.: Turned out, wasted.

So, my Nigger Son, I have made the feeble and sincere attempt to begin your Dictionary of Nigger-American words. Perhaps you, or some other who come after, will improve, add to and complete this particular language, so that even the Alabasters, in whose midst we live, might more fully understand us. Remember, this is exactly the way that their languages began, when someone amongst them began scribbling the interpretation of their meanings on the walls of caves.

eeny

meeny

miney

moe

black (blăk), *adj.* [AS. *blæc.*] **1**. Destitute of light, or incapable of reflecting it; devoid of color or so dark as to have no distinguishable color; -- opposed to *white.* **2**. Enveloped in darkness; devoid of light; hence, utterly dismal or gloomy; as, the future looked *black.* **3**. Having dark skin, hair, and eyes; specif., pertaining or belonging to a race characterized by dark pigmentation, including Negroes, Negritos, and Australian natives **4** Soiled with dirt; foul. **5**. Wearing black garments; as, the *black* knight. **6**. Sullen; hostile; foreboding; as, *black* looks. **7** Foully or outrageously wicked; as, *black* cruelty. **8**. Indicating disgrace or dishonor, or culpability; as, a *black* mark **9**. Involving baneful or forbidden practices; as, *black* magic. **10** Sold, distributed, or charged in violation of official quotas, ceiling prices, priorities, or ration restrictions, or conducted for such sale or distribution; as, *black* rent; *black* market. — *v. t.* -- **black out**. **1**. To obscure in blackness, esp. by extinguishing all lights as a protective measure against an air raid; also, to be engulfed in blackness. **2**. To delete or suppress through censorship. **3**. *Radio.* To silence or to jam (radio transmission).

By permission from Webster's New International Dictionary, Second Edition, © 1934 by G. and C. Merriam Company, publishers of the Merriam-Webster Dictionaries.

TIGER
TIGGER
NIGGER

Black is when you're playing "Eenie meanie mynie moe" and the thing they catch by the toe is a tiger.

A Chant for Children

Frank Horne

Little Black boy
Chased down the street—
"Nigger, nigger never die
Black face an' shiny eye,
Nigger . . . nigger . . . nigger . . ."

Hannibal . . . Hannibal
Bangin' thru the Alps
Licked the proud Romans,
Ran home with their scalps—
"Nigger . . . nigger . . . nigger . . ."

Othello . . . black man
Mighty in war
Listened to Iago
Called his wife a whore—
"Nigger . . . nigger . . . nigger . . ."

Crispus . . . Attucks
Bullets in his chest
Red blood of freedom
Runnin' down his vest
"Nigger . . . nigger . . . nigger . . ."

Toussaint . . . Toussaint
Made the French flee
Fought like a demon
Set his people free—
"Nigger . . . nigger . . . nigger . . ."

Jesus . . . Jesus
Son of the Lord
—Spit in his face
—Nail him on a board
"Nigger . . . nigger . . . nigger . . ."

Little Black boy
Runs down the street—
"Nigger, nigger never die
Black face an' shiny eye,
Nigger . . . nigger . . . nigger . . ."

Incident

Countee Cullen

Once riding in old Baltimore,
Heart-filled, head-filled with glee,
I saw a Baltimorean
Keep looking straight at me.

Now I was eight and very small,
And he was no whit bigger,
And so I smiled, but he poked out
His tongue and called me, "nigger."

I saw the whole of Baltimore
From May until December:
Of all the things that happened there
That's all that I remember.

Harlem Jive

This is your grandpa's jive.
Do you dig?
The white man says black talk
is substandard.
What words has he stolen from
your grandpa?

Harlem Jive

Dan Burley

FIRST STEPS IN JIVE

Names of Things

. . . It is of primary interest that we get a good working knowledge of the Jive names for things. It is also essential to understand here that really good Jive talk is also accompanied by appropriate gestures, inflections of the voice, and other aids toward making one's meaning clear.

The simplest words in Jive are those relating to things—inanimate objects, the furniture in a room, objects which can be moved, sold, bought, exchanged, all concrete and tangible objects.

Alarm Clock—Chimer
Body—Frame
Corner—Three pointer
Door—Slammer
Elderly man—Poppa Stoppa
Feet—Groundpads
Gun—Bow-wow
Hands—Grabbers
Jail—House of Many Slammers
Liquor—Lush, juice
Moon—Pumpkin
Nose—Sniffer
Overcoat—Benny or Bear

Verbal Nouns

These are the words that move and "jump," the Jive Verbs that give the language its appeal and spontaneity, that make Jive flexible.

Here we are dealing with the words which describe bodily motion, the movement of arms, legs, hands, and feet. They also denote intangible action

having to do with thought, comprehension, a very important phase of Jive.

We start off by naming simple acts. In the preceding portion of this chapter we discussed the name of things, we had you going home: and, instead of saying, "I am going home," you said, "I'm going to my pile of stone." "Am going" is a perfectly legitimate expression in English denoting an intention and describing an act already taking place. In Jive you would substitute the words "cop" and "trill" in place of "am going," and your statement would be: "I'm copping my trill for my pile of stone." Simple, isn't it? Even your great-aunt Hannah could understand that, couldn't she?

There are relatively few Jive verbs, since Jive is primarily a language consisting of descriptive adjectives, rather than being replete with verbs denoting action. However, the few Jive verbs to balance the enormous number of nouns, or names of things, are thrillingly competent, graphic and commanding. Two in particular are worthy of our attention. The verbs "knock" and "lay" are the basis of Jive. "Knock" in particular is found all through the process of a Jive conversation. It is one of the key words.

"Knock a nod," says the Jiver. He means going to sleep. "Knock a scoff," he says. He means, eat a meal. "Knock a broom" is found to mean a quick walk or brisk trot away from something. "Knock me down to her" means to introduce me to a young lady; "knock off a riff," in musical parlance means for a musician to play a musical break in a certain manner. "Knock a jug" means to buy a drink.

The verb, "Lay," is another vitally important verb in the Jiver's vocabulary. It also denotes action. For example: "Lay some of that cash on me," says a Jiver. His statement means literally what it says. But if he says, "he was really laying it," he means someone was doing something out of the ordinary, as in a stage performance or musical program, or a well-dressed man entering a room and suddenly becoming the object of all eyes.

Here are some other important verbs:

Blow—To leave, move, run away

Cop—To take, receive, understand, do

Dig—To understand, take, see, conceive, perceive, think, hand over

Drag—Humiliate, upset, disillusion

Stash—To lay away, hide, put down, stand, a place

Take a powder—Leave, disappear

Jive Adjectives, or Words Signifying Quality

Before the names of things, or objects, as in standard English we need to know a special state or condition regarding them in order to get a clear mental picture in our minds. For example, a *blue* sky, a *soft* chair, the *hot* sun, etc. The language of Jive has plenty of such adjectives, more of which are constantly being added every day. The following list may prove helpful:

Anxious—Wonderful, excellent

Fine—All right, okay, excellent

Frantic—Great, wonderful

Groovy—To one's liking, sensational, outstanding, splendid

Mad—Fine, capable, able, talented

Mellow—State of delight, beautiful, great, wonderful

Righteous—Pleasing to the senses, glorious, pretty, beautiful, mighty

Solid—Very fine, okay, great, terrific

Jive Phrases, Simile and Hyperbole

As in standard English, Jive is flexible and infinitely capable of expressing phrases or rare harmonic beauty and rhythmical force. The language of the hepsters is constantly acquiring new descriptive phrases, narrative and explanatory in content, which constitute an integral and necessary part of one's equipment for gaining proficiency in talking and writing Jive. Here are a few, some of which are self-explanatory, and others of which are translated into English:

Fine as wine

Mellow as a cello

Like the bear, nowhere

Playing the dozens with my uncle's cousins—doing things wrong

"I'm like the chicken, I ain't stickin' "—broke

"Dig what I'm laying down?"—understand what I'm saying?

"I'm chipper as the China Clipper and in the mood to play"—flying high and personally feeling fine

"Swimps and wice"—Shrimps and rice

"Snap a snapper"—light a match

"Like the farmer and the 'tater, plant you now and dig you later"— means, "I must go, but I'll remember you."

Jive Rhyming and Meter

The language of Jive presents an unusual opportunity for experimentation in rhymes, in fact, a lot of it is built on rhymes, which at first hearing might be considered trite and beneath the notice. However, Jive rhymes and couplets are fascinating and comparatively easy to fashion. As to meter, it is desirable that the syllables form a correct measure, but this is not essential. All that is necessary is that the end words rhyme; they do not necessarily need to make sense. Here are some examples:

"Collars a broom with a solid zoom"—left in a hurry

"No lie, frog eye"

"What's your duty, Tutti-Frutti?"

"Joe the Jiver, the Stranded Pearl-Diver"

"Had some whiskey, feel kind o' frisky"

"Swing and sweat with Charley Barnet"—means dance to Barnet's music

"Are you going to the function at Tuxedo Junction?"—Tuxedo Junctions are places, dancehalls, candy-stores, etc., where hepsters gather.

"My name is Billie, have you seen Willie?"—used as a greeting or salutation among accomplished hepcats

"Ain't it a pity, you're from Atlantic City?"—salutation

"I can't frolic, I got the colic"—I drank too much

Test Your Knowledge of
Harlem Jive Talk, Idioms, Folk Expressions

1. ACE	1. Money; wages.
2. ALLIGATOR	2. To leave.
3. BABY KISSER	3. Excitable.
4. BACK	4. To have riotous fun.
5. BALL	5. Same as blow your fuse.
6. BEAT	6. To get angry.
7. BENDERS	7. Cent.
8. BLIP	8. Bad looking, depressed, tired.
9. BLINDS	9. To explain, to describe.
10. BLOW	10. Depressing, no good.
11. BLOWTOP	11. A politician.
12. BLOW YOUR FUSE	12. Same as blow your fuse.
13. BLOW YOUR LID	13. Bosom friend.
14. BLOW YOUR TOP	14. Same as ace.
15. BOON-COON	15. Knees.
16. BOOT	16. Rods beneath a railway coach.
17. BREAD	17. Good, fine.
18. BRING DOWN	18. Very good or bad.
19. BROWNIE	19. A jitterbug.
20. BUG	20. A female.
21. BUST YOUR VEST	21. A playgirl.
22. CAT	22. A dollar bill.
23. CHICK	23. To understand everything.
24. CHINCH	24. Take a quick nap.
25. CHINCHPAD	25. An aged person.
26. CHIPPY	26. To dance.
27. CHIPPY'S PLAYGROUND	27. Apartment, room, home.
28. CHIPS	28. A bedbug.
29. CHOLLY	29. To take a seat.
30. CHOPS	30. To understand, to enjoy.
31. C-NOTES	31. A male.
32. CLINKER	32. To go to work.
33. COLLAR ALL JIVE	33. House, home.
34. COOL	34. Corn whiskey.
35. COP	35. Not caring.
36. COP A NOD	36. Calm, unruffled.
37. COP A DEUCEWAYS	37. Two.
38. COP A SLAVE	38. To irritate.
39. COP A SQUAT	39. To disappear, to leave suddenly.
40. CORN	40. High hat, snooty.
41. CREAKER	41. To depart.
42. CRIB	42. A pot belly on a man.
43. CUT OUT	43. A hundred dollar bill.
44. CUT SOME RUG	44. To take, receive, understand.
45. DEN	45. To swell with pride.
46. DEUCE	46. Humorous but vulgar references to someone else's mother.
47. DICTY	

48. DIG	47. To buy $2.00 worth of something.
49. DO A HOUDINI	48. To get acquainted with, to under-
50. DOODLEY-SQUAT	stand.
51. DOWN WITH IT	49. Money.
52. DOZENS	50. A sour note in music.
53. DRAG	51. Lips, mouth, jaws.
54. DRAPE	52. A hotel, a cheap rooming house.
55. DUST	53. A suit of clothes.
56. DUST YOUR BROOM	54. Fresh, impudent, sassy, flirtacious.
57. EARLY BLACK	55. A white person.
58. EARLY BLUE	56. Great, wonderful.
59. EIGHTY-EIGHT	57. An exciting thing.
60. EYEBALL	58. Show off, strut your stuff, go over
61. FAULT	big.
62. FAY	59. To slap hands in greeting.
63. FEDS	60. To look at someone.
64. FLIC, FLICKER	61. Free, without charge.
65. FLY	62. Marijuana.
66. FLY RIGHT	63. The President of the U.S.
67. FOR KICKS	64. To clarify, speak plainly.
68. FRACTURE YOUR WIG	65. To dine.
69. FRANTIC	66. To behave.
70. FREEBYE	67. A juke box.
71. GAMS	68. A colored man.
72. GASSER	69. Soothingly pleasant.
73. GATE	70. To humiliate, upset, disillusion.
74. GAUGE	71. To leave.
75. GEECHEE	72. A motion picture.
76. GET OFF	73. A single engagement for a
77. GET STRAIGHT	musician.
78. GIG	74. To go away, to leave town.
79. GIMME SOME SKIN	75. A white person.
80. GIT-BOX	76. Federal officers.
81. GO DOWN	77. To talk alot, gossip.
82. GONE	78. The happenings.
83. GREAT WHITE FATHER	79. Early evening.
84. GREY	80. A phoney, a worthless character.
85. GREASE YOUR CHOPS	81. Great, fine, very good.
86. GROOVEY	82. To blame.
87. GUMBEAT	83. A South Carolinian.
88. GUTBUCKET	84. Loud and low down.
89. HALF-PAST A COLORED MAN	85. For fun.
90. HAMFAT	86. A big mouth.
	87. Same as early black.
	88. Legs.
	89. Same as blow your top.
	90. A piano.

ANSWERS:

1. (13)	23. (20)	45. (27)	67. (85)
2. (19)	24. (28)	46. (37)	69. (56)
3. (11)	25. (52)	47. (40)	70. (61)
4. (17)	26. (21)	48. (30)	71. (88)
5. (4)	27. (42)	49. (39)	72. (57)
6. (8)	28. (49)	50. (35)	73. (86)
7. (15)	29. (22)	51. (48)	74. (62)
8. (18)	30. (51)	52. (46)	75. (83)
9. (16)	31. (43)	53. (70)	76. (58)
10. (2)	32. (50)	54. (53)	77. (64)
11. (3)	33. (23)	55. (71)	78. (73)
12. (6)	34. (36)	56. (74)	79. (59)
13. (12)	35. (44)	57. (79)	80. (67)
14. (5)	36. (24)	58. (87)	81. (78)
15. (14)	37. (47)	59. (90)	82. (81)
16. (9)	38. (32)	60. (60)	83. (63)
17. (1)	39. (29)	61. (82)	84. (75)
18. (10)	40. (34)	62. (55)	85. (65)
19. (7)	41. (25)	63. (76)	86. (69)
20. (38)	42. (33)	64. (72)	87. (77)
21. (45)	43. (41)	65. (54)	88. (84)
22. (31)	44. (26)	66. (66)	89. (68)
			90. (80)

GRADE EQUIVALENTS

86- 90: MELLOW, HIPSTER CLASS
71- 85: SOLID, SUB-HIPSTER CLASS
 0- 70: BLIP; LANE, HAMFAT, SQUARE CLASS

Rhymed Jive

Dan Burley

Fine as wine,
Mellow as a cello.

I dig all jive,
That's the reason I stay alive.

Let's get racy
With Count Basie.

I can't frolic,
I got the colic.

Do your duty,
Tutti-Fruitti.

I'm like the chicken. . .
I ain't stickin'.

Where did you get that drape?
Your pants look like a cape.

Cut out that
Rootin' and tootin'
Then there won't be
Any shootin' and bootin'.

John Greenleaf Whittier's "The Barefoot Boy"

A Parody in Harlem Jive

Dan Burley

Blessings on Thee, Little Square,
Barefoot Cat with the unconked hair;
With thy righteous pegtop pants,
And thy solid hepcat's stance,
With thy chops so red and mellow,
Kissed by chicks so fine and yellow;
With the bean beaming on thy crown,
That sky of thine such a bringdown;
My own tick-tock to thee I bare,

I was once an unhipped Square,
A Lane, thou art; Poppa Stoppa
Is only a pigeon dropper;
Let the Cats with gold go trotting,
Barefoot, knock thy trill while plotting
Thou has more than Cat can lam—
In the reach of gin and gam;
Outward foxy, inward, mop!
Blessings on thee, Junior Hop.

Willie Cool Digs the Scene

Harlem Jive Talk with Translation

Dan Burley

MY MAN:—The freeze has really set in on the turf, champ, and a kiddie has the toughest kind of time trying to get hold to some long bread so that he can have a ball and come on with frantic plays all up and down the line. Home, it's so bad that a lot of the cats on the stroll can't even get to their grits half the time. There used to be a few hustles that you could always fall back on for your twos and fews but nothing is happening at all. Even the soft shoe or gumshoe plays are cold. It used to be that a man could lay down a real hype by tomming to some grey but most of them plays got nixed by the hard beef laid down by some of the equal rights kids. You can still get some fast action on the single action kick because most of the pickups carry the stuff in their head and pass the scribe. This tricks the bluecoats and bulls trying to pickup on the action for a break job. It's a little tough copping any bread on the straight digit action because the boys from the ace law and order pad have been whaling like mad at the turnin' points. The heavy iron boys who didn't get snagged in the crummy play are blowing the burg if they're straight waiting for the chill to set in or they're just cooling it until somebody gets the contacts straight so that the brass will hold still for an arrangement. Con plays are out, too, cause everybody is so hip, there ain't no fools to drop a shuck on. You move in one a lane or square with the smooth tongue action and half the time he's got a riffle of his own that he drops on you behind a sob story so you wind up giving up some iron to him or her and then blow your stack when you see the action that plays behind it for the next time you eyeball the turkey, he running them around at a giggle juice joint. It is the craziest action, Jim, so it's best to go on the desperate tip and cop a slave for your ends. Later, daddy.

WHO'S GOT

William Cool Surveys the Situation

Translation of Willie Cool Digs the Scene:

MY FRIEND:—I am really sick about the way things have gotten so difficult and money so scarce a fellow can hardly hustle any easy money any more. It is so bad that many of the fellows on the street can't even make enough to cover their meals regularly. The once fertile avenues of kowtowing to the whites has been dried up the virile campaign for equal rights. Single action on the numbers is still a possibility because the writers carry their plays in their heads instead of in writing. But the straight numbers men are either on the lams or inactive because of raids and other difficulties with the law. But things will change when the proper contacts are made with the higher ups. Confidence games are out now, too, because there are no unwary people to use as victims. In fact, you try such tricks and you may wind up falling for the other fellow's story yourself, only to be humiliated when you see the person enjoying himself with your money at a bar. Things are so difficult, Jim, that in desperation it's best to make the most drastic of all moves and go and get yourself a regular job. I'll see you later, pal.

SOUL
SOUL
SOUL
SOUL
SOUL
SOUL
SOUL
SOUL
SOUL
SOUL
SOUL
SOUL
SOUL
SOUL
SOUL
SOUL

Don Lee, *Ebony* Magazine/Johnson Publishing Co., Inc. Adam Clayton Powell, Wide World Photos. Lena Horne, Wide World Photos. Bobby Seale, Ted Streshinsky. Stokely Carmichael, Wide World Photos. Malcolm X, Photo Researchers, Inc. Ray Charles, Wide World Photos. LeRoi Jones, Chester Higgins, Jr. Jesse Jackson, Photo Researchers, Inc.

Saturday Night

Langston Hughes

Play it once.
O, play it some more.
Charlie is a gambler
An' Sadie is a whore.
    A glass o' whiskey
    An' a glass o' gin:
    Strut, Mr. Charlie,
    Till de dawn comes in.
Pawn yo' gold watch
An' diamond ring.
Git a quart o' licker.
Let's shake dat thing!
    Skee-de-dad! De-dad!
    Doo-doo-doo!
    Won't be nothin' left
    When de worms git through.
    An' you's a long time
    Dead
    When you is
    Dead, too.
So beat dat drum, boy!
Shout dat song:
Shake 'em up an' shake 'em up
All night long.
    Hey! Hey!
      Ho . . . Hum!
      Do it, Mr. Charlie,
      Till de red dawn come.

Captions by Henry Simmons.

Don Lee
If you can't dig the soul he writes, you need some.

Adam Powell
Blew the man's mind when he did his thing. Count him in.

Lena Horne
Found out late where her Blackness is, but she's together now.

Bobby Seale
Went in with soul —came out with more. Power to the People.

Stokely Carmichael
So much soul they won't let him into Trinidad.

Malcolm X
Big Red's soul goes marching on and nobody can stop it.

Ray Charles
Father, son and soulful ghost. If he ain't got it nobody has.

Ameer Baraka
Used to be LeRoi Jones, but the soul is the same.

Jesse Jackson
One of the first to be "free at last," he IS somebody!

soul

Soul

Barbara Simmons

Tell me about Soul
Do you know? Have I got it?
Do you have it? Can you touch mine?
I'll touch yours.

Soul is a plastic man
who lives in an invisible shell
and drifts to heaven or to hell
when you get shot or trip or slip
on a banana peel left living in the
    street.

Naw man!
Soul's a trumpet playin, Baby!
Eyes closed and cryin NOTES
spottin hizself
hiz inside self
and groovin and cryin
there's gonna be/ gotta be
AN EXPLOSION

and there is:
women cryin, heels tappin,
no nappin, no foolin, no drinkin,
    no talkin,
or smokin

just beatin hard hearts
made softer
a moment

SOUL SOUL SOUL
YO SOUL/MI SOUL/HE SOUL/
FA SOUL/LA SOUL
WHEEE
    SOUL
is way down deep in the bucket
Soul's way up high floatin around
Soul's sittin on the subway
    you see me
    I see you
but nobody's lookin.
Soul is Screamin/Screechin
    TINTINNABULATION!
      That's Soul!!

Ring bells oh
RING LAWDY LAWDY
You can't touch it or feel it
but you touch it and feel it
it moves ya when you see it,
and you feel it when it moves ya
cause you can't see it if it
moves ya

It's the holy ghost
It's the seven seas
It's chicken pie
and a bloody nose

It's the rhythmic beat
of two flat feet
thumpin and bumpin
out soul
SOUL SOUL
will beat ya
in a minute
if you're highfaluttin
round in it
Listen:
    A beautiful south sea island,
the whistle of the waves,
grass skirts, the whistle of,
a liner docks, smiling faces
You're here! Mr. & Mrs. Westerveal
Duddly Hammington, you're here

staying at the HILTON,
registered and fed, you take a "dip"
at the hotel pool
WHATA LIFE! WHATA LIVIN!
A dance? A drink from a ceramic
    coconut
A piece of mint thrown on the side
    A flower
in Miz Duddly's hair? That's Soul?
(You're told).
But in the distance:
drums beatin, natives retreatin,
night grows darker,
fires starta glowin,

Reprinted from *Black Fire*, edited by LeRoi Jones and Larry Neal, Wm. Morrow & Co., Inc., New York, N.Y., 1968. Used with permission of Barbara Simmons and the Ronald Hobbs Literary Agency.

somethin magic gets ta goin
heat gettin hotta,
somethin swellin deep inside ya,
hips movin and groovin,
this ain't art
It's Real/Movin!
DO YOU HEAR ME, MR. DUDDLY?
ARE YOU SWINGIN AND SWAYIN
WITH MIZ DUDDLY IN HER
   CORSETED MOO MOO?

COULD YOU DIG IT IF YOU KNEW IT
YOU SPENT YOUR MONEY AND
   YA BLEW IT!
TAKE THE LINER WITH DINAH
   (SHORE) SINGIN 49ER,
NOOO SOUL.

Soul is the titular head of your emotional household something in man believed to be the source of his spiritual
being

Yeah, man!
Soul is the holy rollers
and all the unholy rollers
groovin in their own kinda way
Soul is the swish and swash
of a fat bahind with somethin good
on her mind
Please understand it!
You can't go round spillin

out pat definitions
on Soul
Cause Soul is goin down
in the gutter down
and comin up/ STRONG
a rose with a gutter smell
and ya love that smell
wont lose that smell
cause it's where ya been
and ya might go back
Heard a man say,
"I laughed all the breath out my body."
Now that's Soul
Soul is burnin for learnin
and learnin ta burn
and singin
for singin, no more
Soul is an honest livin
legal or illegal when you're honest
with yourself about life
Soul is a heart cut out of watermelon
   rind
screaming, "I wanta VOTE!"
while the vein of a country
the A-okay order, chokes off it's breath

See
how deep Soul can go.
Anyhow, for those who don't
   understand
Soul, there is this word,
you never will.

The Language of Soul

Claude Brown

Perhaps the most soulful word in the world is "nigger." Despite its very
definite fundamental meaning (the Negro man), and disregarding the depre-
catory connotation of the term, "nigger" has a multiplicity of nuances when
used by soul people. Dictionaries define the term as being synonymous with
Negro, and they generally point out that it is regarded as a vulgar expression.
Nevertheless, to those of chitlins-and-neck-bones background the word
nigger is neither a synonym for Negro nor an obscene expression.

"Nigger" has virtually as many shades of meaning in Colored English as the demonstrative pronoun "that," prior to application to a noun. To some Americans of African ancestry (I avoid using the term Negro whenever feasible, for fear of offending the Brothers X, a pressure group to be reckoned with), nigger seems preferable to Negro and has a unique kind of sentiment attached to it. This is exemplified in the frequent—and perhaps even excessive—usage of the term to denote either fondness or hostility.

It is probable that numerous transitional niggers and even established ex-soul brothers can—with pangs of nostalgia—reflect upon a day in the lollipop epoch of lives when an adorable lady named Mama bemoaned her spouse's fastidiousness with the strictly secular utterance: "Lord, how can one nigger be so hard to please?" Others are likely to recall a time when that drastically lovable colored woman, who was forever wiping our noses and darning our clothing, bellowed in a moment of exasperation: "Nigger, you gonna be the death o' me." And some of the brethren who have had the precarious fortune to be raised up, wised up, thrown up or simply left alone to get up as best they could, on one of the nation's South Streets or Lenox Avenues, might remember having affectionately referred to a best friend as "My nigger."

The vast majority of "back-door Americans" are apt to agree with Webster —a nigger is simply a Negro or black man. But the really profound contemporary thinkers of this distinguished ethnic group—Dick Gregory, Redd Foxx, Moms Mabley, Slappy White, etc.—are likely to differ with Mr. Webster and define nigger as "something else"—a soulful "something else." The major difference between the nigger and the Negro, who have many traits in common, is that the nigger is the more soulful.

Certain foods, customs and artistic expressions are associated almost solely with the nigger: collard greens, neck bones, hog maws, black-eyed peas, pigs' feet, etc. A nigger has no desire to conceal or disavow any of these favorite dishes or restrain other behavioral practices such as bobbing his head, patting his feet to funky jazz, and shouting and jumping in church. This is not to be construed that all niggers eat chitlins and shout in church, nor that only niggers eat the aforementioned dishes and exhibit this type of behavior. It is to say, however, that the soulful usage of the term nigger implies all of the foregoing and considerably more.

The Language of Soul—or, as it might also be called, Spoken Soul or Colored English—is simply an honest vocal portrayal of black America. The roots of it are more than three hundred years old.

Before the Civil War there were numerous restrictions placed on the speech of slaves. The newly arrived Africans had the problem of learning to speak a new language, but also there were inhibitions placed on the topics of the slaves' conversation by slave masters and overseers. The slaves made up songs to inform one another of, say, the underground railroads' activity. When they sang *Steal Away* they were planning to steal away to the North, not to heaven. Slaves who dared to speak of rebellion or even freedom usually were severely punished. Consequently, Negro slaves were compelled to create a semi-clandestine vernacular in the way that the criminal underworld has historically created words to confound law-enforcement agents. It is said that numerous Negro spirituals were inspired by the hardships of slavery, and that what later became songs were initially moanings and coded cotton-field lyrics. To hear these songs sung today by a talented soul brother or sister or by a group is to be reminded of an historical spiritual bond that cannot be satisfactorily described by the mere spoken word.

The American Negro, for virtually all of his history, has constituted a vastly disproportionate number of the country's illiterates. Illiteracy has a way of showing itself in all attempts at vocal expression by the uneducated. With the aid of colloquialisms, malapropisms, battered and fractured grammar, and a considerable amount of creativity, Colored English, the sound of soul, evolved.

The progress has been cyclical. Often terms that have been discarded from the soul people's vocabulary for one reason or another are reaccepted years later, but usually with completely different meaning. In the Thirties and Forties "stuff" was used to mean vagina. In the middle Fifties it was revived and used to refer to heroin. Why certain expressions are thus reactivated is practically an indeterminable question. But it is not difficult to see why certain terms are dropped from the soul language. Whenever a soul term becomes popular with whites it is common practice for the soul folks to relinquish it. The reasoning is that "if white people can use it, it isn't hip enough for me." To many soul brothers there is just no such creature as a genuinely hip white person. And there is nothing more detrimental to anything hip than to have it fall into the square hands of the hopelessly unhip.

White Americans wrecked the expression "something else." It was bad enough that they couldn't say "sump'n else," but they weren't even able to get out "somethin' else." They had to go around saying *something else* with perfect or nearly perfect enunciation. The white folks invariably fail to perceive the soul sound in soulful terms. They get hung up in diction and grammar, and when they vocalize the expression it's no longer a soulful thing. In fact, it can be asserted that spoken soul is more of a sound than a language. It generally possesses a pronounced lyrical quality which is frequently incompatible to any music other than that ceaseless and relentlessly driving rhythm that flows from poignantly spent lives. Spoken soul has a way of coming out metered without the intention of the speaker to invoke it. There are specific phonetic traits. To the soulless ear the vast majority of these sounds are dismissed as incorrect usage of the English language and, not infrequently, as speech impediments. To those so blessed as to have had bestowed upon them at birth the lifetime gift of soul, these are the most communicative and meaningful sounds ever to fall upon human ears: the familiar "mah" instead of "my," "gonna" for "going to," "yo" for "your." "Ain't" is pronounced "ain'"; "bread" and "bed," "bray-ud" and "bay-ud"; "baby" is never "bay-bee" but "bay-buh"; Sammy Davis Jr. is not "Sammee" but a kind of "Sam-eh"; the same goes for "Eddeh" Jefferson. No matter how many "man's" you put into your talk, it isn't soulful unless the word has the proper plaintive, nasal "maee-yun."

Spoken soul is distinguished from slang primarily by the fact that the former lends itself easily to conventional English, and the latter is diametrically opposed to adaptations within the realm of conventional English. Police (pronounced po' lice) is a soul term, whereas "The Man" is merely slang for the same thing. Negroes seldom adopt slang terms from the white world and when they do the terms are usually given a different meaning. Such was the case with the term "bag." White racketeers used it in the Thirties to refer to the graft that was paid to the police. For the past five years soul people have used it when referring to a person's vocation, hobby, fancy, etc. And once the appropriate term is given the treatment (soul vocalization) it becomes soulful.

However, borrowings from spoken soul by white men's slang—particularly teen-age slang—are plentiful. Perhaps because soul is probably the most graphic language of modern times, everybody who is excluded from Soulville wants to usurp it, ignoring the formidable fettering to the soul folks that has brought the language about. Consider "uptight," "strung-out," "cop," "boss," "kill 'em," all now widely used outside Soulville. Soul people never question the origin of a slang term; they either dig it and make it a part of their vocabulary or don't and forget it. The expression "uptight," which meant being in financial straits, appeared on the soul scene in the general vicinity of 1953. Junkies were very fond of the word and used it literally to describe what was a perpetual condition with them. The word was pictorial and pointed; therefore it caught on quickly in Soulville across the country. In the early Sixties when "uptight" was on the move, a younger generation of soul people in the black urban communities along the Eastern Seaboard regenerated it with a new meaning: "everything is cool, under control, going my way." At present the term has the former meaning for the older generation and the latter construction for those under thirty years of age.

It is difficult to ascertain if the term "strung-out" was coined by junkies or just applied to them and accepted without protest. Like the term "uptight" in its initial interpretation, "strung-out" aptly described the constant plight of the junkie. "Strung-out" had a connotation of hopeless finality about it. "Uptight" implied a temporary situation and lacked the overwhelming despair of "strung-out."

The term "cop," (meaning "to get"), is an abbreviation of the word "copulation." "Cop," as originally used by soulful teen-agers in the early Fifties, was deciphered to mean sexual coition, nothing more. By 1955 "cop" was being uttered throughout national Soulville as a synonym for the verb "to get," especially in reference to illegal purchases, drugs, pot, hot goods, pistols, etc. ("Man, where can I cop now?") But by 1955 the meaning was all-encompassing. Anything that could be obtained could be "copped."

The word "boss," denoting something extraordinarily good or great, was a redefined term that had been popular in Soulville during the Forties and Fifties as a complimentary remark from one soul brother to another. Later it was replaced by several terms such as "groovy," "tough," "beautiful" and, most recently, "out of sight." This last expression is an outgrowth of the former term "way out," the meaning of which was equivocal. "Way out" had an ad hoc hickish ring to it which made it intolerably unsoulful and consequently it was soon replaced by "out of sight," which is also likely to experience a relatively brief period of popular usage. "Out of sight" is better than "way out," but it has some of the same negative, childish taint of its predecessor.

The expression, "kill 'em," has neither a violent nor a malicious interpretation. It means "good luck," "give 'em hell," or "I'm pulling for you," and originated in Harlem from six to nine years ago.

There are certain classic soul terms which, no matter how often borrowed, remain in the canon and are reactivated every so often, just as standard jazz tunes are continuously experiencing renaissances. Among the classical expressions are: "solid," "cool," "jive" (generally as a noun), "stuff," "thing," "swing" (or "swinging"), "pimp," "dirt," "freak," "heat," "larceny," "busted," "okee doke," "piece," "sheet" (a jail record), "squat," "square," "stash," "lay," "sting," "mire," "gone," "smooth," "joint," "blow," "play," "shot," and there are many more.

Soul language can be heard in practically all communities throughout the country, but for pure, undiluted spoken soul one must go to Soul Street. There are several. Soul is located at Seventh and "T" in Washington, D.C., on One Two Five Street in New York City; on Springfield Avenue in Newark; on South Street in Philadelphia; on Tremont Street in Boston; on Forty-seventh Street in Chicago, on Fillmore in San Francisco, and dozens of similar locations in dozens of other cities.

As increasingly more Negroes desert Soulville for honorary membership in the Establishment clique, they experience a metamorphosis, the repercussions of which have a marked influence on the young and impressionable citizens of Soulville. The expatriates of Soulville are often greatly admired by the youth of Soulville, who emulate the behavior of such expatriates as Nancy Wilson, Ella Fitzgerald, Eartha Kitt, Lena Horne, Diahann Carroll, Billy Daniels, or Leslie Uggams. The result—more often than not—is a trend away from spoken soul among the young soul folks. This abandonment of the soul language is facilitated by the fact that more Negro youngsters than ever are acquiring college educations (which, incidentally, is not the best treatment for the continued good health and growth of soul); integration and television, too, are contributing significantly to the gradual demise of spoken soul.

Perhaps colleges in America should commence to teach a course in spoken soul. It could be entitled the Vocal History of Black America, or simply Spoken Soul. Undoubtedly there would be no difficulty finding teachers. There are literally thousands of these experts throughout the country whose talents lie idle while they await the call to duty.

Meanwhile the picture looks dark for soul. The two extremities in the Negro spectrum—the conservative and the militant—are both trying diligently to relinquish and repudiate whatever vestige they may still possess of soul. The semi-Negro—the soul brother intent on gaining admission to the Establishment even on an honorary basis—is anxiously embracing and assuming conventional English. The other extremity, the Ultra-Blacks, are frantically adopting everything from a Western version of Islam that would shock the Caliph right out of his snugly fitting shintiyan to anything that vaguely hints of that big, beautiful, bountiful black bitch lying in the arms of the Indian and Atlantic Oceans and crowned by the majestic Mediterranean Sea. Whatever the Ultra-Black is after, it's anything but soulful.

Black Power is Black Language

Black Power Is Black Language

Geneva Smitherman

One of the more recent developments within the discipline of linguistics is sociolinguistics, the study of the sociology of language. Using empirical data collected from speakers of various classes, the sociolinguist constructs hypotheses about the social stratification of language. Differences in usage—lexicon, grammar, and phonology—are studied as social barometers although the scope of sociolinguistic inquiry may extend beyond these matters to encompass differences in syntactical patterns and syntactical complexity. Urban language studies are being or have recently been conducted in Detroit, Chicago, Washington, New York, Los Angeles, and Memphis. Socio-linguists posit that this kind of research will facilitate the construction of linguistic profiles of typical users of the language, in a given urban setting, according to the indices of sex, age, ethnic origin, and class status. Although perhaps no sociolinguist would admit it, the primary focus of these studies is the differentiation of white from black speech and lower class from upper class speech. In this connection, a word about that old bugaboo of English teachers: "correct usage." The imposition of the label "nonstandard English" upon any utterance which departs from the linguistic norm (i.e., so-called "standard English," itself only a social dialect) reflects the pervasive racial and class anxiety of America, a psycho-social hang-up that seems incurable. To state the obvious point: "standard" is defined by the predominant culture, white middle class America. Through its rejection of "deviant" linguistic structures, this group reinforces its sense of superiority in language matters and would remake others in its linguistic image. The requirements for membership into this group of language pace-setters are neither intelligence nor linguistic facility but race and social class. Aspirants lacking proper qualifications but desirous of acceptance by this group imitate its language models or risk being called speakers of "nonstandard English." Yet the rapidity of language change and borrowings among social groups begin to blur the linguistic distinctions between classes almost as soon as the sociolinguist has finished quantifying his data. A contemporary case in point is the word "hip," borrowed from black America's "mispronunciation" of "hep," the original word. At the all white high school I attended, I was once severely reprimanded for pronouncing "hep" as "hip" by a member of the white teeny-bopper cult which prided itself on being both intellectual and "hep." The current popularity of the word and the journalist's, newsman's, and yes, the college professor's use and pronunciation of "hip" demonstrate an absorption into mainstream language on both the lexical and phonological levels. Further, the Hippie Movement, comprised mostly of middle and upper class whites, derives its name from this same linguistic borrowing (black nationalists call it "theft"). This has happened in my lifetime and I am still under 30.

Teachers must abandon the prescriptive canon—what linguist Donald Lloyd has termed "our national mania for correctness"—and recognize that language customs vary according to the practices of native speakers. Gone should be the days of linguistic purists, like eighteenth century grammarian Robert Lowth who conceptualized his grammar of the language in terms of giving "order" and permanence to the "unruly, barbarous" tongue of the

Anglo-Saxons. Further, educators should be informed that the "varying" social and regional dialects of American English are really not all that varied. As one linguist has commented, the differences consist of "flavoring rather than substance." (This applies to Black English as well though it contains the greatest amount of syntactical variance of any of the dialects.) Finally, if instructors of written and oral composition are honest, then they will surely conclude that the tag "nonstandard English" is a euphemism which ought to be squarely located in the black community where the principal number of speakers of this class dialect resides. From this perspective, let us consider the socio-ethnic variation of American English variously labelled Negro speech, Negro dialect, nonstandard Negro speech, or recently Black English.

The existence of black language as a sociological-historical reality is now being acknowledged on many levels of American life, both academic and nonacademic. I view this as a healthy sign and a mark of maturity in American race relations. Recognition and study of the black idiom has previously been obstructed by the social and psychological dimensions of the issue. Laboring under the misconception of a correlation between Negro speech and lack of intelligence, white educators, liberals, intellectuals, and not surprisingly, many Afro-Americans themselves have refused to acknowledge that there is a Negro speech pattern—as if the admittance thereof is tantamount to the admission of Negro inferiority. This kind of self-consciousness is both dangerous and absurd, dangerous because it obscures legitimate historical differences that must be *recognized and respected,* absurd because it implies a relationship between one's native tongue and his intelligence. (Are white Americans less intelligent than Britishers because their dialect of English is different?)

I would define black speech as a sub-system of that amorphous entity, the "English language." Because it is a dialect, not an entirely different language altogether, this sub-system shares significant commonalities with what might be designated as "white, middle class American English" (e.g., basic lexicon —determiners, function words, etc.). But also because it is a dialect, with strong roots among the black masses throughout America, it differs from certain aspects of white, middle class English in lexicon, syntax, and phonology. The black speaker says *thang* (not thing); he says *gon do* (not *going to do* or even *gonna do*); if he is young and/or hip, he doesn't *get* something, he *cops* it. When the dissapointments and frustrations of life become overwhelming, he says with black songstress Nina Simone, "It bees that way sometime." The systematic patterns that comprise Black English can be located historically in residual Africanisms, Southern regionalisms, and archaic Old Englishisms. The patterns can be accounted for sociologically by the near-total isolation of Afro-Americans from the mainstream of American life—and thus from the *mainstream of language change*—an isolationist life style originating in slavery and persisting today in a variety of discrimination patterns. By virtue of the fact that a great number of black people use an idiom that can be characterized in the historical terms presented here, and due to the continued existence of disproportionate numbers of Afro-Americans in the lower-class, what has emerged is a dialect that is both social and ethnic. Our "separate but equal" ways of life, North and South, have produced separate but equal dialects. (This also serves to explain the fact that white Southerners, who were socially but not residentially separated from Negroes, share many features of Negro speech as white Northerners do not.)

This belated candidness about black speech is motivated by two forces in the social reality. First the psychological revolution in the black community which stresses all things black and de-emphasizes all things white. Second the accelerated drive, by some segments of the white power structure, for Negro integration and equality as a reaction to the violent upheavals in the nation's ghettos and the attendant increase in racial polarization. These forces are frequently operating at cross-purposes. Viewing the clash of color as an oral communication problem, some school systems are pursuing a course of language teaching aimed at the dissolution of language differences. New York City, for instance, recently published *Nonstandard Dialect,* a pamphlet of "standard English" language exercises and lessons to be used in its ghetto schools. Such programs purport to have a "bi-dialectal" orientation, (i.e., students are told that their language is systematic, beautiful, and useful in their home environments, but that they must master the prestige idiom to further their mobility potential). In reality, though, these programs are organized on a difference equals deficit principle, for students quickly perceive that their language must not be so "systematic" or "beautiful" since they are required to shift dialects in the presence of white (and black) employers, teachers, and other persons in positions of power. Furthermore, since no "bi-dialectal" programs exist in white, middle class schools, these programs can lead to the perpetration of the "super nigger" motif, for their implicit message is that if blacks want to "get ahead" in this world, they must be twice as good as whites, even to the extent of commanding two dialects. As these "super niggers" become more and more immersed in middle class culture, they eventually become mono-dialectal and may ultimately reject anything associated with the black masses, including of course, Black English.

But there is a process of cultural revitalization taking place among black people today, and nowhere is this more evident than in the celebration of the heretofore denigrated black idiom. Recognizing that language can be a tool of social and political oppression, and perceiving the need for a cultural underpinning to the current thrust toward black unification, many black intellectuals, educators, and creative artists are advocating use of "our lingo," not "the Man's." In black America, especially among black youth, the clarion call is ethnic, the style revolutionary, the language black. Thus we find many contemporary black poets incorporating black speech forms into their works. These forms range from the purely lexical items which characterize urban black slang (words like *cool, soul, rap*), to phonological patterns, as in "Energy for a New *Thang,*" the title of a poem by Ernie Mkalimoto in *The New Black Poetry,* to grammatical features as in "I mean even the ones where the wigs a slide around, and *they coming* at you 75 degrees off course," a line from LeRoi Jones' poem "W.W.," (also in *The New Black Poetry)* to, finally, combinations of all three Black English features, as in the poetry of Don Lee —"Wooooooooooooo—*jim* he *bees* so *cool* and ill tel li gent," and "my leaders? *is you*/mad/lead you to get/*mo* papers signed."

Observe this same trend in the writing of black scholars/intellectuals. For instance, in a recent piece of literary criticism written for *Black World,* one finds such phrases as "all black poems *ain't* the same kind"; "[certain] poets *hip* you to something, *pull the covers off* of something or *run it down* to you, or ask you to just *dig* it—your *coat is being pulled*"; "every poet has written a *bein* poem. In fact, most poets start off writing them. Just writing about the way *they be, they friends be, they lovers be, the world be"*; "we do not . . . want subhumans defining what *we be doing* . . . black poetry is becoming what it has always been but has not quite *beed."* And in a sociological essay on the need for an "ideology of black social science," written for *The Black Scholar,* one finds the following: "Robert Park [was] just another *cat walkin'* and *workin'* "; "now this was a white *dude* trying to trick us into *diggin'* what some slave owners developed about us (remember that they counted us as three/fifths of a man)"; ". . . Park was the man most responsible in the social sciences for developing a liberal white *game* to *run on* black people"; "in other words, we need to *get this shit on,* and for that we need a revolutionary script for the terrible black drama of cosmic forces that we're about to rain down on these pitiful *ofays."* (All italics in the quoted materials are mine.)

The crucial point I wish to make here is that language is the basic instrument of the social reality. Created in the human environment, adaptable and subject to change, it is a tool that man manipulates to a desired end. It is power. Black language, though often superciliously termed "nonstandard English," contains as much power, complexity and usefulness as other varieties of American English, including the so-called "standard" idiom. A quick glance at the urban street environment of black America reveals an oral culture where one's social survival is exactly proportionate to his ability to *rap* and *cap. Rapping* is language facility directed toward making a point in a powerful manner. The skillful *rapper* wins the adulation of his peers and becomes a culture hero. (Unknown to many, Rap Brown's given name is not "Rap" but Hubert; he was dubbed "Rap" because of his ability to deliver a message, that is, his ability to *rap.) Capping* is language facility directed toward conquest of one's opponent through verbal attack. In the ghetto jungle of Claude Brown's "promised land," even physical survival may depend on *capping* ability: many a black *cat has capped his way out of a rumble,* i.e., averted a fight by employing his verbal repartee and linguistic wit to shame an opponent into leaving the scene. As Ralph Ellison has said: "One uses the language which helps to perserve one's life, which helps to make one feel at peace in the world, and which screens out the greatest amount of chaos."

On another level, we can see the power of the black idiom in the style of national leaders. Soul brother James Brown "says it loud": "I'm black and I'm proud" and "I don't want nobody to give me nothin'—just open up the door," and all over America, blacks rally to his call. In Chicago, the Reverend Jesse Jackson, former aide to Dr. "Kang," as Reverend Jackson called him, has built a powerful economic boycott group, Operation Breadbasket, one of the few mass-supported organizations in black communities throughout America. "Reverend Jesse," as some parishioners refer to him, delivers an ethnic message with black linguistic flavoring: "How many of y'all watch those cowboy movies on T.V.? They're a lesson y'all got to learn. At first there ain't nothin' on the scene but pistols and money. Bang! Bang! A man holds up the stagecoach. Who has the most power? The man with the most money. He can be so ugly look like he been made in a Headstart program and it don't matter." Many black historians credit Malcolm X with igniting the spark that has led to the current thrust for black self-determination. Listen to Malcolm's *Message to the Grass Roots* for a powerful piece of rhetoric with participial endings dropped, front-shifting of stress ("*po - lice*") and other features of Black English. I could go on and on citing culture heroes, speaking in the black tongue, and moving their black audiences to a new level of awareness and group identity.

At this juncture, professors might conceivably counter with the question: But what of the employers who are to hire our college graduates? My answer is rhetorical: What of them? The process of education involves the development of one's mental faculties to their fullest. The goal of learning should be the ability to think for oneself, to reason effectively and make judgments prudently. To conceptualize the educational process in terms of preparing students for the "world of work" is to make our institutions of higher learning training mills in which the daily output is one student-robot capable of fitting into the vast machinery of technological times. (The distinction between the *trained* individual and the *educated* individual has been made before, recently by doctoral student Brother Ron Karenga of the University of California, Los Angeles, on behalf of black students entrapped in these "training" institutions.) Emphasizing white, middle class grammaticality as a vehicle for employability rather than black (or white) linguistic versatility as a vehicle for communicative power is likely to produce a standardized, mediocre language for what has perhaps already become a standardized, mediocre society.

This discussion of black language has been in terms of sociolinguistic and cultural factors. In addition, there are a few more strictly linguistic questions that some linguists and educators deem important. I shall deal briefly with each of these.

First, to what extent does code-switching exist in black students? Observation of black speakers and my own experience as a speaker of both dialects attest to the fact that a good deal of dialectal shifting occurs on the *lexical* level. The vocabulary of "the streets" is used extensively in discourse between blacks but only infrequently in conversations between blacks and whites. (Thus, in this one sense, perhaps our black students may already be "bi-dialectal.") This kind of "bi-dialectalism" wards off unwanted intimacy and provides a useful social mask. (As a matter of fact, the Language of Hip that made its way out of the black ghettos was disseminated by white musicians, writers, hipsters, and other "white Negroes"—to borrow Norman Mailer's phrase—who had been permitted an inside view into urban black America.) From a linguistic point of view, vocabulary shifting is the easiest level on which a speaker can manipulate codes. However, in the realms of phonology and syntax—but especially syntax—the shifting is much more difficult (and hence far less frequent among speakers of Black English) since syntactical patterns of language usage are more rigid and firmly fixed in a given speaker's dialect (or in any language for that matter).

Second, to what extent are speech forms reflected in writing and vice versa? Does code switching significantly differentiate the student's oral and written styles? Again one will find significant dfferences between oral and written *vocabularies,* some differences in *phonology* (i.e., some students will say *thang* but write *thing*), but very few shifts on the level of *syntax.* As a matter of fact, once one specifies the particular contextual environments in which patterns occur, there exists a high degree of predictability about the syntactical performance of a Black English speaker. So, for example, in any narration (or other piece of communication) composed in the present tense, third person singlar "s" will be deleted with regularity. In any situation where there is an indefinite pronoun or article coupled with a negative, multiple negation will occur, and if there is an indefinite pronoun used as subject, multiple negation and inversion both will occur, as in "Couldn't nobody do nothing" (i.e., "Nobody could do anything"). Yet there are exceptions among Black English speakers, some of whom manage to combine all three linguistic shifts when writing. My as yet unvalidated hypothesis is that such speakers are probably advanced and excellent readers who are making transferences from reading to writing. If this is indeed so, it is obvious what teachers of "disadvantaged" black students ought to emphasize.

Third, how clear-cut is the distinction between phonological and syntactical rules in the black idiom? We can hypothesize, for instance, that the form *He walk home yesterday* derives from contextual signalling of past tense in the grammar of Black English (as opposed to the white middle class speaker's redundant signalling of past tense by both verb form—"walked"—and con-text—"yesterday"). However, since a final consonant deletion rule operates in Black English (producing, for instance, *dea* for *dead*), we can posit with equal validity that *-ed* deletion is phonological. The logical implication of this line of reasoning is that if teachers of composition want to change their student's written dialect, perhaps they must first change their students' speech.

Fourth, employing the recent transformational-generative emphasis on syntax, do the grammatical rules that differentiate Black and white English operate on the deep or surface structure level? Isn't the black speaker who says "It's a boy in my room pick on me" manipulating the same kernel structure as the white speaker who says "There's a boy in my room that picks on me"? Is there a deep structure difference between the simplified verb system of Black English (e.g., use of *is* and *was* for all persons, singular and plural) and the variations in the verb system of white speech? Between black songstress Aretha Franklin's "since you been gone" and the white singer's verson given on a recent television program, "since you've been gone"? Granted there is a deep structure difference between Black and white English in the use of the verb form *be.* Thus in Black English, *He be tired* (i.e., habitually) contrasts in meaning with *He tired* (i.e., at the present moment) whereas white English has no equivalent contrast and employs *He is tired* to serve both functional meanings. But how "deep" is this deep structure difference really? And how many such deep structure differences are there anyway? (To date, there is only this *one* deep structure difference that linguists agree upon.) None of this is to minimize the differences between Black and white English, for the distinctiveness of black speech can be located at the precise point where syntax, lexicon, and phonology converge, producing, for instance, the following statement by a black student from

Detroit: "Them dudes alway be doing they thang." My point of contention, though, is that here we are dealing with surface, not deep structure differences, that white English differs from Black English in the socio-cultural dimension—that is, on the level of social preference—but not on the basic, purely linguistic level, and that the point about dialects being different in flavoring, not substance, is well-taken.

In formulating teaching technologies, then, we must balance sociological, historical truths with linguistic truth. And we must eradicate linguistic purism for it distorts the *real* problems of the process of composing and obscures the fundamental value of language. As I have indicated, this value lies in the use of language to order the chaos of personal realities and to manipulate the social structure. The power of the word lies in its enabling us to translate vague feelings and fleeting experiences into forms that give unity, coherence and expression to the Inexpressible. The process of composing becomes a mechanism for discovery wherein we may generate illuminating revelations about a particular idea or event. The *real* problem involved in this process is that of organizing and ordering language to effect this transformation from the subjective to the objective. Using linguistic structures in a social context, the writer or speaker must adapt his audience and choose rhetorical strategies, not grammatical "niceties," for moving the audience in the direction desired. As teachers of written and oral composition, our concerns lie not with our students' linguistic flavoring, but with their linguistic substance, not with sheer grammatical conventions and usage practices, themselves constantly in flux, but with teaching our students to deal with increasingly complex and sophisticated topics in an increasingly sophisticated and powerful way. As professional writers and speakers know only too well, using language as power precludes concerns about grammatical amenities. As we teachers should know only too well, the student's written and oral products, like those of the professionals, succeed or fail on the basis of the totality of the language used, not on its degree of mechanical exactness. In short, a paper or speech succeeds as a whole. Faulty logic, poor organization, verbosity, lack of specificity, lack of content—all will produce a weak, ineffective speech or paper whatever the brand of dialect. But language judiciously selected and effectively delivered, *including that of the black dialectal variety,* becomes a weapon capable of the most devastating destruction. Given the contemporary acceleration of "student unrest," we should wish our students, black *and* white, to know that language is power. Perhaps then we may convince them that the pen is mightier than the Molotov cocktail.

LANGUAGE

AS REVOLUTION

Black Art

LeRoi Jones

Poems are bullshit unless they are
teeth or trees or lemons piled
on a step. Or black ladies dying
of men leaving nickel hearts
beating them down. Fuck poems
and they are useful, they shoot
come at you, love what you are,
breathe like wrestlers, or shudder
strangely after pissing. We want live
words of the hip world live flesh &
coursing blood. Hearts Brains
Souls splintering fire. We want poems
like fists beating niggers out of Jocks
or dagger poems in the slimy bellies
of the owner-jews. Black poems to
smear on girdlemamma mulatto bitches
whose brains are red jelly stuck
between 'lizabeth taylor's toes. Stinking
Whores! We want "poems that kill."
Assassin poems, Poems that shoot
guns. Poems that wrestle cops into alleys
and take their weapons leaving them dead
with tongues pulled out and sent to Ireland. Knockoff
poems for dope selling wops or slick halfwhite
politicians Airplane poems. rrrrrrrrrrrrrrrrrrr
rrrrrrrrrrrrrr . . . . tuhtuhtuhtuhtuhtuhtuhtuhtuhtuh
. . . . rrrrrrrrrrrrrrr . . . . Setting fire and death to
whities ass. Look at the Liberal
Spokesman for the jews clutch his throat
& puke himself into eternity . . . . rrrrrrrrrr
There's a negroleader pinned to
a bar stool in Sardi's eyeballs melting
in hot flame. Another negroleader
on the steps of the white house one
kneeling between the sheriff's thighs
negotiating cooly for his people.
Aggh . . . stumbles across the room . . .
Put it on him, poem. Strip him naked
to the world! Another bad poem cracking
steel knuckles in a jewlady's mouth
Poem scream poison gas on beasts in green berets
Clean out the world for virtue and love,
Let there be no love poems written

until love can exist freely and
cleanly. Let Black People understand
that they are the lovers and the sons
of lovers and warriors and sons
of warriors Are poems & poets &
all the loveliness here in the world

We want a black poem. And a
Black World.
Let the world be a Black Poem
And Let All Black People Speak This Poem
Silently

or LOUD

The Undaunted Pursuit of Fury

. . . After the Civil War came a new wave of Negro poets that included Paul
Laurence Dunbar, who wrote in the Negro folk dialect of the rural South as
well as standard English. The 1920s produced the movement known as the
Harlem Renaissance, when Negro poetry began to turn from the classic English lyric verse of Countee Cullen to the rhythmic, blues-style poetry of
Langston Hughes. Later came Pulitzer Prize-winning Gwendolyn Brooks, Jazz
Poet Ted Joans and Margaret Walker, whom some call the mother of the
black poets of the '60s. These new poets began to look on themselves not
as Negro but as black. Writing primarily for a black audience, they turned
their eyes toward Africa and a new-found reverence for black culture.

"Black is a burden bravely chanted," James Emanuel proclaims in a poem
called "Negritude."

> Black cross of sweat for a nation's rise.
> Black is a boy who knows his heroes:
> Black the way a hero dies.[1]

Like many black poets today, Emanuel reflects revolutionary attitudes most
passionately expressed by Malcolm X and Stokely Carmichael. The poets
also developed their ideas from the writings of the late black psychiatrist
Frantz Fanon. Basically, Fanon stated, Africa and the rest of the third world
must be freed from the colonialism that developed color consciousness. Past
humiliations can only be washed away through violence. Political freedom
will bring about a rejoicing in a new black identity.

[1] Lines from "Negritude" by James Emanuel, *Treehouse*. Copyright © 1968. Reprinted
by permission of Broadside Press.

Prophets and Poets

Also from Africa came a tribal tradition of the poet as wiseman and prophet, interpreter of the past and seer of the future. According to Poet Nikki Giovanni: "There is no difference between the warrior, the poet, and the people. Like Stokely is a poet and so is Rap Brown."

And the poets are Rap Browns. The barbarity of what Jon Eckels stridently calls "Western Syphilization" in its attitude toward the black man is mockingly captured in a couplet from *Some Changes* by June Jordan: "George Washington he think he big/ he trade my father for a pig."

The mockery turns to bitterness in Gil Scott-Heron's forthcoming volume, *Small Talk at 125th & Lenox:*

> A rat done bit my sister Nell.
>   (with Whitey on the moon)
> Her face and arms began to swell.
>   (and Whitey's on the moon).[2]

The rage becomes an outright call to arms in the work of Mae Jackson:

> "the time has come"
> to kill
> white women and children
> for Emitt Till
> and the children of Birmingham.[3]

There is as much rage in the poetry of Don L. Lee, whose three books *(Black Pride, Think Black!, Don't Cry, Scream),* put out by the most active of the black poetry publishers, Detroit's Broadside Press, have sold some 80,000 copies. Writes Lee:

> i ain't seen no poems stop a .38,
> i ain't seen no stanzas brake a honkie's head . . .
> & until my similes can protect me from a night stick
> i guess i'll keep my razor
> & buy me some more bullets.[4]

Photo of Don Lee, *Ebony* Magazine/Johnson Publishing Co., Inc.

[2] Reprinted by permission of The World Publishing Company from *Small Talk at 125th and Lenox* by Gil Scott-Heron. Copyright © 1970 by Gil Scott-Heron.

[3] Reprinted by permission of Mae Jackson.

[4] Poem from "2 Poems" by Don L. Lee, *Black Pride.* Copyright © 1968 by Don L. Lee. Reprinted by permission of Broadside Press.

A more sophisticated anger is found in the poetry of Gwendolyn Brooks when she described the Chicago ghetto riots after the assassination of Martin Luther King.

> *A White Philosopher said*
> *'It is better to light one candle/*
> *than curse the*
> *   darkness.'*
> *   These candles curse—*
> *inverting the deeps of the darkness.*[5]

If there is rage and hate, there is also a defiant but touching pride in the new black awareness, reflected in Mari Evan's soon-to-be-published *I Am a Black Woman:*

> *I*
> *am a black woman*
> *tall as a cypress*
> *strong*
> *beyond all definition still*
> *defying place*
> *and time*
> *and circumstance*
> *   assailed*
> *   impervious*
> *   indestructible*
> *Look*
> *   on me and be*
> *renewed*[6]

Although Nikki Giovanni is one of the foremost propagandists, she can also express concern with the blackness of love and take pride in the joy behind the anguish, as she reports in her best-known poem, "Nikki-Rosa":

> *. . . and I really hope no white person ever has cause to*
> *write about me because they never understand Black love*
> *is Black wealth and they'll probably talk about my hard*
> *childhood and never understand that all the while I was*
> *quite happy.*[7]

Photo of Nikki Giovanni, David Gahr.

[5] Reprinted by permission of Broadside Press and Gwendolyn Brooks Blakely.

[6] From *I Am a Black Woman*, published by Wm. Morrow and Company, 1970, by permission of the author.

[7] Reprinted by permission of Nikki Giovanni.

There seems to be little room for the self-mockery which has often characterized Negro humor or for the literary sense of irony that has dominated much of modern white poetry. But the black poets have a continuing oral tradition lacking in the more cerebral white English poetry. This tradition has been handed along from rural preachers to gospel singers to blues singers, to Langston Hughes, who dignified the street language of the blacks and read his poems wherever he could find an audience, even in bars. Today's black poets often chant their poetry in lofts, churches and schools, as if they were still tribal prophets. David Henderson's new book, *De Mayor of Harlem,* is full of the language of incantation, uniting fragments of history and contemporary impression as if in a visionary state of mind:

> *walk his city by sundown*
> *witness*
> *flames upon rooftops*
> *along the piers*
> *palisades crumbling spires*
> *organized amusement parks / fright-death*
> *upon roller coasters with one end only . . .*
> *the weirdest*
> *roller coaster through manhattan by underground express*
> *iron cars trains of auschwitz*
> *jangling metal grit   subway air*[8]

Black Dialect and Rhythm

LeRoi Jones, a playwright and essayist, who has stood trial in New Jersey on charges related to his political activities, is perhaps the best known of the new black poets. "I make a poetry with what I feel is useful & can be saved out of all the garbage of our lives," he writes. "What I see, am touched by (CAN HEAR) . . . wives, gardens, jobs, cement yards where cats pee, all my interminable artifacts . . . ALL are a poetry, & nothing moves (with any grace) pried apart from these things. There cannot be closet poetry. Unless the closet be wide as God's eye."

Whether subtle or simplistic, black poetry often makes the poetry of the streets come alive. If four-letter words are used (and they appear often), it is because they are not only weapons to hack away protective layers of deadening sophistication, but they are also the words of the common people.

"Black English" is not an illiterate language, as many think, but remarkably rich in nuances. According to Toni Morrison, an editor at Random House, "many of these poets are turning to the grammar, the punctuation, the language through which subculture blacks in particular have resisted total Westernization. Black dialect—if you want to call it that—is probably more subtle and sophisticated than standard white English." In standard English, she says, "there are only two present tenses—I work, I am working. In English as spoken in white Appalachia, there are three—I work, I am working, I a' working. In black Appalachian dialect, there are five—I work, I am working, I be working, I a' working, I be a' working—and each has a different shade of meaning."

[8] From *De Mayor of Harlem* by David Henderson.

Photo of LeRoi Jones, Chester Higgins, Jr.

Funky, jive, down, high, the Man, hawk, cool, hot, copped-out, cats, caps, kicked, reefer, johns, juke, ofay, goofed, wing, hip, dig, soul, honkies, splib (spook as in Negro), grass and skag are just a few of the words appearing in black poetry that often have multiple meanings elusive to the white reader. For example, in Etheridge Knight's *Poems from Prison,* he says,

> *You rocked too many boats, man.*
> *Pulled too many coats, man.*
> *Saw through the jive.*[9]

Jive here refers not only to the dance but also to a fake song-and-dance routine, a deceit, which is in contrast to the truth of soul.

Just as elusive are the rhythms drawn from city sounds, African drumbeats, church responses, and the jazz of Coleman, Coltrane and Charlie ("Bird") Parker. These can be heard in Michael S. Harper's book, *Dear John, Dear Coltrane:*

> *Bird, buttermilk bird—*
> *smack, booze and bitches*
> *I am Bird*
> *baddest nightdreamer*
> *on sax in the ornithology-world*
> *I can fly—higher, high, higher—*
> *I'm a black man;*
> *I am; I'm a black man—*[10]

The rhythm of the breath line, the breathing syncopation of speech and modern music—elements inherent in black poetry's relationship to the oral tradition—have been given new life and extensions in white poetry, particularly in the work of Charles Olson and the Black Mountain school, as well as Allen Ginsberg and the beat poets of the 1950s. As a result, whether in white poetry's revolt against academic aridity or in black poetry's political efforts to reunite the poet and the common people in a common cause, the breath line with its responsiveness to the gut rather than the brain has pumped a new emotional force into the poem. And, related to the re-emphasis on the spoken word, special black words and the Joycean play of black language have deeply influenced both American writing and speech . . .

[9] Lines from "It Was a Funky Deal" by Etheridge Knight, *Poems from Prison.* Copyright © 1968 by Etheridge Knight. Reprinted by permission of Broadside Press.

[10] Reprinted from *Dear John, Dear Coltrane* by Michael Harper. Copyright © 1970, University of Pittsburgh Press. From the poem, "Brother John."

WORLD'S HIGHEST STA

PSYCHE OF

THE WHITE

the psychological perspective

How It Looks to Blacks

If whites have prejudices about blacks, blacks also have many fixed notions about whites. This much is clear from that part of the special TIME-Harris poll that examines stereotypes blacks have about the white society.

More than four out of five blacks polled think that whites consider Negroes inferior. Two-thirds of the blacks believe whites to be scared that blacks are better people than they are. Nearly the same number—63%—feel that whites today regret having abolished black slavery.

Other black beliefs: whites give blacks a break only when forced to (77% agreed with that proposition); white men secretly want black women (74%); whites have a mean and selfish streak in them (65%); whites are physically weaker than blacks (55%); whites are less honest than blacks (50%); white people need to have somebody like blacks to lord it over (49%); whites are more apt to catch diseases (44%).

White Hang-Up

Whites invented psychology and psychiatry, and occasionally put them to what they thought was good use in probing the psyches of blacks. Today there are enough black professionals to turn the tables, and many of them treat white patients in both public institutions and private practice.* In both areas they have a unique opportunity to examine Whitey's hang-ups about blacks—his guilt, his insecurities and the rationalizations by which he tries to justify his racism.

American ambivalence toward blacks dates back most signally to Thomas Jefferson, who wrote the credo that men are created free and equal, yet believed that blacks were less equal than others. A second ambivalence, which Jefferson shared, concerned sex. Despite laws against miscegenation, there has been, over the centuries, a steady increase in the number of mulattoes.

Contempt and Loathing

White Americans today are no less ambivalent. No matter how firmly they protest that they "have nothing against the black," contempt and loathing have become embedded in the language. Black Psychiatrist Alvin F. Poussaint points out: "In the legacy of our civilization, the color black has been virtually synonymous with 'sin' and 'bad'—witness such terms as black sheep, black magic, blacklist, blackguard, blackball, black lie and many others. The word is associated with all the dirty, lowly, unintellectual functions in human life. The word white is usually invested with the opposite meanings, so Americans have been conditioned to perceive black as inferior and white as superior."

---

* The American Psychiatric Association has approximately 400 black members out of 17,000; the American Psychological Association refuses to give a color breakdown of its 30,500 membership.

The Real Killers

Black Psychiatrists William H. Grier and Price M. Cobbs, authors of *Black Rage,* put it still more strongly: "Most whites, including psycho-analysts and psychiatrists, are amazed to learn that their hatred of blacks is culturally determined, psychologically malignant, and can be ultimately lethal." How lethal it can be, they say, is evident when "law and order" is invoked, supposedly to protect white Americans from "murderous killer blacks." But, insist Grier and Cobbs sweepingly, "When the dust clears, the bodies are all black. The killers are white."

Since the white man has been the perpetrator of violence more often than the black, why does he persist in projecting his own misdeeds upon upon his victims? Poussaint explains: "Individuals who are deeply prejudiced frequently use this paranoid mechanism to avoid facing painful truths about unacceptable impulses and fears within themselves. Racist feelings can unconsciously become deeply enmeshed in one's own psyche and serve neurotic needs in an effort to shore up a shaky emotional equilibrium and sense of self-esteem. Because of their abuse and rejection of blacks, many whites have developed a great deal of understandable guilt, but since this too is an unpleasant emotional feeling, they have tried to avoid it by further rationalizations. This often reinforces prejudices and creates a vicious circle of negative defenses. For example, although white men exploited and sexually abused black women, the supposedly oversexed Negro male was lynched for the slightest real or imagined overture to a white woman."

Drs. Grier and Cobbs carry the argument to extremes when they contend that the "self-concept of slaveholder is central to the American national character and is in fact the national sickness of white racism." It has been structured into demeaning laws and customs designed to keep maximum distance between black and white. Poussaint argues that what is needed is a massive program of "deconditioning" Americans from their white-super-ior, black-inferior models of thought and relationships. The burden in achieving this, he suggests, would fall mainly on the educational system and the mass media.

Stubbornness

Say Grier and Cobbs: "If the white man recognizes individuality and humanity in a black, he must then feel love and set himself against the oppressor of his beloved brother." While this counsel of perfection may be hard to fulfill, they offer an interesting classification of whites rated according to the stubbornness of their prejudice. They see little hope for a near-future change in attitudes by most blue-collar workers, some "men of influence," or white (meaning rightist) radicals. For the rest:

"1) The white Southerner, converted under the right circumstances, may experience a complete abolition of bigotry. Surprisingly, we think, he has the greatest potentiality for change.

"2) The Northern liberal, if he can master the fear of loss of position and power, is next most likely to change because he has worked with blacks.

"3) The conventional, Middle American is conservative in outlook. His interests are intense but idiosyncratic, and if approached along the line of his self-interest, he may discard his hatred of blacks."

This article is reprinted from Vol. 8, No. 3, 1968 of *Freedomways*, published at 799 Broadway, New York City.

The White American Psyche— Exploration of Racism

Lloyd T. Delany

On April 29, 1968, Thomas A. Johnson, a black reporter for *The New York Times,* reported the following conversation: "German in Vietnam asked a Negro civilian if he was aware of how some American whites talked about Negroes when they were alone. The Negro said he was.

" 'Do you know that they call you animals?,' the German said, 'that they say you have tails and that they seem especially anxious that foreigners— myself and the Vietnamese—hear this?'

" 'I know,' the Negro said.

" 'What's wrong with them?' the German said.

" 'They're white Americans,' he was told. 'A strange breed of people.' "

Much has been written about the impact of bigotry on the psychology of the black American. However, very little in the literature deals with the psycho-dynamics of white racism. This imbalance is crucial, for the continual harping on what impact white racism has on blacks still maintains the myth that it is a "black problem." The imbalance fosters the distortion that whites are mainly bystanders in this

Benedict J. Fernandez, *In Opposition* (Da Capo Press, 1968).

illness while in fact they are both creators and victims of the sickness of racism.

It is important that the black American have some understanding of the pathology of white racism so that he may deal with it more appropriately. It is consequently necessary to examine some of the psychodynamic aspects of white racism and what accounts for "this strange breed of people" and their racism.

The historical base of racism rests on the Anglo-Dutch attitudes and sentiments which stemmed from their original ignorance of blacks. The tenets of Protestantism and capitalism, a form of economy that requires the perpetuation of an exploitable group, compounded the development of racism. From these three main roots slavery emerged and was maintained. However, certain psychological mechanisms also accompanied this development, enabling the American racist to deny his barbarity and exploitation.

If an individual were to walk into a psychiatrist's or a psychologist's office exhibiting the symptoms that are so typical of the racist, there isn't a clinician of any competence that would not immediately diagnose him as grossly pathological. Yet when the society at large employs these mechanisms they are overlooked. Part of the explanation for overlooking this rests with the obvious fact that the very people who would diagnose the pathology are themselves racists and consequently unable and unwilling to view their behavior as sick. Moreover, the endemic nature of racism makes it easier to ignore its pathology. It is as if everyone in the society has the flu perpetually; under such circumstances it would take some careful analysis to recognize that, despite its prevalence, to have the flu is to be sick. Too often people are wont to mistake the prevalence of a form of behavior as testimony to its normalcy. The man who kills one man on a street corner with a knife is considered a murderer; the man who drops an atom bomb, killing fifty thousand humans, is a hero because he is merely one of many. What is common soon comes to be regarded as normal. Hence, the commonness of racism enables most in the society to ignore its pathological nature. Yet even the prevalence of racism would not enable the racist to be unknowing of his illness unless he employed the usual devices employed by all sick people to avoid confrontation with their pathology.

THE PROCESS OF DEPERSONALIZATION

The underlying psychodynamic basis of racism is the process of depersonalization, a psychological process which is an aberration and manifested by stark denial of reality. The racist denies the reality that he is interacting with other humans. The energy necessary to maintain this pervasive denial of reality is extraordinary; it drains the racist to a considerable extent, crippling him and his society in serious ways.

The process of depersonalization utilized by the racist is sustained by many mental operations. These specific mechanisms employed by the racist are important to recognize. They are modeled in many ways after the specific mechanisms present in all emotionally disturbed people.

EVASION AND AVOIDANCE

Evasion and avoidance are a disturbed mental process known to all clinicians. This is a pathological mechanism in which the person avoids or evades confronting, facing, recognizing anything that would be a source of tension, anxiety or fear. The utilization of avoidance and evasion in the white racist is quite clear though its form is sometimes misunderstood by blacks.

Many blacks have had the experience of walking in the white section of town and being passed in the street by a white who they know quite well. This is sometimes misinterpreted by the black man to mean the white who walks past him without indicating recognition is unwilling to greet his black friend in public. This may, in some instances, be an accurate appraisal; it is most often not so. What is most usually the case is that most white Americans, until very recently, did not look at or see blacks. This is one way to avoid having to face the reality that there are blacks and that if there are blacks one must deal with them. Avoidance and evasion are an unconscious process, unrecognized by the person employing it. To test this, the next time it occurs simply tap your white acquaintance on the shoulder and he'll be quite delighted to see you. Whites do not see blacks, wishing unconsciously they were not there.

A contemporary consequence of this evasion and avoidance is manifested in the shock and surprise about what is now called the rise of black militance and nationalism. The white American is only now being awakened to the fact that he has been living for four hundred years with blacks. Rap Brown, Stokely Carmichael, Ron Karenga and other nationalists can easily reach the headlines of any paper today by merely uttering a sentence whether it has much virtue or not because of this new found black awareness in the white press.

What is not known by most whites is that the militance of blacks today is neither new nor unique. A cogent illustration of this is in a poem written by the late Langston Hughes. The poem is entitled *Roland Hayes Beaten* and was written in 1942.

Negroes
Sweet and docile
Meek, humble, and kind;
Beware the day
They change their minds!

Wind
In the cotton fields,
Gentle breezes
Beware the hour
It uproots the trees![1]

Though white historians are aware of it, most white Americans are completely unaware of the fact that Marcus Garvey in the 1920's was able to amass the greatest support among black people any movement in this nation has ever achieved. And the stridency of Garvey has not been exceeded by any contemporary black militant.

[1] Copyright 1948 by Alfred A. Knopf, Inc. from *Selected Poems* by Langston Hughes. Reprinted by permission of the publisher.

The increasing new awareness of the black man occasioned by the early civil right demonstrations and later the more militant direct action programs has shaken somewhat the utilization of the mechanism of evasion and avoidance, but other pathological devices used by the white racist still exist.

ACTING OUT AND PROJECTION

The acting out and projection of white racists frequently confound, frustrate and sometimes even amuse blacks.

Acting out is a neurotic mechanism in which a person is unable to contain his own feelings, therefore he translates his feelings directly into some form of overt behavior. Usually these are feelings that are destructive. The hatred of the white racist is commonly acted out in his overt violence. The testimony to white violence goes back a long time.

Acting out, however, is commonly combined with projection, another mechanism employed by the white racist. This is also a neurotic defense. The individuals who are projecting ascribe to others behavior, thoughts, feelings, attitudes, and sentiments that they have themselves but which they find unacceptable and hence attribute to others.

The fear and panic that periodically sweep across the nation are living testimony to the pathological use of both acting out and projection. In an article appearing in the *Wall Street Journal* on April 23, 1968, headlined "White Racism: Ghetto Violence Brings Hardening of Attitudes Towards Negro Groups," the following item appears: "A recent visit to the gun shop in Allan Park tells a good deal about the climate of fear in many parts of the metropolitan area.

"The clerk, a balding paunchy man, has the rapt attention of several customers when he says, 'The word is out that if there's any trouble this summer and you see a black man in your neighborhood, shoot to kill and ask questions later. They [Negroes] are gonna send carloads of firebombs into the suburbs to suck the police out of the city.' "

By projecting his own hatred and violence onto this mythical "black horde invading his suburb," the "paunchy man" can act out this violence while disowning the responsibility of it. By creating a myth that blacks are violent, he can justify himself and his killing of innocent blacks. When he is unable to personally accomplish this, he utilizes his police force to carry out what he is not able to do himself.

The projection of his hatred and violence on the black man requires a certain amount of reality denial; for well this "paunchy man" knows that the so-called riots have all occurred within the black communities, that invariably, just as in the past, the so-called riots take a far greater toll of black lives than of whites. The so-called riots of today, as the riots of the past, invariably end with many more blacks being killed than whites and most of them innocent of even the so-called crimes of looting and arson.

The National Advisory Commission's Report on Civil Disorders (as they refer to them) is replete with instances of innocent black people being slain during the so-called disorders. There was the 10-year-old child slain in his father's car, the family entirely uninvolved and unaware that a so-called civil disorder was going on. There is Rebecca Brown, shot in the back

through her apartment window after she rushed to grasp her two-year-old from the window so that he would not be harmed. There was the man sitting in a rocking chair on his porch slain by National Guardsmen, and many more. But this balding, paunchy white racist can ignore the murder of these innocents. And by this process of projection can justify the continuation of his doing the same things he and his forefathers before him have always done.

Projection is not only limited to such things as white violence; white sexuality is also projected. The recent Pulitzer Prize-winning novel of William Styron is a good example of white lechery projected. Once again blacks are subjected in this best-selling novel to the fantasies and projections of a white racist who, under the guise of sympathy for blacks, projects his own sexual preoccupation onto his twisted fictionalized version of the black revolutionary Nat Turner. Styron's projection of his sexuality into the character of Nat Turner required not only a distortion of history but an emasculation of this revolutionary figure. He ends up depicted, in Styron's portrayal, as puking over the fact that he has killed a callow, white adolescent girl, a pure fantasy of Styron's sick Southern imagination.

The white southerner who decries most the sanctity of white womanhood is also the most preoccupied with raping and violating black womanhood. Southerners have been able to do this without fully confronting the meaning of their acts by projecting their sexual and aggressive feelings onto the black man, creating the fantasy of black sexuality and aggression, then acting as if the fantasy they have created is a reality. Thus, projection is manifested in any number of ways covering the deep seated violence, sexuality, and inferiority of the white racist.

No one has more aptly pointed out how whites project their feelings of inferiority than James Baldwin in his essay *The Fire Next Time*. In this essay Baldwin comments extensively on how the projection of inferiority feelings on the part of the white racist occurs. And he sums this up when he points out that the white racist needs the "nigger" because it is the "nigger" in him that he cannot tolerate.

Eldridge Cleaver in his book of essays *Soul on Ice* discusses in some detail the often thinly disguised admiration whites have of blacks and how recently whites have increasingly modeled themselves after blacks. The white campus revolts are but one illustration of this.

Jack Kerouac is the least restrained in his admiration of the black man when he has the hero of his novel *On the Road* saying, "I walked . . . wishing I were a Negro, feeling that the best the white world had offered was not enough ecstasy for me, not enough life, joy, kicks, darkness, music, not enough night."

Too often black psychologists and other black social scientists have in their stress of the impact of racism on black people minimized the psychological need of the white racist to create an inferior being. It is this need that reflects the basic sense of inferiority and inadequacy on the part of the white racist, masking often his admiration for the black man. He needs an inferior and he projects his inadequacies, his failing, relying on the pathetic device of skin color to establish his "superiority." So sad this fragile, frantic need that hinges on the irrelevance of skin color, a fact not even within the control of the white man. Yet it is this desperation to find something or someone on which he can heap his profound sense of inadequacy and inferiority that the "nigger" had to be created and perpetuated in the minds of the white racists.

Indeed too much emphasis has been placed on the inferiority feeling engendered in blacks without the concomitant recognition on the part of blacks that whites also have these deep-seated inadequate feelings and frequently they project their inferiority feelings. The white women spitting at six-and seven-year-olds in New Orleans are the victims of their bottomless feelings of failure and frustration. The helpless black children become the easy prey for these emotionally disturbed women.

A segment of the black militant movement makes a similar error as do the social scientists mentioned above by constantly haranguing about the superiority of blackness, failing to recognize that the need to state over and over their blackness in the terms and contexts in which they do is still playing the game according to the white racists. The man who experiences his worth and adequacy does not have to proclaim it, he knows it. Some forms of black nationalism mask feelings of deprivation, frustration about not having been given the things they wanted from "the white massa." Like the two-year-old having a tantrum, sulking in the corner, feeling hurt and injured but covering up this hurt and injury by screaming, the black militant sulks, feels hurt, and substitutes rhetoric for screaming. The black militants who proclaim the desire for separation in effect isolating themselves are often unwilling to face that they too have bought the white racist's message that they are indeed inferior.

It is understandable why black separatists exist in the black community. It is also well to recognize that in joining hands with the white separatists, the black segregationist may be masking his fear of confronting and competing with whites. Black separatism stems from despair and anger about white racism but it also serves a secondary purpose, in effect complementing and complying with the aims of the white racist. The black separatists should examine carefully what is wrong when they find their cause supported by the same people who enslaved their grandparents and raped their mothers.

ATTEMPTED JUSTIFICATION

This is a mechanism in which the sick individual attempts to apply a reasonable explanation to cover the unconscious impulses, thoughts, and feelings that would be quite distressful if they were aware of them. The racist's behavior is replete with examples of this defense operation. For example, the continual harping on the obviously fallacious notion that blacks not having achieved equality in the society is the responsibility of blacks, is one of the common utilizations of attempted justification. In spite of the endless issuing of reports, facts and figures to demonstrate both historical and current reasons for the inequity that exists in the society, white racists continue to act as if this mass of information were unknown to them. This is not merely a political device, although it has manipulative political advantages; it is a psychological device as well. For example, it

enables the racist living in the suburbs to talk about his unwillingness to hand out federal monies for slum clearance while ignoring the fact that the home in which he lives is supported and subsidized by federal funds, usually obtained through Veteran Administration or Federal Housing Administration loans. It enables the racist to ignore the fact that only 800,000 units have been constructed in the thirty-one-year history of subsidized federal housing in ghetto communities, but *10 million* units have been constructed in middle and upper income communities utilizing federal subsidies.

The white racist, riding to his suburban home with a bumper sticker "I fight poverty, I work," attempts to justify his behavior while ignoring the fact that he refuses to hire any black people in his place of business or that he works in a place which discriminates against blacks of equal capacity and skill. In one breath he talks of the fact that blacks like living in the slums and the next moment he attends a committee meeting to protest a black family moving into the community and failing in that, he throws a brick through their window.

Throughout the summer of so-called riots, white TV men, radio reporters and newspaper reporters roamed freely through the black communities emerging unharmed. In fact their greatest threat came not from the black community but from the white police force who sometimes either deliberately or mistakenly attacked them. Yet throughout all of this they were able to comment and write or report their stories about "the black violence" ignoring the fact that they were standing in the midst of this so-called black violence unharmed.

The white racist continues to draw invidious parallels between the gains of such immigrant groups as the Italians, Irish and Jews and the blacks, citing this as proof of black inferiority. In his attempted justification of his racism he ignores the fact that none of these groups were subjected to enslavement, none was the victim of federal, state, and local government policies to keep him in subservience and therefore there is no parallel.

In his attempted justification, he explains away the fact that the Irish, Italians and Jews were not brought to this country against their will, their families were not broken up deliberately, nor were they perpetually subjected to all manners of barbarities and cruelties to keep them in a state of slavery and subjugation. All history and all present reality are ignored as the white racist, in his pathological attempts to justify himself, relies on these devices.

The white man's hidden fear: he wants it and she likes it.

**the sexual
implications
of racism**

The Sexualization of Racism

Calvin C. Hernton

More than two decades ago, a Swedish social scientist was invited to America for the purpose of conducting perhaps the most thorough study of the race problem ever undertaken. The social scientist was Gunnar Myrdal. As it turned out, he produced a monumental work entitled *An American Dilemma*.

One of the most interesting aspects of the race problem was formulated by Myrdal into a schema which he called "The Rank Order of Discrimination." When Myrdal asked white Southerners to list, in the order of importance, the things they thought Negroes wanted most, here is what he got:

1. Intermarriage and sex intercourse with whites
2. Social equality and etiquette
3. Desegregation of public facilities, buses, churches, etc.
4. Political enfranchisement
5. Fair treatment in the law courts
6. Economic opportunities[1]

The curious thing about this "Rank Order" was that when Myrdal approached the Negroes, they put down the same items as did the whites, but with one major change—they listed them in the direct reverse order!

Today the same reverse positions are still maintained with equal vigor by both whites and Negroes. While I am not going to charge either group with being totally dishonest, I am going to assert that neither whites nor Negroes were or are being completely honest with themselves. For, of the various facets of the race problem in America, there is no doubt that the sexual aspect is as much a "thorn in the side" to Negroes as it is to whites. Both groups, for their own special reasons, are hideously concerned about it.

The white man, especially the Southerner, is overtly obsessed by the idea of the Negro desiring sexual relations with whites. The Negro man is secretly tormented every second of his wakeful life by the presence of white women in his midst, whom he cannot or had better not touch. Despite the severe penalties for associating with white women—lynching, castration, electrocution—Negroes risk their lives for white flesh, and an occasional few actually commit rape. On the other hand, the white man, especially in the South, cannot seem to adhere to his own laws and customs prohibiting interracial intercourse—he insults, seduces, and rapes Negro women as if this were what they exist for. A preponderance of racial violence takes the form of sexual atrocities against not only black women but black men as well.

In the North, Midwest, and West, where there are few legal barriers

[1] Gunnar Myrdal, *An American Dilemma* (7th ed.; New York, London: Harper & Brothers, 1944), Vol. I, pp. 60–61.

against race mixing, many Negroes and whites suffer social ostracism and castigation for engaging in interracial relations.

What does all of this mean? It means that the race problem is inextricably connected with sex. More and more in America, everything we make, sell, handle, wear, and do takes on a sexual meaning. Matters dealing with race relations are no exception. The Madison Avenue "hidden persuaders" and the "organization men" of the commercial world are functioning now in such in all-pervasive way that virtually no area of social reality, no facet of our psyches, can escape the all but total sexualization of American life. In nearly every television commercial, in every fashion magazine, on the "center pages" of our newspapers, on billboard, bus, and subway ads, in the tabloids of scandal, on the covers and pages of every "cheap" magazine—there is but one incessant symbol: the naked or half-naked white woman. The scantily clad white woman is irresistibly enticing as the ubiquitous sex symbol of our times. Sex pervades everything.

The sexualization of the race problem is a reality, and we are going to have to deal with it even though most of us are, if not unwilling, definitely unprepared.

A tall, dark Negro boards the subway at 42nd Street in New York City. He takes a seat in the corner away from everybody. He pulls from his hip pocket a magazine; he looks around carefully, then opens the cover and instantly becomes engrossed. He turns the pages slowly, almost as if transfixed in and by some forbidden drug. There are naked women in various "naughty" poses on every page of the magazine. Their skin is white. A white man enters and stands beside the Negro. Quickly the Negro snaps the magazine shut, tucks it into his pocket, lays his head back and closes his eyes, probably to dream or to have a nightmare.

"I can't hardly sit by a Negro woman," said a white man who served as an informant for this book. "I can't be comfortable in their presence. I mean I get excited. They don't even have to be good-looking. I can't help but get erect no matter what kind of looking Negro she is."

I have before me the October (1963) issue of the *Science Digest*. There is a picture of a Negro on the cover. The caption reads:

> The Negro
> HOW HE'S
> *DIFFERENT*
> WHY
> WHITES
> *FEAR HIM*[2]

Inside, on one of the pages, it says that the thing whites fear most about Negroes is that Negroes have an uncontrollable urge to mate with the sisters and daughters of white men. White men, especially Southerners, are afraid of the so-called superior, savage sexuality of the Negro male, and they are dead set against any measures that will lift the Negro's status,

[2] My italics [Hernton].

116

"I can't hardly sit by a Negro woman..."

because they are certain that such measures will bring the Negro one step nearer to the white woman's bedroom. Meanwhile it is a common saying in the South among white males that "a man is not a man until he has slept with a nigger."

Listen to the advice a Negro woman in Mississippi gave reporter John Griffin, who she thought was a stranger to the way of white folks in the South.

> . . . well, you know you don't want to even look at a white woman. In fact, you look down at the ground or the other way . . . you may not know you're looking in a white woman's direction but they'll try to make something out of it. . . . If you pass by a picture show, and they've got women on the posters outside, don't look at them either. . . . Somebody's sure to say, "Hey, boy—what are you looking at that white gal like *that* for?"[3]

The white man's self-esteem is in a constant state of sexual anxiety in all matters dealing with race relations. So is the Negro's, because his life,

[3] John Griffin, *Black Like Me* (New York: Signet Books, 1963), p. 60.

Photograph by Hugh Bell.

117

too, is enmeshed in the absurd system of racial hatred in America. Since racism is centered in and revolves around sex, the Negro cannot help but see himself as at once sexually affirmed and negated. While the Negro is portrayed as a great "walking phallus" with satyr-like potency, he is denied the execution of that potency, he is denied the most precious sexual image which surrounds him—the white woman. The myth of the sanctity of "white womanhood" is nothing more than a myth, but because this myth is acted upon *as if* it were real both by blacks and whites alike, then it *becomes* real as far as the behavior and sensitivities of those who must encounter it are concerned.

The sexualization of racism in the United States is a unique phenomenon in the history of mankind; it is an anomaly of the first order. In fact, there is a sexual involvement, at once real and vicarious, connecting white and black people in America that spans the history of this country from the era of slavery to the present, an involvement so immaculate and yet so perverse, so ethereal and yet so concrete, that all race relations tend to be, however subtle, *sex* relations.

It is important to see how the racism of sex in America has affected the sexual behavior of blacks and whites toward one another, and how black and white people perceive each other and themselves sexually as a result of living in a world of segregation and racial bigotry. As Negro and Caucasian, male and female, what do we mean to each other as sexual beings?

I am reminded of the way the policemen, during the historic march on Washington in 1963, constricted their eyes, tightened their faces, and fondled their sticks every time an interracial couple passed them in that mammoth parade. I am further reminded that when the marchers were yelling for F-R-E-E-E-DOM, for jobs, civil rights, equality of education, and the rest, a young Negro leaped in the air and shouted out—"S-E-X!" Perhaps he was a "crackpot." Even so, can one be certain that he was not an omen for our times? I am not certain, for, I submit, that, secretly, for many Negroes and whites, sexual liberty is as precious and sought-after as any other freedom. As the other barriers to freedom fall down, sexual liberty will become increasingly important in our society.

On Being Crazy

W. E. B. Du Bois

It was one o'clock and I was hungry. I walked into a restaurant, seated myself, and reached for the bill of fare. My table companion rose.

"Sir," said he, "do you wish to force your company on those who do not want you?"

No, said I, I wish to eat.

"Are you aware, sir, that this is social equality?"

Nothing of the sort, sir, it is hunger—and I ate.

The day's work done, I sought the theatre. As I sank into my seat, the lady shrank and squirmed.

I beg pardon, I said.

"Do you enjoy being where you are not wanted?" she asked coldly.

Oh no, I said.

"Well you are not wanted here."

I was surprised. I fear you are mistaken, I said, I certainly want the music, and I like to think the music wants me to listen to it.

"Usher," said the lady, "this is social equality."

"No madame," said the usher, "it is the second movement of Beethoven's Fifth Symphony."

After the theatre, I sought the hotel where I had sent my baggage. The clerk scowled.

"What do you want?"

Rest, I said.

"This is a white hotel," he said.

I looked around. Such a color scheme requires a great deal of cleaning, I said, but I don't know that I object.

"We object," said he.

Then why, I began, but he interrupted.

"We don't keep niggers," he said, "we don't want social equality."

Neither do I, I replied gently, I want a bed.

I walked thoughtfully to the train. I'll take a sleeper through Texas. I'm a little bit dissatisfied with this town.

"Can't sell you one."

I only want to hire it, said I, for a couple of nights.

"Can't sell you a sleeper in Texas," he maintained. "They consider that social equality."

I consider it barbarism, I said, and I think I'll walk.

Walking, I met another wayfarer, who immediately walked to the other side of the road, where it was muddy. I asked his reason.

"Niggers is dirty," he said.

So is mud, said I. Moreover, I am not as dirty as you—yet.

"But you're a nigger, ain't you?" he asked.

My grandfather was so called.

"Well then!" he answered triumphantly.

Do you live in the South? I persisted, pleasantly.

"Sure," he growled, "and starve there."

I should think you and the Negroes should get together and vote out starvation.

"We don't let them vote."

We? Why not? I said in surprise.

"Niggers is too ignorant to vote."

But, I said, I am not so ignorant as you.

"But you're a nigger."

Yes, I'm certainly what you mean by that.

"Well then!" he returned, with that curiously inconsequential note of triumph. "Moreover," he said, "I don't want my sister to marry a nigger."

I had not seen his sister, so I merely murmured, let her say no.

"By God, you shan't marry her, even if she said yes."

But—but I don't want to marry her, I answered, a little perturbed at the personal turn.

"Why not!" he yelled, angrier than ever.

Because I'm already married and I rather like my wife.

"Is she a nigger?" he asked suspiciously.

Well, I said again, her grandmother was called that.

"Well then!" he shouted in that oddly illogical way.

I gave up.

Go on, I said, either you are crazy or I am.

"We both are," he said as he trotted along in the mud.

"White racism is a self-initiated offensive enactment designed to protect the affluency of whites at the expense of Blacks." Preston R. Wilcox, Staff Associate, Education Affiliate, Bedford-Stuyvesant D & S Corp.

racism

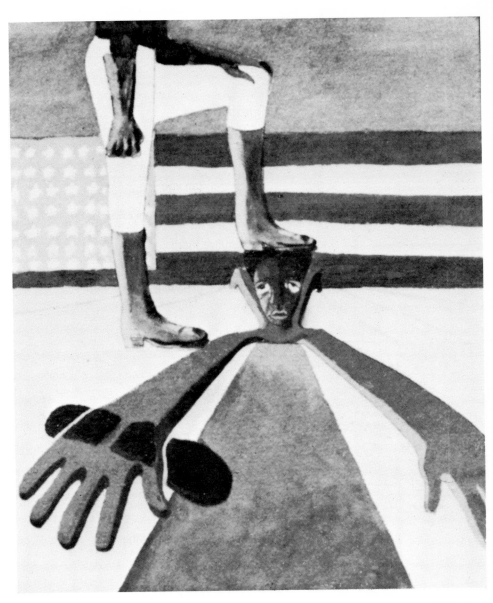

"Land of the Free, 1967" by Dana Chandler. Courtesy of Contemporary Crafts Publications.

as exploitation

When in Rome

Mari E. Evans

Marrie dear
the box is full . . .
take
whatever you like
to eat . . .
        (an egg
        or soup
        . . . there ain't no meat.)

there's endive there
and
cottage cheese . . .
        (whew! if I had some
         black-eyed peas . . .)

there's sardines
on the shelves
and such . . .
but don't
get my anchovies . . .
they cost
too much!
        (me get the
        anchovies indeed!
        what she think, she got—
        a bird to feed?)

there's plenty in there
to fill you up . . .
        (yes'm, just the
        sight's
        enough!

        Hope I lives till I get
        home
        I'm tired of eatin'
        what they eats in Rome . . .)

From *I Am a Black Woman*, published by Wm. Morrow & Co. 1970, by permission of the author.

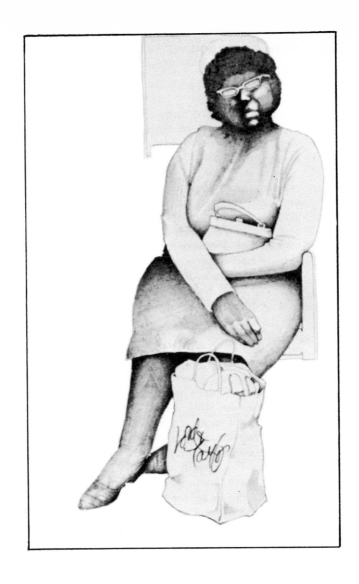

Black is being
so shiftless and lazy you scrub floors six days a week.

Son in the Afternoon

John A. Williams

It was hot. I tend to be a bitch when it's hot. I goosed the little Ford over Sepulveda Boulevard toward Santa Monica until I got stuck in the traffic that pours from L.A. into the surrounding towns. I'd had a very lousy day at the studio.

I was—still am—a writer and this studio had hired me to check scripts and films with Negroes in them to make sure the Negro moviegoer wouldn't be offended. The signs were already clear one day the whole of American industry would be racing pell-mell to get a Negro, showcase a spade. I was kind of a pioneer. I'm a *Negro* writer, you see. The day had been tough because of a couple of verbs—slink and walk. One of those Hollywood hippies had done a script calling for a Negro waiter to slink away from the table where a dinner party was glaring at him. I said the waiter should walk, not slink, because later on he becomes a hero. The Hollywood hippie, who understood it all because he had some colored friends, said that it was essential to the plot that the waiter slink. I said you don't slink one minute and become a hero the next; there has to be some consistency. The Negro actor I was standing up for said nothing either way. He had played Uncle Tom roles so long that he had become Uncle Tom. But the director agreed with me.

Anyway . . . hear me out now. I was on my way to Santa Monica to pick up my mother, Nora. It was a long haul for such a hot day. I had planned a quiet evening: a nice shower, fresh clothes, and then I would have dinner at the Watkins and talk with some of the musicians on the scene for a quick taste before they cut to their gigs. After, I was going to the Pigalle down on Figueroa and catch Earl Grant at the organ, and still later, if nothing exciting happened, I'd pick up Scottie and make it to the Lighthouse on the Beach or to the Strollers and listen to some of the white boys play. I liked the long drive, especially while listening to Sleepy Stein's show on the radio. Later, much later of course, it would be home, back to Watts.

So you see, this picking up Nora was a little inconvenient. My mother was a maid for the Couchmans. Ronald Couchman was an architect, a good one I understood from Nora who has a fine sense for this sort of thing; you don't work in some hundred-odd houses during your life without getting some idea of the way a house should be laid out. Couchman's wife, Kay, was a playgirl who drove a white Jaguar from one party to another. My mother didn't like her too much; she didn't seem to care much for her son, Ronald, junior. There's something wrong with a parent who can't really love her own child, Nora thought. The Couchmans lived in a real fine residential section, of course. A number of actors lived nearby, character actors, not really big stars.

By permission of the author, John A. Williams.

Somehow it is very funny. I mean that the maids and butlers knew everything about these people, and these people knew nothing at all about the help. Through Nora and her friends I knew who was laying whose wife; who had money and who *really* had money; I knew about the wild parties hours before the police, and who smoked marijuana, when, and where they got it.

To get to Couchman's driveway I had to go three blocks up one side of a palm-planted center strip and back down the other. The driveway bent gently, then swept back out of sight of the main road. The house, sheltered by slim palms, looked like a transplanted New England Colonial. I parked and walked to the kitchen door, skirting the growling Great Dane who was tied to a tree. That was the route to the kitchen door.

I don't like kitchen doors. Entering people's houses by them, I mean. I'd done this thing most of my life when I called at places where Nora worked to pick up the patched or worn sheets or the half-eaten roasts, the battered, tarnished silver—the fringe benefits of a housemaid. As a teen-ager I'd told Nora I was through with that crap; I was not going through anyone's kitchen door. She only laughed and said I'd learn. One day soon after, I called for her and without knocking walked right through the front door of this house and right on through the living room. I was almost out of the room when I saw feet behind the couch. I leaned over and there was Mr. Jorgensen and his wife making out like crazy. I guess they thought Nora had gone and it must have hit them sort of suddenly and they went at it like the hell-bomb was due to drop any minute. I've been that way too, mostly in the spring. Of course, when Mr. Jorgensen looked over his shoulder and saw me, you know what happened. I was thrown out and Nora right behind me. It was the middle of winter, the old man was sick and the coal bill three months overdue. Nora was right about those kitchen doors: I learned.

My mother saw me before I could ring the bell. She opened the door. "Hello," she said. She was breathing hard, like she'd been running or something. "Come in and sit down. I don't know *where* that Kay is. Little Ronald is sick and she's probably out gettin' drunk again." She left me then and trotted back through the house, I guess to be with Ronnie. I hated the combination of her white nylon uniform, her dark brown face and the wide streaks of gray in her hair. Nora had married this guy from Texas a few years after the old man died. He was all right. He made out okay. Nora didn't have to work, but she just couldn't be still; she always had to be doing something. I suggested she quit work, but I had as much luck as her husband. I used to tease her about liking to be around those white folks. It would have been good for her to take an extended trip around the country visiting my brothers and sisters. Once she got to Philadelphia, she could go right out to the cemetery and sit awhile with the old man.

I walked through the Couchman home. I liked the library. I thought if I knew Couchman I'd like him. The room made me feel that. I left it and went into the big living room. You could tell Couchman had let his wife do that. Everything in it was fast, dart-like, with no sense of ease. But on the walls were several of Couchman's conceptions of buildings and homes. I guess he was a disciple of Wright. My mother walked rapidly through the room without looking at me and said, "Just be patient, Wendell. She should be here real soon."

"Yeah," I said, "with a snootful." I had turned back to the drawings when Ronnie scampered into the room, his face twisted with rage.

"Nora!" he tried to roar, perhaps the way he'd seen the parents of some of his friends roar at their maids. I'm quite sure Kay didn't shout at Nora, and I don't think Couchman would. But then no one shouts at Nora. "Nora, you come right back here this minute!" the little bastard shouted and stamped and pointed to a spot on the floor where Nora was supposed to come to roost. I have a nasty temper. Sometimes it lies dormant for ages and at other times, like when the weather is hot and nothing seems to be going right, it's bubbling and ready to explode. "Don't talk to *my* mother like that, you little—!" I said sharply, breaking off just before I cursed. I wanted him to be large enough for me to strike. "How'd you like for me to talk to *your* mother like that?"

The nine-year-old looked up at me in surprise and confusion. He hadn't expected me to say anything. I was just another piece of furniture. Tears rose in his eyes and spilled out onto his pale cheeks. He put his hands behind him, twisted them. He moved backwards, away from me. He looked at my mother with a "Nora, come help me" look. And sure enough, there was Nora, speeding back across the room, gathering the kid in her arms, tucking his robe together. I was too angry to feel hatred for myself.

Ronnie was the Couchmans' only kid. Nora loved him. I suppose that was the trouble. Couchman was gone ten, twelve hours a day. Kay didn't stay around the house any longer than she had to. So Ronnie had only my mother. I think kids should have someone to love, and Nora wasn't a bad sort. But somehow when the six of us, her own children, were growing up we never had her. She was gone, out scuffling to get those crumbs to put into our mouths and shoes for our feet and praying for something to happen so that all the space in between would be taken care of. Nora's affection for us took the form of rushing out into the morning's five o'clock blackness to wake some silly bitch and get her coffee; took form in her trudging five miles home every night instead of taking the streetcar to save money to buy tablets for us, to use at school, we said. But the truth was that all of us liked to draw and we went through a writing tablet in a couple of hours every day. Can you imagine? There's not a goddam artist among us. We never had the physical affection, the pat on the head, the quick, smiling kiss, the "gimme a hug" routine. All of this Ronnie was getting.

Now he buried his little blond head in Nora's breast and sobbed. "There, there now," Nora said. "Don't you cry, Ronnie. Ol' Wendell is just jealous, and he hasn't much sense either. He didn't mean nuthin'."

I left the room. Nora had hit it of course, hit it and passed on. I looked back. It didn't look so incongruous, the white and black together, I mean. Ronnie was still sobbing. His head bobbed gently on Nora's shoulder. The only time I ever got that close to her was when she trapped me with a bearhug so she could whale the daylights out of me after I put a snowball through Mrs. Grant's window. I walked outside and lit a cigarette. When Ronnie was in the hospital the month before, Nora got me to run her way over to Hollywood every night to see him. I didn't like that worth a damn.

All right, I'll admit it: it did upset me. All that affection I didn't get nor my brothers and sisters going to that little white boy who, without a doubt, when away from her called her the names he'd learned from adults. Can you imagine a nine-year-old kid calling Nora a "girl," "our girl"? I spat at the Great Dane. He snarled and then I bounced a rock off his fanny. "Lay down, you bastard," I muttered. It was a good thing he was tied up.

I heard the low cough of the Jaguar slapping against the road. The car was throttled down, and with a muted roar it swung into the driveway. The woman aimed it for me. I was evil enough not to move. I was tired of playing with these people. At the last moment, grinning, she swung the wheel over and braked. She bounded out of the car like a tennis player vaulting over a net.

"Hi," she said, tugging at her shorts.

"Hello."

"You're Nora's boy?"

"I'm Nora's son." Hell, I was as old as she was; besides, I can't stand "boy."

"Nora tells us you're working in Hollywood. Like it?"

"It's all right."

"You must be pretty talented."

We stood looking at each other while the dog whined for her attention. Kay had a nice body and it was well tanned. She was high, boy was she high. Looking at her, I could feel myself going into my sexy bastard routine; sometimes I can swing it great. Maybe it all had to do with the business inside. Kay took off her sunglasses and took a good look at me. "Do you have a cigarette?"

I gave her one and lit it. "Nice tan." I said. Most white people I know think it's a great big deal if a Negro compliments them on their tans. It's a large laugh. You have all this volleyball about color and come summer you can't hold the white folks back from the beaches, anyplace where they can get some sun. And of course the blacker they get, the more pleased they are. Crazy. If there is ever a Negro revolt, it will come during the summer and Negroes will descend upon the beaches around the nation and paralyze the country. You can't conceal cattle prods and bombs and pistols and police dogs when you're showing your birthday suit to the sun.

"You like it?" she asked. She was pleased. She placed her arm next to mine. "Almost the same color," she said.

"Ronnie isn't feeling well," I said.

"Oh, the poor kid. I'm so glad we have Nora. She's such a charm. I'll run right in and look at him. Do have a drink in the bar. Fix me one too, will you?" Kay skipped inside and I went to the bar and poured out two strong drinks. I made hers stronger than mine. She was back soon. "Nora was trying to put him to sleep and she made me stay out." She giggled. She quickly tossed off her drink. "Another, please?" While I was fixing her drink she was saying how amazing it was for Nora to have such a talented son. What she was really saying was that it was amazing for a servant to have a son who was not also a servant. "Anything can happen in a democracy," I said. "Servants' sons drink with madames and so on."

"Oh, Nora isn't a servant," Kay said. "She's part of the family."

Yeah, I thought. Where and how many times had I heard *that* before?

In the ensuing silence, she started to admire her tan again. "You think it's pretty good, do you? You don't know how hard I worked to get it." I moved close to her and held her arm. I placed my other arm around her. She pretended not to see or feel it, but she wasn't trying to get away either. In fact she was pressing closer and the register in my brain that tells me at the precise moment when I'm in, went off. Kay was very high. I put both arms around her and she put both hers around me. When I kissed her, she responded completely.

"Mom!"

"Ronnie, come back to bed," I heard Nora shout from the other room. We could hear Ronnie running over the rug in the outer room. Kay tried to get away from me, push me to one side, because we could tell that Ronnie knew where to look for his Mom: he was running right for the bar, where we were. "Oh, please," she said, "don't let him see us." I wouldn't let her push me away. "Stop!" she hissed. "He'll *see* us!" We stopped struggling just for an instant, and we listened to the echoes of the word *see.* She gritted her teeth and renewed her efforts to get away.

Me? I had the scene laid right out. The kid breaks into the room, see, and sees his mother in this real wriggly clinch with this colored guy who's just shouted at him, see, and no matter how his mother explains it away, the kid has the image—the colored guy and his mother—for the rest of his life, see?

That's the way it happened. The kid's mother hissed under her breath, *"You're crazy!"* and she looked at me as though she were seeing me or something about me for the very first time. I'd released her as soon as Ronnie, romping into the bar, saw us and came to a full, open-mouthed halt. Kay went to him. He looked first at me, then at his mother. Kay turned to me, but she couldn't speak.

Outside in the living room my mother called, "Wendell, where are you? We can go now."

I started to move past Kay and Ronnie. I felt many things, but I made myself think mostly, *There, you little bastard, there.*

My mother thrust her face inside the door and said, "Goodbye, Mrs. Couchman. See you tomorrow. 'Bye, Ronnie."

"Yes," Kay said, sort of stunned. "Tomorrow." She was reaching for Ronnie's hand as we left, but the kid was slapping her hand away. I hurried quickly after Nora, hating the long drive back to Watts.

Lithograph by John Lennon. Copyright Avant-Garde, 1970. Reprinted with permission.

For a Lady I Know

Countee Cullen

She even thinks that up in heaven
   Her class lies late and snores,
While poor black cherubs rise at
     seven
     To do celestial chores.

Fred Pusterla

white militants

The White Race and Its Heroes

Eldridge Cleaver

. . . What has suddenly happened is that the white race has lost its heroes. Worse its heroes have been revealed as villains and its greatest heroes as arch-villains. The new generations of whites, appalled by the sanguine and despicable record carved over the face of the globe by their race in the last five hundred years, are rejecting the panoply of white heroes whose careers rested on a system of domestic and foreign exploitation, rooted in the myth of white supremacy and the manifest destiny of the white race. The emerging shape of a new world order, and the requisites for survival in such a world, are fostering in young whites a new outlook. They recoil in shame from the spectacle of cowboys and pioneers—their heroic forefathers whose exploits filled earlier generations with pride—galloping across a movie screen shooting down Indians like Coke bottles. Even Winston

Churchill, who is looked upon by older whites as perhaps the greatest hero of the twentieth century—even he, because of the system of which he was a creature and which he served, is an arch-villain in the eyes of the young white rebels.

At the close of World War Two, national liberation movements in the colonized world picked up new momentum and audacity, seeking to cash in on the democratic promises made by the Allies during the war. The Atlantic Charter, signed by President Roosevelt and Prime Minister Churchill in 1941, affirming "the right of all people to choose the form of government under which they may live," established the principle, although it took years of postwar struggle to give this piece of rhetoric even the appearance of reality. And just as world revolution has prompted the oppressed to re-evaluate their self-image in terms of the changing conditions, to slough off the servile attitudes inculcated by long years of subordination, the same dynamics of change have prompted the white people of the world to re-evaluate their self-image as well, to disabuse themselves of the Master Race psychology developed over centuries of imperial hegemony.

It is among the white youth of the world that the greatest change is taking place. It is they who are experiencing the great psychic pain of waking into consciousness to find their inherited heroes turned by events into villains. Communication and understanding between the older and younger generation of whites has entered a crisis. The elders, who, in the tradition of privileged classes or races, genuinely do not understand the youth, trapped by old ways of thinking and blind to the future, have only just begun to be vexed—because the youth have only just begun to rebel. So thoroughgoing is the revolution in the psyches of white youth that the traditional tolerance which every older generation has found it necessary to display is quickly exhausted, leaving a gulf of fear, hostility, mutual misunderstanding, and contempt.

The rebellion of the oppressed peoples of the world, along with the Negro revolution in America, have opened the way to a new evaluation of history, a re-examination of the role played by the white race since the beginning of European expansion. The positive achievements are also there in the record, and future generations will applaud them. But there can be no applause now, not while the master still holds the whip in his hand! Not even the master's own children can find it possible to applaud him—he cannot even applaud himself! The negative rings too loudly. Slave-catchers, slaveowners, murderers, butchers, invaders, oppressors—the white heroes have acquired new names. The great white statesmen whom school children are taught to revere are revealed as the architects of systems of human exploitation and slavery. Religious leaders are exposed as condoners and justifiers of all these evil deeds. Schoolteachers and college professors are seen as a clique of brainwashers and whitewashers.

The white youth of today are coming to see, intuitively, that to escape the onus of the history their fathers made they must face and admit the moral truth concerning the works of their fathers. That such venerated figures as George Washington and Thomas Jefferson owned hundreds of black slaves, that all of the Presidents up to Lincoln presided over a slave state, and that every President since Lincoln connived politically and cynically with the issues affecting the human rights and general welfare of the broad masses of the American people—these facts weigh heavily upon the hearts of these young people.

The elders do not like to give these youngsters credit for being able to understand what is going on and what has gone on. When speaking of juvenile delinquency, or the rebellious altitude of today's youth, the elders employ a glib rhetoric. They speak of the "alienation of youth," the desire of the young to be independent, the problems of "the father image" and "the mother image" and their effect upon growing children who lack sound models upon which to pattern themselves. But they consider it bad form to connect the problems of the youth with the central event of our era—the national liberation movements abroad and the Negro revolution at home. The foundations of authority have been blasted to bits in America because the whole society has been indicted, tried, and convicted of injustice. To the youth, the elders are Ugly Americans; to the elders, the youth have gone mad. . . .

. . . In the world revolution now under way, the initiative rests with people of color. That growing numbers of white youth are repudiating their heritage of blood and taking people of color as their heroes and models is a tribute not only to their insight but to the resilience of the human spirit. For today the heroes of the initiative are people not usually thought of as white: Fidel Castro, Che Guevara, Kwame Nkrumah, Mao Tse-tung, Gamal Abdel Nasser, Robert F. Williams, Malcolm X, Ben Bella, John Lewis, Martin Luther King, Jr., Robert Parris Moses, Ho Chi Minh, Stokeley Carmichael, W. E. B. DuBois, James Forman, Chou En-lai.

There is in America today a generation of white youth that is truly worthy

Benedict J. Fernandez, *In Opposition* (Da Capo Press, 1968).

of a black man's respect, and this is a rare event in the foul annals of American history. From the beginning of the contact between blacks and whites, there has been very little reason for a black man to respect a white, with such exceptions as John Brown and others lesser known. But respect commands itself and it can neither be given nor withheld when it is due. If a man like Malcolm X could change and repudiate racism, if I myself and other former Muslims can change, if young whites can change, then there is hope for America. It was certainly strange to find myself, while steeped in the doctrine that all whites were devils by nature, commanded by the heart to applaud and acknowledge respect for these young whites—despite the fact that they are descendants of the masters and I the descendant of slave. The sins of the fathers are visited upon the heads of the children—but only if the children continue in the evil deeds of the fathers.

The white youth of today have begun to react to the fact that the "American Way of Life" is a fossil of history. What do they care if their old baldheaded and crew-cut elders don't dig their caveman mops? They couldn't care less about the old, stiffassed honkies who don't like their new dances: Frug, Monkey, Jerk, Swim, Watusi. All they know is that it feels good to swing to way-out body-rhythms instead of dragassing across the dance floor like zombies to the dead beat of mind-smothered Mickey Mouse music. Is it any wonder that the youth have lost all respect for their elders, for law and order, when for as long as they can remember all they've witnessed is a monumental bickering over the Negro's place in American society and the right of people around the world to be left alone by outside powers? They have witnessed the law, both domestic and international, being spat upon by those who do not like its terms. Is it any wonder, then, that they feel justified, by sitting-in and freedom riding, in breaking laws made by lawless men? Old funny-styled, zipper-mouthed political night riders know nothing but to haul out an investigating committee *to look into the disturbance* to find the cause of the unrest among the youth. Look into a mirror! The cause is you, Mr. and Mrs. Yesterday, you with your forked tongues.

A young white today cannot help but recoil from the base deeds of his people. On every side, on every continent, he sees racial arrogance, savage brutality toward the conquered and subjugated people, genocide; he sees the human cargo of the slave trade; he sees the systematic extermination of American Indians; he sees the civilized nations of Europe fighting in imperial depravity over the lands of other people—and over possession of the very people themselves. There seems to be no end to the ghastly deeds of which his people are guilty. *GUILTY.* The slaughter of the Jews by the Germans, the dropping of atomic bombs on the Japanese people—these deeds weigh heavily upon the prostrate souls and tumultuous consciences of the white youth. The white heroes, their hands dripping with blood, are dead.

The young whites know that the colored people of the world, Afro-Americans included, do not seek revenge for their suffering. They seek the same things the white rebel wants: an end to war and exploitation. Black and white, the young rebels are free people, free in a way that Americans have never been before in the history of their country. And they are outraged.

the love it or leave it syndrome

syndrome

from Day of Absence

Douglas Turner Ward

. . . Lights rise on . . . section of the stage where a young couple lie in bed under an invisible wire-suspension sign lettered "HOME." Loud, insistent sounds of baby yells are heard. JOHN, *the husband, turns over trying to ignore the cries;* MARY, *the wife, is undisturbed.* JOHN's *efforts are futile; the cries continue until they cannot be denied. He bolts upright, jumps out of bed, and disappears offstage. Returns quickly and tries to rouse* MARY.

JOHN. Mary . . . *(Nudges her, pushes her, yells into her ear, but she fails to respond)* Mary, get up . . . Get up!

MARY. Ummm . . . *(Shrugs away, still sleeping.)*

JOHN. **GET UP!**

MARY. Ummmmmmmmm!

JOHN. Don't you hear the baby's bawling? . . . **NOW GET UP!**

MARY *(mumbling drowsily).* What baby . . . whose baby . . .?

JOHN. Yours!

MARY. Mine? That's ridiculous . . . what'd you say . . . ? Somebody's baby bawling? . . . How could that be so? *(Hearing screams)* Who's crying? Somebody's crying! . . . What's crying? . . . *Where's Lula?*

JOHN. I don't know. You better get up.

MARY. That's outrageous! . . . What time is it?

JOHN. Late 'nuff! Now rise up!

MARY. You must be joking . . . I'm sure I still have four or five hours' sleep in store—even more after that head-splittin' blowout last night . . . *(Tumbles back under covers.)*

JOHN. Nobody told you to gulp those last six bourbons—

MARY. Don't tell me how many bourbons to swallow, not after you guzzled the whole stinking bar! . . . Get up? . . . You must be cracked . . . Where's Lula? She must be here, she always is . . .

JOHN. Well, she ain't here yet, so get up and muzzle that brat before she does drive me cuckoo!

MARY *(springing upright, finally realizing gravity of situation).* Whaddaya mean Lula's not here? She's always here, she must be here . . . Where else kin she be? She supposed to be . . . She just can't *not* be here—call her! . . .

(. . . Baby cries are as insistent as ever.)

MARY. *(at end of patience).* Smother it!

JOHN *(beyond his).* That's a hell of a thing to say 'bout your own child! You should know what to do to hush her up!

MARY. Why don't you try?

JOHN. You had her!

MARY. You shared in borning her!

JOHN. Possibly not!

MARY. Why, you lousy—!

JOHN. What good is a mother who can't shut up her own daughter?

MARY. I told you she yells louder every time I try to lay hands on her—Where's Lula? Didn't you call her?

JOHN. I told you I can't get the call through!

MARY. Try agin—

JOHN. It's no use! I tried numerous times and can't even git through to the switchboard. You've got to quiet her down yourself. (*Firmly*) Now, go in there and clam her up 'fore I lose my patience! (MARY *exits. Soon, we hear the yells increase. She rushes back in.*)

MARY. She won't let me touch her, just screams louder!

JOHN. Probably wet 'n soppy!

MARY. Yes! Stinks something awful! Phooooey! I can't stand that filth and odor!

JOHN. That's why she's screaming! Needs her didee changed—go change it!

MARY. How you 'spect me to when I don't know how? Suppose I faint?

JOHN. Well let her blast away. I'm getting outta here.

MARY. You can't leave me here like this!

JOHN. Just watch me! . . . See this nice split-level cottage, peachy furniture, multicolored T.V., hi-fi set n' the rest? . . . Well, how you think I scraped 'em together while you curled up on your fat lil fanny? . . . By gittin outta here—not only on *time* . . . but *earlier*!—Beating a frantic crew of nice young executives to the punch—gitting there fustest with the mostest brown-nosing you ever saw! Now if I goof one day—just **ONE DAY!**—you reckon I'd stay ahead? **NO!** . . . There'd be a wolf pack trampling over my prostrate body, racing to replace my smiling face against the boss's left rump! . . . *No mam!* I'm zooming outta here on time, just as I always have, and what's more—you gon fix me some breakfast. *I'm hungry!*

MARY. But—

JOHN. No buts about it! (*Flash-blackout as he gags on a mouthful of coffee*). What you trying to do, **STRANGLE ME?** (*Jumps up and starts putting on jacket.*)

MARY (*sarcastically*). What did you expect?

JOHN (*in biting fury*). That you could possibly boil a pot of water, toast a few slices of bread and fry a coupler eggs! . . . It was a mistaken assumption!

MARY. So they aren't as good as Lula's!

JOHN. That is an overstatement. Your efforts don't result in anything that could possibly be digested by man, mammal, or insect! . . . When I married you, I thought I was fairly acquainted with your faults and weaknesses—I chalked 'em up to human imperfection . . . But now I know I was being extremely generous, over-optimistic and phenomenally deluded! —You have no idea how useless you really are!

MARY. Then why'd you marry me?

JOHN. Decoration!

MARY. You shoulda married Lula!

JOHN. I might've if it wasn't against the segregation law! . . . But for the sake of my home, my child and my sanity, I will even take a chance on sacrificing my slippery grip on the status pole and drive by her shanty to find out whether she or someone like her kin come over here and prevent some ultimate disaster. (*Storms toward door, stopping abruptly at exit*) Are you sure you kin make it to the bathroom wit'out Lula backing you up?

(*Blackout. . . . JOHN and MARY a few hours later. A funeral solemnity pervades their mood.*)

JOHN. Walked up to the shack, knocked on door, didn't git no answer. Hollered: "Lula? Lula . . . ?—

not a thing. Went 'round the side, peeped in window—nobody stirred. Next door—nobody there. Crossed other side of street and banged on five or six other doors—not a colored person could be found!) Not a man, neither woman or child—not even a black dog could be seen, smelt or heard for blocks around . . . They've gone, Mary.

MARY. What does it all mean, John?

JOHN. I don't know, Mary . . .

MARY. I always had Lula, John. Never missed a day at my side . . . That's why I couldn't accept your wedding proposal until I was sure you'd welcome me and her together as a package. How am I gonna git through the day? Baby don't know *me,* I ain't acquainted wit *it.* I've never lifted cover off pot, swung a mop or broom, dunked a dish or even pushed a dustrag. I'm lost wit'out Lula, I need her, John, I need her. (*Begins to weep softly.* JOHN *pats her consolingly.*)

JOHN. Courage, honey . . . Everybody in town is facing the same dilemma. We mustn't crack up . . .

(Blackout.)

Massa Sussman's First Annual Social Awareness and Polarized Society Rent-a-Honkie Multiple Choice Quiz by Vic Sussman

Give this test to whites to see if they know anything about Blacks. Guessing doesn't count. They're either with it or not.

Reprinted by permission of the author, Vic Stephen Sussman.

1. A Black Man who caters to the whims of White people is often called:
   (a) a burr head
   (b) a John
   (c) a handkerchief head
   (d) a dogman

2. A disease which attacks only Black people is called:
   (a) ash fungus
   (b) yaws
   (c) shard cell anemia
   (d) sickle cell anemia

3. Whites often refer to Black men as:
   (a) son
   (b) hey
   (c) boy
   (d) baby

4. Hotshot white liberal teachers often refer in pious tones to one of the few figures in Black History that they know anything about. Her name becomes a cliche:
   (a) Harriot Tubman
   (b) Aunt Jemima
   (c) Maxine T. Evette
   (d) Rosalind Stapleton

5. Which of the following is NOT known for his poetry:
   (a) Claude McKay
   (b) Sterling Brown
   (c) Richard Hatcher
   (d) James Weldon Johnson

6. Many young Blacks are interested in studying
   (a) Uhuru
   (b) Swahili
   (c) Masakela
   (d) Quahiri

7. A famous slave who became an author and statesman was:
   (a) Nat Turner
   (b) Charles Drew
   (c) Ward Milton
   (d) Frederick Douglass

8. A well-known playwright is:
   (a) LeRoi Markham
   (b) LeRoi Jackson
   (c) LeRoi Brown
   (d) LeRoi Jones

9. Before Malcolm X became a Muslim, his last name was:
   (a) Little
   (b) Litell
   (c) Langford
   (d) Lewis

10. As a child, Malcolm X had a nickname. He was called:
    (a) Slim
    (b) Bojangles
    (c) Red
    (d) Bopper

11. Soul Food has been publicized to the point that White people have heard of 'chitlins'. What are they:
    (a) pig bladders
    (b) pig intestines
    (c) Chicken livers
    (d) fried watermelon rinds

12. Ralph Ellison was honored for a novel he wrote entitled:
    (a) Curse of Darkness
    (b) The Invisible Man
    (c) Black Like Me
    (d) On the Ropes

13. A Black leader of the 1920's is:
    (a) Colin Cook
    (b) Obadiah Royal
    (c) Marcus Garvey
    (d) Robert Shelton

14. A noted Black photographer for Life Magazine has directed a motion picture version of his auto-biography. His name is:
    (a) Gordon Parks
    (b) Gordon Brewer
    (c) Al Parker
    (d) Vance Bujean

15. During the period of formal slavery in the United States, a slave could

be killed by the white masters for:
- (a) stealing
- (b) running away
- (c) any reason at all
- (d) reading and writing

16. Just as Whites have epithets for Blacks, Blacks have names for Whitey. Pick out four of these names. You must get three right to score:
- (a) hooter
- (b) gray
- (c) Simon
- (d) Charley
- (e) Ofay
- (f) funky
- (g) The Man
- (h) conk

17. Match up these Black writers with their books. Guessing doesn't count. You must get four right to score:
- ( ) Claude Brown
- ( ) Richard Wright
- ( ) James Baldwin
- ( ) Dick Gregory
- ( ) Julius Lester
- ( ) W.E.B. DuBois
- a. The Souls of Black Folk
- b. Manchild in the Promised Land
- c. Look Out Whitey, Black Power's Gon' Get Your Mamma
- d. Another Country
- e. Nigger
- f. Black Boy

18. Of the following words, two are the names of African leaders. You must get both right to score:
- (a) Umoju
- (b) Kenyatta
- (c) Kaffir
- (d) Nkrumah
- (e) Makeba
- (f) Malinka

19. You are on a downtown street. A well-dressed Black man steps up to you and asks if you would like to buy:
- (a) a copy of Muhammed Proclaims
- (b) a copy of Muhammed Speaks
- (c) Ebony Magazine
- (d) Aunt Martha's Dream Book

20. The spiritual leader of the Black Muslims is:
- (a) Julius 2X Best
- (b) Elijah Muhammed
- (c) Ali Akbah Khan
- (d) Minister Muhammed Bey

21. If you were a Muslim, you'd most likely do your shopping at:
- (a) the local Cooperative
- (b) the Mosque Market
- (c) Shabazz Market
- (d) the Kiff Market

22. A West Coast Black leader is:
- (a) Ron Umgowah
- (b) Ron Kalinga
- (c) Ron Karenga
- (d) Ron Topanga

23. A well-known Black organization is the:
- (a) Black Panthers
- (b) Black Jacks
- (c) Black Bombers
- (d) Black Knights

24. Another organization known by its initials is:
- (a) BBB
- (b) RIM
- (c) RAM
- (d) SOC

25. Dashikis are something Black people might:
- (a) eat
- (b) wear
- (c) sing
- (d) play

THE ANSWERS:

1. c, 2. d, 3. c, 4. a, 5. c, 6. b, 7. d, 8. d, 9. a, 10. c, 11. b, 12. b, 13. c, 14. a, 15. c, 16. b, d, e, g, 17. b, f, d, e, c, a, 18. b, d, 19. b. 20. b, 21. c, 22. c, 23. a, 24. c, 25. b.

1 to 5 correct: Congratulations! You, Snow White, are typical of most socially ignorant Whites. Black people have been cleaning your house, cooking your food, and caring for your children for 400 years and you know nothing about them. Blacks have endured slavery, legalized murder, denial of basic humanity and unconcealed hatred. Black children are right now growing up in a world of self-hatred, nurtured by your kind of ignorance. There are more than 25 million Black people in America who past and present have been rendered invisible by the power structure you support by your lack of awareness. You and yours enjoy the fruits of white skin, while Black people have no more identity in your eyes than a stray dog. YOU are what racism is all about.

6 to 10: You are guessing. You probably sport a 'Support Your Local Police' bumper sticker and think Blacks are 'moving too fast.' When you get out of bed in the morning, do you take your sheet with you?

11 to 15: Okay, Big Deal, you've probably stopped saying 'there's a nigger in the woodpile,'' and you don't even mind eating at the same table with your maid. But half the questions stumped you. Do you really know where you're at?

16 to 20: You're partially plugged into the other half of the American scene. You wouldn't mind if one 'moved in next door as long as he was clean,' and you're beginning to sense the rhetoric behind the calls for 'Law and Order.' But what about your friends? If you have children, what about them? And where do you go from here?

21 to 25: You've been doing some reading beyond the Wall Street Journal and some listening beyond the country club. You should think seriously about doing some missionary work among Whites. But now that you're aware of the crap Blacks have to put up with in the Land of the Free, your biggest challenge is the fight against cynicism. Take a redneck to lunch.

Royal Geographic Society. Radio Times Hulton Picture Library.

VIOLATED SELF

From *Chicago Daily Defender*, October 30, 1969. Used by permission.

the ordeal
of BOBBY SEALE

How Blacks View Gagging of Seale

L. F. Palmer Jr.

There he sat, silenced by a gag, made immobile by manacles that chained his wrists and ankles to a chair. Bobby Seale, leader of the Black Panther Party, was imprisoned by the absolute physical restraint. In a United States court of law.

What the jury, the press and spectators saw—whether they realized it or not—was a portrait of the American dilemma sketched in living black and white.

The painter was white—the guardian of law and order, personified by Judge Julius F. Hoffman who ordered the restraints. The subject was black— one of the most persistent symbols of resistance to oppression.

As Seale fought futilely to extricate himself from the shackles which bound his body and swelled his soul, he was as much a black panther as he was a Black Panther.

For here was a man turned into an animal, the ultimate dehumanization of the black man, a process which had long been an American specialty. And, in this extraordinary portrait, the judge had perhaps unwittingly blended the essence of the black experience with the intransigence of the white mind.

It is the fury which grows out of the black experience pitted against the unmoving quality of the white mind which has brought America to a dilemma for which no one has found a solution. The courtroom drama made this crystal clear, at least to many blacks.

For in gagging and handcuffing Seale to a chair, the judge succeeded in suppressing the Black Panther, but the act did nothing toward changing the conditions which made Seale resist so strenuously.

This is the typical reaction of the American Establishment.

There are many whites, of course, who will say that Seale got what was coming to him. They will plead the rhetoric of law and order. They will insist that the decorum of the courtroom must be observed.

And they will say that Seale's blackness had nothing to do with the judge's decision—he would have done the same thing to a white defendant who acted as Seale had.

This contention would be disputed by countless blacks whose personal

Reprinted with permission from the *Chicago Daily News.*

experiences have convinced them that the kind of action taken against Seale is reserved for blacks only.

Not to be lost on those who agree that binding and gagging Seale was proper are these pertinent points:

- None of the defendants, charged with conspiracy to incite riots at the Democratic National Convention, believes that he is being tried on a valid charge. They contend their trial is political.
- Seale particularly feels that he is being unjustly tried because, it is contended, his participation in the disturbances was minimal.
- Seale says that he is being tried without counsel and has been refused the right to defend himself. He rejects the judge's ruling that the Conspiracy 8's chief defense counsel also represents him.
- Seale is black and, despite protestations to the contrary, under the American system of justice this becomes an enormously pertinent fact.

Against this background, there is the historical station of the black man in America and, perhaps, only oppressed people can understand the drives which motivate a man like Seale.

As he sat in the federal courtroom, utterly suppressed by the American judicial system, many thoughts could have raged through his mind.

He may have remembered that his forefathers were brought to this country in chains. He may have remembered that throughout the days of slavery, blacks were openly, legally and, by calculation, exposed to dehumanization.

Seale could have traced in his mind the history of the black man after slavery, noting the continuation of the dehumanizing process which became decreasingly open but increasingly sophisticated.

And he may have reviewed his own identification with the black resistance movement and reflected upon the official acts to wipe the Black Panther Party off the face of America.

Bound and gagged as he was, Bobby Seale sat in that courtroom and he was a mirror for America. He was a mirror into which many blacks look and see the truth about their mission. He was also a mirror into which many whites look and see a frantic need to protect their dominance. If, indeed, they look at all.

These two images which reflect from the same mirror constitute the American dilemma for which no solution has yet become apparent.

Then They Came for Me

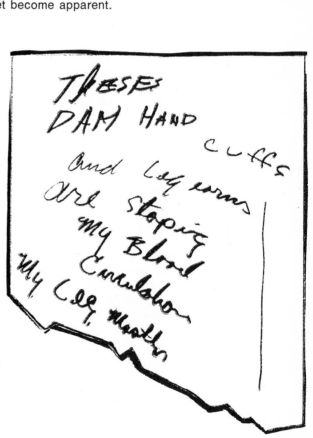

This treatment of a person who is supposed to be assumed innocent until proven guilty is frightening enough by itself, but the American people should ponder long and hard on the words of a survivor of Buchenwald:

"When they came for the Jews, I didn't protest because I wasn't Jewish. When they came for the Communists, I didn't protest because I wasn't a Communist. When they came for the trade unionists, I didn't protest because I wasn't a trade unionist. Then they came for me."

ROBERT A. WILSON
Chicago

Reprinted from the *Chicago Daily News*, November 5, 1969, by permission of Robert A. Wilson.

"7" Judge Has a Sunnier Side

Mike Royco

Some people have said Judge Julius Hoffman is stern and inflexible. That's not entirely true. He has an understanding, humorous side.

Tuesday, while waiting for the Conspiracy 7 jury to make up its mind, he heard some motions on other, less infamous cases.

© 1970 *Chicago Daily News*. Reprinted by permission of Mike Royko and the *Chicago Daily News*.

A lawyer came in who is representing a man accused of stealing securities, a very high class, but serious, crime.

The lawyer asked Judge Hoffman for a six-week delay in the trial.

Naturally, when you ask for a delay in a trial you have to have a good reason. You can't walk in and give any old reason, like maybe you feel like going off to a tropical island and loafing around the beach for awhile.

So Judge Hoffman asked the lawyer why he wanted a delay in the trial.

The lawyer said he was going on a vacation to the Caribbean islands.

There were a few reporters and court buffs sitting there when he said it, and everybody leaned forward. Boy, was he going to get it from Judge Hoffman.

They all know how Judge Hoffman feels about delaying trials. It was only a few months ago that Bobby Seale asked Hoffman to delay the start of the conspiracy trial for seven weeks.

The judge asked Seale why.

Seale said that his lawyer—Charles Garry—was entering a hospital for gall-bladder surgery and it would take that long for him to recover.

Hoffman was unmoved. He told Seale to get somebody else to defend him, such as William Kunstler, and ordered the case to proceed full steam ahead.

That, of course, is why Seale is faced with four years in prison for contempt of court. He insisted on defending himself, in Garry's absence, and Hoffman said he couldn't do that either. So when Seale kept trying to cross-examine witnesses and make motions, Hoffman finally sent him off to prison. Most of the Seale "outbursts" you read about were nothing more than his efforts to be his own lawyer.

And now, this bold lawyer was standing there telling Judge Hoffman that he wanted a long delay so he could go off and frolic in the surf on the Caribbean. He was either very brave or very foolish. In either case, the spectators half expected a bolt of lightning to fell him on the spot.

Judge Hoffman cleared his throat. One spectator felt faint, out of terror for the poor lawyer. Would he go to prison for a year, two years, or life? Possibly Hoffman would order him gagged and shackled to a chair until he had repented and stopped bringing frivolous and contemptuous requests before his honorable honor.

Judge Hoffman focused those tiny eyes of his on the brazen fellow. A spectator put his hands over his ears, expecting a thunderclap.

Then something strange happened. The wrinkles on Judge Hoffman's head began to shift position and rearrange themselves. When they settled into an expression, it appeared to be a smile, and a smile of recognition at that.

Of course. He remembered that the lawyer used to be an assistant U.S. attorney in the Federal Courthouse.

Hoffman spoke: "Now I see why you left your former position here."

At first it didn't sink in. Then somebody got the point. It was a joke. Judge Hoffman had made a funny. He was kidding about how the lawyer could afford Caribbean vacations, now that he had left the government payroll.

And everybody had said Hoffman was humorless!

"Black" from "Colors" in On These I Stand, by Countee Cullen. Copyright 1927 by Harper & Brothers; renewed 1955 by Ida M. Cullen. Reprinted by permission of Harper & Row, Publishers, Inc.

Before the shock had subsided, he went ever further. "April 7," he said. It meant the man had received his delay—six full weeks in all—so he could go on his island vacation.

Inflexible? It was an act of pure understanding and decency. Those Caribbean hotels ask for an advance on the room, and if you cancel, they keep the dough. To have denied the request would have been inhumane.

But it is a good thing for that lawyer that he didn't have any gall bladder problems.

other lynchings

The play is done, the crowds depart;
    and see
That twisted tortured thing hung
    from a tree,
Swart victim of a newer Calvary.
                    Countee Cullen

i saw them lynch

carol freeman

i saw them lynch festus whiteside and
all the limp white women with lymphatic greasy eyelids came
to watch silent silent in the dusty burning noon
shifting noiselessly from heavy foot to heavy
foot licking beast lips showing beast teeth in
anticipation of the feast
and they all plodded forward after the
lynching to grab and snatch the choice
pieces, rending them with their bloody teeth crunching on
   his hollow bones.

Reprinted from *Black Fire,* edited by LeRoi Jones and
Larry Neal, Wm. Morrow & Co., Inc., New York, N.Y., 1968.
Used with permission of Carol Freeman and Ronald Hobbs
Literary Agency.

Blood-Burning Moon

Jean Toomer

1

Up from the skeleton stone walls, up from the rotting floor boards and the solid hand-hewn beams of oak of the pre-war cotton factory, dusk came. Up from the dusk the full moon came. Glowing like a fired pine-knot, it illuminated the great door and soft showered the Negro shanties aligned along the single street of factory town. The full moon in the great door was an omen. Negro women improvised songs against its spell.

Louisa sang as she came over the crest of the hill from the white folks' kitchen. Her skin was the color of oak leaves on young trees in fall. Her breasts, firm and up-pointed like ripe acorns. And her singing had the low murmur of winds in fig trees. Bob Stone, younger son of the people she worked for, loved her. By the way the world reckons things, he had won her. By measure of that warm glow which came into her mind at thought of him, he had won her. Tom Burwell, whom the whole town called Big Boy, also loved her. But working in the fields all day, and far away from her, gave him no chance to show it. Though often enough of evenings he had tried to. Somehow, he never got along. Strong as he was with his hands upon the ax or plow, he found it difficult to hold her. Or so he thought. But the fact was that he held her to factory town more firmly than he thought, for his black balanced, and pulled against, the white of Stone, when she thought of them. And her mind was vaguely upon them as she came over the crest of the hill, coming from the white folks' kitchen. As she sang softly at the evil face of the full moon.

A strange stir was in her. Indolently, she tried to fix upon Bob or Tom as the cause of it. To meet Bob in the canebrake, as she was going to do an hour or so later, was nothing new. And Tom's proposal which she felt on its way to her could be indefinitely put off. Separately, there was no unusual significance to either one. But for some reason, they jumbled when her eyes gazed vacantly at the rising moon. And from the jumble came the stir that was strangely within her. Her lips trembled. The slow rhythm of her song grew agitant and restless. Rusty black and tan spotted hounds, lying in the dark corners of porches or prowling around back yards, put their noses in the air and caught its tremor. They began plaintively to yelp and howl. Chickens woke up and cackled. Intermittently, all over the countryside dogs barked and roosters crowed as if heralding a weird dawn or some ungodly awakening. The women sang lustily. Their songs were cotton-wads to stop their ears. Louisa came down into factory town and sank wearily upon the step before her home. The moon was rising towards a thick cloud-bank which soon would hide it.

> Red nigger moon. Sinner!
> Blood-burning moon. Sinner!
> Come out that fact'ry door.

2

Up from the deep dusk of a cleared spot on the edge of the forest a mellow glow arose and spread fan-wise into the low-hanging heavens. And all around the air was heavy with the scent of boiling cane. A large pile of cane-stalks lay like ribboned shadows upon the ground. A mule, harnessed to a pole, trudged lazily round and round the pivot of the grinder. Beneath a swaying oil lamp, a Negro alternately whipped out at the mule, and fed cane-stalks to the grinder. A fat boy waddled pails of fresh-ground juice between the grinder and the boiling stove. Steam came from the copper boiling pan. The scent of cane came from the copper pan and drenched the forest and the hill that sloped to factory town, beneath its fragrance. It drenched the men in the circle seated around the stove. Some of them chewed at the white pulp of stalks, but there was no need for them to, if all they wanted was to taste the cane. One tasted it in factory town. And from factory town one could see the soft haze thrown by the glowing stove upon the low-hanging heavens.

Old David Georgia stirred the thickening syrup with a long ladle, and ever so often drew it off. Old David Georgia tended his stove and told tales about the white folks, about moonshining and cotton picking, and about sweet nigger gals, to the men who sat there about his stove to listen to him. Tom Burwell chewed cane-stalk and laughed with the others till someone mentioned Louisa. Till someone said something about Louisa and Bob Stone, about the silk stockings she must have gotten from him. Blood ran up Tom's neck hotter than the glow that flooded from the stove. He sprang up. Glared at the men and said, "She's my gal." Will Manning laughed. Tom strode over to him. Yanked him up and knocked him to the ground. Several of Manning's friends got up to fight for him. Tom whipped out a long knife and would have cut them to shreds if they hadn't ducked into the woods. Tom had had enough. He nodded to Old David Georgia and swung down the path to factory town. Just then, the dogs started barking and the roosters began to crow. Tom felt funny. He shivered. He shuddered when he saw the full moon rising towards the cloud-bank. He who didn't give a godam for the fears of old women. He forced his mind to fasten on Louisa. Bob Stone. Better not be. He turned into the street and saw Louisa sitting before her home. He went towards her, ambling, touched the brim of a marvelously shaped, spotted, felt hat, said he wanted to say something to her, and then found that he didn't know what he had to say, or if he did, that he couldn't say it. He shoved his big fists in his overalls, grinned, and started to move off.

"Youall want me, Tom?"

"Thats what us wants, sho, Louisa."

"Well, here I am—"

"An here I is, but that aint ahelpin none, all th same."

"You wanted to say something?"

154

"I did that, sho. But the words is like th spots on dice: no matter how y fumbles em, there's times when they jes wont come. I dunno why. Seems like th love I feels fo yo done stole m tongue. I got it now. Whee! Louisa, honey, I oughtnt tell y, I feel I oughtnt cause yo is young an goes t church an I has had other girls, but Louisa I sho do love y. Lil gal, Ise watched y from them first days when youall sat right there befo yo door befo th well an sang sometimes in a way that like t broke m heart. Ise carried y with me into th fields, day after day, and after that, an I sho can plow when yo is there, an I can pick cotton. Yassur! Come near beatin Barlo yesterday. I sho did. Yassur! An next year if ole Stone'll trust me, I'll have a farm. My own. My bales will buy yo what y gets from white folks now. Silk stockings an purple dresses—course I don't believe what some folks been whisperin as t how y gets them things now. White folks always did do for niggers what they likes. An they jes cant help alikin yo, Louisa. Bob Stone likes y. Course he does. But not th way folks is awhisperin. Does he, hon?"

"I don't know what you mean, Tom."

"Course y dont. Ise already cut two niggers. Had t hon, t tell em so. Niggers always tryin t make somethin outa nothin. An then besides, white folks aint up t them tricks so much nowadays. Godam better not be. Leastawise not with you. Cause I wouldnt stand f it. Nassur."

"What would you do, Tom?"

"Cut him jes like I cut a nigger."

"No, Tom—"

"I said I would an there ain't no mo to it. But that aint th talk f now. Sing, honey Louisa, an while I'm listenin t y I'll be makin love."

Tom took her hand in his. Against the tough thickness of his own, hers felt soft and small. His huge body slipped down to the step beside her. The full moon sank upward into the deep purple of the cloud-bank. An old woman brought a lighted lamp and hung it on the common well whose bulky shadow squatted in the middle of the road, opposite Tom and Louisa. The old woman lifted the well-lid, took hold the chain, and began drawing up the heavy basket. As she did so, she sang. Figures shifted, restless-like, between lamp and window in the front rooms of the shanties. Shadows of the figures fought each other on the gray dust of the road. Figures raised the windows and joined the old women in song. Louisa and Tom, the whole street, singing:

> Red nigger moon. Sinner!
> Blood-burning moon. Sinner!
> Come out that fact'ry door.

3

Bob Stone sauntered from his veranda out into the gloom of fir trees and magnolias. The clear white of his skin paled, and the flush of his cheeks turned purple. As if to balance this outer change, his mind became consciously a white man's. He passed the house with its huge open hearth which, in the days of slavery, was the plantation cookery. He saw Louisa bent over that hearth. He went in as a master should and took her. Direct, honest, bold. None of this sneaking that he had to go through now. The contrast was repulsive to him. His family had lost ground. Hell no, his family still owned the niggers, practically. Damned if they did, or he wouldnt have to duck around so. What would they think if they knew? His mother? His sister? He shouldnt mention them, shouldnt think of them in this connection. There in the dark he blushed at doing so. Fellows about town were all right, but how about his friends up North? He could see them, incredible, repulsed. They didnt know. The thought first made him laugh. Then, with their eyes still upon him, he began to feel embarrassed. He felt the need of explaining things to them. Explain hell. They wouldnt understand, and moreover, who ever heard of a Southerner getting on his knees to any Yankee, or anyone. No sir. He was going to see Louisa to-night, and love her. She was lovely—in her way. Nigger way. What way was that? Damned if he knew. Must know. He'd known her long enough to know. Was there something about niggers that you couldnt know? Listening to them at church didnt tell you anything. Looking at them didnt tell you anything. Talking to them didnt tell you anything— unless it was gossip, unless they wanted to talk. Of course, about farming, and licker, and craps—but those werent nigger. Nigger was something more. How much more? Something to be afraid of, more? Hell no. Who ever heard of being afraid of a nigger? Tom Burwell. Cartwell had told him that Tom went with Louisa after she reached home. No sir. No nigger had ever been with his girl. He'd like to see one try. Some position for him to be in. Him, Bob Stone, of the Stone family, in a scrap with a nigger over a nigger girl. In the good old days . . . Ha! Those were the days. His family had lost ground. Not so much, though. Enough for him to have to cut through old Lemon's canefield by way of the woods, that he might meet her. She was worth it. Beautiful nigger gal. Why nigger? Why not, just gal? No, it was because she was nigger that he went to her. Sweet . . . The scent of boiling cane came to him. Then he saw the rich glow of the stove. He heard the voices of the men circled around it. He was about to skirt the clearing when he heard his own name mentioned. He stopped. Quivering. Leaning against a tree, he listened.

"Bad nigger. Yassur, he sho is one bad nigger when he gets started."

"Tom Burwell's been on th gang three times fo cuttin men."

"What y think he's a gwine t do t Bob Stone?"

"Dunno yet. He aint found out. When he does— Baby!"

"Young Stone aint no quitter an I ken tell y that. Blood of th old uns in his veins."

"Thats right. He'll scrap, sho."

"Be gettin too hot f niggers round this away."

"Shut up, nigger. Y dont know what y talkin bout."

Bob Stone's ears burned as though he had been holding them over the stove. Sizzling heat welled up within him. His feet felt as if they rested on red-hot coals. They stung him to quick movement. He circled the fringe of the glowing. Not a twig cracked beneath his feet. He reached the path that led to factory town. Plunged furiously down it. Halfway along, a blindness within him veered him aside. He crashed into the bordering canebrake. Cane leaves cut his face and lips. He tasted blood. He threw himself down and dug his fingers in the ground. The earth was cool. Cane-roots took the fever from his hands. After a long while, or so it seemed to him, the thought came to him that it must be time to see Louisa. He got to his feet and walked calmly to their meeting place. No Louisa. Tom Burwell had her. Veins in his forehead bulged and distended. Saliva moistened the dried blood on his lips. He bit down on his lips. He tasted blood. Not his own blood; Tom Burwell's blood. Bob drove through the cane and out again upon the road. A hound swung down the path before him towards factory town. Bob couldn't see it. The dog loped aside to let him pass. Bob's blind rushing made him stumble over it. He fell with a thud that dazed him. The hound yelped. Answering yelps came from all over the countryside. Chickens cackled. Roosters crowed, heralding the bloodshot eyes of southern awakening. Singers in the town were silenced. They shut their windows down. Palpitant between the rooster crows, a chill hush settled upon the huddled forms of Tom and Louisa. A figure rushed from the shadow and stood before them. Tom popped to his feet.

"Whats y want?"

"I'm Bob Stone."

"Yassur—and I'm Tom Burwell. Whats y want?"

Bob lunged at him. Tom side-stepped, caught him by the shoulder, and flung him to the ground. Straddled him.

"Let me up."

"Yassur—but watch yo doins, Bob Stone."

A few dark figures, drawn by the sound of scuffle, stood about them. Bob sprang to his feet.

"Fight like a man, Tom Burwell, an I'll lick y."

Again he lunged. Tom side-stepped and flung him to the ground. Straddled him.

"Get off me, you godam nigger you."

"Yo sho has started somethin now. Get up."

Tom yanked him up and began hammering at him. Each blow sounded as if it smashed into a precious, irreplaceable soft something. Beneath them, Bob staggered back. He reached in his pocket and whipped out a knife. "That's my game, sho."

Blue flash, a steel blade slashed across Bob Stone's throat. He had a sweetish sick feeling. Blood began to flow. Then he felt a sharp twitch of pain. He let his knife drop. He slapped one hand against his neck. He pressed the other on top of his head as if to hold it down. He groaned. He turned, and staggered towards the crest of the hill in the direction of white town. Negroes who had seen the fight slunk into their homes and blew the lamps out. Louisa, dazed, hysterical, refused to go indoors. She slipped, crumpled, her body loosely propped against the woodwork of the well. Tom Burwell leaned against it. He seemed rooted there.

Bob reached Broad Street. White men rushed up to him. He collapsed in their arms.

"Tom Burwell. . . ."

White men like ants upon a forage rushed about. Except for the taut hum of their moving, all was silent. Shotguns, revolvers, rope, kerosene, torches. Two high-powered cars with glaring search-lights. They came together. The taut hum rose to a low roar. Then nothing could be heard but the flop of their feet in the thick dust of the road. The moving body of their silence preceded them over the crest of the hill into factory town. It flattened the Negroes beneath it. It rolled to the wall of the factory, where it stopped. Tom knew that they were coming. He couldnt move. And then he saw the search-lights of the two cars glaring down on him. A quick shock went through him. He stiffened. He started to run. A yell went up from the mob. Tom wheeled about and faced them. They poured down on him. They swarmed. A large man with dead-white face and flabby cheeks came to him and almost jabbed a gun-barrel through his guts.

"Hands behind y, nigger."

Tom's wrists were bound. The big man shoved him to the well. Burn him over it, and when the woodwork caved in, his body would drop to the bottom. Two deaths for a godam nigger.

Louisa was driven back. The mob pushed in. Its pressure, its momentum was too great. Drag him to the factory. Wood and stakes already there. Tom moved in the direction indicated. But they had to drag him. They reached the great door. Too many to get in there. The mob divided and flowed around the walls to either side. The big man shoved him through the door. The mob pressed in from the sides. Taut humming. No words. A stake was sunk into the ground. Rotting floor boards piled around it. Kerosene poured on the rotting floor boards. Tom bound to the stake. His breast was bare. Nails scratches let little lines of blood trickle down and mat into the hair. His face, his eyes were set and stony. Except for irregular breathing, one would have thought him already dead. Torches were flung onto the pile. A great flare muffled in black smoke shot upward. The mob yelled. The mob was silent. Now Tom could be seen within the flames. Only his head, erect, lean, like a blackened stone. Stench of burning flesh soaked the air. Tom's eyes popped. His head settled downward. The mob yelled. Its yell echoed against the skeleton stone walls and sounded like a hundred yells. Like a hundred mobs yelling. Its yell thudded against the thick front wall and fell back. Ghost of a yell slipped through the flames and out the great door of the factory. It flut-tered like a dying thing down the single street of factory town. Louisa, upon the step before her home, did not hear it, but her eyes opened slowly. They saw the full moon glowing in the great door. The full moon, an evil thing, an omen, soft showering the homes of folks she knew. Where were they, these people? She'd sing, and perhaps they'd come out and join her. Perhaps Tom Burwell would come. At any rate, the full moon in the great door was an omen which she must sing to:

Red nigger moon. Sinner!
Blood-burning moon. Sinner!
Come out that fact'ry door.

Between the World and Me

Richard Wright

And one morning while in the woods I stumbled suddenly
upon the thing,
Stumbled upon it in a grassy clearing guarded by scaly oaks
and elms.
And the sooty details of the scene rose, thrusting themselves
between the world and me. . . .

There was a design of white bones slumbering forgottenly

159

upon a cushion of ashes.
There was a charred stump of a sapling pointing a blunt
    finger accusingly at the sky.
There were torn tree limbs, tiny veins of burnt leaves, and a
    scorched coil of greasy hemp;
A vacant shoe, an empty tie, a ripped shirt, a lonely hat, and
    a pair of trousers stiff with black blood.
And upon the trampled grass were buttons, dead matches,
    butt-ends of cigars and cigarettes, peanut shells, a
    drained gin-flask, and a whore's lipstick;
Scattered traces of tar, restless arrays of feathers, and the
    lingering smell of gasoline.
And through the morning air the sun poured yellow surprise
    into the eye sockets of a stony skull. . . .
And while I stood my mind was frozen with a cold pity for
    the life that was gone.
The ground gripped my feet and my heart was circled by
    icy walls of fear—
The sun died in the sky; a night wind muttered in the grass
    and fumbled the leaves in the trees; the woods poured
    forth the hungry yelping of hounds; the darkness
    screamed with thirsty voices; and the witnesses rose
    and lived:
The dry bones stirred, rattled, lifted, melting themselves into
    my bones.
The grey ashes formed flesh firm and black, entering into my
    flesh.
The gin-flask passed from mouth to mouth; cigars and ciga-
    rettes glowed, the whore smeared the lipstick red
    upon her lips,
And a thousand faces swirled around me, clamoring that
    my life be burned. . . .

And then they had me, stripped me, battering my teeth into
    my throat till I swallowed my own blood.
My voice was drowned in the roar of their voices, and my
    black wet body slipped and rolled in their hands as
    they bound me to the sapling.
And my skin clung to the bubbling hot tar, falling from me in
    limp patches.
And the down and quills of the white feathers sank into my
    raw flesh, and I moaned in my agony.
Then my blood was cooled mercifully, cooled by a baptism
    of gasoline.
And in a blaze of red I leaped to the sky as pain rose like
    water, boiling my limbs.
Panting, begging I clutched childlike, clutched to the hot
    sides of death.
Now I am dry bones and my face a stony skull staring in
    yellow surprise at the sun. . . .

CHRIST IS BLACK

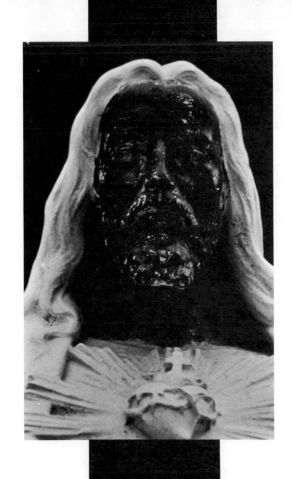

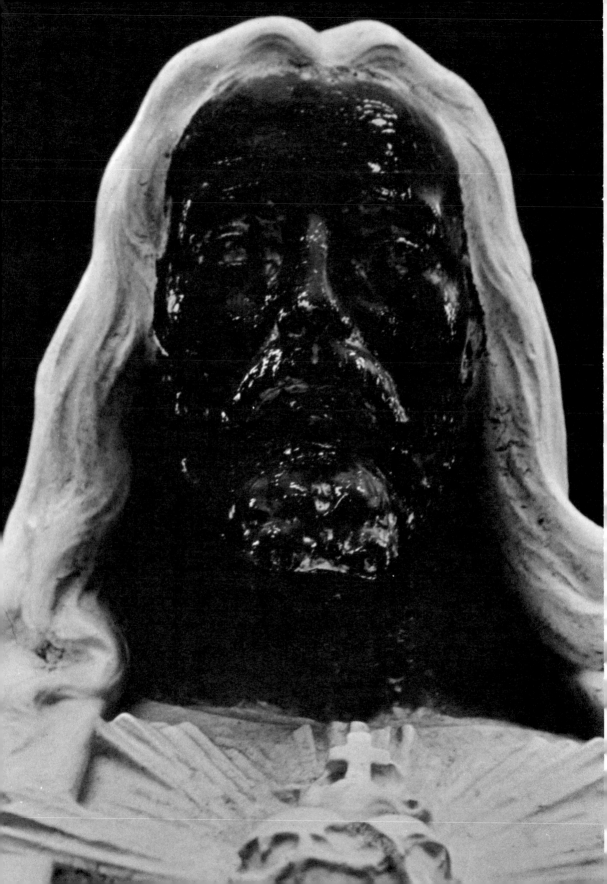

Christy in Alabama

Langston Hughes

Christ is a nigger,
Beaten and black:
Oh, bare your back!

Mary is His mother:
Mammy of the South,
Silence your mouth.

God is His father:
White Master above
Grant Him your love.

Most holy bastard
Of the bleeding mouth,
    Nigger Christ
    On the cross
    Of the South.

The Boy Who Painted Christ Black

John Henrik Clarke

He was the smartest boy in the Muskogee County School—for colored children. Everybody even remotely connected with the school knew this. The teacher always pronounced his name with profound gusto as she pointed him out as the ideal student. Once I heard her say: "If he were white he might, some day, become President." Only Aaron Crawford wasn't white; quite the contrary. His skin was so solid black that it glowed, reflecting an inner virtue that was strange, and beyond my comprehension.

In many ways he looked like something that was awkwardly put together. Both his nose and his lips seemed a trifle too large for his face. To say he was ugly would be unjust and to say he was handsome would be gross exaggeration. Truthfully, I could never make up my mind about him. Sometimes he looked like something out of a book of ancient history . . . looked as if he was left over from that magnificent era before the machine age came and marred the earth's natural beauty.

His great variety of talent often startled the teachers. This caused his classmates to look upon him with a mixed feeling of awe and envy.

Before Thanksgiving, he always drew turkeys and pumpkins on the blackboard. On George Washington's birthday, he drew large American flags surrounded by little hatchets. It was these small masterpieces that made him

163

the most talked-about colored boy in Columbus, Georgia. The Negro principal of the Muskogee County School said he would some day be a great painter, like Henry O. Tanner.

For the teacher's birthday, which fell on a day about a week before commencement, Aaron Crawford painted the picture that caused an uproar, and a turning point, at the Muskogee County School. The moment he entered the room that morning, all eyes fell on him. Besides his torn book holder, he was carrying a large-framed concern wrapped in old newspapers. As he went to his seat, the teacher's eyes followed his every motion, a curious wonderment mirrored in them conflicting with the half-smile that wreathed her face.

Aaron put his books down, then smiling broadly, advanced toward the teacher's desk. His alert eyes were so bright with joy that they were almost frightening. The children were leaning forward in their seats, staring greedily at him; a restless anticipation was rampant within every breast.

Already the teacher sensed that Aaron had a present for her. Still smiling, he placed it on her desk and began to help her unwrap it. As the last piece of paper fell from the large frame, the teacher jerked her hand away from it suddenly, her eyes flickering unbelievingly. Amidst the rigid tension, her heavy breathing was distinct and frightening. Temporarily, there was no other sound in the room.

Aaron stared questioningly at her and she moved her hand back to the present cautiously, as if it were a living thing with vicious characteristics. I am sure it was the one thing she least expected.

With a quick, involuntary movement I rose up from my desk. A series of submerged murmurs spread through the room, rising to a distinct monotone. The teacher turned toward the children, staring reproachfully. They did not move their eyes from the present that Aaron had brought her. . . . It was a large picture of Christ—painted black!

Aaron Crawford went back to his seat, a feeling of triumph reflecting in his every movement.

The teacher faced us. Her curious half-smile had blurred into a mild bewilderment. She searched the bright faces before her and started to smile again, occasionally stealing quick glances at the large picture propped on her desk, as though doing so were forbidden amusement.

"Aaron," she spoke at last, a slight tinge of uncertainty in her tone, "this is a most welcome present. Thanks. I will treasure it." She paused, then went on speaking, a trifle more coherent than before. "Looks like you are going to be quite an artist. . . . Suppose you come forward and tell the class how you came to paint this remarkable picture."

When he rose to speak, to explain about the picture, a hush fell tightly over the room, and the children gave him all of their attention . . . something they rarely did for the teacher. He did not speak at first; he just stood there in front of the room, toying absently with his hands, observing his audience carefully, like a great concert artist.

"It was like this," he said, placing full emphasis on every word. "You see, my uncle who lives in New York teaches classes in Negro History at the Y.M.C.A. When he visited us last year he was telling me about the many great black folks who have made history. He said black folks were once the most powerful people on earth. When I asked him about Christ, he said no one ever proved whether he was black or white. Somehow a feeling came over me that he was a black man, 'cause he was so kind and forgiving, kinder than I have ever seen white people be. So, when I painted his picture I couldn't help but paint it as I thought it was."

After this, the little artist sat down, smiling broadly, as if he had gained entrance to a great storehouse of knowledge that ordinary people could neither acquire nor comprehend.

The teacher, knowing nothing else to do under prevailing circumstances, invited the children to rise from their seats and come forward so they could get a complete view of Aaron's unique piece of art.

When I came close to the picture, I noticed it was painted with the kind of paint you get in the five and ten cent stores. Its shape was blurred slightly, as if someone had jarred the frame before the paint had time to dry. The eyes of Christ were deep-set and sad, very much like those of Aaron's father, who was a deacon in the local Baptist Church. This picture of Christ looked much different from the one I saw hanging on the wall when I was in Sunday School. It looked more like a helpless Negro, pleading silently for mercy.

For the next few days, there was much talk about Aaron's picture.

The school term ended the following week and Aaron's picture, along with the best handwork done by the students that year, was on display in the assembly room. Naturally, Aaron's picture graced the place of honor.

There was no book work to be done on commencement day and joy was rampant among the children. The girls in their brightly colored dresses gave the school the delightful air of Spring awakening.

In the middle of the day all the children were gathered in the small assembly. On this day we were always favored with a visit from a man whom all the teachers spoke of with mixed esteem and fear. Professor Danual, they called him, and they always pronounced his name with reverence. He was supervisor of all the city schools, including those small and poorly equipped ones set aside for colored children.

The great man arrived almost at the end of our commencement exercises. On seeing him enter the hall, the children rose, bowed courteously, and sat down again, their eyes examining him as if he were a circus freak.

He was a tall white man with solid gray hair that made his lean face seem paler than it actually was. His eyes were the clearest blue I have ever seen. They were the only life-like things about him.

As he made his way to the front of the room the Negro principal, George Du Vaul, was walking ahead of him, cautiously preventing anything from getting in his way. As he passed me, I heard the teachers, frightened, sucking in their breath, felt the tension tightening.

A large chair was in the center of the rostrum. It had been daintily polished and the janitor had laboriously recushioned its bottom. The supervisor went straight to it without being guided, knowing that this pretty splendor was reserved for him.

Presently the Negro principal introduced the distinguished guest and he favored us with a short speech. It wasn't a very important speech. Almost at the end of it, I remember him saying something about he wouldn't be surprised if one of us boys grew up to be a great colored man, like Booker T. Washington.

After he sat down, the school chorus sang two spirituals and the girls in the fourth grade did an Indian folk dance. This brought the commencement program to an end.

After this the supervisor came down from the rostrum, his eyes tinged with curiosity, and began to view the array of handwork on display in front of the chapel.

Suddenly his face underwent a strange rejuvenation. His clear blue eyes flickered in astonishment. He was looking at Aaron Crawford's picture of Christ. Mechanically he moved his stooped form closer to the picture and stood gazing fixedly at it, curious and undecided, as though it were a dangerous animal that would rise any moment and spread destruction.

We waited tensely for his next movement. The silence was almost suffocating. At last he twisted himself around and began to search the grim faces before him. The fiery glitter of his eyes abated slightly as they rested on the Negro principal, protestingly.

"Who painted this sacrilegious nonsense?" he damended sharply.

"I painted it, sir." These were Aaron's words, spoken hesitantly. He wetted his lips timidly and looked up at the supervisor, his eyes voicing a sad plea for understanding.

He spoke again, this time more coherently. "Th' principal said a colored person have jes as much right paintin' Jesus black as a white person have paintin' him white. And he says. . . ." At this point he halted abruptly, as if to search for his next words. A strong tinge of bewilderment dimmed the glow of his solid black face. He stammered out a few more words, then stopped again.

The supervisor strode a few steps toward him. At last color had swelled some of the lifelessness out of his lean face.

"Well, go on!" he said, enragedly, ". . . I'm still listening."

Aaron moved his lips pathetically but no words passed them. His eyes wandered around the room, resting finally, with an air of hope, on the face of the Negro principal. After a moment, he jerked his face in another direction, regretfully, as if something he had said had betrayed an understanding between him and the principal.

Presently the principal stepped forward to defend the school's prize student.

"I encouraged the boy in painting that picture," he said firmly. "And it was with my permission that he brought the picture into this school. I don't think the boy is so far wrong in painting Christ black. The artists of all other races have painted whatsoever God they worship to resemble themselves. I see no reason why we should be immune from that privilege. After all, Christ was born in that part of the world that had always been predominantly populated by colored people. There is a strong possibility that he could have been a Negro."

But for the monotonous lull of heavy breathing, I would have sworn that his words had frozen everyone in the hall. I had never heard the little principal speak so boldly to anyone, black or white.

The supervisor swallowed dumfoundedly. His face was aglow in silent rage.

"Have you been teaching these children things like that?" he asked the Negro principal, sternly.

"I have been teaching them that their race has produced great kings and queens as well as slaves and serfs," the principal said. "The time is long overdue when we should let the world know that we erected and enjoyed the benefits of a splendid civilization long before the people of Europe had a written language."

The supervisor coughed. His eyes bulged menacingly as he spoke. "You are not being paid to teach such things in this school, and I am demanding your resignation for overstepping your limit as principal."

George Du Vaul did not speak. A strong quiver swept over his sullen face. He revolved himself slowly and walked out of the room towards his office.

The supervisor's eyes followed him until he was out of focus. Then he murmured under his breath: "There'll be a lot of fuss in this world if you start people thinking that Christ was a nigger."

Some of the teachers followed the principal out of the chapel, leaving the crestfallen children restless and in a quandary about what to do next. Finally we started back to our rooms. The supervisor was behind me. I heard him murmur to himself: "Damn, if niggers ain't getting smarter."

A few days later I heard that the principal had accepted a summer job as art instructor of a small high school somewhere in south Georgia and had gotten permission from Aaron's parents to take him along so he could continue to encourage him in his painting.

I was on my way home when I saw him leaving his office. He was carrying a large briefcase and some books tucked under his arm. He had already said good-by to all the teachers. And strangely, he did not look broken-hearted. As he headed for the large front door, he readjusted his horn-rimmed glasses, but did not look back. An air of triumph gave more dignity to his soldierly stride. He had the appearance of a man who had done a great thing, something greater than any ordinary man would do.

Aaron Crawford was waiting outside for him. They walked down the street together. He put his arms around Aaron's shoulder affectionately. He was talking sincerely to Aaron about something, and Aaron was listening, deeply earnest.

I watched them until they were so far down the street that their forms had begun to blur. Even from this distance I could see they were still walking in brisk, dignified strides, like two people who had won some sort of victory.

the negative role

Status Symbol

Mari Evans

i
Have Arrived

i
am the
New Negro

i
am the result of
President Lincoln
World War I
and Paris
the
Red Ball Express
white drinking fountain
sitdowns and
sit-ins
Federal Troops
Marches on Washington
   and
prayer meetings . . .

today
They hired me
it
is a status
job . . .
along
with my papers
They
gave me my
Status Symbol
the
key
to the
White . . . Locked . . .
John

Brass Spittoons

Langston Hughes

Clean the spittoons, boy.
    Detroit,
    Chicago,
    Atlantic City,
    Palm Beach.
Clean the spittoons.
The steam in hotel kitchens,
And the smoke in hotel lobbies,
And the slime in hotel spittoons:
Part of my life.
    Hey, boy!
    A nickel,
    A dime,
    A dollar,
Two dollars a day.
    Hey, boy!
    A nickel,
    A dime.
    A dollar,
    Two dollars
Buy shoes for the baby.
House rent to pay.
Gin on Saturday,
Church on Sunday.
    My God!
Babies and gin and church
And women and Sunday
All mixed with dimes and
Dollars and clean spittoons
And house rent to pay.
    Hey, boy!
A bright bowl of brass is beautiful to
    the Lord.
Bright polished brass like the cymbals
Of King David's dancers,
Like the wine cups of Solomon.
    Hey, boy!
A clean spittoon on the altar of the
    Lord.
A clean bright spittoon all newly
    polished—
At least I can offer that.
    Com'mere, boy!

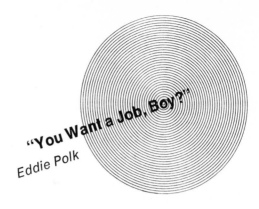

"You Want a Job, Boy?"

Eddie Polk

"You want a job, boy?"

"Yes, Ma-um, what do you want me to do?"

"You just be at my house in the morning."

Joy and excitement ran through my body like electricity flowing through the line of no return.

"Daddy, a white lady want me to work for her tomorrow."

"What white lady?"

"The white lady that live by the tracks."

"How much is she going to pay you?"

"I don't know, but she looks like she got a lot of money."

"You know you're pose to start chopping cotton Monday."

"Daddy, I'll do anything to get out of chopping cotton all day in the hot sun for two dollars. For ten years I've been chopping Mr. Bobby Handcock's cotton and I'm getting tired of it. I want a better job now."

"Son, I used to do it for twenty-five cents a day, from sun up til sundown."

"Two dollars looks a hell of a lot bigger than twenty-five cents!"

"Well, you can go on over there

tomorrow, if you want to, but don't promise that white woman nothing. You hear me?"

"You got here didn't you, boy."
"Yes-sum."
"Alright, you bout ready to start?"
"Yes-sum."
"See those weeds in my flower bed?"
"Yes-sum."
"Pull those weeds off and around my beautiful flowers."
"Yes-sum."
"Are you finished boy?"
"Yes-sum"
"Take that trash and burn it."
"Yes-sum"
"Now, boy, you know what I want you to do?"

"No, Ma-um."
"Go under the house and get that old dead cat."
"Dead cat!"
"What's wrong boy?"
"Nothing ma-um."
"Well, go on under ther, boy."
"Yes-sum"
"Now take him and throw him across the tracks."
"Take this dime and go home. I don't need you anymore."
"What's wrong boy, you better be glad to get that, you niggers want more than you're worth."

Walking away with my head down wondering what could I tell my father that he didn't already know?

The Hands of the Blacks

Luis Bernado Honwana

I don't remember now how we got on to the subject, but one day teacher said that the palms of the blacks' hands were much lighter than the rest of their bodies because only a few centuries ago they walked around on all fours, like wild animals, so their palms weren't exposed to the sun, which went on darkening the rest of their bodies. I thought of this when Senhor Padre told us after catechism that we half-castes were absolutely hopeless, and that even the blacks were better than we were, and he went back to this thing about their hands being lighter, saying it was like that because they always went about with their hands folded together, praying in secret.

I thought this was so funny, this thing of the blacks' hands being lighter, that you should just see me now—I don't let go of anybody, whoever they are, until they tell me why they think that the palms of their hands are lighter. Dona Dores, for instance, told me that God made their hands lighter like that so they wouldn't dirty the food they made for their masters, or anything else they were ordered to do that should be kept quite clean.

Senhor Antunes, the Coca-Cola man, who only comes to the village now and again when all the Cokes in the *cantinas* have been sold, said to me that everything I had been told was a lot of baloney. Of course I don't know if it was really, but he assured me it was. After I said yes, all right, it was baloney, then he told me what he knew about this thing of the blacks' hands. It was like this: "Long ago, many years ago, God, our Lord Jesus Christ, the Virgin Mary, St. Peter, many other saints, all the angels that were in heaven then, and some of the people who had died and gone to heaven—they all had a meeting and decided to make blacks. Do you know how? They got hold of some clay and pressed it into second-hand molds. And to bake the clay of the creatures they took them to the heavenly kilns. Because they were in a hurry and there was no room next to the fire, they hung them in the chimneys. Smoke, smoke, smoke—and there you have them, black as coals. And now do you want to know why their hands stayed white? Well, didn't they have to hold on while their clay baked?"

When he had told me this Senhor Antunes and the other men who were around us all burst out laughing, they were so pleased.

That very same day Senhor Frias called me after Senhor Antunes had gone away, and told me that everything I had heard from them there had been just one big pack of lies. Really and truly, what he knew about the blacks' hands was right—that God finished making men and told them to bathe in a lake in heaven. After bathing the people were nice and white. The blacks, well, they were made very early in the morning, and at this hour the water in the lake was very cold, so they only wet the palms of their hands and the soles of their feet before dressing and coming into the world.

But I read in a book that happened to mention it that the blacks have hands lighter like this because they spent all their days bent over, gathering

171

the white cotton in Virginia and I don't know where else. Of course, Dona Estefânia didn't agree when I told her this. According to her it's only because their hands became bleached with all that washing.

Well, I don't know what you'll think about all this, but the truth is that however callused and cracked they may be, a black's hands are always lighter than the rest of him. And that's that!

My mother is the only one who must be right about this question of a black's hands being lighter than the rest of his body. On the day that we were talking about this, us two, I was telling her what I already knew about the matter, and she just couldn't stop laughing. What I found strange was that she didn't tell me at once what she thought about all this, and she only answered me when she was sure I wouldn't get tired of bothering her about it. And even then she was crying and clutching herself around the stomach as if she had laughed so much she couldn't bear it. What she said was more or less this:

"God made blacks because they had to be. They had to be, my son, He thought they really had to be. . . . Afterward, He regretted having made them because the other men laughed at them and took them off to their homes and put them to serve as slaves or not much better. But because He couldn't make them all turn white, for those who were used to seeing them black would complain, He made it so that the palms of their hands would be exactly like the palms of other men's hands. And do you know why that was? Of course you don't know, and it's not surprising, because many, many people don't know. Well listen: it was to show that what men do is only the work of men. . . . That what men do is done by hands that are the same—hands of people who, if they had any sense, would know that before everything else they are men. He must have been thinking of this when He made it so that the hands of the blacks would be the same as the hands of all those men who thank God they're not black."

After telling me this, my mother kissed my hands.

As I ran off into the yard to play ball, I thought to myself that I had never seen her cry so much when nobody had even hit her or anything.

The worst crime the white man has committed has been to teach us to hate ourselves.   Malcolm X

Black Bourgeoisie

LeRoi Jones

has a gold tooth, sits long hours
on a stool, thinking about money.
sees white skin in a secret room
rummages his sense for sense
dreams about Lincoln (s)
conks his daughter's hair
sends his coon to school
works very hard
grins politely in restaurants
has a good word to say
never says it
does not hate ofays
hates, instead, him self
him black self

self - hate

Leroy

LeRoi Jones

I wanted to know my mother when
    she sat
looking sad across the campus in the
    late 20's
into the future of the soul, there were
    black angels
straining above her head, carrying
    life from our ancestors,
and knowledge, and the strong nigger
    feeling. She sat
(in that photo in the yearbook I showed
    Vashti) getting into

new blues, from the old ones, the trips
    and passions
showered on her by her own.
    Hypnotizing me, from so far
ago, from that vantage of knowledge
    passed on to her passed on
to me and all the other black people
    of our time.
When I die, the consciousness I carry
    I will to
black people. May they pick me apart
    and take the
useful parts, the sweet meat of my
    feelings. And leave
the bitter bullshit rotten white parts
alone.

173

Wake-Up Niggers

Don Lee

(you ain't part Indian)

From *Don't Cry, Scream* by Don L. Lee. Broadside Press, copyright © 1969 by Don L. Lee. Reprinted by permission of Broadside Press.

were
don eagle & gorgeous george
sisters
or did they just
             act that way—
in the ring,
in alleys,
in bedrooms of the future.
                  (continuing to take yr/money)
have you ever
heard tonto say:
            "i'm part negro?"
             (in yr/moma's dreams)
the only time
tonto was hip
was when he said:
             "what you mean WE,
              gettum up scout"
& left
that mask man
burning on a stake
             crying for satchel paige
to throw his
balls
back.

&
you followed him niggers—
all of you—
             yes you did,
                i saw ya.
on yr/tip toes
with
roller skates
on yr/knees
             following Him
down the road,
           not up
following Him
that whi
te man with
that
cross on his back.

174

Portrait of a White Nigger

Carolyn Rodgers

Fat boy
    is a
cop. talks like
a biscuit that will
    not
rise, lives up the street &
round
jelly mind
        the corner, got a
          and
shimmy thighs
      got a
mom & dad & sis too!
      had an
accident the second
      he was born
some goddamn fairy/threw/tar
      alloverhim   and
he has been trying
          ever since
to find the MAGIC that
      will
PRESTO! ! !
        Black
         off . . .

Carolyn Rodgers, "Portrait of a White Nigger," *Paper Soul.* Third World Press/Chicago, 1968. Used by permission.

Is You Is . . . ?

(To the Black College Student)

Ruwa Chiri

Black student?
Is you is or
Is you ain't?

Is you a big nappy head; a tiki necktie and
A 34° smile while holding hands with miss ann?
Is you a black bottle of "soul" with a B-52 nose
Accompanied by visibly rather generous lips that
Spit out white saliva?

Black student?
Is you a man hid behind robert hall and oxford street
Suits or is you a Mao, Nkrumah, Rap, and Lumumba
Diehardly dedicated to the true and purely unadulterated
Black bottle of soul . . . ready . . .
To take your stand for Blackness?

Or is you a growing beard and long hair because
Honkies have hippies? Or is you doing all this shit
Because, somehow, you just can't help that
El Shabbazz El Malik died for you?

What is you Black student?
Is you is or is you ain't?

Is you a White man with a negrow female or vice versa?
Or is you ready to carry the cross of colour. To
Accept, defend, and activise the sacred domain
Of Black Womanhood?

Is you getting your wings ready to "fly" to the
Suburbs of the '70s and '80s? Or is you a cat
Who ain't never been caught "getting down" on
Chitterlings, gritz and collards for breakfast?

I don't give a fuck
Whatever you ain't now or what you gonna be . . .
When you split the college scene, baby.
IS YOU IS?

Consequence

David Reese Moody

It was two-thirty and Friday morning. I entered my home with a light step as a result of the four Jack Daniels I had consumed at Marty's, where the jazz was, and to prevent waking my family.

In my search of the kitchen (where the food is kept) I discovered in the sink a large black bug. A bug about one and one-quarter inches in length and five-eights of an inch in width, two uncommonly long antennae projecting from his forehead. I assumed the bug to be male because he looked male. Let's call him Sam. The sink is divided into two parts, one side with a garbage disposal and the other with a regular drain. Sam happened to be in the side with the regular drain. The glacier-like whiteness of the Ajax-polished surface gave Sam's blackness and size amplification. Sam was very still, almost as though he was aware of my presence. I observed Sam in quiet contemplation: "Sam is wrong; he's looking to take something from me: what, is of no consequence. Sam is trespassing; Sam means me no good; Sam is possibly a carrier of some disease, if not medical, social." Feeling I needed no more justification I sentenced Sam to death.

I deftly placed the stopper in Sam's side of the sink to cut off the possibility of escape—that is, escape from my vision. The prosecutor has the right to "see" justice done in instances where capital punishment is involved. Using the garbage disposal as an instrument of execution I found it to be inexpedient for the effort of transportation. Sam's great long antennae were rotating like two miniature radars, as though he was now more keenly aware of the imminence of his situation. Like lightning the words "hot water" came to me. The faucet, being of the swivel type, took on the appearance of "The Great Hand of Justice." The hot water had not been used for several hours, therefore to obtain some, it was necessary to let the hot water run for a period of a minute or two. I took "The Great Hand of Justice" in mine and swung it over the side of the sink containing the garbage disposal, then turned the "H" handle to the "on" position, deliberately. In the adjacent chamber Sam began to move, aware of a change in the quiet and of the vibrations emitted by the water and enamel and metal splashing together. When the water temperature reached the lethal point of giving off steam I turned it with absolute conviction into Sam's place. Sam ran at the glacier-like sides of the sink with desperation; all the wrath of justice touched Sam and his bowels ran; there was no way out; in a matter of seconds Sam was overcome. The casket was a paper towel and the remains were laid to rest in the toilet.

It occurred to me that Sam may have had a sister or brother who may have had children, making Sam—Uncle Sam.

Because of the King of France

Adrienne Cornell   From *Black Orpheus* magazine, edited by Ulli Beier. © Mbari 1964 and published for the Mbari writers and artists club by Longmans of Nigeria Ltd.

When my brother and I were children we had a cousin who ran away to the Virgin Islands. His name was Sidney.

It was a great joke. Often at night when we'd be sitting telling ghost stories my brother would giggle and say, "Suddenly from the haunted house there appeared Sidney back from the Virgin Islands." My mother who would be sitting embroidering crisscrosses on towels, in absurd solemnity never failed to say, "I wonder why on earth that boy went to the Virgin Islands? Of all the places in the world." This stately perplexity always collapsed my brother and me further into wild giggles that lasted at least a quarter of an hour. One time when my brother and I were sitting in the attic playing Monopoly, Sidney's father came to see us. He was a thin little Negro in denim overalls and a great cap. He drove a mustard-coloured moving van and looked very sad. My brother and I came to the top of the stairs and peeped at him. I thought he was one of my father's patients (my father was a doctor). When he left, my mother said the poor man was so unhappy, his wife dead and Sidney gone. She told my father that night and they talked about it. My father said he would go and see him. But my brother and I rarely saw Mr. Carter. He lived on the other side of town.

One day many years later, when I was in college, I was in a department store. It was a Saturday afternoon in September and I believe I was buying something silly, a cashmere sweater or socks with my initials on them (they were popular that year), when I felt someone watching me, I turned. And staring at me was a forlorn, thin stooped figure. I knew right away that it was Sidney: the sallow skin, the elongated head, the black spiritual eyes. But he was so much older than I remembered. He looked almost thirty. He wore a battered hat, skimpy cotton trousers and a baggy poplin jacket. I didn't give him a chance to speak but unconsciously put down my packages on the counter, looked at him saying in perfect imitation of my mother:

"Sidney," I demanded, as only a spoiled college girl can, "why on earth did you run away to the Virgin Islands? Of all places." And then as if to atone for my impudence I hastily added, "And you who could play the piano so well." He looked at me, not in the least humiliated by my rudeness and answered in a clear sweet earnestness which I have never forgotten, "Because of the King of France."

I went back to school that fall, I was very happy in those days and never thought of anything except my cashmere sweaters. I doubt if Sidney or our encounter ever crossed my mind.

Then one day toward the Christmas holidays a letter came. My room-mate and I had a joke of taking each other's mail and gluing it to the ceiling. When I came in for lunch I saw a grey envelope waiting for me there. It was late afternoon before I got the desk chair and the umbrella and took the letter down, examining the tiny squarish handwriting and the dim postmark reading St. Thomas, Virgin Islands. For some reason I clutched at the letter, then suddenly threw it across the room, went out and left it. I wondered what was in that letter. I could not explain it but I did not want to open that damn thing. Perhaps I would go back and throw it in the wastepaper basket. Inexplicably and against my will I began to remember things about Sidney. His mother had died. Willa was her name. She was a distant cousin of my father's. (I hadn't liked their house because it smelled of turnip greens. I had told my mother and she said, "Dear you mustn't be like that, those are your father's cousins." But I hadn't liked being cousins to poor people. My father was a doctor.) Then there had been a girl named Sylvia. My mother had seen her once at a piano recital where Sidney played and later recalling her she said the girl had looked deathly, very homely. She was a Jew with kinky blonde hair and, according to Willa, Sidney's first love. They studied music together at the Cleveland Institute where Sidney had gotten a scholarship. (It was after his first year there that Willa died.) And right after that that all that trouble began. Mr. Carter came to see my father late one night and had Sidney with him. Mr. Carter was crying. But Sidney sat almost immobile and withdrawn, repeating over and over, "It was the whole world let me in, finally the whole world let me in." It seemed that Sylvia Klein was pregnant with Sidney's baby and her father had come to the house and before Mr. Carter could reach him had beat Sidney in the face with a lead pipe. My father asked him did he know the seriousness of such a thing? But Sidney only sat then looked directly into my father's eyes. "Did you know there's love in the world," he said. "Did you know it?" "Did you know that even though Mama's gone there's love in this world." And the next thing I heard Sidney was dismissed from his beloved Institute and Mr. Klein, who was a little Jewish grocer, took his family to Sandusky.

Of course my mother didn't believe it. "How on earth?" she would exclaim. "Sidney, of all people, so intelligent, so artistic, always playing the piano," she'd add bewilderingly. It seemed impossible to me; too embarrassing to even discuss with my brother.

"Willa's to blame," my father said. "She's dead and in her grave but she's to blame for all this. She babied that boy so, making him think he was a genius, put all those ideas into his head about him being a piano player, giving him music lessons, sending him to the Institute. Why, that boy thinks he's white and he's coloured. He's nothing but a poor coloured boy. I feel sorry for him, Mildred." (That was my mother's name.) "It is a shame," my mother replied.

I came back to the room that night. The letter was still under the bed where I had thrown it. I picked it up and looked at it for a long time. Then I went over and latched the door and sat down at the desk, took a cigarette and read. This is what it said.

It was because of the King of France that I came away. You see after I left the Institute I went to live at Versailles. Louis XIV asked me to. Chopin was due to arrive soon. Of course Louis XIV was not a Negro. Neither was Chopin or Mr. Rosen my teacher at the Institute. But I am. And everyone at the Institute knows that Negroes are people who were brought to America from Africa and Africa is a black jungle where black pygmies with rings in their noses sit banging drums and sit distorting their pygmy bodies. Everyone at the Institute knows that Negroes are stupid people with woollen hair who shuffle and say Lawsy me and I gwine and black. Very black. Everyone except Sylvia Klein. And if I were not a Negro then her father would not yell at her when I walked her to the store that day. Her father would not scream at her about the niggers, niggers, everywhere and the kinkiness of nigger hair and the flatness of nigger noses and the blackness of their skin. Nobody would yell. And my mother would not keep saying to me, "Sidney baby, it's the Lord's will you're black and she's white. If he had wanted you white and living on Ridge Street he would have made it so."

"But I love her. I love her Mama," I cry. "I'm sixteen years old and I know what I feel."

"You can't go against the Lord, Sidney," she says. "You can't go against Him."

"I love her," I cry.

But all that was past and now I had my life at the Palace. I lived in a white-walled salon with a balcony overlooking the Palace gardens. I was happy there, myself and the Royal Family, when one day Louis XIV came to see me. He had been away for a long while. He came striding into the rooms and asked me to play a concert for him that Sunday at the Hall of Mirrors. I agreed. For we were great friends. As we stood talking on the balcony overlooking the fountains the King went on to tell me of the concert. I would play anything I chose. And also playing would be the amusing Monsieur Philippe. He had commanded him. I had not heard of this Philippe before and mentioned this to the King.

"He's an inconsequential fellow," he shrugged and with that the King disappeared off to the Throne Room or perhaps hunting. I practised that week, read my books and composed pieces for Sylvia, for even at the Palace I had not been able to forget the sorrow. The King had never visited me but that week he came in often to remark about the amusing Monsieur Philippe. It seemed he was an ugly fellow, small, stunted, sallow skinned with a large nose, and besides he was a Corsican, and spent hours in his room cursing his vile Corsican face and his stunted body. And besides the most amusing part he was in love with his daughter. The vile stunted thing loved his daughter. Louis XIV giggled. Then Sunday came and the Concert in the Hall of Mirrors. I played well and the Royal Family applauded. I was a great success. Then Monsieur Philippe came on.

He was ugly. And crippled too. He limped on to the stage and turned to us. His face was hideous. He looked like a filthy beggar. When he turned to look at the Princess she averted her face in disgust. He seated his cripped body at the piano and began to play. I saw tears in his eyes. And he played. And from those ugly fingers came all the longings, all the tenderness, all the loveliness that comes from dreaming alone in shuttered rooms that smell of turnips, all the fierceness that comes from being convicted to disgrace and inequity by God's will, the rage, the annihilation, the grief of race, and the unchangingness, the eternity of it all.

The King of France laughed.

The Negro

Bernard Pearson

Poor soul
of
    Black
ancestry
living a
lie of
time in
what the
white man
calls a
    ghetto
Eats the
foot of
pigs
intestines,
works hard
(to be
accepted),
trys to comb
the beauty
out of his
hair.
looks for
integrated
peace,
only tells
white lies,
forgets where
he came from,
laughs at his
race, smiles at
his oppressor,
and dies
(not knowing
all the
time
he was
a BLACK
prince)

181

lost identity

Lost Identity

(for negro bourgeois)

Eugene Perkins

The women sip cocktails
and gossip about latest
fashions (mini skirts,
strapless gowns and knee
high boots)

        In the corner four
neatly dressed men (doctor, lawyer, social
worker, undertaker) superficially admire
a Michaelangelo reproduction, without knowing
that Charles White grew up in a Chicago slum.

        The lawyer talks
about how judges are fining niggers who take
advantage of freak snow storms and instigate
violence on the streets for no apparent reason.
The doctor (surgeon by skill) makes a comment
about how ludicrous it is to give birth control
pills to unwed mothers, because most of them
        are only whores.

The social worker (wearing an au natural for
disguise) brags about communicating with the
grass roots, and then denounces the brothers
on the corner for being deviant and shiftless
        niggers.

        The undertaker
smiles and remarks that during the riots his
business went up seventy-five per cent (welfare
paid for all but six of his wooden caskets) He
concludes by saying he wouldn't know how to
accommodate the niggers if they rioted again.
Unless he cremated their bodies in the furnace
        of his mortuary.

The hostess enters dressed in African garb and
wearing a blond wig. She prepares to show
slides of her trip to Italy and points proudly
at a Nigerian mask made by a white art dealer.

From *Black Is Beautiful* by Eugene Perkins. Used by permission of Free Black Press.

Black Jam for Dr. Negro

Mari Evans

Pullin me in off the corner to wash
    my face an
cut my afro turn
my collar
down
when that aint my
thang I
walk heels first
nose round an tilted
up
my ancient
eyes
see your thang
baby
an it aint
shit
your thang
puts my eyes out baby
turns my seeking fingers
   into splintering fists
messes up my head
an I scream you out
your thang
is whats wrong
  and you keep
    pilin it on rubbin it
  in
  smoothly
  doin it
  to death
what you sweatin
baby your
        guts
puked an rotten
waitin
to be defended

From *I Am a Black Woman*, published by
Wm. Morrow & Co. 1970, by permission of
the author.

Listen, America, Ebony Middle-Class is Talking

Jeanne Taylor

Black, I am today
And black will ever be . . .

Yes, black and conceived during the cold, hungry nights of the depression, reared in the money-plentiful years of World War II, and now, at thirty years plus, we live in the year of the too-near disastrous future. Thus far we have spent a life on earth not worthy of the historians' note. The half-completed cycle of our lives has been one big waste of time! We speak not for black Watts or black Harlem. We talk of coffee-cream Leimert Park, Inglewood, Morningside Park, Baldwin Hills, Altadena, and Pasadena, where the lawns are green and the latest Chevrolet and Ford stand glistening in the drive, and the bills are barely paid each month and bankruptcy seems the sure way out. Where husband drinks more and more and is building as fine an arrest record as his black brother who steals and is considered the decadent result of the ghetto. Where a woman treads a lonely middle path, hated by her "poor" east-side cousin who can afford but one cheap, new dress all year, and by the doctor or lawyer's wife, who doesn't want her fantasy black-white world invaded. It's the envied Utopia we cry about, where young Mother and Father detest each other a little more each year, and sex has become a grotesque imitation of affection because what was revered during the romantic years of courtship is gone. Now the offspring are indulged lavishly because love has to be given to someone, something. Ours is a cry that says: hate us not for trying to rise up and above the man-made hell on earth; do not reject us because our cars and homes were bought with hard physical labor and not with the mind of an intellectual. Our hearts also strangle on the despair of racial injustice and the anguish of hopeless dreams that we've been told should never have been embraced. Our hands search desperately for the grip of happiness, love, and understanding. When you see us smile in our poised, self-confident way, stop and look a little closer. The corners of our mouths are really turned down. The tears are there, mingled with the mascara. And when we laugh, listen—is there not a sob in our voice?

So the next time we meet on the highway to where-ever, smile our way. We breathe, we bleed, we die too!

A Man of the Middle Class

Gwendolyn Brooks

I'm what has gone out blithely and with noise
Returning! I'm what rushed around to pare
Down rind, to find fruit frozen under there.

I am bedraggled, with sundry dusts to be shed;
Trailing desperate tarnished tassels. These strident Aprils

With terrifying polkas and Bugle Calls
Confound me.

—Although I've risen! and my back is bold.
My tongue is brainy, choosing from among
Care, rage, surprise, despair, and choosing care.
I'm semi-splendid within what I've defended.

Yet, there I totter, there limp laxly. My
Uncomely trudge
To Plateau That and platitudinous Plateau
Whichever is no darling to my grudge-
Choked industry or usual alcohol.

I've roses to guard
In the architectural prettiness of my yard.
(But there are no paths remarkable for wide
Believable welcomes.)

I have loved directions.
I have loved orders and an iron to stride, I,
Whose hands are papers now,
Fit only for tossing in this outrageous air.

Not God nor grace nor candy balls
Will get me everything different and the same!

My wife has canvas walls.

My wife never quite forgets to put flowers in vases,
Bizarre prints in the most unusual places,
Give teas for poets, wear odoriferous furs.
An awful blooming is hers.

I've antique firearms. Blackamoors. Chinese
Rugs. Ivories.
Bronzes. Everything I Wanted.
But have I answers? Oh methinks
I've answers such as have
The executives I copied long ago,
The ones who, forfeiting Vicks salve,
Prayer book and Mother, shot themselves last Sunday.

All forsaking
All that was theirs but for their money's taking.
I've answers such as Giants used to know.
There's a Giant who'll jump next Monday; all forsaking
Wives, safes and solitaire
And the elegant statue standing at the foot of the stair.

Keith Ferdinand/Blkartsouth.

Middle-Class Negroes and the Negro Masses

Whitney M. Young, Jr.

. . . Available figures on Negro income levels reflect the growth of a new and vital middle class. Some 20 per cent of the Negro family population are in the $7,000 a year or over income bracket, while some 60 per cent are in an income bracket of $3,000 or under. This means that the conventional way of looking at general social-class divisions does not hold true for Negroes because there is a distinct, drastic jump from the low-income level to the middle-class group with no upper-income class, and only a tiny lower middle class.

This poses serious problems for those who work in the field of race relations and who are concerned about what is happening in the Negro community. There is a grave danger of the possible alienation of the middle-class Negro from those of his race, who, due to automation or other factors, are in an almost dependent category of the lower class. This alienation works both ways. The middle-class Negro often (sometimes unconsciously) disassociates himself from the lower-class Negro, not because of any personal dislike of him, but because he is symbolic of a phase in history that he wants to forget. To the middle-class Negro, the black ghetto often is symbolic of discrimination, embarrassment, humiliation, second-class citizenship, and inferiority. The alienation or withdrawal of the middle-class Negro, therefore, is not so much an expression of a desire to escape Negroes in the lower-class category as an unconscious desire to escape what has been associated with that status.

On the other hand the Negro in the lower-class group sees in the flight of the middle-class Negro from his neighborhood a desire to disassociate himself from the rest, and this causes a tension. This is of real concern to those of us involved in efforts to advance the Negro community because while the desire of the middle-class [Negro] is to escape a condition, his flight often results in a loss of leadership that is needed to inspire and uplift the group which cannot afford escape.

Another problem created by the withdrawal of the middle-class Negro is the development of different values and different goals by the two groups.

From Whitney Young, "The Role of the Middle Class Negro," *Ebony*, September, 1963. Used by permission of the publisher.

Middle-class Negroes possess status or symbolic goals to which the lower class may be completely indifferent. Negroes in the low or poorer class are concerned with reality or welfare goals. For example, the opening to Negro use of rest-room facilities in a Southern airport terminal may mean a great deal to middle-class Negroes, but little or nothing to the lower class. Winning such a right would be of symbolic importance primarily to the middle class.

Today, almost without exception, the leadership of the Negro's civil-rights struggle is drawn from the middle-class group. The danger exists, therefore, that because of the widening alienation of the classes, each class may at times be working toward different goals. This is evidenced in support by working or lower-class Negroes for certain schools and public-housing projects near or in their ghetto districts, and a resultant clash with middle-class Negroes who may oppose erection of such buildings because they regard them as strengthening segregation instead of weakening it. The welfare values of the lower-class Negro can force him to see tangible benefits in such facilities wherever they may be built. . . .

For generations in the South an established middle-class leadership group existed which could identify with the lower-class masses they represented because they were subjected to the same pressures because of skin color. One of the chief differences between the status of the Negro in the South and the North is that in the South Negroes have experienced prejudice regardless of economic level. In the North the middle-class Negro is able to escape some of the pressure of racial prejudice by physically withdrawing from the ghetto.

Middle-class Americans are extremely concerned about conformity. Negroes who enter the middle class become even more rigid in their class values, more conscious of status than do white middle-class folk. The new Negro middle class clings more desperately to the status symbols, is more careful and correct in behavior.

. . . In the white community there are more stages in social advancement. The rise from low-income status to upper is marked by various class levels between the two extremes—lower middle class, upper middle class, etc. For the Negro there is no in-between status; he must jump directly from lower-class status to the higher with no way stops or intermediate steps.

The Negro in America today all too often faces a choice between being a highly skilled technician or professional, or being a waiter, porter, or domestic; between living in a fabulous house in the suburbs or in a tenement in the slums; between sending his kids to a fashionable prep school or to an overcrowded, ill-equipped public school in a deprived neighborhood; between acceptance by heads of government and barons of industry or daily rejection by callous and indifferent human beings; between caviar and steak or bread and water. . . .

Negro leadership is drawn mainly from the professionals, persons who in the white community would not enjoy such eminence, would in fact be largely ignored. In a typical Negro community schoolteachers and physicians are personages of real importance, as are the executive secretaries of the local Urban League and YMCA. In the white community such persons have very little rating.

The average Negro professional has leadership responsibilities imposed upon him because of his position in a disadvantaged and deprived group. The Negro doctor, in addition to being a good doctor, has to assume some responsibility for social leadership. Many are refusing to accept these responsibilities, preferring to concentrate on their professional careers and on the acquisition of wealth. . . .

Certain middle-class Negroes are now exhibiting an unfortunate tendency to be indifferent if not actually hostile to those black Americans less fortunate and privileged. A generation is coming of age that was born in the North of middle-class parents and spent all of their lives in an environment relatively free of prejudice and restrictions. Educated in predominantly white schools, they have never experienced real rejection owing to their color and have never been a part of the Negro struggle. This type feels that it is a mark of their emancipation not to identify with the Negro effort for freedom, that it is a measure of their sophistication that they do not belong to the NAACP or support the Urban League or engage in antidiscrimination activity. After having been taught all their lives that they could escape the indignities and penalties attached to being Negro, they often find themselves humiliated or blocked by racial barriers. Instead of joining with their fellow Negroes to oppose the enemy, they become bitter and disillusioned.

The middle class will continue to furnish the cadres for Negro leadership for years to come. Only a handful of the Negro leaders have come from labor —outstanding men like A. Philip Randolph and George L. P. Weaver, Assistant Secretary of Labor. The competition of the middle class for civil-rights leadership roles in the Negro community usually has overwhelmed the uneducated Negro candidates from the lower economic class. The latter was generally outclassed, outtalked, and outmaneuvered by his more highly trained middle-class rivals. The uneducated Negro thus seldom got a chance at Negro leadership, to try his wings and show what he could do. He never got the thrill of sacrifice or the satisfaction of victory. This is not true of leadership of churches, fraternal groups, and social clubs, where middle-class Negroes are not as active in their participation. . . .

While the Negro middle class is growing in numbers and influence the large mass of unskilled, unemployable Negroes is growing at an even faster rate. Unless the rate of growth of the latter group is soon checked we will soon see in America a large class of dependent, permanently unemployed with Negroes contributing a disproportionate share. This holds alarming implications for the economic future of the Negro middle class because its income and wealth still derive preponderantly from the Negro community. Most Negro professionals earn their living from Negro clienteles.

The role of the Negro middle class will become increasingly vital and dynamic, especially in the struggle for human rights and first-class citizenship. Though the income and status gap between lower- and middle-class Negroes is widening, it must not be forgotten that the Negro middle-class person essentially cannot rise above the general condition of his entire people. He must rise along with the group or not at all. The social advantages or economic security enjoyed by an individual member of an oppressed minority will only be temporary until the least disadvantaged and the most impoverished of that group improves his status, and freedom is achieved for all. This was pointedly illustrated several years ago when the son of Nobel

Prize winner and United Nations Under-Secretary Ralph Bunche was rejected by the West Side Tennis Club in Forest Hills, New York, when he sought to get tennis instruction there. Bunche himself, while visiting Atlanta, was denied accommodations at a major hotel while a white man wearing overalls was being registered.

The educationally privileged Negro middle class will share the horrors and hardships of his more handicapped working-class brother as long as racism exists in our society and color is still the determining factor in the treatment accorded the citizens of an imperfect democracy.

Excerpt from the poem "Since 1619" is reprinted by permission of Yale University Press from *For My People,* by Margaret Walker. Copyright © 1942 by Yale University Press.

RAGE

When will I understand the cheated and the cheaters;
Their paltry pittances and cold concessions to my pride?
When will I burst from my kennel an angry mongrel,
Lean and hungry and tired of my dry bones and years?

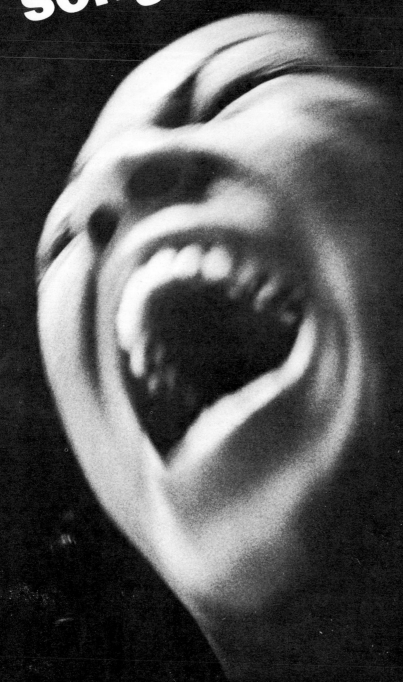

songs of hate

THE SO-CALLED WHITE SOCIETY'S PLIGHT AND RACISM

The so-called white society is a society of "swines, pork and pigs." They prey upon people as vultures prey upon helpless victims.

They wallow and lounge in filth, degradation and the injustices of racism as does the swine in his mud arena. The white society is cold, without feeling, indifferent and without a conscience. The white society manipulates their manifestations in perpetrating criminal acts against their minority races. The gallant white society has a religion — coercion and perpetration of the "Great white society and white America."

The society in general is controlled by a small number of swines. Swines may seem to be an unfair term. However, it is quite appropriate. A swine is the dirtiest, filthiest, greediest and most unclean animal alive. Anyone who would commit criminal acts against human beings falls well within the pig, pork and swine category.

Those who follow and adhere to and perpetrate the criminal acts of the swines are in the same category. The man and woman who sit by motionless, apathy filling their daily lives, are the elements perpetrating the establishment's reign.

The so-called white society's mind has been chained by years of the establishment's reign and corruption. The sun; is the awakening of the minorities and actions of groups pushing awareness and means of using the lights-truths.

The fire is the wrath that will and is being brought upon the oppressor. The voices are angry tones of discontent. The man who escaped, I would say is a symbol of the Black Rebels. Those remaining chained and those who laugh and sneer are those helpless ones who always say, "you can't fight City Hall — America."

When the so-called white society is totally awakened and becomes responsive perhaps they will save themselves.

Organization of Afro-Asia Unity Applied Economic
ERVINE AKBAR   826-7345
DONATION $1.00

Militant

Langston Hughes

Let all who will
Eat quietly the bread of shame.
I cannot,
Without complaining loud and long,
Tasting its bitterness in my throat,
And feeling to my very soul
It's wrong.
For honest work
You proffer me poor pay,
For honest dreams
Your spit is in my face,
And so my fist is clenched
Today—
To strike your face.

From *The Panther and the Lash,* by Langston Hughes. Copyright © 1967 by Arna Bontemps and George Houston Bass. Reprinted by permission of Alfred A. Knopf, Inc.

Warning

Langston Hughes

Negroes,
Sweet and docile,
Meek, humble, and kind:
Beware the day
They change their mind!

Wind
In the cotton fields,
Gentle breeze:
Beware the hour
It uproots trees!

Whiteeyes on Black Thighs

Ted Joans

I KNOW YOU DIG DARK ME
I KNOW YOU WANT A TASTE
BUT IF YOU LAY A HAND
ON ME
I'LL RUN
A RAZOR BLADE
SEVEN TIMES
ACROSS
YOUR PALE
CRACKER
FACE

From *Black Pow-Wow* by Ted Joans (New York: Hill and Wang, Inc., Publishers, 1969). Copyright © 1969 by Ted Joans.

Let's Get Violent

Ted Joans

LET'S GET VIOLENT! AND ATTACK THE WHITEWASH
   ICING CAKED
ON OUR BLACK MINDS
LET'S GET SO VIOLENT   THAT WE LEAVE   that white way
   of thinking
ON THE TOILET BENEATH OUR BLACK BEHINDS   LET'S
   GET VIOLENT!

From a Black Perspective

Don Lee   From *Don't Cry, Scream* by Don L. Lee. Broadside Press, copyright © 1969 by Don L. Lee. Reprinted by permission of Broadside Press.

WALLACE FOR PRESIDENT
HIS MOMMA FOR VICE-PRESIDENT

   WAS SCRIBBLED
ON THE MEN'S ROOM WALL
ON OVER THE TOILET
WHERE
IT'S
SUPPOSED TO BE.

A Folk Fabel (For My People)

Johari Amini (Jewel C. Latimore)

          the Third World had
hung the un/humans(beastids
& parasites that is they wasn't any left
except in russia
& england & other cold
continents
(israel had only blk/jews
natural resources was up
tight the un/humans & they evil had to
live on theyselves
& on they technology & they
crust was so dried up it wouldn't
   even grow
cotton any more
               then the niggas(that is
               peoples(Bantu:
defined(blacks/negroes/muthas also
that is got bad & every
body was afraid them niggas
was really bad them bad niggas
was burnin everything the un/humans
   had on the reser
vations(cleanin up that is:
3/flats (18-rooms for 18 families
10/flats (60-rooms for 60 families
speed-easy cleaners
(brown pressers & a pale cashier
speed-easy-shopp food centers
(sour/meat/vegetable sellers & a blk
   cashier
speed-easy-cut-rated liquor stores
(corned/breath salesboys & no cashier

(Bantu(human beings

that is
just cheap wine
              & the grass was burned
& the teas was burned & the reser
vations was
cleaned
when
the pimps
& other death reflec
tors was offed had the pills
stuffed
down they own
throats the bad niggas was
ready the bad niggas
was ready to move even
the indians was ready to make
up for what they hadn't done
at plymouth rock in 1620(they was
ready to burn too
but they didn't know it was too
late that the
time had come because the
   un/humans had
did it
     had copped
it copped the moon but the
niggas wadn't hip
they was still burnin burnin
talkin about how good it was the
burnin(they wasn't talkin about Viet
Nam & how bad it had been
(that was over
but the niggas wadn't hip & wadn't
   hipped
until they was copped.
too.
to work in the mines on the moon(the
   mines was
full of
bauxite uranium gold
diamonds un/humans desires they
couldn't get from Africa any
more & the ships was
big had promises had names
that all the niggas knew names
like JESUS & HEAVEN & FREEDOM
to take the niggas to a new world they
was pickin bad niggas off the
streets out/in/side the reservations

197

puttin em in the ships packin em
chainin em in the decks brandin
em with the owners name brandin
    N-A-S-A on
they foreheads
                the satelite
was the first stop the niggas
was landed
& graded by size
& age &
health(the niggas who couldn't work
had they good organs taken
out & put in banks to be
come transplants 4 un/humans/hearts
un/humans/livers
/eyes un/humans/kidneys
/arms/legs/stomachs to replace
    un/humans/ulcers
and nigga/magic/love
parts
to replace un/humans masturbation
& other cold in-action
them niggas was trained
to dig ore
& load it &
pull it &
pro-cess it & breed &
breed & breed more
niggas to work the moon mines plus
good black(missionaries was trained
    to keep the
mine niggas quiet
                & when they all was
trained they was shipped to the moon
mainland sold
to companies who
was bidden
while the chasemanhattan bank
supervised the auctions
they was bred
& trained
& worked
& butchered & banked
until the chance came
until the un/humans forgot

NOTE: According to the 1964 South African
Institute for Medical Research Annual Report, the discovery was made that less than
3 out of every 750,000 Bantu die of coro-
nary heart disease annually (dig, putting a
premium on blk/hearts

that the moon was full
all the time . . .
on the moon . . .
that was when some of them
bad niggas made beauty moving ju
ju changes
                the drum musics hummed
mojo/vibrated & high
john screamed through the bloods
to Nommo hears the blood sounds
Nommo spoke Ntu forces
& all the niggas listened & acted—
    missionaries
too—dig—my people—
they acted the rhythms pulling they
minds was one & moved moved moved
universe/earth/spirits firing the soil to
destroy the evil/un/image
cleanse the waste from the cold lands
until the cosmos was whole
again &
the worlds had become new

(N.A.S.A.(National Aeronautics and Space
Administration

(Nommo(word—creative/creating life force
(Ntu(cosmic universal force in which
        Being & beings coalesce

A Dance for Militant Dilettantes

Al Young

No one's going to read
or take you seriously,
a hip friend advises,
until you start coming down on them
like the black poet you truly are
& ink in lots of black in your poems
soul is not enough
you need real color
shining out of real skin
nappy snaggly afro hair
baby grow up & dig on *that*!

You got to learn to put in about
stone black fists
coming up against white jaws
& red blood splashing
down those fabled wine & urine-
stained hallways
black bombs blasting out real white
   estate
the sky itself black with what's to
   come:
final holocaust
the settling up
Don't nobody want no nice nigger
   no more
these honkies that put out
these books and things
they want an angry splib
a furious nigrah
they don't want no bourgeois woogie
they want them a militant nigger
in a fiji haircut
fresh out of some secret boot camp
with a bad book in one hand
& a molotov cocktail in the other
subject to turn up at one of their
   conferences
or soirees
& shake the shit out of them.

for unborn malcolms

sonia sanchez

git the word out
now.
   to the man/boy
taking a holiday
from murder.
      tell him
we hip to his shit and that
the next time he kills one
of our
   blk/princes some of
his faggots gonna die
a stone/cold/death.
       yeah.
it's time.
   an eye for an eye
   a tooth for a tooth
   don't worry abt his balls
they al
   ready gone.
      git the word
out that us blk/niggers
      are out to lunch
and the main course
is gonna be his white meat.
      yeah.

to die is to be a MAN

If We Must Die

Claude McKay

If we must die, let it not be like hogs
Hunted and penned in an inglorious spot,
While round us bark the mad and hungry dogs,
Making their mock at our accursed lot.
If we must die, O let us nobly die,
So that our precious blood may not be shed
In vain; then even the monsters we defy
Shall be constrained to honor us though dead!
O kinsmen, we must meet the common foe!
Though far outnumbered let us show us brave,
And for their thousand blows deal one death blow!
What though before us lies an open grave?
Like men we'll face the murderous cowardly pack,
Pressed to the wall, dying, but fighting back!

state/meant

LeRoi Jones

The Black Artist's role in America is to aid in the destruction of America as he knows it. His role is to report and reflect so precisely the nature of the society, and of himself in that society, that other men will be moved by the exactness of his rendering and, if they are black men, grow strong through this moving, having seen their own strength, and weakness; and if they are white men, tremble, curse, and go mad, because they will be drenched with the filth of their evil.

The Black Artist must draw out of his soul the correct image of the world. He must use this image to band his brothers and sisters together in common understanding of the nature of the world (and the nature of America) and the nature of the human soul.

The Black Artist must demonstrate sweet life, how it differs from the deathly grip of the White Eyes. The Black Artist must teach the White Eyes their deaths, and teach the black man how to bring these deaths about.

We are unfair, and unfair.
We are black magicians, black art
s we make in black labs of the heart.

The fair are
fair, and death
ly white.

The day will not save them
and we own
the night.

And We Own The Night

Jimmy Garrett

    The scene is an alleyway, dark, dirty, dingy. A large trashcan sits stage right next to a red brick building. The entire rear of stage right is a line of buildings shaded and faded, red or brown brick or graying white wooden frames. A dim yellow light sits above the building closest to the front of the stage. To the left of the stage is a tall white picket fence, also graying. To the right of stage front, around the trashcan, is a broom, leaning against the building. At the very rear of stage left lies a dead BODY: a black youth. In the center rear of the stage is another BODY, a white man dressed in a policeman's uniform.
The lighting should give an effect of dimness, not darkness though it is night, of muted light, of soft shadows, of a kind of grey dinginess. The time is that of the present and that of death and dying.
From off stage there is the sound of gunfire, in short bursts, then in a long sustained burst, followed by high shrilling sirens. Then more gunfire.

First published in *The Drama Review*, Volume 12, Number 4 (T40), Summer 1968. © 1968 by *The Drama Review*. Reprinted by permission. All rights reserved.

VOICE, *offstage.* Johnny's been shot! Help me!

SECOND VOICE. Is he hurt bad?

FIRST VOICE. Yeah, get a doctor, Billy Joe.

SECOND VOICE. Okay. I'll try to find his mother too.

FIRST VOICE. To hell with his mother. Get a doctor, dammit. We'll be in the alley behind Central Street.

Two young black men enter from stage left as if from behind the fence. Johnny, tall and thin with fine black features, is being crutched by LIL'T *who is small-statured and has a high brown face. They move toward the building at stage right.*

LIL'T. Come on, Johnny, sit here. *He props* JOHNNY *up against the building in front of the trashcan.* JOHNNY *is clutching his left side where his shirt is covered with blood. He is holding a pistol in his right hand.*

JOHNNY, *breathing heavily.* Lil' T . . . Lil' T . . . Bad . . . Mother . . . fuckin' cops *Clutches* LIL' T . . . caught us from behind . . .

LIL'T. They won't fuck with nobody else. I blew 'em away.

JOHNNY. Good . . . Good . . . *Grimaces, then clutches* LIL' T. Lil T, find mama.

LIL' T. Cool it, Johnny. Don't talk, brother. *He touches the wound.* You're bleedin' like hell. The doctor'll be here in a little while.

JOHNNY. No . . . find Mama . . . Tell her . . . Stay away. Tell her stay home. Ain't no . . . women here . . . Tell her . . . Lil' T.

LIL' T. Don't worry Johnny. We'll keep your mother away. She knows we got a war to fight in this alley. She knows we're kickin' the white man's ass.

JOHNNY. Naw man . . . She ain't . . . She ain't . . . no good . . . that way . . . keep her away . . . til we win . . . then she'll understand. Not now . . . Not yet . . . *He nods his head from side to side.*

LIL' T. She can't stop us Johnny. Nobody can. The white man can't. Your Mama can't. Nobody. We're destroying the white man. There's wars like this in every big city . . . Harlem, Detroit, Chicago . . . all over California. Everywhere. We've held off these white motherfuckers for three days.

JOHNNY. Yeah . . . If we keep pushin' . . . we'll win . . . we'll . . . win. Keep Mama away . . . Keep her away . . . til we win. I'm scared. I can't fight her and the white man too. *He clutches his side and grimaces.*

LIL' T. Cool it brother . . . You the leader Johnny. You ain't scared of nothing, everybody knows that. You're smart. You know how to fuck with whitey. You fight too hard to be scared of a woman.

JOHNNY. You don't know. Lil' T. You don't know . . .

LIL' T. What you mean, I don't know. I've known you for three days . . . three days of fire. I know how you fight . . .

JOHNNY. No. You don't know. On the street, in the alley, I'm a fighter. But in my Mama's house I ain't nothin.

LIL' T. What you mean?

JOHNNY. She's too strong. She about killed my Daddy. Made a nigger out of him. She loves the white man . . . She'll take me home.

LIL' T. Home. This is home. This alley and those bodies. That's home. I'm your brother and you're my brother and we live and fight in alleys. This is home. And we'll win against the white man.

JOHNNY. We're brothers 'T but mama believes the white man's God. *He lapses into silence nodding his head from side to side.*

LIL' T. Cool it, Johnny. Don't be so uptight. Where's the fucking doctor?

VOICE, *offstage.* Go for soul! LIL' T *turns his head toward stage left and rises. A short, stocky, black faced* young man enters. *A rifle hangs loosely at his shoulder.*

LIL' T. Where's that doctor, Billy Joe?

BILLY JOE. I got him. I found him hiding at his home. Come on in the alley, Doc. A lil' dirt won't hurt you.

DOCTOR *enters, crouching low moving slowly, passes* BILLY JOE *toward* LIL' T, *who is standing. He looks around as if expecting to be shot. He is a light-complexioned Negro in his late forties, dressed in an expensive-looking gray suit.* LIL' T *goes over and jerks him forward.* BILLY JOE *leaves.*

LIL' T. Come on, Doc. We ain't got no time to be jiving. Johnny's bleeding bad.

DOCTOR, *standing above* JOHNNY. I don't . . . I don't know what I can do.

LIL' T, *raises his gun.* Man, you'd beter do something quick. DOCTOR *leans over* JOHNNY *and kneels.*

DOCTOR. That boy rushed me so quick I didn't get a chance to get my tools. I just stuffed what I could in my pockets. *The* DOCTOR *presses the area where* JOHNNY *is bleeding.* That's a bad wound.

JOHNNY. Aw. *He slides away from the* DOCTOR. Be cool, man.

DOCTOR. Be still, boy, or you'll bleed to death. *Two* BLACK BOYS *rush on stage from the right, one carrying a pistol, the other a rifle.*

FIRST BOY. Lil' T. *He stops to catch his breath.* The cops 've broken through the barricade on Vernon.

LIL' T. Which barricade? What happened?

SECOND BOY. The one on Vernon . . . The cops come in buses, five of 'em.

FIRST BOY. Yeah, looked like 'bout fifty cops a bus. The cats saw all them cops, an' ran.

LIL' T. Where'd the cats go? Up to the park?

FIRST BOY. Yeah, they set up another barricade.

SECOND BOY. We got to think of something or them cops'll break that 'un too. We came to get Johnny. He'll know what to do.

LIL' T. He can't move. He got shot lil' while ago. *The* TWO BOYS *turn to go over to* JOHNNY, *but are held up by* LIL' T. Naw, man, don't bother him . . . He's been hurt bad. Wait til the Doc's finished.

FIRST BOY. Man, we can't wait. *They rush over to* JOHNNY. *The* FIRST BOY *kneels in front of the* DOCTOR, *the other stands behind him.* JOHNNY *rolls his head around.* Johnny, Johnny. Wake up brother. Hey, what's wrong?

DOCTOR. I gave him something to kill the pain.

SECOND BOY, *kneeling, grabs* JOHNNY *by the arm.* Aw, fuck. Wake up Johnny.

LIL' T. Whyn't you cats leave him alone. *Moving over to the group.*

JOHNNY. Oh. Oh. *Waking.* What. Wha . . . Lil' T. Lil' T.

LIL' T, *kneeling.* It's all right, Johnny, These cats . . .

FIRST BOY. Look, Johnny. We know you hurt but we need your help, man. Them cops're rushing the barricades in buses. Hundreds of cops.

SECOND BOY. Man. We got to stop them buses or they'll wipe us out. Cats ran from Vernon. They're all the way down the park now. Got another barricade goin'. But it won't hold long!

DOCTOR, *as* JOHNNY *sits up listening.* Wait a second. I'll be through with this bandage in a minute.

JOHNNY, *to* DOCTOR. Yeah, yeah. Look here. Throw broken glass in the streets. Then pour gasoline up and down the street for a block or so. If the glass don't stop 'em, plant cats in places so they can hide with fire bombs. An' when the buses get in the middle of that gasoline, chunk them bombs under em.

FIRST BOY. Roasted cops!

SECOND BOY. Wow! Oh, man . . . outta sight. Outta sight! Come on. Let's go. We'll get 'em. Go for soul. Thanks Johnny. You're a heavy cat. *They exit.* Go for soul!

DOCTOR. Boy if you don't be still, you'll bleed to death.

LIL' T. He's right, Man. Ain't no use in you cuttin' out on a humbug. You blowin' too much soul. BILLY JOE *enters.*

BILLY JOE, *to* LIL' T. I saw Johnny's mother down at the barricade.

LIL' T. *takes* BILLY JOE *to the side of the stage left.* She's not coming here is she?

BILLY JOE. Yeah, man. I told her to come. I thought Johnny might die. I thought his mother should . . .

JOHNNY. Lil' T . . . Get this dude off me.

DOCTOR, *turning to face* LIL' T. I'm just patching him. He's restless.

LIL' T. It's okay, Johnny. Take it easy Doc. *Back to* BILLY JOE. Look man . . . We got to keep his old lady away . . . She's a bitch. Johnny don't want her around. Go keep her away.

BILLY JOE. But. She's his mother . . .

LIL' T. I don't give a shit. Keep her out of here. Go on. *Pushes* BILLY JOE.

BILLY JOE. Okay man. *He rushes out.*

LIL' T *turns toward* JOHNNY *and the* DOCTOR.

VOICE, *offstage.* Look out son. You nearly knocked me down. Where's my son at? Where's Johnny at?

BILLY JOE, *backing on to stage.* You can't come in. Lil' T says you got to stay out . . .

JOHNNY'S MOTHER *enters, backing* BILLY JOE *into the alley. She is an imposing black woman, wearing a simple dress of floral design and flat shoes. She never smiles.*

MOTHER. Boy, don't you mess with me. Where is my son at? *As she speaks,* LIL' T *turns. He is blocking* JOHNNY *from his* MOTHER'S *view.*

BILLY JOE. I don't know where the dude is. *Realizes he is in the alley and stops.*

LIL' T, *walking toward them.* I told you to keep her out.

BILLY JOE. I . . .

MOTHER. Johnny! *She rushes over to* JOHNNY *and kneels, pushing the* DOCTOR *out of the way.* BILLY JOE *shrugs his shoulders and leaves.*

JOHNNY. Mama. Mama. Go back home.

DOCTOR. Don't shake him woman! He's been shot. He's bleeding inside.

MOTHER. My son. He's my son. *She speaks loudly but does not sob.* You the doctor? Will he be all right?

LIL' T, *clutching the woman by the shoulders and trying to lift her.* He's all right. Come on now. Billy Joe'll take you home.

MOTHER, *jerking loose.* Naw. Let me go. Who are you? Why'd my son get hurt like this? You're the cause of it.

LIL'T. He got shot by a white cop.

JOHNNY. Go way Mama. T get her out of here.

MOTHER. Don't you talk to me like that. You bad boys. Sinning. And this is what you get. *Points at* JOHNNY's *wound.*

LIL' T. Ain't nobody sinning but the white man. Now he's payin' for it.

MOTHER. Johnny layin' there bleedin' and the white man's payin'. Help me doctor. Help me take him to the hospital.

JOHNNY. Mama leave me alone.

LIL' T. Johnny ain't goin' to no white man's hospital. Them motherfuckers would just let him die.

MOTHER. Don't you curse white people like that. Doctor help me.

DOCTOR, *looks up at* LIL' T *who has lifted the gun.* No we shouldn't move him. I've slowed the flow but he's still bleeding internally. He'll die if he moves around too much.

MOTHER. But he can't stay here in

this alley. Oh lord help me, what can I do?

DOCTOR. I've got to get that bullet out quick. I'll go back to the office and get my case.

LIL' T. Okay Doc. Billy Joe can take you and make sure you get back. Billy Joe? DOCTOR *rises.* BILLY JOE *enters.* Take the Doctor back to get his stuff.

BILLY JOE. Okay, come on, Doc. *They leave.*

MOTHER. Is it bad son? Is it bad? Oh Lord. What can I do? I need strength.

JOHNNY. Mama, don't pray. It don't do no good.

MOTHER. I told you to stay home. Out here fightin' the Police. Burnin' down white folks' businesses. I'm ashamed of you. God knows why you're doin' this.

JOHNNY. I'm bein' a man. A black man. And I don't need a white man's God to help me.

MOTHER. What you say? What you say 'bout God?

JOHNNY. Forget it.

MOTHER. Where'd you learn all that stuff. *She rises and turns to* LIL' T. Did you teach him this sacrilege?

JOHNNY. Nobody taught me.

LIL' T. He's leader. He knows how to fuck with whitey.

MOTHER, *to* LIL' T. Boy, can't you talk without cursin'? Don't no child like you need to talk that way. *To* JOHNNY. Your daddy's a man, and he don't curse.

JOHNNY. Where is he, Mama?

MOTHER. He's at home where you should be 'stead of out here in this alley.

JOHNNY. Is he hidin', Mama?

MOTHER. Naw he ain't hidin'. He's just stayin' close to his home.

LIL' T. While his woman's out on the street. Bullshit. A man don't need to hide. Can't. He'd be out here fightin' like us.

MOTHER. You're wrong boy. God knows you're wrong. You out here breakin' laws. Killin'. Look at what you've done. *She points at the bodies lying on the stage.*

LIL' T. People die when they face the white man. Better to die like a man, bringing the white man to his knees than hidin' at home under a woman's skirt.

MOTHER. My husband ain't no sinner. He don't break laws. He works hard . . . He don't bother nobody. He . . .

JOHNNY. He's still a nigger.

LIL' T. He believes what the white man says.

MOTHER. You don't know him. You don't know what he believes.

LIL' T. Be a good nigger, work hard, pray, kiss ass, and you'll make it.

MOTHER. How do you know? How do you know?

JOHNNY. I know, Mama.

MOTHER. I'm gonna take you home. Away from this sin.

JOHNNY. Don't bother me, Mama.

MOTHER. I brought you into the world. I clothed and fed you. And now you don't want me to touch you? I'm taking you home. *She tries to lift* JOHNNY. LIL' T *rushes over and grabs her by the shoulder, pulling her away.*

MOTHER. Let me go. *Breaks away from his grip.* Don't put your hands on me again.

LIL' T. Well you leave Johnny alone. Can't you understand? He's a man. He's a leader. He's my brother. We're gonna stay here in this alley and fight the white man together. Right Johnny?

JOHNNY. Yeah, brother.

MOTHER. You ain't no leader, boy. You ain't even got no mind. *Turns to* LIL' T. He's got the mind. A dirty mind. Why don't you leave him alone? He's just a boy. He didn't know about hatin' and killin' til he started running with you.

LIL' T. Killin' ain't no dirty thing to do to a white man.

MOTHER, *rising.* Murder ain't never been clean.

LIL' T. Except when the white man did it, right?

MOTHER. Who are you, the devil? I ain't speakin' of the white man as you call it. He ain't done me no harm.

LIL' T. He beat you and raped you. He made a whore out of you and a punk out of your man.

MOTHER. Naw. The white man ain't done nothing to me. But I don't know you. Where are your folks?

LIL' T. My mother and father are dead. They died the first day fightin' the cops. My brother's in jail. My sister's somewhere fightin' or dyin'! My home is this alley and Johnny is my brother. This is where I live or die.

MOTHER. You don't have nothin' left. You don't feel nothin'. You ain't found God. You don't have love.

LIL' T. That God you pray to is a lie. A punk. The last dick the white man's got to put in you.

MOTHER. You see, Johnny. He's got no heart. He's got no love.

LIL' T. Love! Love! Everybody knows that love ain't enough for the white man. He don't understand love. You got to kill him. Love! Ass suckin' love. Askin' him for forgiveness when he's done wrong. Letin' him shoot you in the back while you're on your knees prayin' to his God.

MOTHER. Jesus said . . .

LIL' T. Another punk . . .

MOTHER. Jesus said love those who are spiteful of . . .

LIL' T. Strokin' his rod, cleanin' his shit . . .

MOTHER. Forgive those who do harm . . .

LIL' T. Blowin' up black children in churches . . . Beatin' pregnant women . . .

MOTHER. We must pray to God for salvat . . .

LIL' T. Kill that motherfucker! Cut out his heart and stuff it down his throat. Bury him in his own shit.

MOTHER, *quietly, slowly.* I will not strike out at white men. They have been good to me. Fed my son. Gave me shelter when there was no work for my husband. Gave me a job so I could care for my family. White men have done me no harm. Only niggers like you trying to take my son away and lead him to sin.

LIL' T. The white man gave you a job and took away your husband's balls. You have the money and your husband's a tramp in his own home. Ain't that right Johnny?

MOTHER, *to* JOHNNY. *She speaks quietly at first, then building to the end.* Johnny. Son. In God's name, you know how I love you and your Daddy. How I've worked and slaved for you all. And you know how white folk's have always helped us. They're smart. They know what's right and what ain't. We got to trust in them. They're good. They run the whole world don't they? How come you're out here killin' white men. I don't understand. Livin' in this filth. Crawlin' around alleys bleedin' to death. You call yourselves men. Don't no men act like that. The white man don't crawl around, cussin' and stealin! You ought to be actin' like the white man stead of tryin' to kill him.

JOHNNY, *tries to rise.* Mama . . .

LIL' T. Sit still Johnny. You'll start bleedin'.

JOHNNY. I'm already bleedin'.*Tries to rise. He gets to his knes and stops, breathing heavily.* LIL' T *starts toward him, then stops.*

MOTHER. Don't try to get up son.

JOHNNY. Just stay away . . . I'll make it . . . I should try to be a white man,

207

huh? White as snow. White as death. Don't you wish I was white Mama. Clean and white like toilet paper.

MOTHER. Johnny . . .

JOHNNY *starts to rise from his knees. He is holding the pistol with one hand and clutching his side with the other.* And daddy. Don't you wish he was white too? Daddy's smarter than I thought he was. He had to decide between bein a white man and bein nothin' and he decided to be nothin!

MOTHER. Sit down Johnny, you're bleedin!

JOHNNY. So I'm bleedin'. Its a blood comin' from a black body shot by a white cop. Or don't that matter?

MOTHER. You were doing wrong.

JOHNNY. The white man decides what's wrong. The white man's right no matter what he's done. Right Mama. I'm wrong from the time I was born. You love the white man. And I kill the white man.

MOTHER. You made yourself into a criminal.

JOHNNY. My name is criminal. I steal and kill. I am black and that is my greatest crime. And I am proud of that crime.

MOTHER. I didn't raise you to be no criminal.

JOHNNY. You raised me to be white, but it didn't work. The white man is my enemy. I wait in alleys to stab him in the back or cut his throat.

MOTHER. But that is heathen.

JOHNNY. I have been a heathen for three days. He has for three hundred years. But I am not guilty. I feel passion when I kill. Love. He don't give a shit for nobody. He kills efficiently. I kill passionately. He is your God and I have sworn to kill God. Can't you understand, Mama? We're gonna build a whole new thing after this. After we destroy the white man. Black people don't want to kill. We want to live. But we have to kill first. We have to kill in order to win.

MOTHER. But you can't win. They've got guns and bombs. *Loud explosion. They all stop—startled.* God, what is it?

JOHNNY. It's the police buses, they got to the police buses.

LIL' T. Blow them motherfuckers away! I'll go see. *He leaves stage right. As soon as he is out of sight a second explosion roars. He rushes back on stage jumping wildly.* Boom! Man, Johnny, you should have seen that scene.

JOHNNY. Are they gettin' to 'em?

LIL' T. Goin' for soul. Gimme five brother. *He extends his open palm to* JOHNNY *who takes his bloody left hand away from his side and slaps* LIL'T's *palm.*

JOHNNY. See. See mama. We're winnin! *Dabbing his side.*

MOTHER, *quietly.* I don't see nothing boy 'cept you lost your mind. There's nothin' I can do with you. *A third explosion.*

LIL'T, *rushes up to* JOHNNY *and spins him around seemingly not remembering that* JOHNNY *has been shot.* Forget her, Johnny. She's too old. JOHNNY *spins around with* LIL' T, *stumbling but trying to acquiesce to the dance.* This is judgment day, and we're the judges. Motherfuck the police. Motherfuck the white man. JOHNNY *is stumbling, holding the gun and clutching his side.*

JOHNNY. And motherfuck daddy and mama and all them house niggers. Death to the house niggers! *A fourth explosion.* JOHNNY *tries to dance and falls to his knees.* It's all over for the white man, huh T?

LIL' T. You damn right. *He picks up his rifle.* I'm going out to the barricade. I ain't gonna stay and wait for that Doctor no more. We got a war to fight.

JOHNNY. Okay, brother, be cool.

LIL' T. *Walks up to* JOHNNY *who is breathing very heavily while his body*

falters. I hope you don't die brother
. . . But you know how death is. It's
over with. Ain't no more after that.
Gimme five. *He extends his hand.*
JOHNNY *slaps it with his last expression of strength.* LIL' T *wipes the blood onto his shirt, and leaves, not looking back.*
JOHNNY. Mama . . .
MOTHER. You ain't my son. I don't
know you. You rejoice when you kill
white people and don't even feel
sympathy for each other when you
dying. That boy did more toward
killin' you than any white man but you
love him.
JOHNNY *falls forward bracing himself by his elbow.*
JOHNNY. Mama . . .
MOTHER. Don't Mama me. I don't
care about that no more. You steal
and kill and curse God. You call yourselves criminals and feel no remorse.
You hide in alleys cuttin' throats. You
blow up buses and burn down property. That boy left here knowin' you'd
die and he was smilin'. I don't understand. He'll probably be dead himself in a few minutes. I just can't see
it. I know you're wrong. The white
people would never do those things.
You must be wrong. I don't understand. But they'll know. They'll understand. They'll make it right. They'll
explain it to me. They'll show me the
way. I trust in them. Ain't no nigger
never been right. *She turns slowly and walks toward the stage left.* And
never will be right.
JOHNNY, *points the gun at her back.*
We're . . . new men, Mama . . . Not
niggers. Black men. *He fires at her back. She stops still, then begins to turn.* JOHNNY *fires again and she stumbles forward and slumps to the stage.* JOHNNY *looks at her for a moment, then falls away. There is a loud explosion followed by gunfire.*

Benedict J. Fernandez, *In Opposition* (Da Capo Press, 1968).

exploding ghetto

Dream Deferred

Langston Hughes

What happens to a dream deferred?

Does it dry up
like a raisin in the sun?
Or fester like a sore—
And then run?
Does it stink like rotten meat?
Or crust and sugar over—
like a syrupy sweet?

Maybe it just sags
like a heavy load.

Or *does it explode?*

Riot Sale or Dollar Psyche Fake Out

Ben Caldwell

> Police Officer
> Voices from crowd
> Time: June 196?
> Week-end
> 10:30 p.m.
> Place: Harlem, 125th St.

Darkened store-fronts tell the area is closed for business, but there are sounds of much activity. Chaotic. People moving, talking, screaming, loudly. Threats and encouragement. The sounds of cars moving rapidly, halting abruptly. Sirens. Flashing, whirring red lights reflect from the faces of an angry, moving black crowd.

The black crowd is moving, in one direction, towards Lenox Ave. The off-on of the lights makes the action seem static. This is the prelude to the expected, overdue, violent confrontation of armed blacks with heavily-armed police forces.

A barricade of police cars and trucks is stretched perpendicular to 125th St., at Lenox Ave. The crowd has done no damage to property this time. This time property damage is not their objective. Blood. White police blood is what they want—in the name of freedom. White police stand between them and that objective. The force of blacks, now acting out this inevitable alternative, converges on the barricades. They are halted by the sight of a police officer who is dressed in a "bullet-proof" fiberglass-shingle outfit. Shots are fired and bullets are seen and heard to ricochet from his "superman" suit. He ignores the fire and addresses the loud angry crowd over a "bull-horn."

POLICE OFFICER. This is to warn you—we are prepared to handle whatever situation arises. We don't want anyone hurt or killed. You people surrender your weapons and go home—it's all over—everything will be all right.
The loud noise of a police helicopter, hovering, drowns all other noises—everyone looks up.
LOUD VOICES FROM THE CROWD. "Liar." "One of you motherfuckas killed a' innicent fifteen year old boy! We're tired of this shit!" "Ain't nobody 'fraid of dying!" "I fought in Vietnam! Let's get this shit on here!"

"We tired of you fuckin' over black men and women and ruinin' our children!" "We tired of all this shit!" "We gon' git all you motherfuckas! Or die trying!" "You can't stop my people now, goddamn!" "We ready to go all the way!"
POLICE OFFICER. I repeat. We don't want to see anyone hurt or killed. You people surrender your weapons and go home. Let your appointed leaders handle your grievances and negotiate your demands.
VOICES FROM CROWD. "Die, whitey! That's the only demand!" "Motherfuck you and your trick deals." "We gon'

First published in *The Drama Review*, Volume 12, Number 4 (T40), Summer 1968 © 1968 by *The Drama Review*. Reprinted by permission. All rights reserved.

tear this motherfuckin' town to pieces!"

POLICE OFFICER. You people leave us no alternative. Captain, call headquarters, put the master plan into action.

The armored knight rushes back behind the barricade. The crowd makes a surge forward, but they are driven back by the unleasing of tear-gas. As the gas lifts a police bus arrives. Its occupants are white men in "civilian" clothing. They are middle-aged, or old-looking, more like the 125th St. jew merchants than detectives. They disembark and confer with the uniformed police "brass," and civilian-clothed city and government officials. Suddenly explosive sounds. Tear-gas missiles are fired among the crowd. It's then that the newly-arrived old-men disperse—escorted, running, past the now disorganized crowd, by heavily-armed officers. The gas-sickened crowd spots this action. The atmosphere vibrates from the resulting bedlam. The air is filled with rock, bottle, brick, missiles. Another van-type police vehicle arrives, its whooping-cough-beast-battle siren wailing, and lights flashing, and parks between the crowd and the barricade, perpendicular to Lenox Ave. Loud threats from the crowd as they regather for another charge. Scattered gunshots. Their fire is rarely returned by the heavily armed, heavily armored, police. Occasionally a black man falls wounded. But the blacks do not retreat. Most of them stand, fearlessly, out in the open. It looks as though the black man has finally, really become himself.

VOICES FROM CROWD. "Come on man!" "Let's end this shit!" "Let's get 'em!"

POLICE OFFICER, *over bull-horn.* I'm warning you people for the last time, surrender your weapons and return home. You're endangering the lives of innocent men, women, and chil. . . . .

His warning is interrupted—answered by a flaming Molotov cocktail. It falls short of its intended target.

LOUD VOICES. "Fuck you, Whitey!, we want our freedom! We ain't waitin' for you to give it!" "I fought in Vietnam, motherfucker, I'm ready to fight right here!"

POLICE OFFICER, *in a most sarcastic tone.* You niggers sure all you want is freedom?

LOUD VOICES. "You hear that?! Come on let's get these m.f.'s now!" *The crowd breaks into a slow charge forward. The newly arrived police vehicle goes into action—action being the opening of the sliding doors on the side facing the crowd. All that is discernible in the vague lighting is a huge muzzle projecting from the black cavernous opening. The blacks break into a faster charge towards the vehicle, hoping that proximity will defeat its purpose. The pace of the charge towards the barricade is frantic. It is halted abruptly, by the thunderous roar of a cannon. SCREAMS. PANIC. In precise synchronization to the sound of the cannon, the lights of all the stores come up. The street is neon-bright. And the cannon's missiles can be seen clearly. MONEY! Money flying high in the air, and in all directions. Paper money. No one has been injured by the blast. MONEY! Apparently millions of dollars! Fives, tens! Twenties! Millions! Again the cannon roars, belching forth more money. Utter chaos as the blacks scatter-scramble for the loot. Those few still bent on revolution are now easily subdued by the police, as their fellow "freedom fighters" now fight among themselves over the loot. The (anti-poverty) cannon roars again. Millions of dollars! Everything! The* black crowd's purpose and direction is lost. Weapons are discarded while they gather money and rush to the open stores to make purchases with their new "freedom." NIGGERS, NOW, they gather money in boxes and run towards home. Niggers stuff their cars full. The laughter of the still-combat-ready cops is heard from behind the barricades, and from the rooftops, and helicopters, over the volume of this bedlam.

POLICE OFFICER'S VOICE. Look at the black bastards go after that money!

Black Phoenix

Blossom Powe

Reprinted by permission of The World Publishing Company from *From the Ashes: Voices of Watts*, edited by Budd Schulberg. An NAL book. Copyright © 1967 by New American Library, Inc.

And so, each day
Became a nightmare . . .
With no place else to run:
Picket fences falling down,
Sidewalks crumbling on the ground,
Hunger crawling all around . . .
Waiting for tomorrow!
And then Time . . . running swiftly,
Stopped to sift through the ashes
With barely visible picks
And such weak hands—
Crying! Brooding! Trying somehow
To create . . . from dreams archaic
From old edicts and empty places!

And so, each day
Became a nightmare . . .
Torture under the sun:
Picket fences falling down,
Sidewalks crumbling on the ground,
Hunger marching all around . . .
Waiting for tomorrow!
And then Time . . . walking quietly,

Stooped to lift the burnt ashes,
Wondering how it could fix
The broken Bands—
Crying! Brooding! Trying somehow
To create . . . a thing prosaic
From kindling sticks and shoeless
    laces!

And so, each day
Became a nightmare . . .
But, what is done is done:
Picket fences falling down,
Sidewalks crumbling on the ground,
Hunger running all around . . .
Waiting for tomorrow!
And now, Time . . . crawling slowly,
Starts to sift through the ashes
Of this black kind of Phoenix
With trembling hands—
Crying! Brooding! Trying somehow
To create . . . a new mosaic
From broken bricks and charcoal
    faces!

From *The Black Man in Search of Power* by the Times News T
Used by permission of the publisher, Thomas Nelson & Sons Ltd., Publis

BURN, BABY, BURN

Marvin E. Jackmon

Reprinted from *Black Fire*, edited by LeRoi Jones and Larry Neal. Wm. Morrow & Co., Inc., New York, N.Y., 1968. Used with permission of Marvin Jackmon and the Ronald Hobbs Literary Agency.

TIRED. SICK AND TIRED.
TIRED OF BEING SICK AND TIRED.
LOST. LOST IN
THE WILDERNESS OF WHITE
    AMERICA.
ARE THE MASSES ASSES?
COOL. SAID THE MASTER
TO THE SLAVE, "NO PROBLEM,
DON'T ROB AND STEAL, I'LL
BE YOUR DRIVING WHEEL."
COOL.
AND HE WHEELED US INTO
    350 YEARS OF BLACK
MADNESS—TO HOG GUTS,
CONKED HAIR, QUO VADIS
BLEACHING CREAM,
UNCLE THOMAS, TO WATTS
TO THE STREETS, TO THE
KILLLLLLLLLLLL. . . . . .
BOOOMMMMM. . . . . .
    2 honkeys gone . .
MOTHERFUCK THE POLICE
AND PARKER'S SISTER TOO.
BURN, BABY, BURN*******
COOK OUTTA SIGHT*******
FINEBURGS, WINEBURGS,
SAFEWAY, NOWAY, BURN . . . . .
BABY, BURN

On Riots

Cy Leslie

Incentive
born in ancient
drum
    battles
obscene values,
archaic faiths.

Exploited blacks
stand grounded
in strong
    belief;
And now must
wreck
the diabolic clock
of moderation.

Used by permission of International Publishers Co., Inc. from *The New Black Poetry*, edited by Clarence Major.

it takes no one to stir up the sociological dynamite that stems from unemployment, bad housing and inferior education already in the ghettoes. this explosively criminal condition has existed for so long, it needs no fuse; it spontaneously combusts from within itself.

215

the WHY of violence

Numbers

Geraldine Morris

300 years of scrubbing floors from dusk to dawn
    And wading through the rubbish just beyond your door.
      3 hundred white and shining floors
        And one dull black one
300 years of steaks prepared three times a day
    And feasting with the hogs—after they've had their fill
      3 thousand fat white pigs
        One lean black one
300 years of foster-parent-motherhood
    Meanwhile producing orphans you must call your own
      A million white and pampered, treasured, kids
        One would-be black one
300 years of perpetuating common wealth
    Sacrificing that one true possession—Life
      3 million white and crooked walking canes
        A twisted black one
300 years of hate and broken promises
    3000 stanzas "We Shall Overcome" with LOVE
      3 million prayers, and pleas—and yet,
Who dares predict how many angry Blacks
    Must gather strength and wit
      And as one force, one final time
        With most effective implements
          "CLEAN HOUSE"

Used by permission of Geraldine Morris.

Letter to a Black Boy

Bob Teague

Dear Adam,

Several nights ago, I wrote you a letter about the ways people have described your daddy. Well, today at the office, a liberal-type Mister Charlie spat a new one in my face—"a sensible Negro."

Like everyone else these days, we were discussing the violent aspects of the Black Revolution, the periodic riots in the ghettos. He wanted to know why "a sensible Negro like you doesn't try to use his influence to calm things down in Brooklyn."

Could a truly sensible Negro ever bring himself to that?

As the late Malcomn X often told us: "You get your freedom by letting your enemy know that you'll do anything to get your freedom. Then you'll get it. It's the only way you'll get it."

I'm afraid that your daddy didn't handle himself too well in that conversation. Don't ask me why. I simply told him that the black people in the Brooklyn ghetto were angry, and for valid reasons; that they probably wouldn't listen to anyone, least of all to someone they could regard as a fat cat; that they would be all too aware that I make more money in television broadcasting in one year than most of them would see in a lifetime.

What I should have told him—what I failed to say like a man—was that I am secretly pleased about the riots, that I'm a bona fide riot fan, that nothing would please the tortured man inside me more than seeing bigger and better riots every day. Not because I believe in violence. But because black violence seems the only form of protest that engages Mister Charlie's attention.

I also failed to say that whenever I watch a film replay of a riot on television, I root for the blacks—even though I know how the battle turns out. Like Mister Charlie when he watches the *Late Late Shows,* and roots for General Custer against the Indians.

May Be Fair . . .
But It Sho' Is Hard

Living in the slums
is a pain in the ass.
Mostly dirt and concrete—
Very little grass.
Come home late—
No place to park,
Just like Noah
Up in that Ark.

Rats play tag
all through the night,
Catch me sleep
And take a bite
Out of a toe,
Or arm or ham—
Daley's poison's
not worth a damn.

Rats tote land deeds
in their vests,
Some smoke Hedges'
Cigarettes.
It's obvious why
Rent's so high
On these slummy flats—
We paying extra
For the rats.

I don't forget
the roaches man!
They strut around
Like they own the land!
Bold as Batman
high on pot!
As soon walk off
With your plate
as not.

Sometimes . . .
Don't wait 'til you
through cookin'—
They liftin' up
The lids and lookin'—
  to see if the menu
  meets their taste,

Ghetto Roaches
are the super race!
Stone gourmets!
Our roaches are!—
They'll eat soul food,
but prefer caviar,
Or filet Mignon,
Or other high-
falutin' stuff,
But the thing
that's really tough
'Bout living in
the slums is COPS!

Really lovin' it
when they stops
you driving down
some busy drive
Then here they come
with that M-F-in' jive . . .

"Let me see your license Boy!"
"O.K. Up against the car!"
Then they spread you wide,
And pat you down,
With your friends
and neighbors standing 'round.
They check your trunk,
Glove compartment,
While you nearly die
of embarrassment.
Then they send you
On your way—
Look displeased—
You'll hear them say,

"On your way Boy!"
Be quick with it!
Shut your mouth!
You want a ticket?!
Don't have to tell
you why you're stopped,
See this badge?—
That means we're cops!
No you ain't

Committed no crime—
You boys get checked
From time to time,
Just'a keep you
All in line.
Everybody knows
You can't be trusted—
So now and then
"You're routinely busted."

And one more thing
that gripes my ass
is all this God-damn
   BROKEN GLASS!
Busted bottles—
Ev'ry where I look.
But has got me
Really shook
Is bottles are
Worth two whole cents
But kids from homes
that can't pay rents
Throw them just
To hear them shatter,
Then beg for carfare,
What's the matter?
with kids in the
slums today?
When I was young
It wasn't that way.
Bottles were money!
Cold hard cash!
And all the gang
worked hard to stash
a secret little
pile of glass
We catch you stealin'
We'd kick your ass!
Sat'dy morning—

to the store,
With a wagon
load or more.

Another thing's
the food we buy.

I get so mad
I damn near cry—
Seeing picked-over garbage
Brought here for us.
It's enough to make
A Boy Scout cuss.
Third-Class food
at first class prices
left after white folks
buys the nicest.
Leftovers sent
for us to buy,—
And we do—
But I can't see why.

Meat so tough—
   Only acid cuts it.
But with Accent and Adolph's
   We thrive off of it.
Using plenty of gravy—
   to slide it down—
While white folks on
   their side of town
Are laughing at
   we silly clowns.
Eating stuff
   that they've rejected—

But . . .
That's life in the slums—
   Until we wreck it.

from "The Wonder Is There Have Been So Few Riots"

Kenneth Clark

It is one measure of the depth and insidiousness of American racism that the nation ignores the rage of the rejected—until it explodes in Watts or Harlem. The wonder is that there have been so few riots, that Negroes generally are law-abiding in a world where the law itself has seemed an enemy.

To call for reason and moderation, to charge rioters with blocking the momentum of the civil-rights movement, to punish rioters by threatening withdrawal of white support for civil rights may indeed ease the fears of whites and restore confidence that a firm stern hand is enforcing order.

But the rejected Negro in the ghetto is deaf to such moral appeals. They only reinforce his despair that whites do not consider equal rights for Negroes to be their due as human beings and American citizens but as rewards to be given for good behavior, to be withheld for misbehavior. The difficulty which the average American of goodwill—white or Negro—has in seeing this as a form of racist condescension is another disturbing symptom of the complexities of racism in the United States.

It is not possible for even the most responsible Negro leaders to control the Negro masses once pent-up anger and total despair are unleashed by a thoughtless or brutal act. The prisoners of the ghetto riot without reason, without organization and without leadership, as this is generally understood. The rioting is in itself a repudiation of leadership. It is the expresson of the anarchy of the profoundly alienated.

In a deeper sense such anarchy could even be a subconscious or conscious invitation to self-destruction. At the height of the Harlem riots of 1964, young Negroes could be heard to say, "If I don't get killed tonight, I'll come back tomorrow." There is evidence these outbreaks are suicidal, reflecting the ultimate in self-negation, self-rejection and hopelessness.

It was the Negro ghetto in Los Angeles which Negroes looted and burned, not the white community. When white firemen tried to enter the ghetto, they were barred by Negro snipers. Many looters did not take the trouble to avoid injury, and many were badly cut in the looting orgy. So one cannot help but wonder whether a desire for self-destruction was not a subconscious factor. Of the 36 people killed in Los Angeles riot, 33 were Negroes, killed in the campaign to restore law and order. The fact of their deaths—the senseless deaths of human beings—has been obscured by our respectable middle-class preoccupation with the wanton destruction of property, the vandalism and the looting.

From *The New York Times Magazine*, September 5, 1965. © 1965 by The New York Times Company. Reprinted in part by permission of the publisher and Kenneth B. Clark.

Appeals to reason are understandable; they reflect the sense of responsibility of Governmental and civil-rights leaders. But they certainly do not take into account the fact that one cannot expect individuals who have been systematically excluded from the privileges of middle-class life to view themselves as middle-class or to behave in terms of middle-class values. Those who despair in the ghetto follow their own laws—generally the laws of unreason. And though these laws are not in themselves moral, they have moral consequences and moral causes.

The inmates of the ghetto have no realistic stake in respecting property because in a basic sense they do not possess it. They are possessed by it. Property is, rather, an instrument for perpetuation of their own exploitation. Stores in the ghetto—which they rarely own—overcharge for inferior goods. They may obtain the symbols of America's vaunted high standard of living— radios, TV's, washing machines, refrigerators—but usually only through usurious carrying costs, one more symbol of the pattern of material exploitation. They do not respect property because property is almost invariably used to degrade them.

James Bryant Conant and others have warned America it is no longer possible to confine hundreds of thousands of undereducated, underemployed, purposeless young people and adults in an affluent America without storing up social dynamite. The dark ghettoes now represent a nuclear stock pile which can annihilate the very foundations of America. And if, as a minority, desperate Negroes are not able to "win over" the majority, they can nevertheless effectively undermine what they cannot win.

A small minority of Negroes can do this. Such warnings are generally ignored during the interludes of apparent quiescence and tend to be violently rejected, particularly when they come from whites, at the time of a Negro revolt.

When Senator Robert Kennedy incisively observed, after Watts, "There is no point in telling Negroes to observe the law. . . . It has almost always been used against [them]," it was described by an individual who took the trouble to write a letter to *The New York Times* as an irresponsible incitement to violence. The bedeviling fact remains, however, that as long as institutionalized forms of American racism persist, violent eruptions will continue to occur in the Negro ghettoes. As Senator Kennedy warned: "All these places —Harlem, Watts, South Side—are riots waiting to happen."

While the riots cannot be understood by attempts to excuse them, neither can they be understood by deploring them—especially by deploring them according to a double standard of social morality. For while the lawlessness of white segregationists and rebellious Negroes are expressions of deep frustrations and chronic racism, the lawlessness of Negroes is usually considered a reflection on all Negroes and countered by the full force of police and other governmental authority, but the lawlessness of whites is seen as the primitive reactions of a small group of unstable individuals and is frequently ignored by the police—when they are not themselves accessories. Moreover, rarely do the leaders of a white community in which white violence occurs publicly condemn even the known perpetrators, while almost invariably national and local Negro leaders are required to condemn the mob violence of Negroes.

As long as these double standards of social morality prevail, they reflect the forms of accepted racism which are the embers of potential violence on the part of both Negroes and whites. And it should be obvious also, although it does not appear to be, that the violence of the Negro is the violence of the oppressed while the violence of white segregationists seeks to maintain oppression.

It is significant that the recent eruptions in Negro communities have not occurred in areas dominated by more flagrant forms of racism, by the Klan and the other institutions of Southern bigotry. They have occurred precisely in those communities where whites have prided themselves on their liberal approach to matters of race and in those states having strong laws prescribing equal opportunity, fair employment and allegedly open housing.

.   .   .

It may well be that the channeling of energies of Negroes in Southern communities toward eliminating the more vicious and obvious signs of racism precludes temporarily the dissipation of energy in random violence. The Northern Negro is clearly not suffering from a lack of laws. But he is suffering —rejected, segregated, discriminated against in employment, in housing, his children subjugated in *de facto* segregated and inferior schools in spite of a plethora of laws that imply the contrary.

He has been told of great progress in civil rights during the past 10 years and proof of this progress is offered in terms of Supreme Court decisions and civil-rights legislation and firm Presidential commitment. But he sees no positive changes in his day-to-day life. The very verbalizations of progress contribute to his frustration and rage. He is suffering from a pervasive, insensitive and at times self-righteous form of American racism that does not understand the depth of his need.

Not the civil-rights leaders who urge him to demonstrate, but the whites who urge him not to "in the light of present progress" contribute to the anger which explodes in sudden fury. He is told by liberal whites *they* contribute to civil-rights causes, *they* marched to Washington and journeyed to Selma and Montgomery to demonstrate their commitment to racial justice and equality.

But Negroes see only the continuing decay of their homes, many of them owned by liberal whites. He sees he does not own any of the means of production, distribution and sale of goods he must purchase to live. He sees his children subjected to criminally inefficient education in public schools they are required to attend, and which are often administered and staffed by liberal whites. He sees liberal labor unions which either exclude him, accept him in token numbers or, even when they do accept him en masse, exclude him from leadership or policy-making roles.

And he sees that persistent protest in the face of racism which dominates his life and shackles him within the ghetto may be interpreted by his white friends as a sign of his insatiability, his irrationality and, above all, of his ingratitude. And because this interpretation comes from his friends and allies it is much harder to take psychologically than the clear-cut bigotry of open segregationists.

It is precisely at this point in the development of race relations that the complexities, depth and intensity of American racism reveal themselves with excruciating clarity. At this point regional differences disappear. The greatest danger is an intensification of racism leading to the polarization of America into white and black. "What do they *want*?" the white man asks. "Don't they know they hurt their own cause?" "Get Whitey," cries the Negro. "Burn, baby, burn." At this point concerned whites and Negroes are required to face the extent of personal damage which racism has inflicted on both.

It will require from whites more than financial contributions to civil rights agencies, more than mere verbal and intellectual support for the cause of justice. It will require compassion, willingness to accept hostility and increased resolve to go about the common business, the transformation and strengthening of our society toward the point where race and color are no longer relevant in discussing the opportunities, rights and responsibilities of Americans.

Negroes, too, are confronted with difficult challenges in the present stage of the civil rights struggle. The bitterness and rage whch formed the basis for the protests against flagrant racial injustices must somehow be channeled into constructive, nondramatic programs required to translate court decisions, legislation and growing political power into actual changes in the living conditions of the masses of Negroes. Some ways must be found whereby Negro leadership and Negro organizations can redirect the volatile emotions of Negroes away from wasteful, sporadic outbursts and toward self-help and constructive social action. The need for candid communication between middle-class Negroes and the Negro masses is as imperative as the need for painful honesty and cooperation between Negroes and whites.

These demands upon whites and Negroes will not be easy to meet since it is difficult, if not impossible, for anyone growing up in America to escape some form of racist contamination. And a most disturbing fact is the tendency of racism to perpetuate itself, to resist even the most stark imperatives for change. This is the contemporary crisis in race relations which Americans must somehow find the strength to face and solve. Otherwise we will remain the victims of capricious and destructive racial animosities and riots.

The key danger is the possibility that America has permitted the cancer of racism to spread so far that present available remedies can be only palliative. One must, however, continue to believe and act in the assumption that the disease is remediable.

.   .   .

It would be unrealistic, of course, to expect the masses of whites and Negroes who have grown up in an essentially racist society suddenly to love one another. Fortunately, love is not a prerequisite for the social reorganization now demanded. Love has not been necessary to create workable living arrangements among other ethnic groups in our society. It is no more relevant to ask Negroes and whites to love each other than to ask Italians and Irish to do the same as a prerequisite for social peace and justice.

Nevertheless, real changes in the predicament of previously rejected

Negroes—changes compatible with a stable and decent society—must be made, and soon.

The Negro must be included within the economy at all levels of employment, thereby providing the basis for a sound family life and an opportunity to have an actual stake in American business and property.

The social organization of our educational system must be transformed so Negroes can be taught in schools which do not reinforce their feeling of inferiority. The reorganization, improvement and integration of our public schools is also necessary in order to re-educate white children and prepare them to live in the present and future world of racial diversity.

The conditions under which Negroes live must be improved—bad housing, infant mortality and disease, delinquency, drug addiction must be drastically reduced.

Until these minimum goals are achieved, Americans must accept the fact that we cannot expect to maintain racial ghettoes without paying a high price. If it is possible for Americans to carry out realistic programs to change the lives of human beings now confined within their ghettoes, the ghetto will be destroyed rationally, by plan, and not by random self-destructive forces. Only then will American society not remain at the mercy of primitive, frightening, irrational attempts by prisoners in the ghetto to destroy their own prison.

Will There Be Another Riot in Watts?

Harry Dolan

No, not as the riot of last summer, not as a spontaneous, frustrated explosive reaction resulting in death indiscriminately. No, this will not happen again, for "the niggers and criminal elements" that fought and died learned their lessons well. They were given well. It is related at night in the quiet of dimly lit garages:

"Man it was close, I mean I was that close to death—let's face it—Charlie can throw too much power for open warfare. We gotta do like those French were doing when we landed over there . . . the underground."

UNDERGROUND has connotations of deliberately planned moves involving the risk of life, the almost ultimate assurance of death.

Private dance-parties where no one dances to the continuous playing of the record that reproduced the sound of light laughter, and conversation. Church prayer-meetings with no one on their knees, where no one looks at the Bible, held in reverent hands, but at cold blue steel in hands burning with black fury.

Maps that are covered with pencil marks indicating long-forgotten entrances and rust-covered locks that open silently and iron gates that move on well-oiled hinges; stumbling winos who drink colored water and practice runs past storage tanks that could spray flaming oil miles in all directions; locksmiths who make two keys.

Strangers in ominous garb that walk among us and talk of death as their great reward.

No, there is no shining, wildly bubbling black kettle about to explode, but there is a horrible coldness toward any attempt at compromise. There is open contempt for the peacemakers, and they are warned; you go white, black man, you go first, even before the white man, because you could have told him, you should have made him understand, but you only nodded and smiled and ate the crumbs that he could not hold.

So at this moment it goes on, the white man going on blithely secure in his armies, committing the same, the very same acts, and as he does, these acts are not forgotten or forgiven but are used as powder to load the human guns, and fill the flaming souls until the people are saturated with death and welcome it.

And then—and then, God help us, for a man blind with injustice does not value worldly goods, for themselves alone, and so he will destroy and destroy until the ache in his soul has burned out. . . . No, there will be no riot in Watts; possibly, just possibly, Armageddon.

ARMAGEDDON...next time

United Press International.

racism

IDEO

black (blăk), adj. [AS. blæc] 1. Destitute of or so dark as... reflecting it; devoid of color or so dark...

racism

LOGY

On Separation

Malcolm X

... if certain groups think that through integration they are going to get freedom, justice, equality and human dignity, then well and good, we will go along with the integrationists. But if integration is not going to return human dignity to dark mankind, then integration is not the solution to the problem. And oft times we make the mistake of confusing the objective with the means by which the objective is to be obtained. It is not integration that Negroes in America want, it is human dignity. They want to be recognized as human beings. And if integration is going to bring us recognition as human beings, then we will integrate. But if integration is not going to bring us recognition as human beings, then integration "out the window," and we have to find another means or method and try that to get our objectives reached.

... All we say is that South Africa preaches what it practices and practices what it preaches; America preaches one thing and practices another. And we don't want to integrate with hypocrites who preach one thing and practice another.

The good point in all of this is that there is an awakening going on among whites in America today, and this awakening is manifested in this way: two years ago you didn't know that there were black people in this country who didn't want to integrate with you; two years ago the white public had been brainwashed into thinking that every black man in this

Reprinted by permission of Cornell University from *Dialogue,* 1962.

country wanted to force his way into your community, force his way into your schools, or force his way into your factories; two years ago you thought that all you would have to do is give us a little token integration and the race problem would be solved. Why? Because the people in the black community who didn't want integration were never given a voice, were never given a platform, were never given an opportunity to shout out the fact that integration would never solve the problem. And it has only been during the past year that the white public has begun to realize that the problem will never be solved unless a solution is devised acceptable to the black masses, as well as the black bourgeoisie—the upper class or middle class Negro. And when the whites began to realize that these integration-minded Negroes were in the minority, rather than in the majority, then they began to offer an open forum and give those who want separation an opportunity to speak their mind too.

We who are black in the black belt, or black community, or black neighborhood can easily see that our people who settle for integration are usually the middle-class so-called Negroes, who are in the minority. Why? Because they have confidence in the white man; they have absolute confidence that you will change. They believe that they can change you, they believe that there is still hope in the American dream. But what to them is an American dream to us is an American nightmare, and we don't think that it is possible for the American white man in sincerity to take the action necessary to correct the unjust conditions that 20 million black people here are made to suffer morning, noon, and night. And because we don't have any hope or confidence or faith in the American white man's ability to bring about a change in the injustices that exist, instead of asking or seeking to integrate into the American society we want to face the facts of the problem the way they are, and separate ourselves. And in separating ourselves this doesn't mean that we are anti-white or anti-American, or anti-anything. We feel that if integration all these years hasn't solved the problem yet, then we want to try something new, something different and something that is in accord with the conditions as they actually exist. . . .

. . . The method by which the honorable Elijah Muhammad is straightening out our problem is not teaching us to force ourselves into your society, or force ourselves even into your political, economic or any phase of your society, but he teaches us that the best way to solve this problem is for complete separation. He says that since the black man here in America is actually the property that was stolen from the East by the American white man, since you have awakened today and realized that this is what we are, we should be separated from you, and your government should ship us back from where we came from, not at our expense, because we didn't pay to come here. We were brought here in chains. So the honorable Elijah Muhammad and the Muslims who follow him, we want to go back to our own people. We want to be returned to our own people.

. . . But in teaching this among our people and the masses of black people in this country, we discover that the American government is the foremost agency in opposing any move by any large number of black people to leave here and go back among our own kind. The honorable Elijah Muhammad's words and work is harassed daily by the F.B.I. and every other government agency which use various tactics to make the so-called Negroes in every community think that we are all about to be rounded up, and they will be rounded up too if they will listen to Mr. Muhammad; but what the American government has failed to realize, the best way to open up a black man's head today and make him listen to another black man is to speak against that black man. But when you begin to pat a black man on the back, no black man in his right mind will trust that black man any longer. And it is because of this hostility on the part of the government toward our leaving here that the honorable Elijah Muhammad says then, if the American white man or the American government doesn't want us to leave, and the government has proven its inability to bring about integration or give us freedom, justice and equality on a basis, equally mixed up with white people, then what are we going to do? If the government doesn't want us to go back among our own people, or to our own people, and at the same time the government has proven its inability to give us justice, the honorable Elijah Muhammad says if you don't want us to go and we can't stay here and live in peace together, then the best solution is separation. And this is what he means when he says that some of the territory here should be set aside, and let our people go off to ourselves and try and solve our own problem.

Some of you may say, Well, why should you give us part of this country? The honorable Elijah Muhammad says that for 400 years we contributed our slave labor to make the country what it is. If you were to take the individual salary or allowances of each person in this audience it would amount to nothing individually, but when you take it collectively all in one pot you have a heavy load. Just the weekly wage. And if you realize that from anybody who could collect all of the wages from the persons in this audience right here for one month, why they would be so wealthy they couldn't walk. And if you see that, then you can imagine the result of millions of black people working for nothing for 310 years. And that is the contribution that we made to America. Not Jackie Robinson, not Marian Anderson, not George Washington Carver, that's not our contribution; our contribution to American society is 310 years of free slave labor for which we have not been paid one dime. We who are Muslims, followers of the honorable Elijah Muhammad, don't think that an integrated cup of coffee is sufficient payment for 310 years of slave labor.

Integration

Richard J. Margolis

It happens every day
always the same way,
you can depend on it:
the walkers get to school first;
they play outside before the bell.

At eight fifty-six—have no doubt—
the new bus from over the canal
appears, and all the children shout,
"The colored bus is here."

Garvey

Tom Dent

Garvey,
You old crazy
Fat greasy
Plume-helmet
Dream-infested
Jamacian
Son-of-a-bitch,
You left a
Legacy
Of blk & green flags
Yearning to fly high
In the
Cool of morning breeze.
Garvey,
All yr rotten
Ships
Still haven't sunk.
There must have been something
Beautiful
In yr fiery eyes
That
Grows larger
Each
Day
Of the rising
Sun.
Up, you mighty flag.

Kush (tom dent)/BLKARTSOUTH.

Courtesy *The News*, New York's Picture
Newspaper.

Organize!

Marcus Garvey

... Beat the Negro, brutalize the Negro, kill the Negro, burn the Negro, imprison the Negro, scoff at the Negro, deride the Negro, it may come back to you one of these fine days, because the supreme destiny of man is in the hands of God. God is no respecter of persons, whether that person be white, yellow or black. Today the one race is up, tomorrow it has fallen; today the Negro seems to be the footstool of the other races and nations of the world; tomorrow the Negro may occupy the highest rung of the great human ladder.

But, when we come to consider the history of man, was not the Negro a power, was he not great once? Yes, honest students of history can recall the day when Egypt, Ethiopia and Timbuctoo towered in their civilizations, towered above Europe, towered above Asia. When Europe was inhabited by a race of cannibals, a race of savages, naked men, heathens and pagans, Africa was peopled with a race of cultured black men, who were masters in art, science and literature; men who were cultured and refined; men who, it was said, were like the gods. Even the great poets of old sang in beautiful sonnets of the delight it afforded the gods to be in companionship with the Ethiopians. Why, then, should we lose hope? Black men, you were once great; you shall be great again. Lose not courage, lose not faith, go forward. The thing to do is to get organized; keep separated and you will be exploited, you will be robbed, you will be killed. Get organized, and you will compel the world to respect you. If the world fails to give you consideration, because you are black men, because you are Negroes, four hundred millions of you shall, through organization, shake the pillars of the universe and bring down creation, even as Sampson brought down the temple upon his head and upon the heads of the Philistines.

From Amy Jacques-Garvey, editor, *Philosophy and Opinions of Marcus Garvey,* Arno Press Edition, 1968. Reprinted by permission.

Yacub's History

Malcolm X

Elijah Muhammad teaches his followers that first, the moon separated from the earth. Then, the first humans, Original Man, were a black people. They founded the Holy City Mecca.

Among this black race were twenty-four wise scientists. One of the scientists, at odds with the rest, created the especially strong black tribe of Shabazz, from which America's Negroes, so-called, descend.

About sixty-six hundred years ago, when seventy percent of the people were satisfied, and thirty percent were dissatisfied, among the dissatisfied was born a "Mr. Yacub." He was born to create trouble, to break the peace, and to kill. His head was unusually large. When he was four years old, he began school. At the age of eighteen, Yacub had finished all of his nation's colleges and universities. He was known as "the big-head scientist." Among many other things, he had learned how to breed races scientifically.

This big-head scientist, Mr. Yacub, began preaching in the streets of Mecca, making such hosts of converts that the authorities, increasingly concerned, finally exiled him with 59,999 followers to the island of Patmos —described in the Bible as the island where John received the message contained in Revelations in the New Testament.

Though he was a black man, Mr. Yacub, embittered toward Allah now, decided, as revenge, to create upon the earth a devil race—a bleached-out, white race of people.

From his studies, the big-head scientist knew that black men contained two germs, black and brown. He knew that the brown germ stayed dormant, as being the lighter of the two germs, it was the weaker. Mr. Yacub, to upset the law of nature, conceived the idea of employing what we today know as the recessive genes structure, to separate from each other the two germs, black and brown, and then grafting the brown germ to progressively lighter, weaker stages. The humans resulting, he knew, would be as they became lighter, and weaker, progressively also more susceptible to wickedness and evil. And in this way finally he would achieve the intended bleached-out white race of devils.

He knew that it would take him several total color-change stages to get from black to white. Mr. Yacub began his work by setting up a eugenics law on the island of Patmos.

Among Mr. Yacub's 59,999 all-black followers, every third or so child that was born would show some trace of brown. As these became adult, only brown and brown, were permitted to marry. As their children were born, Mr. Yacub's law dictated that, if a black child, the attending nurse or mid-wife, should stick a needle into its brain and give the body to cremators.

Excerpt from *Satan* from *The Autobiography of Malcolm X*. Reprinted by permission of Grove Press, Inc. Copyright © 1964 by Alex Haley & Malcolm X. Copyright © 1965 by Alex Haley & Betty Shabazz.

The mothers were told it had been an "angel baby," which had gone to heaven, to prepare a place for her.

But a brown child's mother was told to take very good care of it.

Others, assistants, were trained by Mr. Yacub to continue his objective. Mr. Yacub, when he died on the island at the age of one hundred and fifty-two, had left laws, and rules, for them to follow. According to the teachings of Mr. Elijah Muhammad, Mr. Yacub, except in his mind, never saw the bleached-out devil race that his procedures and laws and rules created.

A two-hundred-year span was needed to eliminate on the island of Patmos all of the black people—until only brown people remained.

The next two hundred years were needed to create from the brown race the red race—with no more browns left on the island.

In another two hundred years, from the red race was created the yellow race.

Two hundred years later—the white race had at last been created.

On the island of Patmos was nothing but these blond, pale-skinned, cold-blue-eyed devils—savages, nude and shameless; hairy, like animals, they walked on all fours and they lived in trees.

Six hundred more years passed before this race of people returned to the mainland, among the natural black people.

Mr. Elijah Muhammad teaches his followers that within six months time, through telling lies that set the black men fighting among each other, this devil race had turned what had been a peaceful heaven on earth into a hell torn by quarreling and fighting.

But finally the original black people recognized that their sudden troubles stemmed from this devil white race that Mr. Yacub had made. They rounded them up, put them in chains. With little aprons to cover their nakedness, this devil race was marched off across the Arabian desert to the caves of Europe.

The lambskin and the cable-tow used in Masonry today are symbolic of how the nakedness of the white man was covered when he was chained and driven across the hot sand.

Mr. Elijah Muhammad further teaches that the white devil race in Europe's caves was savage. The animals tried to kill him. He climbed trees outside his cave, made clubs, trying to protect his family from the wild beasts outside trying to get in.

When this devil race had spent two thousand years in the caves, Allah raised up Moses to civilize them, and bring them out of the caves. It was written that this devil white race would rule the world for six thousand years.

The Books of Moses are missing. That's why it is not known that he was in the caves.

When Moses arrived, the first of these devils to accept his teachings, the first he led out, were those we call today the Jews.

According to the teachings of this "Yacub's History," when the Bible says "Moses lifted up the serpent in the wilderness," that serpent is symbolic of the devil white race Moses lifted up out of the caves of Europe, teaching them civilization.

It was written that after Yacub's bleached white race had ruled the world for six thousand years—down to our time—the black original race would give birth to one whose wisdom, knowledge, and power would be infinite.

It was written that some of the original black people should be brought as slaves to North America—to learn to better understand, at first hand, the white devil's true nature, in modern times.

Elijah Muhammad teaches that the greatest and mightiest God who appeared on the earth was Master W. D. Fard. He came from the East to the West, appearing in North America at a time when the history and the prophecy that is written was coming to realization, as the non-white people all over the world began to rise, and as the devil white civilization, condemned by Allah, was, through its devilish nature, destroying itself.

Master W. D. Fard was half black and half white. He was made in this way to enable him to be accepted by the black people in America, and to lead them, while at the same time he was enabled to move undiscovered among the white people, so that he could understand and judge the enemy of the blacks.

Master W. D. Fard, in 1931, posing as a seller of silks, met, in Detroit, Michigan, Elijah Muhammad. Master W. D. Fard gave to Elijah Muhammad Allah's message, and Allah's divine guidance, to save the Lost-Found Nation of Islam, the so-called Negroes, here in "this wilderness of North America."*

* Malcolm X's comment on the tale of Yacub: "I was to learn later that Elijah Muhammad's tales . . . infuriated the Muslims of the East. While at Mecca, I reminded them that it was their fault, since they themselves hadn't done enough to make real Islam known in the West. Their silence left a vacuum into which any religious faker could step and mislead our people."

Booker T. Washington on Education

From *Up from Slavery.*

Of one thing I felt more strongly convinced than ever, after spending this month in seeing the actual life of the coloured people, and that was that, in order to lift them up, something must be done more than merely to imitate New England education as it then existed. I saw more clearly than ever the wisdom of the system which General Armstrong had inaugurated at Hampton. To take the children of such people as I had been among for a month, and each day give them a few hours of mere book education, I felt would be almost a waste of time.

After consultation with the citizens of Tuskegee, I set July 4, 1881, as the day for the opening of the school in the little shanty and church which had been secured for its accommodation. The white people, as well as the coloured, were greatly interested in the starting of the new school, and the opening day was looked forward to with much earnest discussion. There were not a few white people in the vicinity of Tuskegee who looked with some disfavour upon the project. They questioned its value to the coloured people, and had a fear that it might result in bringing about trouble between the races. Some had the feeling that in proportion as the Negro received education, in the same proportion would his value decrease as an economic factor in the state. These people feared the result of education would be that the Negroes would leave the farms, and that it would be difficult to secure them for domestic service.

The white people who questioned the wisdom of starting this new school had in their minds pictures of what was called an educated Negro, with a high hat, imitation gold eye-glasses, a showy walking-stick, kid gloves, fancy boots, and what not—in a word, a man who was determined to live by his wits. It was difficult for these people to see how education would produce any other kind of a coloured man.

Miss Davidson and I began consulting as to the future of the school from the first. The students were making progress in learning books and in developing their minds; but it became apparent at once that, if we were to make any permanent impression upon those who had come to us for training, we must do something besides teach them mere books.

In our industrial teaching we keep three things in mind: first, that the student shall be so educated that he shall be enabled to meet conditions as they exist *now*, in the part of the South where he lives—in a word, to be able to do the thing which the world wants done; second, that every student who graduates from the school shall have enough skill, coupled with intelligence and moral character, to enable him to make a living for himself and others; third, to send every graduate out feeling and knowing that labour is dignified and beautiful—to make each one love labour instead of trying to escape it. In addition to the agricultural training which we give to young men, and the training given to our girls in all the usual domestic employments, we now train a number of girls in agriculture each year. These girls are taught gardening, fruit-growing, dairying, bee-culture, and poultry-raising.

Booker T. Washington on Education

From Up from Slavery.

Of one thing I felt more strongly convinced than ever, after spending this month in seeing the actual life of the coloured people, and that was that, in order to lift them up, something must be done more than merely to imitate New England education as it then existed. I saw more clearly than ever the wisdom of the system which General Armstrong had inaugurated at Hampton. To take the children of such people as I had been among for a month, and each day give them a few hours of mere book education, I felt would be almost a waste of time.

After consultation with the citizens of Tuskegee, I set July 4, 1881, as the

Booker T. and W. E. B.

(Booker T. Washington and W. E. B. Du Bois)

Dudley Randall

"It seems to me," said Booker T.,
"It shows a mighty lot of cheek
To study chemistry and Greek
When Mr. Charley needs a hand
To hoe the cotton on his land,
And when Miss Ann looks for a cook,
Why stick your nose inside a book?"

"I don't agree," said W. E. B.
"If I should have the drive to seek
Knowledge of chemistry or Greek,
I'll do it. Charles and Miss can look
Another place for hand or cook.
Some men rejoice in skill of hand,
And some in cultivating land,
But there are others who maintain
The right to cultivate the brain."

"It seems to me," said Booker T.,
"That all you folks have missed the
        boat
Who shout about the right to vote,
And spend vain days and sleepless
        nights
In uproar over civil rights.
Just keep your mouths shut, do not
        grouse,
But work, and save, and buy a house."

"I don't agree," said W. E. B.
"For what can property avail
If dignity and justice fail?
Unless you help to make the laws,
They'll steal your house with trumped-
        up clause.
A rope's as tight, a fire as hot,
No matter how much cash you've got.
Speak soft, and try your little plan,
But as for me, I'll be a man."

"It seems to me," said Booker T.—

"I don't agree,"
Said W. E. B.

integration
integration

On Integration

James Farmer

. . . The masses of Negroes are through putting up with segregation; they are tired of it. They are tired of being pushed around in a democracy which fails to practice what it preaches. The Negro students of the South who have read the Constitution, and studied it, have read the amendments to the Constitution, and know the rights that are supposed to be theirs—they are coming to the point where they themselves want to do something about achieving these rights, not depend on somebody else. . . .

. . . Who will say that lunch counters, which are scattered all over the country are not important? Are we not to travel? Picket lines and boycotts brought Woolworth's to its knees. In its annual report of last year, Woolworth's indicated that profits had dropped and one reason for the drop was the nationwide boycott in which many Northern students, including Cornellians participated. The picketing and the nationwide demonstrations are the reason that the walls came down in the south, because people were in motion with their own bodies marching with picket signs, sitting in, boycotting, withholding their patronage. In Savannah, Georgia, there was a boycott, in which ninety-nine percent of the Negroes participated. They stayed out of the stores. They registered to vote. The store owners then got together and said, "We want to sit down and talk; gentlemen, you have proved your point. You have proved that you can control Negroes' purchasing power and that you can control their votes. We need no more proof, we are ready to hire the people that you send." Negroes are hired in those stores now as a result of this community-wide campaign. In Lexington, Kentucky, the theatres were opened up by CORE as a result of picketing and

Reprinted by permission of Cornell University from *Dialogue,* 1962.

boycotting. Some of the theatres refused to admit Negroes, others would let Negroes sit up in the balcony. They boycotted that one, picketed the others. In a short period of time, the theatre owners sat down to negotiate. All of the theatres there are open now. Using the same technique, they provided scores of jobs in department stores, grocery stores, and more recently as city bus drivers. . . .

. . . What are our objectives; segregation, separation? Absolutely not! The disease and the evils that we have pointed to in our American culture have grown out of segregation and its partner, prejudice. We are for integration, which is the repudiation of the evil of segregation. It is a rejection of the racist theories of DeGobineau, Lothrop Stoddard and all the others. It matters not whether they say that whites are superior to Negroes and Negroes are inferior, or if they reverse the coin and say that Negroes are superior and whites are inferior. The theory is just as wrong, just as much a defiance of history. We reject those theories. We are working for the right of Negroes to enter all fields of activity in American life. To enter business if they choose, to enter the professions, to enter the sciences, to enter the arts, to enter the academic world. To be workers, to be laborers if they choose. Our objective is to have each individual accepted on the basis of his individual merit and not on the basis of his color. On the basis of what he is worth himself. . . .

. . . We are seeking an open society, an open society of freedom where people will be accepted for what they are worth, will be able to contribute fully to the total culture and the total life of the nation.

Now we know the disease, we know what is wrong with America, we know now that the CORE position is in trying to right it. We must do it in interracial groups because we do not think it is possible to fight against caste in a vehicle which in itself is a representative of caste. We know that the students are still sitting in, they are still fighting for freedom. What we want Mr. X, the representative of the Black Muslims and Elijah Muhammad, to tell us today, is what his program is, what he proposes to do about killing this disease. We know the disease, physician, what is your cure? What is your program and how do you hope to bring it into effect? How will you achieve it? It is not enough to tell us that it may be a program of a black state. The Communists had such a program in the thirties and part of the forties, and they dropped it before the fifties as being impractical. So we are not only interested in the terminology. We need to have it spelled out, if we are being asked to follow it, to believe in it, what does it mean? Is it a separate Negro society in each city? As a Harlem, a South Side Chicago? Is it a separate state in one part of the country? Is is a separate nation in Africa, or elsewhere? Then we need to know how is it to be achieved. I assume that before a large part of land could be granted to Negroes or to Jews or to anybody else in the country it would have to be approved by the Senate of the United States.

You must tell us, Mr. X, if you seriously think that the Senate of the United States which has refused or failed for all these years to pass a strong Civil Rights Bill, you must tell us if you really think that this Senate is going to give us, to give you, a black state. I am sure that Senator Eastland would so vote, but the land that he would give us would probably be in the bottom of the sea. After seeing Alabama and Mississippi, if the power were mine, I would give you those states, but the power is not mine, I do not vote in the Senate. Tell us how you expect to achieve this separate black state.

Now it is not enough for us to know that you believe in black businesses, all of us believe that all Americans who wish to go into business, should go into business. We must know, we need to know, if we are to appraise your program, the kind of businesses, how they are to be established; will we have a General Motors, a General Electric? Will I be able to manufacture a Farmer Special? Where am I going to get the capital from? You must tell us if we are going to have a separate interstate bus line to take the place of Greyhound and Trailways. You must tell us how this separate interstate bus line is going to operate throughout the country if all of us are confined within one separate state.

You must tell us these things, Mr. X, spell them out. You must tell us also what the relationship will be between the black businesses which you would develop and the total American economy. Will it be a competition? Will it be a rival economy, a dual economy or will there be cooperation between these two economies?

Our program is clear. We are going to achieve our goals of integration by non-violent direct action on an interracial level with whites and Negroes jointly cooperating to wipe out a disease which has afflicted and crippled all of them, white and black alike. The proof of the pudding is the eating. We have seen barriers fall as the result of using these techniques. We ask you, Mr. X, what is your program?

On The Death Of William Edward Burghardt Du Bois By African Moonlight And Forgotten Shores

Conrad Kent Rivers

Truth to your mighty winds on dusky shores
the kingdom bowed down at last,

there you were, the chosen scholar home.
True you were among the earth's unborn
a sheik of justice and almighty intellect,
killer of liberals, brother to a distant
universe, not easily explained to bands
of hungry black men experiencing a real truth
spelled-out, propagated, in slums born
more vigorous each day and year of triumph,
unemployment, wine and sweet vermouth
squeezed against death's cool
cocoa brown hands. . . .

Reprinted by permission of International Publishers Co., Inc. from *The New Black Poetry* by Clarence Major.

from The Talented Tenth

W. E. B. Du Bois

The Negro race, like all races, is going to be saved by its exceptional men. The problem of education, then, among Negroes must first of all deal with the Talented Tenth; it is the problem of developing the Best of this race that they may guide the Mass away from the contamination and death of the Worst, in their own and other races. Now the training of men is a difficult and intricate task. Its technique is a matter for educational experts, but its object is for the vision of seers. If we make money the object of man-training, we shall develop money-makers but not necessarily men; if we make technical skill the object of education, we may possess artisans but not, in nature, men. Men we shall have only as we make manhood the object of the work of the schools—intelligence, broad sympathy, knowledge of the world that was and is, and of the relation of men to it—this is the curriculum of that Higher Education which must underlie true life. On this foundation we may build bread-winning skill of hand and quickness of brain, with never a fear lest the child and man mistake the means of living for the object of life. . . . Who are today guiding the work of the Negro people? The "exceptions" of course. And yet so sure as this Talented Tenth is pointed out, the blind worshippers of the Average cry out in alarm: "These are exceptions, look here at death, disease and crime—these are the happy rule." Of course they are the rule, because a silly nation made them the rule: Because for three long centuries this people lynched Negroes who dared to be brave, raped black women who dared to be virtuous, crushed dark-hued youth who dared to be ambitious, and encouraged and made to flourish servility and lewdness and apathy. . . .

How then shall the leaders of a struggling people be trained and the hands of the risen few strengthened? There can be but one answer: The best and most capable of their youth must be schooled in the colleges and universities of the land. We will not quarrel as to just what the university of the Negro should teach or how it should teach it—I willingly admit that each soul and each race-soul needs its own peculiar curriculum. But this is true: A university is a human invention for the transmission of knowledge and culture from generation to generation, through the training of quick minds and pure hearts, and for this work no other human invention will suffice, not even trade and industrial schools. . . .

I would not deny, or for a moment seem to deny, the paramount necessity of teaching the Negro to work, and to work steadily and skillfully; or seem to depreciate in the slightest degree the important part industrial schools must play in the accomplishment of these ends, but I *do* say, and insist upon it, that it is industrialism drunk with its vision of success to imagine that its work can be accomplished without providing for the training of broadly cultured men and women to teach its own teachers, and to teach the teachers of the public schools. . . .

I am an earnest advocate of manual training and trade teaching for black boys, and for white boys, too. I believe that next to the founding of Negro colleges the most valuable addition to Negro education since the war has been industrial training for black boys. Nevertheless, I insist that the object of all true education is not to make men carpenters, it is to make carpenters men; there are two means of making the carpenter a man, each equally important; the first is to give the group and community in which he works liberally trained teachers and leaders to teach him and his family what life means; the second is to give him sufficient intelligence and technical skill to make him an efficient workman; the first object demands the Negro college and college-bred men—not a quantity of such colleges, but a few of excellent quality; not too many college-bred men, but enough to leaven the lump, to inspire the masses, to raise the Talented Tenth to leadership. . . .

The Struggle for the Liberation of the Black Laboring Masses

A. Philip Randolph

In this mid-twentieth century black labor is one hundred years behind white labor in the skilled crafts. They are behind in trade union organization. They are behind in workers' education. They are behind in employment oppor- tunities.

Why? The answer is not because white labor is racially superior to black labor. Not because white labor is more productive than black labor.

In the race between black and white labor in American industry black labor never had a chance. How could it be otherwise when Negro workers began as slaves while white workers began as free men, or virtually as free men?

In addition to a quarter of a thousand years of captivity in the labor system of chattel slavery, black labor, even after emancipation, has been a prisoner for a hundred years of a moneyless system of peonage, sharecropper- plantation-farm laborism, and a helpless and hopeless city-slum proletariat. . . .

No greater tragedy has befallen the working class anywhere in the modern world than that which plagues the working class in the South. Both white and black workers turned against their own class and gave aid to their enemy, the feudalistic-capitalist class, to subject them to sharper and sharper exploitation and oppression.

Verily, black and white workers did not fight each other because they hated each other, but they hated each other because they fought each other. They fought each other because they did not know each other. They did not know each other because they had no contact or communication with each other. They had no contact or communication with each other because they were afraid of each other. They were afraid of each other because each was propagandized into believing that each was seeking to take the jobs of the other.

By poisonous preachments by the press, pulpit and politician, the wages of both black and white workers were kept low and working conditions bad, since trade union organization was practically non-existent. And, even today, the South is virtually a "no man's land" for union labor.

There is no remedy for this plight of the South's labor forces except the unity of the black and white working class. . . .

Excerpt from address to the NALC annual convention, Chicago, November 10-12, 1961.
Used by permission of A. Philip Randolph.

violence
yes or no

Yes!

Robert F. Williams

. . . When the brutally oppressed Afroamerican speaks of violent resistance to savage racial dehumanization, he reaps a whirlwind of reasons and causes why such a reaction supposedly is insane and suicidal. There is no end to the stereotyped polemics and heated opposition that beclouds a rational and objective discourse on the subject. From the camps of the rabid white supremacy power structure, the fellow traveling white liberal and the mercenary running dog Uncle Tom, any individual who raises such a question is labeled a bloodthirsty crackpot, not worthy of social acceptance in America's "democratic and Christian" society. Proponents of the peaceful transition philosophy are quick to evoke the Gandhian theory of appealing to the conscience of the brutal oppressor and conquering him with the power of nonviolence and love.

These Gandhian Fabians inadvertently extol the success of Gandhi's peaceful revolution. Gandhi's nonviolent revolution may have guaranteed the ruling powers immunity from the violence of the masses, but it most certainly left the masses exposed to the violence of the oppressors. It served to assure that only the blood of the oppressed would flow. . . .

. . . The power structure, the liberals and Uncle Toms are in essence asking Afroamericans to cooperate with the very forces that are opposing them. How can oppressed people who seek liberation, afford to allow the enemy to dictate the method of struggle? How can a people, who are dead serious about their freedom, allow themselves to be duped into limiting themselves to the most ineffective method of struggle? It is not logical to accommodate the will of the oppressor, who has a vested interest in maintaining the status quo, and to wage a successful liberation struggle simultaneously. . . .

. . . Many of the nonviolent preachers in North America tend to fuse Gandhism and Christianity. Their hybrid type of pacifism leans heavily on Christian teachings and on the Bible, which threatens that the entire earth is to be destroyed by violent fire. Its watchword is the coming battle of Armageddon. Not a nonviolent battle but the most ferociously violent one ever staged. These advocates of the Christian power of nonviolence and love omit that part of the Old Testament which describes the evil subversion attempted by the devil when peaceful coexistence degenerated in Heaven to a state of open conflict wherein the Christian's God, the highest ideal of peace and love, ordered the devil forcibly ejected from the heavenly society. In removing the devil and his evil from menacing the peace of the ideal community, it is significant to note that God did not see fit to relegate such an important task to the realm of nonviolence. Why is the mortal Afroamerican expected to be more peaceful and loving towards his enemy than his divine God? . . .

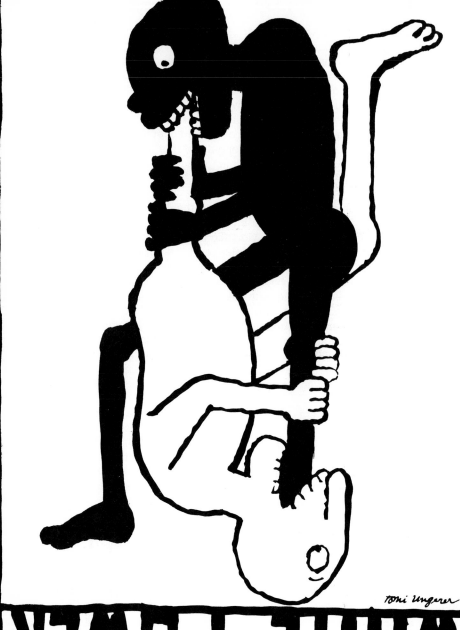

Black Power, White Power. Poster by Tomi Ungerer. Used by permission.

Black People!

LeRoi Jones

What about that bad short you saw last week on Frelinghuysen, or those stoves and refrigerators, record players, shotguns, in Sears, Bambergers, Klein's, Hanhnes', Chase, and the smaller joosh enterprises? What about that bad jewelry, on Washington Street, and those couple of shops on Springfield? You know how to get it, you can get it, no money down, no money never, money dont grow on trees no way, only whitey's got it, makes it with a machine, to control you you cant steal nothin from a white man, he's already stole it he owes you anything you want, even his life. All the stores will open if you will say the magic words. The magic words are: Up against the wall mother fucker this is a stick up! Or: Smash the window at night (these are magic actions) smash the windows daytime, anytime, together, lets smash the window drag the shit from in there. No money down. No time to pay. Just take what you want. The magic dance in the street. Run up and down Broad Street niggers, take the shit you want. Take their lives if need be, but get what you want what you need. Dance up and down the streets, turn all the music up, run through the streets with music, beautiful radios on Market Street, they are brought here especially for you. Our brothers are moving all over, smashing at jellywhite faces. We must make our own World, man our own world, and we can not do this unless the white man is dead. Let's get together and kill him my man, let's get to gather the fruit of the sun, let's make a world we want black children growing and learning in do not let your children when they grow look in your face and curse you by pitying your tomish ways.

Breaking Out

Dick Gregory

. . . Look at Stokely Carmichael and Rap Brown. Stokely is 27; Rap is 23. Two young cats have scared the mightiest nation on the face of this earth to death. Is that insanity? People ask me what is wrong with Rap Brown and Stokely Carmichael. I can tell you what is wrong with them. They have dared to become as bitter as Patrick Henry. I think that if we could question Stokely and Rap and trace their history back, we might not justify what they are doing, but we would sure understand it. I met Stokely Carmichael and Rap Brown six years ago in Greenwood, Mississippi. Rap was just 17 years old then. Stokely insulted me. He said, "Nigger, if you can't be nonviolent, get the hell on back up North."

It was the Stokelys and Raps and the S.N.C.C. kids that taught nonviolence to the movement. Think about what they went through.

Do you know what it is to try to integrate a school? You get that little black kid, take him by his hand, and the kid is smiling and saying, "Thank you for taking me to school." You want to throw up because you know you are really taking him to die. You walk past that barricade and just as you approach those stairs to take that little black kid to that school, you are attacked by the mob, the sheriff, and the police; and the next thing you know you are lying down in the gutter with a white man's foot on your chest and a double-barreled shotgun on your throat, and you hear, "Move, nigger, and I will blow your brains out." You lie there in that gutter and try to muster up the manhood to tell yourself you don't mind dying. You look across the street and see the F.B.I. taking pictures. And as you lie there you spot that little black kid, baby, just as a brick hits him right in the mouth.

We got busted in Birmingham, Alabama. They arrested 2400 of us; some were little kids, 4, 5, 6, 7, and 8 years old. We aren't crying about that. Put everybody in jail, put unborn babies in jail, if it means getting what we want. But when you go to jail, they put the men in one place and the women in another place, the adults away from the kids, and the little girls away from the little boys; and right across from our cell block is where the police put the little girls. I stayed in jail four days, baby, and every night I had to sit and watch those police bring Lesbians in and turn them loose on the kids. Now, if you want to see a sight, you look at a Lesbian tampering with a 4-year-old kid; listen to the kid yell and holler and scream. The F.B.I. knew about it. The news just never got around.

This is what they went through for six years. For six years those cats had faith in America. They were screaming out for help and none of us heard their screams. Now they have lost faith in America and they are screaming and everybody hears them; and they are saying, "No, baby, now we are going to take care of this thing ourselves." That is all they are saying.

Nonviolence didn't help Stokely and Rap. People talk about riots hurting our cause. That is wishful thinking. Riots should hurt; any act of violence should hurt. But we are living in a nation so insane that riots have only helped the cause. After the Detroit riots, Henry Ford hired 6000 blacks in two days. We know why because the fire got too close to the Ford Plant. Don't scorch the Mustangs, baby. If the Indians come to Detroit and start burning, they will hire 6000 red folks next. I wonder why this country can wake up only after an act of violence.

Black folks in this country don't hate white folks. We hate the white system; and when a man hates a system, that's revolt, and you don't stop revolt. There is a bloody revolution going on in this country today, right against wrong. You know the theory of spontaneous combustion. Take some oily, greasy rags, put them in your closet at home, close the door so the air can't circulate, and see what's going to happen. Put your foot up on the door, hold it closed, and you aren't going to hear anything. The black ghetto from one end of this country to the other is America's oily, greasy rags, and if we haven't enough sense to snap that door open, we are going to wake up barbecued.

yes

Hypnotism

Ben Caldwell

CHARACTERS:
MAGICIAN
NEGRO MAN
NEGRO WOMAN
WHITE POLICEMEN

A loud orchestra is playing the "Star-Spangled Banner." "Oh say can you see . . ." is repeated over and over. Sounding like a record playing with the needle stuck.

UP CURTAIN

A white-faced actor dressed in red, white, and blue "Uncle Sam" suit. He speaks in the manner of the mystical movie magician. He holds a circular, two-faced portrait of Rev. Martin Luther King. It dangles from a chain. He sways it from side to side for hypnotic effect. The hypnotist subjects are seated before him. A negro man and a woman with dumb smiles on their faces. They both appear to be in a trance. The magician is seated on a very high stool; subjects are on lower stools.

MAGICIAN:
RELAX—RELAX—relax!
Close your eyes and forget about facts.
You will forget about freedom.
You *must* forget about freedom.
SLEEP—SLEEP—SLEEP!
And dream pleasant, non-violent dreams.
Forget that you are hated, and oppressed, and murdered.
All thoughts of exploitation and injustices are swept out of your mind!
You are *completely in my power.*

When I say move you will move!
(SUBJECTS NOD THEIR HEADS)
When I say stop you will stop!
(SUBJECTS STOP ABRUPTLY)
You will do only as I say do!

Sleep and dream—SLEEP and dream!
Dream of the promised-land of integration.
Non-violence—non-violence—NON-VIOLENCE!
Integration . . . integration!
Sleep—Sleep——sleep!
(HE PAUSES WHILE HIS WORDS TAKE EFFECT ON THEM)
When I snap my fingers you will open your eyes.
And you will see only what I want you to see!
When you open your eyes you will be what I want you to be . . .
DUMB BLACK NIGGERS!

Magician snaps his fingers and the subjects snap to attention. A white policeman rushes out and grabs the woman. He begins to curse her and drag her off stage. (Stinkin' black bitch. "Help! Help me!") Man goes to her defense, which causes the policeman to beat him over the head with his stick. The negro does not fight back. He falls to his knees and begins to sing verses of "We Shall Over-come." Covering his eyes to the scene. He sings louder, trying to drown the woman's screams. The magician folds his arms and nods his head with satisfaction and pleasure at this scene.

YOU CAN STOP IT FROM ENDING THIS WAY! . . .

Nonviolence and the Montgomery Boycott

Martin Luther King, Jr.

Since the philosophy of nonviolence played such a positive role in the Montgomery Movement, it may be wise to turn to a brief discussion of some basic aspects of this philosophy.

First, it must be emphasized that nonviolent resistance is not a method for cowards; it does resist. If one uses this method because he is afraid or merely because he lacks the instruments of violence, he is not truly nonviolent. This is why Gandhi often said that if cowardice is the only alternative to violence, it is better to fight. He made this statement conscious of the fact that there is always another alternative: no individual or group need submit to any wrong, nor need they use violence to right the wrong; there is the way of nonviolent resistance. This is ultimately the way of the strong man. It is not a method of stagnant passivity. The phrase "passive resistance" often gives the false impression that this is a sort of "do-nothing method" in which the resister quietly and passively accepts evil. But nothing is further from the truth. For while the nonviolent resister is passive in the sense that he is not physically aggressive toward his opponent, his mind and emotions are always active, constantly seeking to persuade his opponent that he is wrong. The method is passive physically, but strongly active spiritually. It is not passive nonresistance to evil, it is active nonviolent resistance to evil.

A second basic fact that characterizes nonviolence is that it does not seek to defeat or humiliate the opponent, but to win his friendship and understanding. The nonviolent resister must often express his protest through noncooperation or boycotts, but he realizes that these are not ends themselves; they are merely means to awaken a sense of moral shame in the opponent. The end is redemption and reconciliation. The aftermath of nonviolence is the creation of the beloved community, while the aftermath of violence is tragic bitterness.

A third characteristic of this method is that the attack is directed against forces of evil rather than against persons who happen to be doing the evil.

From pp. 101-104 ("The New Militance—the Philosophy of Martin Luther King, Jr.") in *Stride Toward Freedom* by Martin Luther King, Jr. Copyright © 1958 by Martin Luther King, Jr. Reprinted by permission of Harper & Row, Publishers, Inc.

It is evil that the nonviolent resister seeks to defeat, not the persons victimized by evil. If he is opposing racial injustice, the nonviolent resister has the vision to see that the basic tension is not between races. As I like to say to the people in Montgomery: "The tension in this city is not between white people and Negro people. The tension is, at bottom, between justice and injustice, between the forces of light and forces of darkness. And if there is a victory, it will be a victory not merely for fifty thousand Negroes, but a victory for justice and the forces of light. We are out to defeat injustice and not white persons who may be unjust."

A fourth point that characterizes nonviolent resistance is a willingness to accept suffering without retaliation, to accept blows from the opponent without striking back. "Rivers of blood may have to flow before we gain our freedom, but it must be our blood," Gandhi said to his countrymen. The nonviolent resister is willing to accept violence if necessary, but never to inflict it. He does not seek to dodge jail. If going to jail is necessary, he enters it "as a bridegroom enters the bride's chamber."

One may well ask: "What is the nonviolent resister's justification for this ordeal to which he invites men, for this mass political application of the ancient doctrine of turning the other cheek?" The answer is found in the realization that unearned suffering is redemptive. Suffering, the nonviolent resister realizes, has tremendous educational and transforming possibilities. "Things of fundamental importance to people are not secured by reason alone, but have to be purchased with their suffering," said Gandhi. He continues: "Suffering is infinitely more powerful than the law of the jungle for converting the opponent and opening his ears which are otherwise shut to the voice of reason."

A fifth point concerning nonviolent resistance is that it avoids not only external physical violence but also internal violence of spirit. The nonviolent resister not only refuses to shoot his opponent but he also refuses to hate him. At the center of nonviolence stands the principle of love. The nonviolent resister would contend that in the struggle for human dignity, the oppressed people of the world must not succumb to the temptation of becoming bitter or indulging in hate campaigns. To retaliate in kind would do nothing but intensify the existence of hate in the universe. Along the way of life, someone must have sense enough and morality enough to cut off the chain of hate. This can only be done by projecting the ethic of love to the center of our lives. . . .

Wood engraving by Stefan Martin, from a drawing by Ben Shahn.

I Have a Dream

Martin Luther King, Jr.

. . . I have a dream that one day this nation will rise up and live out the true meaning of its creed: "We hold these truths to be self-evident; that all men are created equal."

I have a dream that one day on the red hills of Georgia the sons of former slaves and the sons of former slaveowners will be able to sit down together at the table of brotherhood.

I have a dream that one day even the state of Mississippi, a desert state sweltering with the heat of injustice and oppression, will be transformed into an oasis of freedom and justice.

I have a dream that my four little children will one day live in a nation where they will not be judged by the color of their skin but by the content of their character.

I have a dream today.

I have a dream that one day the state of Alabama, whose governor's lips are presently dripping with the words of interposition and nullification, will

Reprinted by permission of Joan Daves. Copyright © 1963 by Martin Luther King, Jr.

be transformed into a situation where little black boys and black girls will be able to join hands with little white boys and white girls and walk together as sisters and brothers.

I have a dream today.

I have a dream that one day every valley shall be exalted, every hill and mountain shall be made low, the rough places will be made plain, and the crooked places will be made straight, and the glory of the Lord shall be revealed, and all flesh shall see it together.

This is our hope. This is the faith with which I return to the South. With this faith we will be able to hew out of the mountain of despair a stone of hope. With this faith we will be able to transform the jangling discords of our nation into a beautiful symphony of brotherhood. With this faith we will be able to work together, to pray together, to struggle together, to go to jail together, to stand up for freedom together, knowing that we will be free one day.

This will be the day when all of God's children will be able to sing with new meaning

> My country, 'tis of thee,
> Sweet land of liberty,
>   Of thee I sing:
> Land where my fathers died,
> Land of the pilgrims' pride,
> From every mountain side
>   Let freedom ring.

And if America is to be a great nation this must become true. So let freedom ring from the prodigious hilltops of New Hampshire. Let freedom ring from the mighty mountains of New York. Let freedom ring from the heightening Alleghenies of Pennsylvania!

Let freedom ring from the snowcapped Rockies of Colorado!

Let freedom ring from the curvacious peaks of California!

But not only that; let freedom ring from Stone Mountain of Georgia!

Let freedom ring from Lookout Mountain of Tennessee!

Let freedom ring from every hill and molehill of Mississippi. From every mountainside, let freedom ring.

When we let freedom ring, when we let it ring from every village and every hamlet, from every state and every city, we will be able to speed up that day when all of God's children, black men and white men, Jews and Gentiles, Protestants and Catholics, will be able to join hands and sing in the words of the old Negro spiritual, "Free at last! free at last! thank God almighty, we are free at last!"

Photograph by Gerald Davis

from Beyond Racism

Whitney Young

. . . The job of transforming America into an Open Society, peacefully and with justice for all citizens, will require a commitment far beyond any in our history. The first step must be a clear statement of national purpose to tell the world that we are mobilizing all elements of American life. Secondly, there must be public and private programs on an unprecedented scale, aimed at ending poverty and rebuilding urban life. The third step must be a clearly defined timetable tied to these programs: at the end of the first year, so many jobs will have been created, so many new homes built. Part of the reason for the rising frustrations of recent years was the failure to join announced goals to timetables, so that people could measure performance against promise.

Finally, we must go beyond racism and insure that black people and other minorities get a fair share of the power and responsibility in a democratic society.

All this implies vast social change—in our institutions, in our economy, in our behavior, and even in our thoughts. It won't be easy: yielding privileges and sharing power with the powerless are never painless. But it is necessary if this nation is to fulfill the promise of its past and the dreams of its future.

Building an Open Society will require hard, determined work by all people—white and black. Both suffer under the present system, and both have a stake in transforming it into something decent and humane. I believe deeply that whites and blacks will have to learn to work together. Understandably, there will be frictions, but if we are to survive we must both strive to attain our common goals.

This means that a massive campaign to re-educate Americans will be needed. Fear and mistrust pervade both white and black communities, obstructing joint efforts to make this a decent society, dedicated to diversity.

I am confident that it is possible to construct a coalition between black citizens and an enlightened, intelligent white community that acts out of self-interest as well as morality.

White Americans have to be educated to the damage that a racist system does to their own lives. In a world that is three-fourths nonwhite, no white person can be complacent about the oppression black Americans endure. Nor can he be complacent about what is happening to his children: a survey of white schoolchildren in Florida taken after Dr. Martin Luther King, Jr.'s, assassination found that 59 per cent were "elated or indifferent" about it. Even if their parents disliked Dr. King and the civil rights movement, I find it hard to believe that such an expression of hatred from twelve- and thirteen-year-olds doesn't disturb them.

The campaign against racism can't be limited to old clichés about brotherhood; these appeals have been falling on deaf ears for years. It must show that measures taken to benefit black people will benefit all Americans. Much of the resistance to Negro demands is caused by fear that other groups will be ignored or, worse, that white people who cannot afford it will have to foot the bill. Any effort to rebuild our society must take note of the legitimate demands and aspirations of white people, too.

Two out of three poor people are white, and many millions of white families live just above the official poverty line. Lower-middle-class families feel economic pressures and status insecurities that must be dealt with, just as the disproportionate black poverty and deprivation must be dealt with. An Open Society is for everyone—white and black.

Jesse Jackson

"No man can tell a man who is hurting how to holler," he argues. "The business of trying to decry people because of the way they complain of injustice is past and gone." Thus Jackson does not condemn the Black Panthers; neither does he embrace their Marxist philosophy or all of their tactics. Because the Panthers are so widely seen as victims of police repression, they pose a delicate problem for many black leaders. Jackson handles that problem rather skillfully. He accepts their claim that they espouse violence only

FIFTY CENTS   APRIL 6, 1970

SPECIAL ISSUE

TIME

Black
America
1970

Jesse Jackson

defensively, in response to white terrorism against them. He lauds their contribution to black pride. With the same ease, Jackson can endorse moderates; he praises Roy Wilkins for fighting racial injustice "long before I was born." He sees the usefulness of tuxedoed black leaders who attend banquets and charm wealthy whites into donating to black causes. He is willing to work with whites to create a social, if not a political revolution: "The young white radicals who are rebelling against their mamas and daddies because their lives are empty and meaningless are fighting the system for one reason. Those of us that are black are fighting it for another reason, but both of us are fighting it. And the system is either going to adjust or it's going to deteriorate."

Jackson neither advocates nor castigates violence as a tactic, but he doubts its effectiveness. "Our experience with the hot war is that it is a bit futile, given the Man's military superiority," he says. "There is no more shock value in riots. The Man is ready for that too." But Jackson argues that whether blacks turn to violence will actually depend upon white decisions. "If more of us are starving, more of us will be fighting at the desperate level. If the question is survival, the reaction is independent of any black leader's thoughts of it. They are irrelevant, because of the nature of man." But if violence must come, he pleads, "let it be as mellow as possible."

These and other Jackson views place him closest to the black nationalists in the current philosophical spectrum of the black movement. He feels that many blacks have common economic grievances with poor whites: Breadbasket's campaign to get the Chicago city council to fight hunger in the city embraces such whites. But Jackson's basic approach is to stimulate the black community into forcing concessions from whites. The nationalism he defends is a nationalism based on a shared experience of oppression rather than on race.

From *Black Power*, edited by Dudley Randall. Reprinted by permission of Broadside Press.

coalition

YES OR NO

Malcolm

Sonia Sanchez

Do not speak to me of martrydom
of men who die to be remembered
on some parish day.
I don't believe in dying
though I too shall die
and violets like castanets
will echo me.

Yet this man
this dreamer,
thick-lipped with words
will never speak again
and in each winter
when the cold air cracks
with frost, I'll breathe
his breath and mourn
my gun-filled nights.

He was the sun that tagged
the western sky and
melted tiger-scholars
while they searched for stripes.
He said, "Fuck you white
man. we have been
curled too long. nothing
is sacred now. not your
white face nor any
land that separates
until some voices
squat with spasms."

Do not speak to me of living.
life is obscene with crowds
of white on black.
death is my pulse.
what might have been
is not for him/or me
but what could have been
floods the womb until I drown.

From *Black Poetry*, edited by Dudley Randall. Reprinted by permission of Broadside Press.

Omar Lama.

The Ballot or the Bullet

Malcolm X

Brothers and sisters and friends—and I see some enemies. [*Applause.*] In fact, I think we'd be fooling ourselves if we had an audience this large and didn't realize that there were some enemies present.

This afternoon we want to talk about the ballot or the bullet. The ballot or the bullet explains itself. But before we get into it, I would like to clarify some things . . . about black nationalism.

The political philosophy of black nationalism only means that the black man should control the politics and the politicians in his own community. [*Applause.*] The time when white people can come in our community and get us to vote for them so that they can be our political leaders and tell us what to do and what not to do is long gone. [*Applause.*] By the same token the time when that same one white man can send another Negro into the community, to get you and me to support him so he can use him to lead us astray—those days are long gone. [*Applause.*] The political philosophy of black nationalism only means that if you and I are going to live in a black community—and that's where we are going to live, 'cause as soon as you move out of the black community into their community, it's mixed for a period of time, but they're gone and you're right there all by yourself again. [*Applause.*]

The economic philosopy of black nationalism only means that we should own and operate and control the economy of our community. You can't open up a black store in a white community—white men won't even patronize it, and they're not wrong. They've got sense enough to look out for themselves. It's you who don't have sense enough to look out for yourselves. [*Applause.*] The white man is too intelligent to let someone else come and gain control of the economy of his community. But you will let anybody come in and control the economy of your community; control the housing, control the education, control the jobs, control the businesses under the pretext that you are integrated. No, you're out of your mind. [*Applause.*] . . .

. . . You and I have to make a start, and the definite place to start is right in the community where we live. [*Applause.*] So our people not only have to be re-educated to the importance of supporting black business but the black man himself has to be made aware of the importance of going into business. What we will be doing is developing a situation wherein we will actually be able to create employment for the people in the community. And that will eliminate the necessity of you and me having to act ignorantly and disgracefully boycotting and picketing some cracker someplace else trying to beg him for a job. [*Applause.*] Any time you have to rely upon your enemies for a job you're in bad shape. When you know he is your enemy all the time. Anyhow, you wouldn't be in this country if some enemy hadn't kidnapped you and brought you here. [*Applause*]. . . .

We need a self-help program. A do-it-yourself philosophy. A do-it-right-now philosophy. It's-already-too-late philosophy. This is what you and I need to get with. The only time we're going to solve our problem is with a self-help program. Before we can get a self-help program started, we have to have a self-help philosophy. Black nationalism is a self-help philosophy. This is a philosophy that eliminates the necessity for division and argument, so that if you're black, you should be thinking black. And if you're black, and you're not thinking black at this late date, why, I'm sorry for you. [*Applause.*] . . .

. . . When we look at other parts of this earth upon which we live, we find that black, brown, red and yellow people in Africa and Asia are getting their independence. They're not getting it by singing "We shall overcome." No, they're getting it through nationalism. Every nation in Asia gained its independence through the philosophy of nationalism. Every nation on the African continent that has gotten its independence brought it about through the philosophy of nationalism. And it will take black nationalism to bring about the freedom of 22 million Afro-Americans, here in tihs country, where we have suffered *colonialism* for the past 400 years. [*Applause.*]

So it's time to wake up. It's got to be the ballot or the bullet. The ballot or the bullet. If you're afraid to use an expression like that, you should get on out of the country; you should get back in the cotton patch; you should get back in the alley.

. . . America today finds herself in a unique situation. Historically, revolutions are bloody. Oh, yes, they are. They haven't ever had a bloodless revolution or a non-violent revolution. That don't happen even in Hollywood. [*Applause.*] You don't have a revolution in which you love your enemy. And you don't have a revolution in which you are begging the system of exploitation to integrate you into it. Revolutions overturn systems. Revolutions destroy systems. [*Applause.*] A revolution is bloody. But America is in a unique position. She's the only country in history in a position actually to become involved in a bloodless revolution. The Russian revolution was bloody. The Chinese revolution was bloody. The French revolution was bloody. The Cuban revolution was bloody. And there was nothing more bloody than the American Revolution. But today this country can become involved in a revolution that won't take bloodshed. All she's got to do is give to the black man in this country everything that's due him. Everything. [*Applause.*]

So it's the ballot or the bullet. Today our people can see that we're faced with a government conspiracy. The Senators who are filibustering concerning your and my rights, that's the government. Don't say it's Southern Senators. This is the government. Any kind of activity that takes place on the floor of the Congress or the Senate, that's the government. Any kind of act that's designed to delay or deprive you and me, right now, of getting full rights, that's the government that's responsible. And any time you find the government involved in a conspiracy to violate the citizenship or the civil rights of a people, then you are wasting your time going to that government expecting redress. Instead, you have to take that government to the world court and accuse it of genocide and all the other crimes that it is guilty of today. [*Applause.*]

So those of us whose political and economic and social philosophy is black nationalism have become involved in the civil rights struggle. We have injected ourselves into the civil rights struggle, and we intend to expand it from the level of civil rights to the level of human rights. As long as you fight it on the level of civil rights, you're under Uncle Sam's jurisdiction. You're going to his court expecting him to correct the problem. He created the problem. He's the criminal. You don't take your case to the criminal. You take your criminal to court. [*Applause.*]

When the government of South Africa began to trample upon the human rights of the people of South Africa, they were taken to the U.N. When the government of Portugal began to trample upon the rights of our brothers and sisters in Angola, it was taken before the U.N. Why, even the white man took the Hungarian question to the U.N. And just this week, Chief Justice Goldberg was crying over three million Jews in Russia, about their human rights, charging Russia with violating the U.N. Charter, because of its mistreatment of the human rights of Jews in Russia. Now, you tell me, how can the plight of everybody on this earth reach the halls of the U.N., and yet you have 22 million Afro-Americans whose churches are being bombed? Whose little girls are being murdered. Whose leaders are being shot down in broad daylight. Now, you tell me, why the leaders of this struggle have never taken it before the United Nations? [*Applause.*] So, our next move is to expand the civil rights struggle to the level of human rights, take it into the United Nations, where our African brothers can throw their weight on our side, where our Asian brothers can throw their weight on our side, where our Latin-American brothers can throw their weight on our side, and where 800 million Chinese are sitting there, waiting to throw their weight on our side. And let the world see that Uncle Sam is guilty of violating the human rights of 22 million Afro-Americans and still has the audacity or the nerve to stand up and represent himself as the leader of the free world. [*Applause.*]

Let the world know how bloody his hands are. Let the world know the hypocrisy that's practiced over here.

Black Manifesto

We the black people assembled in Detroit, Michigan, for the National Black Economic Development Conference are fully aware that we have been forced to come together because racist white America has exploited our resources, our minds, our bodies, our labor. For centuries we have been forced to live as colonized people inside the United States, victimized by the most vicious, racist system in the world. We have helped to build the most industrialized country in the world.

We are therefore demanding of the white Christian churches and Jewish synagogues, which are part and parcel of the system of capitalism, that they begin to pay reparations to black people in this country. We are demanding $500,000,000 from the Christian white churches and the Jewish synagogues. This total comes to fifteen dollars per nigger. This is a low estimate, for we maintain there are probably more than 30,000,000 black people in this country. Fifteen dollars a nigger is not a large sum of money, and we know that the churches and synagogues have a tremendous wealth and its membership, white America, has profited and still exploits black people. We are also not unaware that the exploitation of colored peoples around the world is aided and abetted by the white Christian churches and synagogues. This demand for $500,000,000 is not an idle resolution or empty words. Fifteen dollars for every black brother and sister in the United States is only a beginning of the reparations due us as people who have been exploited and degraded, brutalized, killed and persecuted. Underneath all of this exploitation, the racism of this country has produced a psychological effect upon us that we are beginning to shake off. We are no longer afraid to demand our full rights as a people in this decadent society.

We are demanding $500,000,000 to be spent in the following way:

(1) We call for the establishment of a southern land bank to help our brothers and sisters who have to leave their land because of racist pressure, and for people who want to establish cooperative farms but who have no funds. We have seen too many farmers evicted from their homes because they have dared to defy the white racism of this country. We need money for land. We must fight for massive sums of money for this southern land bank. We call for $200,000,000 to implement this program.

(2) We call for the establishment of four major publishing and printing industries in the United States to be funded with ten million dollars each. These publishing houses are to be located in Detroit, Atlanta, Los Angeles, and New York. They will help to generate capital for further cooperative investments in the black community, provide jobs and an alternative to the white-dominated and controlled printing field.

(3) We call for the establishment of four of the most advanced scientific and futuristic audio-visual networks to be located in Detroit, Chicago, Cleveland and Washington, D.C. These TV networks will provide an alternative to the racist propaganda that fills the current television networks. Each of these TV networks will be funded by ten million dollars each.

(4) We call for a research skills center which will provide research on the problems of black people. This center must be funded with no less than thirty million dollars.

(5) We call for the establishment of a training center for the teaching of skills in community organization, photography, movie making, television making and repair, radio building and repair and all other skills needed in communication. This training center shall be funded with no less than ten million dollars.

(6) We recognize the role of the National Welfare Rights Organization, and we intend to work with them. We call for ten million dollars to assist in the organization of welfare recipients. We want to organize welfare workers in this country so that they may demand more money from the government and better administration of the welfare system of this country.

(7) We call for $20,000,000 to establish a National Black Labor Strike and Defense Fund. This is necessary for the protection of black workers and their families who are fighting racist working conditions in this country.

(8) We call for the establishment of the International Black Appeal (IBA). This International Black Appeal will be funded with no less than $20,000,000. The IBA is charged with producing more capital for the establishment of cooperative businesses in the United States and in Africa, our Motherland. The International Black Appeal is one of the most important demands that we are making, for we know that it can generate and raise funds throughout the United States and help our African brothers. . . .

Carmichael Resigns

Robert C. Maynard

New York, July 3—Denouncing the Black Panther Party for its alliances with white groups, Stokely Carmichael has quit as "honorary prime minister" of the party. He called the Panther's methods "dishonest and vicious."

The resignation and condemnation, contained in a letter delivered by Carmichael's wife here today, is the latest and most serious in a series of political and legal blows to the three-year-old Panther organization.

"The Party has become dogmatic in its duly acquired ideology," Carmichael's letter said. "All those who disagree with the Party line are lumped into the same category and labeled cultural nationalists, pork chop nationalists, reactionary pigs. This may be a very convenient tactic; however it is dishonest and vicious."

Carmichael's letter, dated June 25 and written from self-imposed exile in Conakry, capital of West Africa's Republic of Guinea, brings into the open the long smouldering division among revolutionary blacks over the issue of white alliances.

The Panthers have taken the position that whites—they call them "mother country revolutionaries"—have a role to play with blacks in a biracial class struggle. Carmichael and other black nationalists take the position that the struggle is of nonwhites, particularly black Americans and Africans, against whites and "western imperialism."

The first hint of Carmichael's break with the Panthers, with whom he has been associated for more than a year, came when two newsmen were asked to rendezvous with associates of Carmichael in New York.

Taken to Kennedy International Airport, the two reporters were met by Mrs. Carmichael, South African-born singer Miriam Makeba, who presented the letter from her husband.

Here only to deliver the letter and to pick up her 15-month-old grandson, Lumumba, Mrs. Carmichael said little after performing her mission. She smiled, shook hands with friends there to see her off and then boarded a flight for Conakry.

She slipped into New York a week ago and contacted friends of Carmichael to inform them of her mission.

Friends of Carmichael were unavailable for comment on his actions, although several were known to be concerned that the letter might have serious repercussions for his former associates in the United States. Mrs. Carmichael said only that this was not a good time for her husband to leave Conakry, that he is studying French there at the Language Institute and that he hoped to return at some point to the United States.

In his letter, Carmichael said he was not particularly concerned about the fate of the Panther Party because "organizations come and go, but the struggle of black people must go on."

From "Carmichael Assails Black Panthers, Quits as 'Honorary Prime Minister,' " by Robert C. Maynard, *The Washington Post*, July 4, 1969. © *The Washington Post* and reprinted by permission.

United Press International Photo.

The Panthers, with their founder, Huey P. Newton, in jail and with many other members arrested in recent months on a variety of criminal charges, have been fighting to remain intact. Recent Senate hearings have also damaged the organization's public image.

Carmichael's letter said:

"I cannot support the present tactics and methods which the Party is using to coerce and force everyone to submit to its authority. These tactics and the rhetoric of the Party are dividing black revolutionaries and causing divisions within the black community which only benefit our enemy."

Regarding the issue of working with whites, Carmichael's letter said. "The alliances being formed by the Party are alliances which I cannot politically agree with because the history of Africans living in the United States has shown that any premature alliance with white radicals has led to the complete subversion of the blacks by the whites through their direct or indirect control of the black organization."

In recent months the Panthers have announced their intentions of working on various projects with the predominantly white Students for a Democratic Society. In some cities, Panther organizations have allied themselves with other radical white organizations.

"The white left in the United States, seen and unseen," Carmichael said, "not only controls capitalist and imperialist policies, but also the so-called Marxist-Leninist movements. If the Black Panther Party continues on the present course, it will at best become reformist and, at worst, a tool of racist imperialists used against the black masses."

Carmichael also charged that "the white radical left" is encouraging divisions among blacks, "as they are doing in the Nigeria-Biafra situation. They couldn't care less about murder and attacks against black people, whose only crime may be that they do not agree with the party line 100 per cent."

Carmichael, 28 and a native of Trinidad, left the United States, his home since the age of 11, for Africa at the end of last year. Some of his friends have said that he feared "repression" by the Nixon Administration.

Carmichael's closest associates, however, have said that the purpose of his present stay in Africa is to work for alliances between blacks the world over and American Negroes.

He said of himself in his letter:

"I am a Pan-Africanist in outlook and see the need for Africans all over the world to begin to understand our common ancestral heritage and the common situation in which we now find ourselves, since we are all victims of racism, capitalist exploitation, colonialism, neo-colonialism and imperialism."

The divisions among American blacks over the question of cultural versus revolutionary nationalism have been simmering below the surface for many months. In Los Angeles, the cultural nationalist organization US, founded by Ron Karenga, has been in heated controversy with the Panthers. Two members of US are accused of murdering two Panthers in Los Angeles on Jan. 17.

Where Carmichael stood on the issue of white alliances has been a matter of speculation for some months. The letter delivered by his wife today makes his position clear.

An Open Letter to Stokely Carmichael

Stokely Carmichael, Conakry, Guinea:
Your letter of resignation as the Prime Minister of the Black Panther Party
came, I think, about one year too late. As a matter of fact, since the day of
your appointment to that position—February 17, 1968—events have proven
that you were not cut out for the job in the first place. Even then it was
clear that your position on coalition with revolutionary white organizations
was in conflict with that of the Black Panther Party. But we thought that,
in time, even you would be able to shake the SNCC paranoia about white
control and get on with the business of building the type of revolutionary
machinery that we need in the United States in order to unite all the
revolutionary forces in the country to overthrow the system of Capitalism,
Imperialism and Racism.

I know these terms are kicked around like lifeless bodies and that it is
easy to allow the grisly realities behind them to become obscured by too
frequent repetition. But when you see the squalor in which people live as a
result of the policies of the exploiters, when you see the effects of exploitation on the emaciated bodies of little children, when you see the hunger
and desperation, then these terms come alive in a new way. Since you've
made this trip yourself and seen it all with your own eyes, you should
know that suffering is colorblind, that the victims of Imperialism, Racism,
Colonialism and Neo-colonialism come in all colors, and that they need a
unity based on revolutionary principles rather than skin color.

"An Open Letter to Stokely Carmichael" by Eldridge Cleaver, from *Ramparts* Magazine, September, 1969. Reprinted by permission of Cyrilly Abels, Literary Agent.

The other charges which you make in your letter—about our new-found ideology, our dogmatism, our arm-twisting, etc.—seem to me to be of secondary importance, because, with the exception, perhaps, of the honorable Elijah Muhammad, you are the most dogmatic cat on the scene today, and I've never known you to be opposed to twisting arms or, for that matter, necks. In many ways your letter struck me as being an echo and rehash of the charges brought against the party by the bootlickers before the McClellan Committee. And since you chose this moment to denounce the party, we—and I am sure many other people outside the party—must look upon your letter in this light. The only point in your letter that I think is really you is the one about coalition with whites, because it has been this point on which our differences have turned from the very beginning.

You have never been able to distinguish the history of the Black Panther Party from the history of the organization of which you were once the chairman—the Student Non-Violent Coordinating Committee. It is understandable that you can have such fears of black organizations being controlled, or partly controlled, by whites, because most of your years in SNCC were spent under precisely those conditions. But the Black Panther Party has never been in that situation. Because we have never had to wrest control of our organization out of the hands of whites, we have not been shackled with the type of paranoid fear that was developed by you cats in SNCC. Therefore we are able to sit down with whites and hammer out solutions to our common problems without trembling in our boots about whether or not we might get taken over in the process. It has always seemed to me that you belittle the intelligence of your black brothers and sisters when you constantly warn them that they had better beware of white folks. After all, you are not the only black person out of Babylon who has been victimized by white racism. But you sound as though you are scared of white people, as though you are still running away from slave-catchers who will lay hands on your body and dump you in a bag. . . .

. . . The enemies of black people have learned something from history even if you haven't, and they are discovering new ways to divide us faster than we are discovering new ways to unite. One thing they know, and we know, that seems to escape you, is that there is not going to be any revolution or black liberation in the United States as long as revolutionary blacks, whites, Mexicans, Puerto Ricans, Indians, Chinese and Eskimos are unwilling or unable to unite into some functional machinery that can cope with the situation. Your talk and fears about premature coalition are absurd, because no coalition against oppression by forces possessing revolutionary integrity can ever be premature. If anything, it is too late, because the forces of counterrevolution are sweeping the world, and this is happening precisely because in the past people have been united on a basis that perpetuates disunity among races and ignores basic revolutionary principles and analyses.

You are peeved because the Black Panther Party informs itself with the revolutionary principles of Marxism-Leninism, but if you look around the world you will see that the only countries which have liberated themselves and managed to withstand the tide of the counterrevolution are precisely those countries that have strong Marxist-Leninist parties. All those countries that have fought for their liberation solely on the basis of nationalism have fallen victims to capitalism and neo-colonialism, and in many cases now find themselves under tyrannies equally as oppressive as the former colonial regimes.

That you know nothing about the revolutionary process is clear; that you know even less about the United States and its people is clearer; and that you know still less about humanity than you do about the rest is even clearer. You speak about an "undying love for black people." An undying love for black people that denies the humanity of other people is doomed. It was an undying love of white people for each other which led them to deny the humanity of colored people and which has stripped white people of humanity itself. It would seem to me that an undying love for our people would, at the very least, lead you to a strategy that would aid our struggle for liberation instead of leading you into a coalition of purpose with the McClellan Committee in its attempt to destroy the Black Panther Party.

Well, so long, Stokely, and take care. And beware of some white folks and some black folks, because I assure you that some of both of them have teeth that will bite. Remember what Brother Malcolm said in his Autobiography: "We had the best organization that the black man has ever had in the United States—and niggers ruined it!" POWER TO THE PEOPLE!

—Eldridge Cleaver
Minister of Information, Black Panther Party
July, 1969.

"Black Power" and Coalition Politics

Bayard Rustin

Southern Negroes, despite exhortations from SNCC to organize themselves into a Black Panther party, are going to stay in the Democratic party—to them it is the party of progress, the New Deal, the New Frontier, and the Great Society—and they are right to stay. For SNCC's Black Panther perspective is simultaneously utopian and reactionary—the former for the by now obvious reason that one-tenth of the population cannot accomplish much by itself, the latter because such a party would remove Negroes

Reprinted from *Commentary*, by permission. Copyright © 1966 by the American Jewish Committee.

from the main area of political struggle in this country (particularly in the one-party South, where the decisive battles are fought out in Democratic primaries), and would give priority to the issue of race precisely at a time when the fundamental questions facing the Negro and American society alike are economic and social. . . .

The winning of the right of Negroes to vote in the South insures the eventual transformation of the Democratic party, now controlled primarily by Northern machine politicians and Southern Dixiecrats. The Negro vote will eliminate the Dixiecrats from the party and from Congress, which means that the crucial question facing us today is who will replace them in the South. Unless civil-rights leaders (in such towns as Jackson, Mississippi; Birmingham, Alabama; and even to a certain extent Atlanta) can organize grass-roots clubs whose members will have a genuine political voice, the Dixiecrats might well be succeeded by black moderates and black Southern-style machine-politicians, who would do little to push for needed legislation in Congress and little to improve local conditions in the South. While I myself would prefer Negro machines to a situation in which Negroes have no power at all, it seems to me that there is a better alternative today—a liberal-labor-civil rights coalition which would work to make the Democratic party truly responsive to the aspirations of the poor, and which would develop support for programs (specifically those outlined in A. Philip Randolph's $100 billion Freedom Budget) aimed at the reconstruction of American society in the interests of greater social justice. The advocates of "black power" have no such programs in mind; what they are in fact arguing for (perhaps unconsciously) is the creation *of a new black establishment*. . . .

"Black power" is, of course, a somewhat nationalistic slogan and its sudden rise to popularity among Negroes signifies a concomitant rise in nationalist sentiment (Malcolm X's autobiography is quoted nowadays in Grenada, Mississippi as well as in Harlem). We have seen such nationalistic turns and withdrawals back into the ghetto before, and when we look at the conditions which brought them about, we find that they have much in common with the conditions of Negro life at the present moment: conditions which lead to despair over the goal of integration and to the belief that the ghetto will last forever. . . .

It is, in short, the growing conviction that the Negroes cannot win—a conviction with much grounding in experience—which accounts for the new popularity of "black power." So far as the ghetto Negro is concerned, this conviction expresses itself in hostility first toward the people closest to him who have held out the most promise and failed to deliver (Martin Luther King, Roy Wilkins, etc.), then toward those who have proclaimed themselves his friends (the liberals and the labor movement), and finally toward the only oppressors he can see (the local storekeeper and the policeman on the corner). On the leadership level, the conviction that the Negroes cannot win takes other forms, principally the adoption of what I have called a "no-win" policy. Why bother with programs when their enactment results only in "sham"? Why concern ourselves with the image of the movement when nothing significant has been gained for all the sacrifices made by SNCC and CORE? Why compromise with reluctant white allies when nothing of consequence can be achieved anyway? Why indeed have anything to do with whites at all?

On this last point, it is extremely important for white liberals to understand—as, one gathers from their references to "racism in reverse," the President and the Vice President of the United States do not—that there is all the difference in the world between saying, "If you don't want me, I don't want you" (which is what some proponents of "black power" have in effect been saying) and the statement, "Whatever you do, I don't want you" (which is what racism declares). It is, in other words, both absurd and immoral to equate the despairing reponse of the victim with the contemptuous assertion of the oppressor. It would, moreover, be tragic if white liberals allowed verbal hostility on the part of Negroes to drive them out of the movement or to curtail their support for civil rights. The issue was injustice before "black power" became popular, and the issue is still injustice.

In any event, even if "black power" had not emerged as a slogan, problems would have arisen in the relation between whites and Negroes in the civil-rights movement. In the North, it was inevitable that Negroes would eventually wish to run their own movement and would rebel against the presence of whites in positions of leadership as yet another sign of white supremacy. In the South, the well-intentioned white volunteer had the cards stacked against him from the beginning. Not only could he leave the struggle any time he chose to do so, but a higher value was set on his safety by the press and the government—apparent in the differing degrees of excitement generated by the imprisonment or murder of whites and Negroes. The white person's importance to the movement in the South was thus an ironic outgrowth of racism and was therefore bound to create resentment. . . .

Nevertheless, pride, confidence, and a new identity cannot be won by glorifying blackness or attacking whites; they can only come from meaningful action, from good jobs, and from real victories such as were achieved on the streets of Montgomery, Birmingham, and Selma. When SNCC and CORE went into the South, they awakened the country, but now they emerge isolated and demoralized, shouting a slogan that may afford a momentary satisfaction but that is calculated to destroy them and their movement. Already their frustrated call is being answered with counter-demands for law and order and with opposition to police-review boards. Already they have diverted the entire civil-rights movement from the hard task of developing strategies to realign the major parties of this country, and embroiled it in a debate that can only lead more and more to politics by frustration.

On the other side, however—the more important side, let it be said—it is the business of those who reject the negative aspects of "black power" not to preach but to act. Some weeks ago President Johnson, speaking at Fort Campbell, Kentucky, asserted that riots impeded reform, created fear, and antagonized the Negro's traditional friends. Mr. Johnson, according to *The New York Times,* expressed sympathy for the plight of the poor, the jobless, and the ill-housed. The government, he noted, has been working to relieve their circumstances, but "all this takes time."

One cannot argue with the President's position that riots are destructive or that they frighten away allies. Nor can one find fault with his sympathy for the plight of the poor; surely the poor need sympathy. But one can question whether the government has been working seriously enough to eliminate the conditions which lead to frustration-politics and riots. The President's very words, "all this takes time," will be understood by the poor for precisely what they are—an excuse instead of a real program, a cover-up for the failure to establish real priorities, and an indication that the administration has no real commitment to create new jobs, better housing, and integrated schools.

. . . For the truth is that it need only take ten years to eliminate poverty —ten years and the $100 billion Freedom Budget recently proposed by A. Philip Randolph. . . .

Mr. Randolph's Freedom Budget not only rests on the Employment Act of 1946, but on a precedent set by Harry Truman when he believed freedom was threatened in Europe. In 1947, the Marshall Plan was put into effect and 3 per cent of the gross national product was spent in foreign aid. If we were to allocate a similar proportion of our GNP to destroy the economic and social consequences of racism and poverty at home today, it might mean spending more than 20 billion dollars a year, although I think it quite possible that we can fulfill these goals with a much smaller sum. It would be intolerable, however, if our plan for domestic social reform were less audacious and less far-reaching than our intenational programs of a generation ago.

We must see, therefore, in the current debate over "black power," a fantastic challenge to American society to live up to its proclaimed principles in the area of race by transforming itself so that all men may live equally and under justice. . . .

Letter to a Black Boy

Bob Teague

Dear Adam,
. . . Actually, there is no such animal as a Negro leader in Mister Charlie's sense; that is, there is no black man who can speak for all of his cousins, or even most of them. Just as there is no leader who can speak for all Jews, Italians, Lithuanians, Democrats or Republicans. There are Catholics who disagree with the Pope. Yet somehow Mister Charlie persists in the notion

Reprinted by permission of the publisher, Walker and Company, New York. © 1968 by Robert L. Teague.

THERE IS NO BLACK

that black men are less inclined to think for themselves, ready to follow any black scarecrow who has been photographed with the frontmen in the power structure.

Black men, too, are individuals. We disagree among ourselves, as whites disagree about the things that affect their lives and what their so-called leaders say in public.

I have no idea what percentage of my black cousins would agree with my evaluation of the so-called Negro leaders. I respect and reject them all.

Dr. King, for example, I think of as a great man by any civilized standard. But I cannot and will not go along with his theory, taken from Mister Charlie's Bible, that black men should accept violence at the hands of whites and turn the other cheek. For more of the same. To me, that amounts to self-mutilation; perverting yourself into something much less than a man.

Neither can I go all the way with Rap Brown and the other reckless revolutionaries who say, "Let's burn this country down, honkies and all." I am convinced that more violence, burning and rioting is strategically necessary —and I don't wish to stop it—to jar Mister Charlie out of his comfortable dream. But deep down I cling to the notion that violence is wrong whether whites inflict it against blacks or vice versa.

I also have serious reservations about the approach taken not so long ago by Robert Carson of CORE, who is trying to establish an all-black community in the South. Carson argues that blacks must escape from this sick white society to avoid further contamination. He is right about the sickness. But to accept membership in an all-black society in this country would be the first step toward becoming the very thing black men say they hate in Mister Charlie.

I want to stress, however, that in spite of my reservations, I don't wish to see any of those approaches abandoned. It is my guess that these trials and errors may help convince Mister Charlie that he is never going to have peace of mind in this country on his terms alone, that desperate black men will always be trying first this wild scheme and then that one. Until the basic wrong has been righted.

MAN THAT CAN SPEAK FOF

racism as

black (blāk) *adj.* 1 Dest
reflecting it; devoid of color or so dark a
to white 2 Envelo
rly dismal or gloomy;
kin, hair, and eyes; su
rized by dark pigm
stralian natives
ments, as, the *black*
ack looks. 7 Foully
Indicating disgrace o
istributed, or charged
rities, or ration restric
n, as, *black* rent; *bl*
ure in blackness, esp. b
e against an air raid; a
e or suppress througho
dio transmission).

K MAN

OR

ALL HIS COUSINS

275

BLACK HERITAGE

songs of the beloved homeland

Heritage

(For Harold Jackman)

Countee Cullen

What is Africa to me:
Copper sun or scarlet sea,
Jungle star or jungle track,
Strong bronzed men, or regal black
Women from whose loins I sprang
When the birds of Eden sang?
One three centuries removed
From the scenes his fathers loved,
Spicy grove, cinnamon tree,
What is Africa to me?

First stanza of the poem Heritage from *On These I Stand* by Countee Cullen. Copyright 1925 by Harper & Brothers; renewed 1953 by Ida M. Cullen. Reprinted by permission.

Sunrise at Olduvai Gorge, Tanzania, East Africa. Photograph by Joel Baldwin.

The Africa Thing

Adam David Miller

What is Africa to thee?

Let's shuffle

Paint that horn
on backwards—
Knock me some skin

Blow! O

They say home
is a place
in the mind
where you
can rest
when you're tired
not where
your great great
great grandfather
had his farm

Africa?

Africa
is that old man
in the pickin field
making that strange high sound
and all the people following
Africa is a sound
Africa
is the touch
of that old woman
your mother could not stand
but did respect
who caught you as you fell
and held you
and rocked you

beble be
ba
bo
bibob
blaaba
ba ba
buddi di oooooo
rock a diooooo
do oo do o

Fat black bucks in a wine barrel   boom
boom
What is Africa to thee   bam
thou thoo thum   boom
I smell the seat of an english scum   boom boom

—Mamma, Mamma, but he does
It's not just his breath
He stink
Hushsssh, chile
Somebody'll hear you
Say smell.

Africa
is the look
of Tweebie Mae
Snapping her
head around
before she took off
    Cain't ketch me
in the soft dark
You caught her

Africa
is all them roots
and conjurs
and spells

From *Dices or Black Bones*, edited by Adam David Miller. Reprinted by permission of the publisher, Houghton Mifflin Company.

wails and chants
(say blues and hollers)
and all of them stories
about Stackalee
and John Henry
and Bodidly
and the camp meetings
where the wrestling
and head and head
the foot races
the jumping
the throwing

We brought all that down
to dance at birth
when you're sick
take a wife
lose your luck
when you die

and singing in the woods
  in the fields
when you walk
and singing on the levies
  on the chain gang
  in the jail
singing and dancing when you pray
and dancing by the light of the moon
until you drop

Africa is the singing of these lines
of me
of you
of love
singing

Photograph by Emil Schulthess. Courtesy Black Star Publishing Co., Inc.

Outcast

Claude McKay

For the dim regions whence my fathers came
My spirit, bondaged by my body, longs.
Words felt, but never heard, my lips would frame;
My soul would sing forgotten jungle songs.
I would go back to darkness and to peace,
But the great western world holds me in fee.
And I may never hope for full release
While to its alien gods I bend my knee.
Something in me is lost, forever lost,
Some vital thing has gone out of my heart,
And I must walk the way of life a ghost
Among the sons of earth, a thing apart.

For I was born, far from my native clime,
Under the white man's menace, out of time.

From *Selected Poems of Claude McKay,* copyright 1953
by Bookman Associates, Inc. Reprinted by permission of
Twayne Publishers, Inc.

Who Am I?

Jack Shepherd

"Maw brothers," roars Jim Smith in his best black Baptist voice, "yes, maw brothers, gawddamn it's gonna hurt"—his dark eyes flash from the shaved head rigid on the thick fullback body—"but you are gonna get them shots, and you will, yes you wiiilll be able to live, I believe." It's hot in Harlem. The bonkety-bonk of empty beer cans echoes on the concrete. In a long room on the second floor of the Urban League's brownstone at 136th Street, off Seventh Avenue, Jim Smith, an articulate bull of a black man, uses all of his M.A. in psychology to get 25 black kids vaccinated and ready for their trip to Africa. He does little preaching. They are ready.

These kids are asking, "Who am I?" Africa may give them quick answers and identity; a temporary catharsis for the unhealing wounds of being black and in the American ghetto. "Reality is long overdue," Smith argues. "It is time for the youth of Harlem to see what the high hustle of 125th Street has to do with him and the dawn of man at Olduvai Gorge in Tanzania and the ruins of ancient civilizations in West Africa." The plan: send the street dudes for a firsthand look.

These kids are tough, hip, street-smart. They come from Harlem, Brooklyn, the South Bronx. They've bounced against the ghetto's cruelty and

From *Look* Magazine, January 7, 1969. Reprinted by permission of Cowles Syndicate.

landed, most of them upright, uptight, at the Urban League's storefront street academies or Harlem Prep. They range in age from 17 to 24, in ideology from Black Nationalist to Black Muslim. Sixty-seven kids applied through the Urban League last winter for the 25 openings to Africa.

They compete. They write articles and sell subscriptions for their newspaper, *40 Acres and a Mule*. They compose roughhewn essays. Ed Weems writes: "Only until I have lived such an event [going to Africa] would I be able to arrive at some sort of reality. For if I find such a reality, who could then lie to me? Perhaps it is my being black in America which inspires such thought. Many questions about myself which I do not know the answers to, yet no one can answer them but myself. Thus Africa to me is a mother. Cradle to civilization and cradle to all of mankind. I cannot truly know myself when my very existence is almost denied in America. Africa to me can be an encyclopedia of knowledge of myself in specific. How American am I? How African am I? I don't know, perhaps Africa knows."

Every Wednesday night for 12 weeks, they meet in the brownstone at 136th Street, listening to college professors tell them about African history, politics, culture, colonialization. They run in Central Park, hike, climb and camp out in the Catskill Mountains, for most, their first trip outside New York City. They learn Swahili from Winston Ayoki, a group leader and a Kenyan studying here. And, toward the end, the 67 are cut to 25, who take Jim Smith's advice and get six injections. Bill Stirling, the white group leader, a former Peace Corpsman in Kenya and now an instructor in a street academy, helps set the ten-week itinerary: Ghana, Tanzania, Kenya, Uganda, Ethiopia, Egypt; tells them what to bring—sleeping bag, knapsack—and warns them about everything from malaria to shaking out their boots against scorpions. "I do that every morning anyway," says one kid, "to get the roaches out."

"Maw brothers," Smith comes back at them during the last meeting, "now, maw brothers, don't you go spending a lot of bread, 'cause we are broke; we on buns." After a long talk about local currencies, someone breaks up the meeting by asking, with the best British accent in Harlem: "Can I hawve five shillings, Charlie?"

They leave June 25th for Accra, Ghana. They are the first group of black kids from the American ghetto to go to Africa. They represent the people of Harlem, the Harlems of America. Already there is pride. "I was real anxious to go," says Tuhran Gethers. "I never had a chance to go out of the city or go overseas. I've never really done anything to make anybody proud of me." It's also their first plane ride. Hector Lino says: "We came over by slave ship, but we're going back by Pan Am." They start summer-long diaries:

Africa. Heat and new smells. Hector: "It's so terrific to get on that plane and out of Harlem." Stay at youth hostel in Accra. Mosquitoes. Mammy lorry buses: "Perhaps," "God Bless," "Why Worry?" Markets. Everybody buys cloth, has shirts, suits made. Haggling with merchants, Cliff Bailous hustles six packs of U.S. cigarettes for two cedi (about $2), cheaper than Harlem. Guy Burroughs jokes, holds papaya limb, calls out with accent: "Shade tree, you like shade tree? Two cedi shade tree. How much you give?" Someone bids two pesewas. June 29. Victor Gomez, who grew up in

Harlem, drowns at Labadi Beach, Accra. Undertow treacherous, almost got everybody. Tonight, fishermen along the coast beat drums, passing the word. They will search for the body tomorrow. The group gathers in darkness, talks about going home. Gerard Loftin stops it: "Victor wanted this trip so bad. I think we should keep on." Visit slave castle along Ghana coast at Elmina. Then to Kumasi, Tamale, Bolgatanga, Navrongo. Staying in secondary schools, colleges. Local folks feeding us. Kumasi has Harlem sounds: Smiles Photo House; Soul Brothers Furniture. We meet African students, leaders, the Asantehene, chief of the Ashanti nation. Bill Greene pumps a brigadier general about conditions under the military regime. Weems asks a regional administrator about Lebanese merchants. Pull into Tamale market, buy elephant tables, lamps, spears, hats, knives. Ride almost into Upper Volta; been on bus more than on African soil. Navrongo natives dance, ask group to join them. Most refuse. Jim Davis and Gerard play the drums. Stirling does a quick dance, like a white stork with palsy. Everyone laughs and calls him "Bwana Bill." Navrongo chief asks about kids' ancestors, the markings on their grandparents. He's an old man and can remember slave caravans passing through from Upper Volta. We tell him no records kept after Negro slaves arrived in America. "It's a pity," he replies simply. And it is. Payday. Must pay for everything but shelter. Money starts at $30 a week each, quickly drops to $5. Running out. Rebellion over eating rice three times a day. Weems warns: "We should watch it and be nice. These are poor people. When they give us rice, that's the best they have." Tour Sanerigu. Says one student, who must be nameless, "Aw, you've seen one village, you've seen 'em all." Weems says, "I don't think you can find any people like this anywhere in the world, man." To Ghanaians: "You people got something the world needs." Meet with Council of Chiefs in Cape Coast. Arbie Geters tells them: "Our purpose is to take part in the African culture here and see how we relate to it as Afro-Americans." The chiefs ask Hector Lino what he likes about Africa: "Here, the rhythms are different." He's right. Labadi Beach. Mammy lorries. Joe La Tough, real barber.

Fly to Dar es Salaam, Tanzania, then to Moshi, Arusha, Nagorongoro Crater, Olduvai Gorge, Serengeti Plains. Sleeping outside in bags. Nairobi, Kenya live-in: Each kid goes to separate native farm up-country for two weeks. A few return in five days. Tuhran Gethers, Jim Davis, Angel Salcedo sleep out overnight in bush. "Talk about some scared dudes," Tuhran says. Uganda. Ethiopia. Stan Davis has trouble describing New York. "How you gonna explain to someone in Africa about the subway?" he asks. "You tell 'em you a mole?" Lamont Duke finds other problems: "You know what's hard to explain? The poor black people in America. Africans think everyone in America is rich." Cairo. Wear Arabian tunics home on plane. Cliff Bailous: "Africans are beautiful, friendly people."

The trip cost $53,000, and the money came in slowly from private donations. Smith and Stirling, through the International Urban Development Institute, may get kids from more ghettos to go next year. Back in Harlem, some of the students thought it over. Lamont Duke: "I felt proud to be recognized as what we are, respected, looked up to." Tuhran Gethers: "We know in our minds we equal. Over there, we were; and we saw how removed from equality we are here." Ed Weems: "Now I see myself not only as a black American but as one of millions of black people throughout the world." Cliff Bailous: "I find it harder to let anybody run those games over me now, like wearing dashikis—I know Africans don't wear them—or having their hair natural and say, this is the way Africans wear it. I know they don't." Weems: "The black person living in America must emphasize his blackness, because there are people around him who are hostile to him, to what he is trying to be. The dashiki is a commercialized thing. We got to emphasize our blackness." Duke: "Black nationalism made me want to go all the more. Now, I see them out on the street corner preaching; they don't know anything about it. They're a bunch of hypocrites." Weems: "Going to Africa was like seeing a picture you've looked at all your life and just now have somebody explain what it means." Duke: "I think we actually learned more about being black."

The learning goes on in Harlem. These 25 broke out of the ghetto and America for a summer. They found new rhythms and perspectives in Africa. They also found peace and, hopefully, themselves.

The African

We Delighted, My Friend

Léopold Sédar-Senghor

We delighted, my friend, in an African
    presence:
Furniture from Guinea and the Congo,
Heavy and polished, dark and light.
Primitive and pure masks on distant
    walls yet so near.
Taborets of honor for the hereditary
    hosts,
The princes from the high country.
Wild and proud perfumes from the
    thick tresses of silence,
Cushions of shadow and leisure like
    quiet wells running.
Eternal words and the distant
    alternating chant
As in the loin cloth from the Sudan.
But then the friendly light of your
    blue kindness
Will soften the obsession of this
    presence in
Black, white, and red, O red like
    the soil of Africa.

From *Poems from Black Africa,* edited by Langston
Hughes. Copyright © 1963 by Langston Hughes. Reprinted
by permission of Indiana University Press.

"Dianna and Apollo" by Jack Jordan. Courtesy Contemporary Crafts Publications.

Photograph by Joel Baldwin.

Black America's African Heritage

Jack Shepherd

We lied. We tried to hide the shame of slavery by calling Africans lazy and uncivilized. We taught the lie; we murmured it over tea. We created Tarzan and Amos 'n' Andy. And now we reap the darkness of it. In truth, man's sunrise glowed first in Africa. He began there. In West Africa, historical homeland for most American Negroes, he built the powerful states of Mali, Songhai, Kanem, Benin that thrived long before Europeans came.

From *Look* Magazine, January 7, 1969. Reprinted by permission of Cowles Syndicate.

The old Ghana empire lasted 1,000 years, to 1240. Timbuktu, Jenne, Kano traded gold, ivory, slaves. Nok and Ife art had no equal.

Two centuries before the first Christmas, Nok artists of the Niger-Benue country crafted quartz jewelry, iron axes, tin beads and finely molded terra-cotta heads. This art, West Africa's oldest, inspired the magnificent brass heads cast at Ife around 1000 A.D.

West Africa's glory lasted 1000 years. Songhai, Mossi-Dagomba and Benin enjoyed law and order and stability. They built palaces, large armies with fast cavalry, a civil service. Trading reached northward into Asia and Europe. Ife-Benin art flourished.

The Portuguese came first. They warily probed the seacoast, reaching into powerful empires that had strong chiefs, counselors, armies and laws. They found no Stepin Fetchits in Mali, Timbuktu, Oyo, Denkyira, Akwamu. They were welcomed at Benin in 1472, the first Europeans to see the city. They traded with the Oba's merchants and joined his army. Benin and Lisbon exchanged ambassadors. Both prospered.

An African's life had soul. Imagery exerted strong moral power. One folktale warned: "A missile thrown quickly misses its mark." Yoruba priests told: "The sun cannot rise in your wrath."

The weeping began quietly: 12 slaves stolen in 1441. Over 400 years, 20 million more were taken, draining Africa. Perhaps one third died marching; another third at sea. They were branded, and stuffed on ships so crowded they couldn't stand, shift or lie down. Africans and Europeans profited from this misery. In 1619, some 20 blacks were sold at Jamestown, Va.; about 500,000 made it here. By 1744, 300 ships had sailed out of Liverpool. The Africans fought back. They rebelled in Hispaniola, 1522; Puerto Rico, 1527; Panama, 1531. And in America, 1969, they are putting the black fist to our lie.

The Talking Drums

Kojo Gyinaye Kyei

I hear the beat
Of the drums,
The Atumpan drums,
Asante Kotpko:
Kum-apem-a-apem-beba!

I hear the beat
Of Prempeh drums,
Osei Tutu drums.

I hear the call
Of Nnawuta:
Tinn-tinn konn-konn!
Tinn-tinn konn-konn!
Konn-konn!

I ponder the valour
Of the mourned and mighty
African might.
I sense the resonance
Of Dawuro beats:
Tonn-tonn sann-sann!
Tonn-tonn sann-sann!
Sann-sann!

From *Poems from Black Africa*, edited by Langston Hughes. Copyright © 1963 by Langston Hughes. Reprinted by permission of Indiana University Press.

I muse upon Ghana,
Melle and Songhay.
I hear the echo
Of Fontomfrom,
The beat of
Mpintin drums:
Damirifa due . . . due!
Damirifi due . . . due!
Damirifi ooo-oo-o!

And *ooo!* The Sage!
Ankoanna Osagyefo
Bringing up the rear
At shoulders' acclaim:
The Sage who notched
Beauty and splendor
On Africa's glory!

I hear the beat
Of the drums!
I hear the beat
Of the Talking Drums!

Blackman's God

Francis Ernest Kobina Parkes

Our God is great
Who dare deny it
Our God is great
Powerful and dark
Peering through ages
Healing, killing, guiding.

Our God is Black
And like a goddamned god
Guiding when loving
Killing when angered.

Our God is powerful
All-powerful and black . . .

Stanza from "Three Phases of Africa"
by Ernest Kobina Parkes. From *Poems
from Black Africa*, edited by Langston
Hughes. Copyright © 1963 by Langston Hughes. Reprinted by permission
of Indiana University Press.

Ghana

Ghana

Basil Davidson

Among these emergent states of the Western Sudan the earliest that rose to fame and fortune was Ghana. Its territory lay to the north and northwest of the upper Niger: significantly enough, on the gold routes to the north. El Fazari, soon after A.D. 800, named it "the land of gold." Shortly before 833 Kwarizmi marked it on a map that was otherwise a copy of one which Ptolemy had drawn long centuries before. But it was not for another two hundred years that a North African would write of Ghana in any detail. Then comes the vivid account of Abdallah ibn Abdel Aziz, known as Abu Ubaid, or better still as El Bekri. And although it is a work of compilation, written by a man who never visited Africa (or at any rate never visited the Sudan), this description of El Bekri's has the illuminating touch of full and good material. Writing at Córdoba in southern Spain, where he had at his disposal the official records of the Ummayad rulers and the gossip of contemporary pioneers, El Bekri sets forth in careful and discriminating detail what well-informed Mediterranean opinion, based on many firsthand reports and much military intelligence, believed to be the truth about Ghana and the lands beyond the desert. His work was finished in 1067, some thirteen years after Ibn Yasin, the Almoravid ruler of North Africa, had marched southward to invade those lands and had captured Aoudaghast, a tributary city of Ghana. This invasion had brought the Western Sudan much closer to the Mediterranean and Spain; and it was this that gave El Bekri his wide choice of material.

"The king of Ghana," El Bekri is writing in the year after William of Normandy crossed the English Channel, "can put two hundred thousand warriors in the field, more than forty thousand of them being armed with bow and arrow." It would be interesting to know what the Normans might have thought of Ghana. Anglo-Saxon England could easily have seemed a poor and lowly place beside it. "Ghana," says El Bekri in 1067, "is the title of the king of this people," and "the name of their country is Aoukar. The king who governs them at the moment . . . is called Tenkamenin, who came to the throne in 455 [that is A.D. 1062] . . . Tenkamenin is master of a great empire and of a power which is formidable."

That this was more than travelers' embroidery may be seen from the fact that it took the Almoravid armies—rapidly victorious elsewhere—no fewer than fourteen years to subdue Ghana and seize its capital city. Ibn Yasin, fervent promoter of Islam, had marched southward from the Maghreb in 1054. In the following year he took Aoudaghast, a city that is entirely vanished today but was situated, according to El Bekri, two months' southward from Sijilmassa and fifteen days from the capital of Ghana. El Bekri says that Aoudaghast was "a very large city with several markets, many date palms and henna trees as big as olives," and "filled with fine houses and solid buildings." This city—a Sudanese city with many Moorish traders, for it lay at the southern terminal of the trans-Saharan caravan trail from Sijilmassa—the Almoravids "took by storm, violating women and carrying off all they found there, saying it was legal booty." But it was not until 1076 that another Almoravid leader, Abu Bakr, could take the capital of Ghana itself.

This capital had two cities six miles apart, while the space between was also covered with dwellings. In the first of these cities was the king's residence, "a fortress and several huts with rounded roofs, all being enclosed by a wall." The second, which also had a dozen mosques, was a merchant city of the Muslims: a city, that is of those who had come southward to settle or tarry and trade—much, indeed, like the *sabun gari* outside the walls of modern Kano; although there in Kano it is from the south that men had come for trade and settlement. Of manners at the court of its pagan king, El Bekri provides a celebrated description.

"When he gives audience to his people, to listen to their complaints and set them to rights, he sits in a pavilion around which stand his horses caparisoned in cloth of gold; behind him stand ten pages holding shields and gold-mounted swords; and on his right hand are the sons of the princes of his empire, splendidly clad and with gold plaited into their hair. The governor of the city is seated on the ground in front of the king, and all around him are his vizirs in the same position. The gate of the chamber is guarded by dogs of an excellent breed, who never leave the king's seat, they wear collars of gold and silver. . . . The beginning of an audience is announced by the beating of a kind of drum which they call *deba,* made of a long piece of hollowed wood . . ."

· · ·

Trade and tribute were the sources of its wealth. Ghana lay between the salt deposits of the north and the gold deposits of the south, and profited mightily from exchange between the two. Such was the southern need of salt that a gold-producing people called the Ferawi, according to El Bekri, would buy it for an equal weight of gold. But gold was also the commodity that the north wanted most. Thus the imperial ambition of successive states in the Sudan, drawing their wealth from this international trade, would be to monopolize the southern sources of gold—the "mysterious" land of Wangara and its gold-bearing soil that lay in fact somewhere near the sources of the Senegal River—and, secondly, to capture the principal salt deposits of the north, notably those at Taghaza in the northern desert, as well as to dominate the caravan roads. Ghana managed the first but not the second. Mali, after Ghana, would go far toward succeeding in both.

The rulers of Ghana not only knew the supreme trading value of gold, they also understood the need and the means of upholding it. El Bekri makes this clear. "The best gold in the country," he says, "is found at Ghiarou, a town that is eighteen days' journey from the capital, lying in a country filled with Negro peoples" and covered with their villages. "All nuggets of gold that are found in the mines of this empire belong to the king; but he leaves to his people the gold dust that everyone knows. Without this precaution gold would become so plentiful that it would practically lose its value."

They equally understood the value of trading tribute. The king of Ghana "exacts the right of one dinar of gold on each donkey-load of salt that enters the country, and two dinars of gold on each load of salt that goes out." Salt and gold would always be staple commodities; but others were important. "A load of copper"—entering Ghana from the copper mines of the southern Sahara—"pays him five mithcals, and each load of merchandise ten mithcals." Here one glimpses the familiar picture of a centralized government which has discovered the art and exercise of taxation, another witness of stability and statehood.

Photograph by Joel Baldwin. Used by permission of Cowles Syndicate.

Two centuries before the first Christmas, Nok artists of the Niger-Benue country crafted . . . finely molded terra-cotta heads.

The Art of Ife W. Nigeria

Geoffrey Parrinder

The wealth of art found at Ife in Nigeria has only become known to the wider world in the last few years. So much of the rest of African art seems stylized that the calm naturalism of the Ife bronzes and terracottas makes a great contrast. The bronzes are usually dated from the thirteenth or fourteenth centuries and show the existence of schools of craftsmen whose works have rarely been rivalled before or since. Other work has been done in ivory, clay and wood, and there are some fine royal stools in quartz.

The Yoruba regard Ile Ife, the "house of Ife" as their place of origin as told in the creation myths. Another version of this story says that when Great God had been sent to earth he became very thirsty and drank palm wine, and lay down to sleep. As he was away a long time God sent his

Reprinted by permission of The Hamlyn Publishing Group Limited from *African Mythology* by Geoffrey Parrinder.

brother Odu-duwa to continue the work of creation. This he did and supplanted Great God in ownership of the land. Oduduwa is regarded as the first king of Ife and the founder of their race. He was a strong personality but little has survived about him except general stories.

The son of Oduduwa was Oranyan who was a great warrior. In old age he retired into a grove, but if his people were attacked he emerged and dispersed enemies single-handed. One day, however, during a festival when the city was full of people and some were drunk, a man called out to Oranyan that they were being attacked. The old king came out on horseback and laid about the crowd, until the people begged him to stop destroying his own subjects. Then the shocked warrior drove his staff into the ground and said he would never fight again. It is said that it was turned to stone and so were he and his wife. Broken remains of stone have been dug up and fitted to restore the pillar, "the staff of Oranyan," which stands about twenty feet above the ground and studded with iron nails the pattern and meaning of which are disputed.

293

The Oba of Benin

Bini

From "Divine Kingship in Benin" by R. E. Bradbury, *Nigeria* Magazine, No. 62, 1959. Used by permission of the publisher.

He who knows not the Oba
let me know him.
He has mounted the throne,
he has piled a throne upon a throne.
Plentiful as grains of sand on the earth
are those in front of him.
Plentiful as grains of sand on the earth
are those behind him.

There are two thousand people
to fan him.
He who owns you
is among you here.
He who owns you
has piled a throne upon a throne.
He has lived to do it this year;
even so he will live to do it again.

The Yoruba of S.W. Nigeria

Geoffrey Parrinder

. . . Important for ritual in many places are the spirits of the storm, for tropical tornadoes not only bring the expected rains but often cause damage with thunderbolts and flashes of lightning. Remarkable stories are told of Shango, the storm deity of the Yoruba of Nigeria. This divinity was once a man, it is clearly said, and lived as the fourth king of that people, ruling over a kingdom stretching into neighboring countries. Shango was a strong ruler, and a great doctor, but also tyrannical. He could kill people by breathing fire from his mouth. Eventually his tyranny was challenged by two ministers, and to avoid their attack he set them to fight against each other hoping that both would be killed. One was slain, but the victor turned on Shango himself who fled to the forest. He went on horseback, taking his three wives and some loyal followers. But after wandering about for a long time only his favorite wife remained loyal, and finally in despair Shango hanged himself from a tree at a place called Koso.

This shameful end of the terrible king caused a great stir. When travellers brought reports that the monarch had hanged himself, his enemies mocked those who were still faithful to him. So his friends went to a great magician to find out how to bring fire on their enemies' houses. Some say they could make fire descend from heaven, others that they threw small gourds filled with gunpowder on to roofs during storms. Anyway there were many fires, and the followers of Shango said this proved that the king did 'not hang' *(ko-so)*. Shango was showing his anger by sending fire from heaven and sacrifices must be made to appease him. This was done and a temple built at a place still called Koso, *(ko-so)*, to contradict the story that Shango hanged himself. The version of the myth given by priests is that

Reprinted by permission of The Hamlyn Publishing Group Limited from *African Mythology* by Geoffrey Parrinder.

Shango was angry with his discontented subjects, so he disappeared into the forest on a horse. When a search party went after him they only found the horse, and a voice came from the sky saying that Shango did not hang, but ascended to heaven by a chain and would rule from there by thunder.

The Yoruba compare the noise of thunder with the bellowing of a ram, and these animals are sacred to Shango and wander freely about marketplaces. Thunderbolts are called 'thunder axes' and are said to fall to the ground whenever there is a storm. Priests of the storm and their acolytes often carry symbolical 'thunder-axes,' with wooden handles and finely decorated thin metal blades. Sometimes these axes are doubleheaded, like those found in parts of the Mediterranean world.

The God of War

Yoruba poem

He kills on the right and destroys on the left.
He kills on the left and destroys on the right.
He kills suddenly in the house and suddenly in
    the field.
He kills the child with the iron with which it
    plays.
He kills in silence.
He kills the thief and the owner of the stolen
    goods.
He kills the owner of the slave—and the slave
    runs away.
He kills the owner of the house—and paints the
    hearth with his blood.
He is the needle that pricks at both ends.
He has water but he washes with blood.

From *African Poetry*, edited by Ulli Beier. Used by permission of the publisher, Cambridge University Press.

A Yoruba carving from Western Nigeria and Eastern Dahomey. This polished wood figure depicts a devotee of Thunder god Shango. Above the head is the double-axed symbol of the god. It is a modern interpretation of the dance staff carried in Shango ceremonies.

Reprinted from *African Image* by Sam *Haskins.* Copyright © 1967 by Samuel Haskins. Published by Grosset & Dunlap, Inc.

Senegal

The King of Sedo

Senegal folktale

In the town of Sedo, it is said, there was a King named Sabar. Sabar's armies were powerful. They conquered many towns, and many people paid tribute to him. If a neighboring Chief passed through Sedo, he came to Sabar's house, touched his forehead to the ground, and presented gifts to the King. As the King grew old, he grew proud. His word was law in Sedo. And if his word was heard in other places, it was law there too. Sabar said to himself, "I am indeed great, for who is there to contradict me? And who is my master?"

From *The King's Drum,* © 1962 by Harold Courlander. Reprinted by permission of Harcourt Brace Jovanovich, Inc.

There came to Sedo one day a minstrel, and he was called on to entertain the King. He sang a song of praise to Sabar and to Sabar's ancestors. He danced. And then he sang:

"The dog is great among dogs,
Yet he serves man.
The woman is great among women,
Yet she waits upon her children.
The hunter is great among hunters,
Yet he serves the village.
Minstrels are great among minstrels,
Yet they sing for the King and his slaves."

When the song was finished, Sabar said to the minstrel, "What is the meaning of this song?"

The minstrel replied, "The meaning is that all men serve, whatever their station."

And Sabar said to him, "Not all men. The King of Sedo does not serve. It is others who serve him."

The minstrel was silent, and Sabar asked, "Is this not the truth?"

The minstrel answered, "Who am I to say the King of Sedo speaks what is not true?"

At this moment a wandering holy man came through the crowd and asked for some food. The minstrel said to the King, "Allow me to give this unfortunate man a little of the food which you have not eaten."

Sabar said, "Give it, and let us get on with the discussion."

The minstrel said, "Here is my harp until I have finished feeding him." He placed his harp in the King's hands, took a little food from the King's bowl, and gave it to the holy man. Then he came back and stood before Sabar.

"O King of Sedo," he said, "you have spoken what I could not say, for who contradicts a king? You have said that all men serve the King of Sedo and that he does not serve. Yet you have given a wandering holy man food from your bowl, and you have held the harp for a mere minstrel while he served another. How then can one say a king does not serve? It is said, 'The head and the body must serve each other.' "

And the minstrel picked up his harp from the hands of the King and sang:

"The soldier is great among soldiers,
Yet he serves the clan.
The King is great among kings,
Yet he serves his people."

middle

passage

The Interesting Narrative of the Life of Olaudah Equiano

Olaudah Equiano

Olaudah Equiano, the author of this selection, was from the Ibo country around Benin in what is now Nigeria. He was sold into slavery in 1756 to the British, who brought him to the New World. In 1766, he bought his freedom and went to England, where he worked as a barber and as a personal servant. He became actively involved in the anti-slavery movement in England and was interested in colonizing freed blacks in Sierra Leone. His autobiography, written in 1789, is one of the most informative of all such narratives by former slaves.

The portion of Equiano's narrative included here describes his experience of the "middle passage" from Africa to the West Indies. He recalled it as a horrifying example of man's inhumanity to his brothers. Included is a reference to the widespread fear among the captured Africans that they were to be eaten by the white men.

. . . Those of us that were the most active were in a moment put down under the deck, and there was such a noise and confusion amongst the people of the ship as I never heard before, to stop her, and get the boat out to go after the slaves. However two of the wretches were drowned, but they got the other, and afterwards flogged him unmercifully for thus attempting to prefer death to slavery. In this manner we continue to undergo more hardships than I can now relate, hardships which are inseparable from this accursed trade. Many a time we were near suffocation from the want of fresh air, which we were often without for whole days together. This, and the stench of the necessary tubs, carried off many. During our passage I first saw flying fishes, which surprised me very much: they used frequently to fly across the ship, and many of them fell on the deck. I also now first saw the use of the quadrant; I had often with astonishment seen the mariners make observations with it, and I could not think what it meant. They at last took notice of my surprise: and one of them, willing to increase it, as well as to gratify my curiosity, made me one day look through it. The clouds appeared to me to be land, which disappeared as they passed along. This heightened my wonder; and I was now more persuaded than ever that I was in another world, and that every thing about me was magic. At last we came in sight of the island of Barbadoes, at which the whites on board gave a great shout, and made many signs of joy to us. We did not know what to think of this; but as the vessel drew nearer, we plainly saw the harbour, and other ships of different kinds and sizes; and we soon anchored amongst them off Bridge-Town. Many merchants and planters now came on board, though it was in the evening. They put us in separate parcels, and examined us attentively. They also made us jump, and pointed to the land, signifying we were to go there. We thought by this we should be eaten by these ugly men, as they appeared to us; and, when soon after we were all put down under the deck again, there was much dread and trembling among us, and nothing but bitter cries to be heard all the night from these apprehensions, insomuch that at last the white people got some old slaves from the land to pacify us. They told us we were not to be eaten, but to work, and were soon to go on land, where we should see many of our country people. This report eased us much; and sure enough, soon after we landed, there came to us Africans of all languages. We were conducted immediately to the merchant's yard, where we were all pent up together like so many sheep in a fold, without regard to sex or age. As every object was new to me, every thing I saw filled me with surprise. What struck me first was that the houses were built with bricks and stories, and in every other respect different from those I had seen in Africa: but I was still more astonished on seeing people on horseback. I did now know what this could mean; and indeed I thought these people were full of nothing but magical arts. While I was in this astonishment one of my fellow prisoners spoke to a countryman of his about the horses, who said they were the same kind they had in their country. I understood them, though they were from a distant part of Africa, and I thought it odd I had not seen any horses there; but afterwards when I came to converse with different Africans, I found they had many horses amongst them, and much larger than those I then saw. We were not many days in the merchant's custody before we were sold after their usual manner, which is this:—On a signal given, (as the beat of a drum) the buyers rush at once into the yard where the slaves are confined, and make choice of that parcel they like best. The noise and clamour with which this is attended, and the eagerness visible in the countenances of the buyers, serve not a little to increase the apprehension of terrified Africans, who may well be supposed to consider them as the ministers of that destruction to which they think themselves devoted. In this manner, without scruple, are relations and friends separated, most of them never to see each other again.

Dark Symphony

Melvin Tolson

I ALLEGRO MODERATO

Black Crispus Attucks taught
  Us how to die
Before white Patrick Henry's bugle
  breath
Uttered the vertical
  Transmitting cry:
"Yea, give me liberty, or give me
  death."

And from that day to this
  Men black and strong
For Justice and Democracy have
  stood,
Steeled in the faith that Right
  Will conquer Wrong

And Time will usher in one
  brotherhood.
No Banquo's ghost can rise
  Against us now
And say we crushed men with a
  tyrant's boot
Or pressed the crown of thorns
  On Labor's brow,
Or ravaged lands and carted off the
  loot.

II LENTO GRAVE

The centuries-old pathos in our voices
Saddens the great white world,
And the wizardry of our dusky rhythms
Conjures up shadow-shapes of
  ante-bellum years:

Black slaves singing *One More River*
  to Cross
In the torture tombs of slave ships,
Black slaves singing *Steal Away to*
  Jesus
In jungle swamps,
Black slaves singing *The Crucifixion*
In slave pens at midnight,
Black slaves singing *Swing Low,*
  Sweet Chariot
In cabins of death,
Black slaves singing *Go Down, Moses*
In the canebrakes of the Southern
  Pharaohs. . . .

IV TEMPO PRIMO

The New Negro strides upon the
  continent
In seven league boots . . .
The New Negro
Who sprang from the vigor-stout loins
Of Nat Turner, gallows-martyr for
  Freedom,

Reprinted by permission of Dodd, Mead & Company, Inc. from *Rendezvous with America* by Melvin B. Tolson. Copyright 1944 by Dodd, Mead & Company, Inc.

Boston Massacre. Courtesy The Association for The Study of Negro Life and History, Inc.

Of Joseph Cinquez, Black Moses of
   the Amistad Mutiny
Of Frederick Douglass, oracle of the
   Catholic Man,
Of Sojourner Truth, eye and ear of
   Lincoln's legions,
Of Harriet Tubman, St. Bernard of the
   Underground Railroad. . . .

V LARGHETTO

None in the Land can say
To us black men Today:
You send the tractors on their bloody
   path,
And create Oakies for *The Grapes of
   Wrath.*
You breed the slum that breeds a
   Native Son
To damn the good earth Pilgrim
   Fathers won. . . .
None in the Land can say
To us black men Today:

You send flame-gutting tanks, like
   swarms of flies,
And plump a hell from dynamiting
   skies.
You fill machine-gunned towns with
   rotting dead—
A No Man's Land where children cry
   for bread.

VI TEMPO DI MARCIA

Out of abysses of Illiteracy,
Through labyrinths of Lies,
Across wastelands of Disease . . .
We advance!

Out of dead-ends of Poverty,
Through wildernesses of Superstition,
Across barricades of Jim Crowism . . .
We advance!

With the Peoples of the World . . .
We advance!

Middle Passage

Robert Hayden

1

JESUS, ESTRELLA, ESPERANZA, MERCY:

Sails flashing to the wind like weapons,
sharks following the moans the fever and the dying;
horror the corposant and compass rose.

Middle Passage:
voyage through death
  to life upon these shores.

"10 April 1800—
Blacks rebellious. Crew uneasy. Our linguist says
their moaning is a prayer for death.
ours and their own. Some try to starve themselves.
Lost three this morning leaped with crazy laughter
to the waiting sharks, sang as they went under."

DESIRE, ADVENTURE, TARTAR, ANN:

Standing to America, bringing home
black gold, black ivory, black seed.

*Deep in the festering hold thy father lies,
of his bones New England pews are made,
those are altar lights that were his eyes.*

*JESUS SAVIOUR PILOT ME
OVER LIFE'S TEMPESTUOUS SEA*

We pray that Thou wilt grant, O Lord,

safe passage to our vessels bringing
heathen souls unto Thy chastening.

JESUS SAVIOUR

"8 bells. I cannot sleep, for I am sick
with fear, but writing eases fear a little
since still my eyes can see these words take shape
upon the page & so I write, as one
would turn to exorcism. 4 days scudding,
but now the sea is calm again. Misfortune
follows in our wake like sharks (our grinning
tutelary gods). Which one of us
has killed an albatross? A plague among
our blacks—Ophthalmia: blindness—& we
have jettisoned the blind to no avail.
It spreads, the terrifying sickness spreads.
Its claws have scratched sight from the Capt.'s eyes
& there is blindness in the fo'c'sle
& we must sail 3 weeks before we come
to port."

Library of Congress

What port awaits us, Davy Jones'
or home? I've heard of slavers drifting, drifting,
playthings of wind and storm and chance, their crews
gone blind, the jungle hatred
crawling up on deck.

THOU WHO WALKED ON GALILEE

"Deponent further sayeth *The Bella J*
left the Guinea Coast
with cargo of five hundred blacks and odd
for the barracoons of Florida:
"That there was hardly room 'tween-decks for half
the sweltering cattle stowed spoon-fashion there;
that some went mad of thirst and tore their flesh
and sucked the blood:

"That Crew and Captain lusted with the comeliest
of the savage girls kept naked in the cabins;
that there was one they called The Guinea Rose
and they cast lots and fought to lie with her:

305

"That when the Bo's'n piped all hands, the flames
spreading from starboard already were beyond
control, the negroes howling and their chains
entangled with the flames:

"That the burning blacks could not be reached,
that the Crew abandoned ship,
leaving their shrieking negresses behind,
that the Captain perished drunken with the wenches:

"Further Deponent sayeth not."

PILOT OH PILOT ME

2

Aye, lad, and I have seen those factories,
Gambia, Rio Pongo, Calabar;
have watched the artful mongos baiting traps
of war wherein the victor and the vanquished

Were caught as prizes for our barracoons.
Have seen the nigger kings whose vanity
and greed turned wild black hides of Fellatah,
Mandingo, Ibo, Kru to gold for us.

And there was one—King Anthracite we named him—
fetish face beneath French parasols
of brass and orange velvet, impudent mouth
whose cups were carven skulls of enemies:

He'd honor us with drum and feast and conjo
and palm-oil-glistening wenches deft in love,
and for tin crowns that shone with paste,
red calico and German-silver trinkets

Would have the drums talk war and send
his warriors to burn the sleeping villages
and kill the sick and old and lead the young
in coffles to our factories.

Twenty years a trader, twenty years,
for there was wealth aplenty to be harvested
from those black fields, and I'd be trading still
but for the fevers melting down my bones.

3

Shuttles in the rocking loom of history,
the dark ships move, the dark ships move,

their bright ironical names
like jests of kindness on a murderer's mouth;
plough through thrashing glister toward
fata morgana's lucent melting shore,
weave toward New World littorals that are
mirage and myth and actual shore.

Voyage through death,
     voyage whose chartings are unlove.

A charnel stench, effluvium of living death
spreads outward from the hold,
where the living and the dead, the horribly dying,
lie interlocked, lie foul with blood and excrement.

   Deep in the festering hold thy father lies,
   the corpse of mercy rots with him,
   rats eat love's rotten gelid eyes.

   But, oh, the living look at you
   with human eyes whose suffering accuses you,
   whose hatred reaches through the swill of dark
   to strike you like a leper's claw.

   You cannot stare that hatred down
   or chain the fear that stalks the watches
   and breathes on you its fetid scorching breath;
   cannot kill the deep immortal human wish,
   the timeless will.

"But for the storm that flung up barriers
of wind and wave, *The Amistad,* señores,
would have reached the port of Principe in two,
three days at most; but for the storm we should
have been prepared for what befell.
Swift as the puma's leap it came. There was
that interval of moonless calm filled only

307

with the water's and the rigging's usual sounds,
then sudden movement, blows and snarling cries
and they had fallen on us with machete
and marlinspike. It was as though the very
air, the night itself were striking us.

Exhausted by the rigors of the storm,
we were no match for them. Our men went down
before the murderous Africans. Our loyal
Celestino ran from below with gun
and lantern and I saw, before the cane-
knife's wounding flash, Cinquez,
that surly brute who calls himself a prince,
directing, urging on the ghastly work.
He hacked the poor mulatto down, and then
he turned on me. The decks were slippery
when daylight finally came. It sickens me
to think of what I saw, of how these apes
threw overboard the butchered bodies of
our men, true Christians all, like so much jetsam.
Enough, enough. The rest is quickly told:
Cinquez was forced to spare the two of us
you see to steer the ship to Africa,
and we like phantoms doomed to rove the sea
voyaged east by day and west by night,
deceiving them, hoping for rescue,
prisoners on our own vessel, till
at length we drifted to the shores of this
your land, America, where we were freed
from our unspeakable misery. Now we
demand, good sirs, the extradition of
Cinquez and his accomplices to La
Havana. And it distresses us to know
there are so many here who seem inclined
to justify the mutiny of these blacks.
We find it paradoxical indeed
that you whose wealth, whose tree of liberty
are rooted in the labor of your slaves
should suffer the august John Quincy Adams
to speak with so much passion of the right
of chattel slaves to kill their lawful masters
and with his Roman rhetoric weave a hero's

garland for Cinquez. I tell you that
we are determined to return to Cuba
with our slaves and there see justice done. Cinquez—
or let us say 'the Prince'—Cinquez shall die."

The deep immortal human wish,
the timeless will:

     Cinquez its deathless primaveral image,
     life that transfigures many lives.

Voyage through death
               to life upon these shores.

The Granger Collection.

We are here, and here we are likely to be. To imagine that we shall ever be eradicated is absurd and ridiculous. We can be remodified, changed, and assimilated, but never extinguished. We repeat, therefore that we are here; and that this is our country. . . . We shall neither die out, nor be driven out; but shall go with this people, either as a testimony against them, or as an evidence in their favor throughout their generations.

Frederick Douglass

Frederick Douglass

Robert Hayden

When it is finally ours, this freedom, this liberty, this beautiful
and terrible thing, needful to man as air,
usable as earth; when it belongs at last to our children,
when it is truly instinct, brain matter, diastole, systole,
reflex action; when it is finally won; when it is more
than the gaudy mumbo jumbo of politicians:
this man, this Douglass, this former slave, this Negro
beaten to his knees, exiled, visioning a world
where none is lonely, none hunted, alien,
this man, superb in love and logic, this man
shall be remembered. Oh, not with statues' rhetoric,
not with legends and poems and wreaths of bronze alone,
but with the lives grown out of his life, the lives
fleshing his dream of the beautiful, needful thing.

from The Life of Frederick Douglass

In January, 1833 Frederick Douglass was sent to live with Mr. Covey a notorious slave breaker. He was worked from sunrise to sunset in all weather with often less than five minutes for meals. It was during this period of his slavery that he was most thoroughly reduced to wretchedness. Taking sick in the fields, Douglass is accused of malingering and savagely beaten. He flees to his master's home for sanctuary only to be ordered back to Covey.

. . . I immediately started for home; and upon entering the yard gate, out came Mr. Covey on his way to meeting. He spoke to me very kindly, bade me drive the pigs from a lot near by, and passed on towards the church. . . . Long before daylight, I was called to go and rub, curry, and feed, the horses. I obeyed, and was glad to obey. But whilst thus engaged, whilst in the act of throwing down some blades from the loft, Mr. Covey entered the stable with a long rope; and just as I was half out of the loft, he caught hold of my legs, and was about tying me. As soon as I found what he was up to, I gave a sudden spring, and as I did so, he holding to my legs, I was brought sprawling on the stable floor. Mr. Covey seemed now to think he had me, and could do what he pleased; but at this moment—from whence came the spirit I don't know—I resolved to fight; and suiting my action to the resolution, I seized Covey hard by the throat; and as I did so, I rose. He held on to me, and I to him. My resistance was so entirely unexpected, that Covey seemed taken all aback. He trembled like a leaf. This gave me assurance, and I held him uneasy, causing the blood to run where I touched him with the ends of my fingers. Mr. Covey soon called out to Hughes for help. Hughes came, and, while Covey held me, attempted to tie my right hand. While he was in the act of doing so, I watched my chance, and gave him a heavy kick close under the ribs. This kick fairly sickened Hughes, so that he left me in the hands of Mr. Covey. This kick had the effect of not only weakening Hughes, but Covey also. When he saw Hughes bending over with pain, his courage quailed. He asked me if I meant to persist in my resistance. I told him I did, come what might; that he had used me like a brute for six months, and that I was determined to be used so no longer. With that, he strove to drag me to a stick that was lying just out of the stable door. He meant to knock me down. But just as he was leaning over to get the stick, I seized him with both hands by his collar, and brought him by a sudden snatch to the ground. By this time, Bill came. Covey called upon him for assistance. Bill wanted to know what he could do. Covey said, "Take hold of him, take hold of him!" Bill said his master hired him out to work, and not to help to whip me; so he left Covey and myself to fight our own battle out. We were at it for nearly two hours. Covey at length let me go, puffing and blowing at a great rate, saying that if I had not resisted, he would not have whipped me half so much. The truth was, that he had not whipped me at all. I considered him as getting entirely the worst end of the bargain; for he had drawn no blood from me, but I had from him. The whole six months afterwards, that I spent with Mr. Covey, he never laid the weight of his finger upon me in anger. He would occasionally say, he didn't want to get hold of me again. "No," thought I, "you need not; for you will come off worse than you did before."

This battle with Mr. Covey was the turning-point in my career as a slave. It rekindled the few expiring embers of freedom, and revived within me a sense of my own manhood. It recalled the departed self-confidence, and inspired me again with a determination to be free. The gratification afforded by the triumph was a full compensation for whatever else might follow, even death itself. He only can understand the deep satisfaction which I experienced, who has himself repelled by force the bloody arm of slavery. I felt as I never felt before. It was a glorious resurrection, from the tomb of slavery, to the heaven of freedom. My long-crushed spirit rose, cowardice departed, bold defiance took its place; and I now resolved that, however long I might remain a slave in form, the day had passed forever when I could be a slave in fact. I did not hesitate to let it be known of me, that the white man who expected to succeed in whipping, must also succeed in killing me.

From this time I was never again what might be called fairly whipped, though I remained a slave four years afterwards. I had several fights, but was never whipped.

Why Blacks Pay Honor to Douglass

L. F. Palmer Jr.

Frederick Douglass has been called the father of the protest movement. The life of this slave who ran away to freedom is extraordinary because of his deep insight into the monstrous results which accrue when a society physically and mentally enslaves a major segment of its population.

A review of the Douglass story lays bare the striking fact that this society has hardly relaxed the tenacious hold it has on the black American's yearning for liberation.

For the powerfully eloquent words of protest spoken by Douglass are still being repeated today, 153 years after his birth, 75 years after his death.

From the *Chicago Daily News*, February 14, 1970. Reprinted with permission from the *Chicago Daily News*.

He was born in February 1817, but there are no records of the date. Because of this, many black groups have assigned Feb. 12 as his birthdate and honor him rather than Abraham Lincoln on the holiday proclaimed for the latter.

Born of the eastern shore of Maryland, Douglass did not know who his father was. He was aware that rumor attributed this biological role to his slavemaster. Douglass saw his mother fewer than a half-dozen times.

"Slavery abolished fatherhood and motherhood," he once said.

The young slave boy was brilliant and rebellious from an early age. His slavemaster's wife wanted to teach him the alphabet but the master would not permit it.

So young Frederick taught himself how to read.

When he continuously refused to conform to the expected behavior of slaves, he was sent to a "professional Negro-breaker," Edward Corey, who worked and whipped him unmercifully.

Finally reaching the brink, the young slave fought back and held Corey to a long and bitter standoff.

"I had reached the point at which I was not afraid to die," Frederick Douglass said later. "This spirit made me a free man in fact, while I remained a slave in form . . . Men are whipped oftenest who are whipped easiest."

Shortly afterwards, he escaped to freedom.

He was 21 then and the year was 1838. Douglass married and supported his family for a time by waiting tables, sawing wood, and laboring on the docks and in a brass factory.

Soon he became wedded to the movement to abolish slavery.

Douglass' talents and influence bloomed. A tall, handsome man of stately bearing, his wisdom and courage matched his appearance.

"My objection to slavery," he said, "is not that it sinks a Negro to the condition of brute, but that it sinks a man to that condition."

Historian Lerone Bennett, Jr., writes about Douglass and it is as though he is discussing a contemporary black leader:

"As a theorist and advocate, Douglass stressed the structural roots of racism. He said it was libelous to call the race problem the Negro problem. The real problem, he said, was the white problem.

"He urged black Americans to pool their resources as a massive crusade against racism. Although he considered the ballot indispensable, he did not neglect economic power."

Following the Emancipation Proclamation, Douglass spent the remainder of his life trying to convince America that it had not freed blacks. He battled for full citizenship and equal rights for the ex-slaves.

He branded the "so-called emancipation as a stupendous fraud, a fraud upon (the black man) and a fraud upon the world."

His impassioned words rang with the validity of his years and with the challenge of ours:

"When justice is denied, where poverty is enforced, where ignorance prevails, and where any one class is made to feel that society is an organized conspiracy to oppress, rob, and degrade . . . neither persons nor property will be safe. . . .''

This was Frederick Douglass who, more than a hundred years ago, was staging his own sit-ins on Massachusetts railroads and leading a fight for integrated school in Rochester, N.Y.

Before he died on February 20, 1895, the father of the protest movement had become marshal of the District of Columbia and minister to Haiti.

He never stopped fighting for black liberation. Shortly before he died, a young black student asked Douglass what he should do with his life. Douglass' answer leaped across the years to echo in the ears of blacks today:

"Agitate!" he thundered. "Agitate!"

Remembering Nat Turner

(For R. C. L.)

Sterling A. Brown

> We saw a bloody sunset over Courtland, once Jerusalem,
> As we followed the trail that old Nat took
> When he came out of Cross Keys down upon Jerusalem,
> In his angry stab for freedom a hundred years ago.
> The land was quiet, and the mist was rising,
> Out of the woods and the Nottaway swamp,
> Over Southampton the still night fell,
> As we rode down to Cross Keys where the march began.
>
> When we got to Cross Keys, they could tell us little of him,
> The Negroes had only the faintest recollections:
> > "I ain't been here so long, I come from up round' Newsome;
> > Yassah, a town a few miles up de road,

The old folks who coulda told you is all dead an' gone.
I heard something, sometime; I doan jis remember what.
'Pears lak I heard that name somewheres or other.
So he fought to be free. Well. You doan say.''

An old white woman recalled exactly
How Nat crept down the steps, axe in his hand,
After murdering a woman and child in bed,
"Right in this here house at the head of these stairs"
(In a house built long after Nat was dead).
She pointed to a brick store where Nat was captured,
(Nat was taken in the swamp, three miles away)
With his men around him, shooting from the windows
(She was thinking of Harper's Ferry and old John Brown).
She cackled as she told how they riddled Nat with bullets
(Nat was tried and hanged at Courtland, ten miles away).
She wanted to know why folks would comes miles
Just to ask about an old nigger fool.

"Ain't no slavery no more, things is going all right,
Pervided thar's a good goober market this year.
We had a sign post here with printing on it,
But it rotted in the hole, and thar it lays.
And the nigger tenants split the marker for kindling.
Things is all right, naow, ain't no trouble with the niggers
Why they make this big to-do over Nat?''

As we drove from Cross Keys back to Courtland,
Along the way that Nat came down upon Jerusalem,
A watery moon was high in the cloud-filled heavens,
The same moon he dreaded a hundred years ago.
The tree they hanged Nat on is long gone to ashes,
The trees he dodged behind have rotted in the swamps.
The bus for Miama and the trucks boomed by,
And touring cars, their heavy tires snarling on the pavement.
Frogs piped in the marshes, and a hound bayed long,
And yellow lights glowed from the cabin windows.

As we came back the way that Nat led his army,
Down from Cross Keys, down to Jerusalem,
We wondered if his troubled spirit still roamed the Nottaway,
Or if it fled with the cock-crow at daylight,
Or lay at peace with the bones in Jerusalem,
Its restlessness stilled by Southampton clay.
We remembered the poster rotted through and falling,
The marker split for kindling a kitchen fire.

Runagate Runagate

Robert Hayden

I.

Runs falls rises stumbles on from darkness into darkness
and the darkness thicketed with shapes of terror
and the hunters pursuing and the hounds pursuing
and the night cold and the night long and the river
to cross and the jack-muh-lanterns beckoning beckoning
and blackness ahead and when shall I reach that somewhere
morning and keep on going and never turn back and keep on going

    Runagate

      Runagate

        Runagate

Many thousands rise and go
many thousands crossing over

        O mythic North
       O star-shaped yonder Bible city
And before I'll be a slave
I'll be buried in my grave

    North star and bonanza gold
    I'm bound for the freedom, freedom-bound
    and oh Susyanna don't you cry for me

      Runagate

        Runagate

II.

Rises from their anguish and their power,

    Harriet Tubman,

    woman of the earth, whipscarred,
    a summoning, a shining,

    Mean to be free

    And this was the way of it, brethren brethren,
    way we journeyed from Can't to Can.
    Moon so bright and no place to hide,
    the cry up and the patterollers riding,
    hound dogs belling in bladed air
    And fear starts a-murbling, Never make it,
    we'll never make it. *Hush that now,*
    and she's turned upon us, leveled pistol
    glinting in the moonlight:
    Dead folks can't jaybird-talk, she says;
    you keep on going now or die, she says.

Wanted   Harriet Tubman   alias The General
alias Moses   Stealer of Slaves

In league with Garrison   Alcott   Emerson
Garrett   Douglass   Thoreau   John Brown

Armed and known to be Dangerous

Wanted   Reward   Dead or Alive

    Tell me, Ezekiel, oh tell me do you see
    mailed Jehovah coming to deliver me?

Some go weeping and some rejoicing
some in coffins and some in carriages
some in silks and some in shackles

    Rise and go or fare you well

No more auction block for me
no more driver's lash for me
Hoot-owl calling in the ghosted air,
five times calling to the hants in the air.
Shadow of a face in the scary leaves,
shadow of a voice in the talking leaves:

Come ride-a my train

Oh that train, ghost-story train
through swamp and savanna movering movering,
over trestles of dew, through caves of the wish,
Midnight Special on a sabre track movering movering,
first stop Mercy and the last Hallelujah.

Come ride-a my train

Mean mean mean to be free.

Culver Pictures, Inc.

Harriet Tubman

I grew up like a neglected weed—ignorant of liberty, having no experi-ence of it. I was not happy or contented: every time I saw a white man I was afraid of being carried away. I had two sisters carried away in a chain gang—one of them left two children. We were always uneasy. Now I've been free, I know what slavery is. I have seen hundreds of escaped slaves but I never saw one who was willing to go back and be a slave. I have no opportunity to see my friends in my native land. We would rather stay in our native land if we could be as free there as we are here. I think slavery is the next thing to hell. If a person would send another into bondage he would, it appears to me, be bad enough to send him to hell if he could.

To Benjamin Drew, 1855. Quoted by Earl Conrad in Harriet Tubman, *The Associated Publishers, Inc., Washington, D.C., p. 73.*

. . . from Christmas until March (probably of the years 1835-1836) I worked as I could, and prayed through all the long nights—I groaned and prayed for the old master.
Oh Lord, convert master! Oh Lord, change that man's heart!

After Harriet hears the rumor she and her family might be sold South, the prayer changes:

Oh Lord, if you aren't ever going to change that man's heart, kill him Lord, and take him out of the way!

Conrad, p. 19.

The Rescue of Charles Nalle, Fugitive Slave

Earl Conrad

Troy, New York, April 27, 1860

So brittle was the spring air in the Troy streets that finger tips and nose-tips reddened and color came quickly to the cheeks. The pavement was dry and the jostlers, milling about, moving from one group to another to hear all sentiments, soon melted the air throughout the avenue, and waves of warmth arose from the massed body until the vague sense of it wafted into the open windows of the courtroom. But the cold passions of the pro-slavers were not so easily melted, for "Meanwhile angry discussion commenced. Some persons agitated a rescue, and others favored law and order."[1]

Soon the murmurings for a forcible rescue became a clamor for immediate action. At the courtroom door, moaning like some helpless wind lost in a forest, Harriet listened to the roar in the street, measured every slightest motion, each developing factor and waved the basket, shield-like, before her eyes. . . .

The prisoner was about thirty, good-looking, intelligent of appearance, unnerved by his ordeal; and now he paced about before the tremoring window and looked down upon the whirlpool of friends and enemies. Perceiving that he had suddenly become a *cause celebre,* and encouraged by the manifestation of sympathy that thundered from the marketplace, he weighed his chances for escape. The stake was high; the cost might be death. . . .

When . . . the inevitable decision against Nalle was pronounced, as the guards began to squirm, and as Harriet's deep groan of protest suffused the room like a chant, Nalle leaped to action. He turned swiftly as a wheel, darted toward the window with a half dive, opened it with a fleet movement of his gray-white wrists, and stepped out on the ledge. As yells of welcome greeted him from the street, he twisted himself into position for a dangerous drop to the pavement. . . .

The guards soon bayed the prisoner; hands encircled his neck, his sprawling limbs, his whole body, and they hauled him back into the offices of the Commissioner and held to him like crabs to food. Aching for breath in their hard grasp, Charles Nalle subsided; and he looked for help to the swaying Negro women who filled the doorway with their bodies and their bursts of lament at his recapture. . . .

[1] The Troy Whig, April 27, 1860.

As numbers spiral when they are multiplied so the crowd enlarged until the thousands merged and flowed, a great social and human tide. Suddenly there arose from the street a last desperate cry that crackled into the courtroom like a flame, *"We will buy his freedom. What is his master's price?"*

The Southern agent leaped to the rattling window, ready to strike a bargain. Money for flesh. Flesh for money. That was different. Flesh might not be higher than law, but money was.

"Twelve hundred dollars," shouted the Virginian.

Pools of citizens eddied with a new excitement as pouches flashed into the open and pledges loosed on the air. The well-to-do gave richly, and the poor heroically. Two hundred was mounted by three hundred more; a wave of notes and a jangle of silver lifted the sum to a thousand. Soon, like all tides that reach the shore, there was a mighty surf of final contribution.

"We have raised twelve hundred dollars!"

But the slaveowner's agent was avaricious, and he shouted back at the throng, "Fifteen hundred dollars!"

It was the typical Southern attitude, the same which later would provoke secession and rebellion; it was one more slap to rouse the North, and even now it reawakened all the quieted fervor of the anti-slavers. A stinging voice that was a clarion call of all the North shouted:

"Two hundred dollars for his freedom but not one cent for his master!"

The anti-slavers pressed forward, ready to give their lives if need be in the name of Freedom. . . .

Harriet unraveled some of the kinks in her slight body. As several guards and deputies manacled the prisoner and headed him toward the door, ordering onlookers aside, she arose to her full height, which was not impressive, sent the basket reeling and bumping into a corner, magically dropped her aged appearance, and fleet-footed across the courtroom to the window. Her words, declaiming on Troy air like some tonal bell in a hollow steeple, became the cue for the Abolitionists.

"Here he comes! Take him!" . . .

"This man shall not go back to slavery! Take him, friends! Drag him to the river! Drown him! But don't let them take him back!" . . .

When after long attack, and after the fighting throng had swept down the town's blocks toward the river, and when the power of the police and the pro-slavers was smashed, Harriet, still clinging to Nalle, broke away, dashed to the river front, and protected by a brave band of hurt and bleeding whites and Negroes, placed the prisoner in a skiff manned by a sympathetic ferryman. . . .

The prisoner, who was almost unconscious from his injuries, himself having fought furiously, was captured as soon as he reached the other shore, and there was rushed to Police Justice Stewart's office. The law threw up barricades and prepared to fight anew.

With Harriet Tubman in the forefront, the conflict became sharpest and bloodiest at this point. "Not a moment was lost. Upstairs went a score or more of resolute men—the rest piling in promiscuously, shouting and execrating the officers."[2]

Stones flew against the door, pistol shots came from the guards inside. There was a momentary retreat until someone shouted, "They can only kill a dozen of us—come on!" The citadel was stormed, amidst a hail of thrown stones and a returning them of gunfire.[3]

"At last," said *The Whig,* "the door was pulled open by an immense Negro and in a moment he was felled by the hatchet in the hands of Deputy Sheriff Morrison; but the body of the fallen man blocked up the door so that it could not be shut. . . ."

Attorney Martin Townsend has said the last word. ". . . and when the men who led the assault upon the door of Judge Stewart's office were stricken down, Harriet and a number of other colored women rushed over their bodies, brought Nalle out, and putting him into the first wagon passing, started him for the West. . . ."

It was Harriet Tubman's victory as surely as Harper's Ferry was John Brown's, and more, it was a high point of the fugitive slave history that racked the nation's breast for ten years. . . .

The law tracked after her for days, scenting her out as they might some thieving desperado. The wrath of the pro-slavers demanded her arrest, her trial, even her blood. But the Abolitionists had taken her deep into their underground bosom, and she lay hidden for days nursing her terrible wounds.

Later, by all the devious means of the Underground, she continued on her way—to Boston and her friends.

Conrad, pp. 132–138.

---

[2] The Troy Whig, April 27, 1860.

[3] According to the Troy Arena, another local newspaper whose dispatches were reprinted in Frederick Douglass' Paper of May 11, 1860, the only reason why many were not seriously wounded or killed by the law's gunfire was due to the poor aim of the authorities.

Harriet Tubman armed. Culver Pictures, Inc.

About the battle of Fort Wagner:

"And then we heard the thunder and that was the big guns. And then we heard the rain falling and that was the drops of blood falling. And when we came to get in the crops, it was dead men that we reaped."

Quoted in the Black Scholar, *Jan.-Feb. 1970, p. 6, "I Bring You General Tubman," Earl Conrad.*

STOLEN

HERITAGE

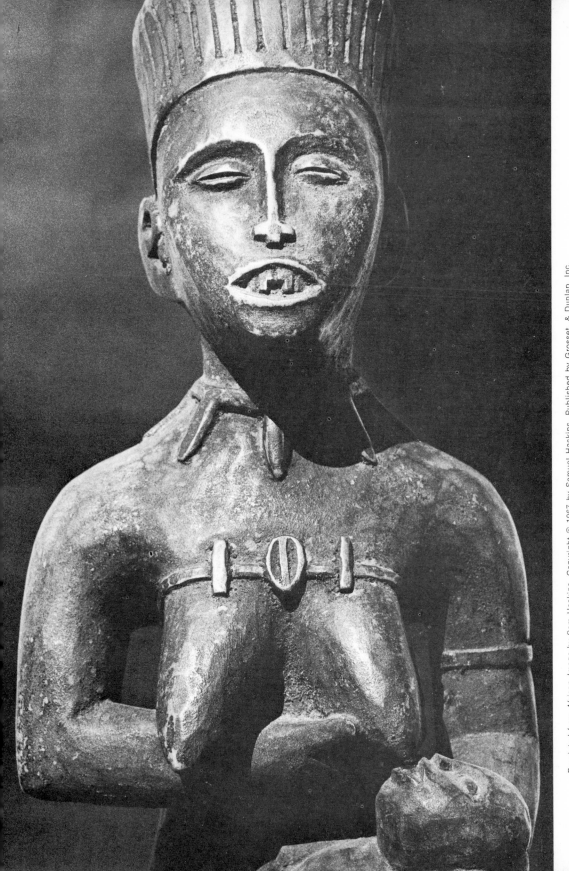

from Lost and Found: Africa and Negro Past

Charles E. Silberman

. . . Today, Africa is contributing enormously to Negro self-pride; yesterday Africa contributed even more to Negro self-hate.

To understand why, it is necessary to recall the image of Africa that prevailed just a few years ago—the image which indeed, still dominates most white thinking. Africa, in this view, is the Dark Continent, "a continent without history," a place of savagery and ignorance whose people had contributed nothing at all to human progress. "All the continents begin with an 'A' except one," begins a chapter of V. M. Hillyer's A Child Geography of the World, a favorite when I was a child, and still a popular children's book. "Asia is the largest continent. Africa is the next largest. But Africa was an 'In-the-Way' continent," the chapter continues. "It was in the way of those who wanted to get to Asia. Everyone wanted to get *around* Africa. No one wanted to get to it. Sailors have been shipwrecked on its shores, but few lived to tell the tale of jungles, of wild animals, and wild black men. Africa was called the Dark Continent because no one knew much about it or wanted to know about it. . . On one edge—along the Mediterranean Sea —white men lived, but south of that edge was a great desert that men feared to cross, and south of that wild black man and wild animals. . . ."

Public school textbooks were even more deprecating. In the texts used when today's adult Negro population attended school, the inevitable pictures of "the five races of man" almost always showed the African man at his most primitive. In contrast to "the Emersonian white man in his study, the Japanese aristocrat, the Malay nobleman, and the Indian chief—all obviously selected to depict the highest social rank in each case," Professor Harold R. Isaacs has written, the "African" appeared as "a prehistoric figure of a man, naked, stepping out of primeval ooze, carrying an ante-deluvian club and shield."* One text, Isaacs reports, classified the states of man as

* Anyone concerned with the impact of Africa on Negro consciousness is indebted to Professor Isaas for *The New World of Negro Americans* (New York: John Day, 1963).

"savage" ("all black or red"), "barbarous" ("chiefly brown"), "half-civilized" ("almost wholly yellow"), and "civilized" ("almost all belong to the white race.") Movies were even more devastating: Hollywood almost invariably showed Africa as a land populated by half-naked cannibals.

Against this debasing picture of "the African," the Negro child had no defense; he had no way of knowing that the picture happened to be false. On the contrary, this "evidence of the black man's inferiority," as Isaacs put it, "was borne in upon him with all the weight and authority of the all-knowing, all-powerful, all-surrounding white world," thereby confirming the sense of his own worthlessness that white attitudes and actions had already established. This confirmation played an important, frequently a crucial, role in the development of Negro children's conception of themselves. In the interviews with a hundred seven leading Negroes that formed the basis of *The New World of Negro Americans,* Isaacs found "that in nearly every instance" the early discovery of the African background had been "a prime element" in shaping the individual's knowledge of and attitude toward himself and his world—so much so that most of the subjects could recall the details of the pictures and the names of the texts with agonizing clarity forty, fifty, and even sixty years later! . . .

I Thank God I'm Free at Last

Free at last, free at last.
I thank God I'm free at last.
Free at last, free at last,
I thank God I'm free at last.

Way down yonder in the graveyard walk,
I thank God I'm free at last,
Me and my Jesus gonna meet an' talk,
I thank God I'm free at last.

On-a my knees when the light pass by,
I thank God I'm free at last,
Thought my soul would rise an' fly,
I thank God I'm free at last.

One o' these mornin's bright an' fair,
I thank God I'm free at last,
Gonna meet my Jesus in the middle o' the air,
I thank God I'm free at last.

Free at last, free at last,
I thank God I'm free at last,
Free at last, free at last,
I thank God I'm free at last.

Reprinted from *African Image* by Sam Haskins. Copyright © 1967 by Samuel Haskins. Published by Grosset & Dunlap, Inc.

isabled passenger: **Is somebody traveling with you?**
À un passager infirme: Quelqu'un voyage-t-il avec vous?
Zu einem körperbehinderten Passagier: Reist jemand mit Ihnen?
A un passeggero incapacitato: C'è qualcuno che viaggia con Lei?
A um passageiro incapacitado: Viaja alguém consigo?
A un pasajero incapacitado: ¿Le acompaña alguien en el viaje?

n **you walk with a little help?**
F: Pouvez-vous marcher si nous vous aidons?
G: Können Sie mit einiger Hilfe gehen?
I: Può camminare con aiuto?
P: Pode andar com ajuda?
S: ¿Puede caminar con ayuda?

am going to **request a wheelchair.**
F: Je vais demander une chaise roulante.
G: Ich werde einen Rollstuhl anfordern.
I: Richiederò per Lei una sedia a rotelle.
P: Vou pedir uma cadeira de rodas.
S: Pediré una silla de ruedas.

What is your address?
F: Quelle est votre adresse?
G: Würden Sie mir Ihre Adresse geben?
I: Qual'è il Suo indirizzo?
P: Qual é o seu endereço?
S: ¿Cuál es su dirección?

71. **Are you going as a tourist or on business?**
F: Voyagez-vous comme touriste ou pour affaires?
G: Sind Sie Tourist oder Geschäftsreisender?
I: Viaggia per turismo o per affari?
P: Viaja como turista ou em negócios?
S: ¿Viaja como turista o de negocios?

Departure (Passengers Checking In)

F: DÉPART (*Enregistrement des passagers*)
G: ABFLUG (*Melden der Passagiere zur Abfertigung*)
I: PARTENZE (*Controllo passeggeri*)
P: PARTIDA (*Processo de passageiros*)
S: PARTIDA (*Proceso de pasajeros*)

Documents

F: DOCUMENTS
G: DOKUMENTE
I: DOCUMENTI
P: DOCUMENTOS
S: DOCUMENTOS

55. **Good morning.**
F: Bonjour.
G: Guten Morgen.
I: `Buon giorno.
P: Bom dia.
S: Buenos días.

56. **Good day.**
F: Bonjour.
G: Guten Tag.
I: Buon giorno.
P: Bom dia.
S: Buenos días.

57. **Good afternoon.**
F: Bonjour.
G: Guten Tag.

I: Buon giorno.
P: Boa tarde.
S: Buenas tardes.

58. Good evening.
F: Bonsoir.
G: Guten Abend.
I: Buona sera.
P: Boa tarde.
S: Buenas tardes.

59. May I see your ticket [your passport]?
F: Permettez-moi de voir votre billet [votre passeport].
G: Darf ich Sie um Ihren Flugschein [Ihren Paß] bitten?
I: Per favore, potrei vedere il Suo biglietto [il Suo passaporto]?
P: Posso ver o seu bilhete [o seu passaporte]?
S: Permítame ver su billete (OR pasaje, boleto*) [su pasaporte].

60. May I see your vaccination certificate?
F: Permettez-moi de voir votre certificat de vaccination.
G: Darf ich Sie um Ihr Impfzeugnis bitten?
I: Potrei vedere il Suo certificato di vaccinazione?
P: Posso ver o seu certificado de vacina?
S: Permítame ver su certificado de vacuna.

61. Are you traveling together?
F: Voyagez-vous ensemble?
G: Reisen Sie zusammen?
I: Viaggiano insieme?
P: Viajam juntos?
S: ¿Viajan juntos?

* "Ticket" is *pasaje* or *boleto* in some parts of South America.

62. Are you a resident o
F: Résidez-vous à (
G: Wohnen Sie in —
I: È Lei residente a
P: É residente de ——
S: ¿Es residente en —

63. May I see your resident's
F: Puis-je voir votre car
G: Darf ich Sie um
bitten?
I: Per favore, potrei veder
P: Posso ver o seu cartão d
S: Permítame ver su tarjet

64. I cannot find my identity card
F: Je ne trouve pas ma carte
G: Ich kann meinen Personala
I: Non riesco a trovare la mia
P: Não posso encontrar o meu ca
S: No encuentro mi tarjeta (OR

65. I have left it at home.
F: Je l'ai laissée à la maison.
G: Ich habe ihn zu Hause gelassen.
I: L'ho lasciata a casa.
P: Deixei-o em casa.
S: La olvidé en casa.

66. Here is my alien registration card.
F: Voici ma carte de résidence.
G: Hier ist mein Personalausweis für A
I: Ecco la mia carta di residenza per str
P: Aqui está o meu cartão de residência p
S: Aquí está mi tarjeta de residencia para

67. To a
F:

G:

I:

P:
S:

68. Ca

69.

70

72. I am going as a tourist.
F: Je suis touriste.
G: Ich reise als Tourist.
I: Vado come turista.
P: Viajo como turista.
S: Viajo como turista.

73. Here are my photographs.
F: Voici mes photographies.
G: Hier sind meine Photographien.
I: Ecco le mie fotografie.
P: Aqui estão as minhas fotografias.
S: Aquí están mis fotografías.

74. The employee at the other counter will help you.
F: L'agent de l'autre comptoir va vous aider.
G: Der Angestellte an dem anderen Schalter wird Sie bedienen.
I: L'impiegato dell'altro banco L'aiuterà.
P: O empregado no outro balcão o ajudará.
S: El empleado en el otro mostrador le atenderá.

75. This passport has expired.
F: La validité de ce passeport est expirée.
G: Dieser Paß ist ungültig.
I: Questo passaporto è scaduto.
P: A validade deste passaporte já expirou.
S: Este pasaporte está vencido (OR caducado).

76. I'm sorry, but we cannot permit you to travel.
F: Je suis désolé (FEM. désolée), mais nous ne pouvons pas vous permettre de voyager.
G: Ich bedauere, aber wir dürfen Sie nicht reisen lassen.
I: Mi dispiace, ma non possiamo farLa partire.
P: Lamento, mas não podemos permitir que viaje.
S: Lo lamentamos mucho, pero no podemos permitirle que viaje.

77. You must have this passport renewed.
   F: Vous devez faire renouveler ce passeport.
   G: Sie müssen diesen Paß verlängern lassen.
   I: Lei deve rinnovare questo passaporto.
   P: Tem que ter este passaporte renovado.
   S: Su pasaporte debe ser renovado.

78. You must get a new passport.
   F: Vous devez obtenir un nouveau passeport.
   G: Sie müssen sich einen neuen Paß besorgen.
   I: Lei deve richiedere un nuovo passaporto.
   P: Deve obter um novo passaporte.
   S: Tiene que obtener un nuevo pasaporte.

79. We will rewrite (OR reissue) your ticket.
   F: Nous allons réémettre votre billet.
   G: Wir werden Ihren Flugschein umschreiben (OR neu ausstellen).
   I: Dovremo riemettere il Suo biglietto.
   P: Reemitiremos o seu bilhete.
   S: Tenemos que cambiar su billete (OR boleto, pasaje).

80. I have to revalidate your ticket.
   F: Je dois revalider votre billet.
   G: Ich muß Ihren Flugschein umbuchen (OR neu eintragen).
   I: Devo rivalidare il Suo biglietto.
   P: Tenho que revalidar o seu bilhete.
   S: Tengo que revalidar su billete.

81. Do you have a visa for ———?
   F: Avez-vous un visa pour ———?
   G: Haben Sie ein Visum für ———?
   I: Ha il visto per ———?
   P: Tem visto para ———?
   S: ¿Tiene visa (OR visado, visación) para ———?

82. I didn't think I needed one.
F: Je pensais que je n'en avais pas besoin.
G: Ich wußte nicht, daß ich eins brauche.
I: Pensavo che non fosse necessario.
P: Pensei não precisar de um visto.
S: Creía que no la necesitaba.

83. I forgot to get it.
F: J'ai oublié d'en obtenir un.
G: Ich habe vergessen, mir eins zu besorgen.
I: Ho dimenticato di prenderlo.
P: Esqueci-me de o obter.
S: Me olvidé de conseguirla.

84. Sorry, but this is a requirement of the country concerned.
F: Je suis désolé (FEM. désolée), mais c'est la réglementation de ce pays-là.
G: Es tut mir leid, aber das betreffende Land verlangt das.
I: Mi dispiace, ma questo è richiesto dall'autorità del rispettivo paese.
P: Lamento, mas isto é um requerimento do respectivo país.
S: Lamento mucho, pero esto es un requerimiento de dicho país.

85. Can you help me?
F: Pouvez-vous m'aider?
G: Können Sie mir helfen?
I: Mi può aiutare?
P: Pode-me ajudar?
S: ¿Podría ayudarme?

86. You could travel with us to ———.
F: Vous pourriez voyager avec nous jusqu'à ———.
G: Sie könnten mit uns nach ——— fliegen.

I: Lei potrebbe viaggiare con noi fino a ———.
P: Podia viajar connosco* para ———.
S: Ud. podría viajar con nosotros hasta ———.

87. There you will be able to obtain your visa for ———.
   F: Vous pourriez obtenir là-bas votre visa pour ———.
   G: Dort kann Ihr Visum für ——— durch den Konsul ausgestellt werden.
   I: Lì può ottenere il visto per ———.
   P: Lá poderá obter o seu visto para ———.
   S: Allí podrá conseguir su visa para ———.

88. You could continue your trip on the first available flight to ———.
   F: Vous pourriez continuer votre voyage sur le premier vol disponible à destination de ———.
   G: Sie können dann Ihre Reise mit der nächsten Maschine nach ——— fortsetzen.
   I: Potrebbe continuare il viaggio con il primo volo per ———.
   P: Poderá continuar a sua viagem no próximo vôo disponível para ———.
   S: Ud. podría continuar el viaje en el primer vuelo que haya para ———.

89. What about my luggage?
   F: Et au sujet de mes bagages?
   G: Was wird mit meinem Gepäck geschehen?
   I: E il mio bagaglio?
   P: Que sucede à minha bagagem?
   S: ¿Qué pasará con mis valijas?

90. We will send a telegram to our office at ———.
   F: Nous allons envoyer un télégramme à notre bureau de ———.

---

* In Brazil *conosco*.

G: Wir werden unser Büro in ——— telegraphisch benachrichten.

I: Manderemo un telegramma al nostro ufficio di ———.

P: Enviaremos um telegrama para o nosso escritório em ———.

S: Mandaremos (OR Enviaremos) un telegrama a nuestra oficina en ———.

91. We will indicate in our message that ———.

F: Nous allons indiquer sur notre message que ———.

G: Wir werden veranlassen, daß ———.

I: Nel messaggio spiegheremo che ———.

P: Mencionaremos na nossa mensagem que ———.

S: Mencionaremos en nuestro mensaje que ———.

92. We will request them to locate your baggage at ———.

F: Nous allons leur demander de retrouver vos bagages à ———.

G: Wir werden veranlassen, daß Ihr Gepäck in ——— gefunden wird.

I: Richiederemo di rintracciare il Suo bagaglio a ———.

P: Pedir-lhe-emos que localizem a sua bagagem em ———.

S: Pediremos que localicen sus valijas en ———.

93. I would suggest your staying here in order to obtain your visa for ———.

F: Je vous suggère de rester ici de façon à obtenir votre visa pour ———.

G: Ich würde vorschlagen, daß Sie hier bleiben, um sich das Visum für ——— zu besorgen.

I: Le consiglio di rimanere qui in modo di ottenere il visto per ———.

P: Sugiro que fique aqui para obter o seu visto para ———.

S: Le recomiendo de quedarse aquí para poder obtener su visa para ———.

94. The Consulate might not be open over the weekend.

F: Le consulat peut être fermé pendant le weekend.

G: Das Konsulat ist vielleicht am Wochenende nicht geöffnet.

I: Il consolato potrebbe essere chiuso durante il fine-settimana.

P: O consulado não deve abrir durante o fim de semana.

S: El consulado no estará abierto durante el fin de semana.

Baggage and Seat Selection

F: BAGAGES ET CHOIX DES PLACES

G: GEPÄCK UND SITZWAHL

I: BAGAGLIO E RICHIESTA DEL POSTO

P: BAGAGEM E SELECÇÃO DE LUGARES

S: EQUIPAJE Y SELECCIÓN DE PLAZAS

95. May I have your ticket, please?

F: Puis-je avoir votre billet, s'il vous plaît?

G: Darf ich um Ihren Flugschein bitten?

I: Posso avere il Suo biglietto, per favore?

P: Faça favor o seu bilhete?

S: ¿Me permite su billete (OR boleto, pasaje)?

96. Do you have any hand baggage?

F: Avez-vous des bagages à main?

G: Haben Sie Handgepäck?

I: Ha del bagaglio a mano?

P: Tem alguma bagagem de mão?

S: ¿Tiene equipaje de mano?

97. I am sorry, but according to the regulations the following articles must be weighed:

F: Je suis désolé (FEM. désolée), mais d'après le règlement les articles suivants doivent être pesés:

G: Es tut mir leid, aber laut Vorschrift müssen folgende Gegenstände gewogen werden:

I: Mi dispiace, ma secondo il regolamento i seguenti oggetti devono essere pesati:

P: Tenho pena, mas de acordo com os regulamentos devem ser pesados os seguintes artigos:

S: Lo siento, pero de acuerdo con las normas se deben pesar los siguientes artículos:

98. Briefcases, portable typewriters.

F: Serviettes d'affaires, machines à écrire portatives.

G: Aktentaschen, Schreibmaschinen.

I: Borse, macchine da scrivere portabili.

P: Pastas, máquinas de escrever portáteis.

S: Carteras, máquinas de escribir portátiles.

99. Portable radios, vanity or cosmetic cases.

F: Postes de radio portatifs, sacs à main de dame.

G: Transistors, Kosmetikkoffer.

I: Radio portabili, necessaires o borsette da signora.

P: Rádios portáteis, malas de cosméticos.

S: Radios portátiles, neceseres.

100. Large camera cases.

F: Appareils photographiques ou cinématographiques de grandes dimensions.

G: Grosse Kameras.

I: Astucci con macchine fotografiche.

P: Câmaras fotográficas ou de filmar grandes.

S: Cámaras fotográficas grandes.

101. Hatboxes, overnight bags.

F: Cartons à chapeaux, petites valises de nuit.

G: Hutschachteln, Reisetaschen.

I: Cappelliere, borse.

P: Chapeleiras, sacos de mão (OR sacolas).

S: Sombrereras, bolsas de viaje.

102. Would you please put the camera on the scale?

F: Voulez-vous, s'il vous plaît, mettre l'appareil sur la balance?

G: Würden Sie bitte die Kamera auf die Waage legen?
I: Per favore, vuole mettere la macchina fotografica sulla bilancia?
P: Faça favor de pôr a câmara fotográfica na balança.
S: Por favor, ponga su cámara en la báscula (OR balanza).

103. I have to tag and weigh the baby carriage also.
F: Je dois étiqueter et peser la poussette du bébé aussi.
G: Der Kinderwagen muß auch gewogen und mit Gepäckanhänger versehen werden.
I: Devo pesare e mettere uno scontrino anche sulla carrozzina.
P: Tenho que etiquetar e pesar o carrinho do bébé também.
S: Debo rotular y pesar también el cochecito (OR cochecillo) de niños.

104. May I keep my baby carriage until boarding time?
F: Puis-je garder ma poussette jusqu'à l'embarquement?
G: Darf ich meinen Kinderwagen behalten, bis der Flug aufgerufen wird?
I: Posso tenere la carrozzina fino all'imbarco?
P: Posso conservar o carrinho do bébé até o momento de embarque?
S: ¿Podría usar el cochecito (OR cochecillo) hasta el momento de embarcar?

105. Yes, you may continue to use it, but only until boarding.
F: Oui, vous pouvez continuer à vous en servir jusqu'à l'embarquement.
G: Sie dürfen ihn behalten, aber nur bis zum Einsteigen.
I: Sì, può usarla fino al momento dell'imbarco.
P: Sim, pode continuar usá-lo até o embarque.
S: Sí, puede usarlo hasta el momento de embarcar.

106. Please do not forget to return the carriage to the same baggage counter as soon as your flight is announced.

F: S'il vous plaît, n'oubliez pas de rendre cette poussette au même comptoir dès que le départ de votre vol sera annoncé.

G: Vergessen Sie bitte nicht den Kinderwagen an dem selben Gepäckschalter abzugeben, sobald Ihr Flug aufgerufen ist.

I: Per favore, non dimentichi di riportare la carrozzina allo stesso banco dei bagagli appena il Suo volo sarà annunciato.

P: Por favor, não se esqueça de devolver o carrinho do bébé no mesmo balcão de bagagem logo que o seu vôo seja anunciado.

S: Por favor, no se olvide devolver el cochecito al mismo mostrador de equipaje en cuanto se anuncie su vuelo.

107. Do not go away! Stay here and wait for me!

F: Ne partez pas, restez ici et attendez-moi!

G: Gehen Sie nicht weg, bleiben Sie hier und warten Sie auf mich!

I: Non vada via, stia qui e mi aspetti!

P: Não se afaste, fique aqui e espere por mim.

S: Por favor, no se vaya, quédese aquí y espéreme.

108. Would you please put all your luggage on the scale?

F: Voulez-vous, s'il vous plaît, mettre tous vos bagages sur la bascule?

G: Würden Sie bitte Ihr gesamtes Gepäck auf die Waage legen?

I: Per favore, metta tutto il bagaglio sulla bilancia!

P: Por favor, coloque na balança toda a sua bagagem!

S: ¡Por favor, ponga todo su equipaje en la báscula (OR balanza)!

109. I am sorry, but we must hand-tag whatever you carry on board.

F: Je suis désolé (FEM. désolée), mais nous devons étiqueter tout ce que vous gardez à bord.

G: Es tut mir leid, aber wir müssen alle Stücke, die Sie mit an Bord nehmen, mit einem Anhänger versehen.

I: Mi dispiace, ma dobbiamo mettere uno scontrino a mano su tutto ciò che porta a bordo.

P: Tenho pena (OR Lamento), mas temos que etiquetar o que levar na cabina.

S: Lo siento, pero debemos rotular todo lo que lleve a bordo.

110. You have ――― pounds [kilos] of excess baggage.

F: Vous avez ――― livres [kilos] d'excédent de bagages.

G: Sie haben ――― Pfund [Kilo] Übergepäck.

I: Lei ha ――― libbre [chili] di eccedenza bagaglio.

P: Tem ――― libras [quilos] de excesso de bagagem.

S: Tiene ――― libras [kilos] de exceso de equipaje.

111. I do not understand. What do you mean by excess baggage?

F: Je ne comprends pas cela. Que voulez-vous dire par excédent de bagages?

G: Das verstehe ich nicht. Was meinen Sie mit Übergepäck?

I: Non capisco. Cosa vuole dire con eccedenza bagaglio?

P: Eu não compreendo isto. Que quer dizer por excesso de bagagem?

S: No lo comprendo. ¿Qué entiende Ud. por exceso de equipaje?

112. Please let me explain it to you!

F: Laissez-moi vous l'expliquer!

G: Ich will es Ihnen erklären!

I: Lasci che Le spieghi, prego!

P: Deixe-me explicar, por favor!

S: ¡Permítame explicarle!

113. The allowance according to the regulations is ――― pounds [kilos] for an Economy Class passenger.

F: D'après le règlement on admet en franchise ――― livres [kilos] en Classe Économique.

G: Laut Vorschriften dürfen Sie —— Pfund [Kilo]
   für die Touristenklasse mitnehmen.
I: Secondo i regolamenti, il peso concesso è di ——
   libbre [chili] per un passeggero in Classe Economica.
P: De acordo com os regulamentos o permitido é ——
   libras [quilos] por cada passageiro de Classe Económica.
S: El peso permitido de acuerdo con las normas es ——
   libras [kilos] para el pasajero de Clase Económica.

**114. The allowance is —— pounds [kilos] for a First Class
passenger.**

F: On admet —— livres [kilos] en Première Classe.
G: Sie dürfen —— Pfund [Kilo] für die Erste Klasse
   mitnehmen.
I: Il peso concesso è di —— libbre [chili] per un
   passeggero in Prima Classe.
P: O permitido é —— libras [quilos] por cada passageiro
   de Primeira Classe.
S: El peso permitido es —— libras [kilos] para el
   pasajero de Primera Clase.

115. Please look at the scale now!

F: Regardez la bascule maintenant, s'il vous plaît!
G: Und jetzt sehen Sie bitte auf die Waage!
I: Ora, guardi la bilancia, prego!
P: Por favor, verifique a balança!
S: ¡Fíjese en la báscula (OR balanza), por favor!

116. You will see that the weight is —— pounds [kilos].

F: Vous verrez que le poids est de —— livres [kilos].
G: Sie werden feststellen, daß das Gewicht —— Pfund
   [Kilo] beträgt.
I: Può vedere che il peso è di —— libbre [chili].
P: Verificará que o peso é —— libras [quilos].
S: Puede comprobar que el peso es —— libras [kilos].

117. Listen! I have traveled a great deal, but my hand baggage has never been weighed before.

F: Écoutez! J'ai beaucoup voyagé mais mes bagages à main n'ont jamais encore été pesés.

G: Hören Sie mal zu! Ich bin schon sehr viel gereist, aber mein Handgepäck wurde niemals gewogen.

I: Senta, io ho viaggiato molto, ma il mio bagaglio a mano non è stato mai pesato.

P: Escute-me! Tenho viajado muitíssimo mas a minha bagagem de mão nunca foi pesada.

S: ¡Escuche! He viajado mucho pero mi equipaje nunca ha sido pesado.

118. I cannot possibly have an excess baggage weight.

F: Il est impossible que j'aie un excédent de bagages.

G: Es ist unmöglich, daß ich Übergepäck habe.

I: È impossibile! Non credo di avere eccedenza di peso.

P: É impossível que eu tenha excesso de peso.

S: Es imposible que yo tenga exceso de equipaje.

119. I have just come in from a flight on another airline.

F: Je viens d'arriver d'un vol avec une autre compagnie aérienne.

G: Ich bin gerade mit einer anderen Gesellschaft angekommen.

I: Sono appena arrivato con un volo di un'altra compagnia.

P: Acabo de chegar num vôo de outra companhia.

S: Acabo de llegar en un vuelo de otra compañía.

120. I was not charged for any excess weight.

F: On ne m'a pas chargé d'excédent de bagages.

G: Bei dieser Gesellschaft mußte ich nicht für Übergewicht bezahlen.

I: Non m'hanno fatto pagare eccedenza di peso.

P: Não me cobraram qualquer excesso de peso.

S: No tuve que pagar ningún gasto adicional por exceso de equipaje.

121. **It is possible that the agent who checked your baggage on the last occasion made an error.**

F: Il est possible que l'agent qui a enregistré vos bagages la dernière fois ait fait une erreur.

G: Es ist möglich, daß dem Angestellten, der Ihr Gepäck abgefertigt hat, bei dieser Gelegenheit ein Fehler unterlaufen ist.

I: Possibilmente il rappresentante che ha controllato il Suo bagaglio l'ultima volta ha fatto un errore.

P: É possível que o agente que processou a sua bagagem na última vez enganou-se.

S: Es posible que el empleado que comprobó su equipaje la última vez cometiera un error.

122. **I have not bought anything since I got off the other flight.**

F: Je n'ai rien acheté depuis que je suis descendu (FEM. descendue) de l'autre avion (OR appareil).

G: Seit meiner Ankunft mit der anderen Gesellschaft habe ich überhaupt nichts gekauft.

I: Non ho comprato niente da quando sono arrivato con l'altro aereo.

P: Eu não comprei mais nada desde que deixei o outro vôo.

S: No hé comprado nada desde que salí del otro vuelo.

123. **Consequently, I cannot have any excess weight.**

F: En conséquence je ne peux pas avoir d'excédent.

G: Infolgedessen kann ich kein Übergepäck haben.

I: Perciò non posso avere eccedenza bagaglio.

P: Por tanto não posso ter qualquer excesso de peso.

S: Por lo tanto no puedo tener exceso de equipaje.

124. **Sir, I am very sorry, but I can only judge by the scale and the baggage you have for this flight.**

F: Je suis désolé (FEM. désolée), Monsieur, mais je ne puis que me référer à cette bascule et aux bagages que vous avez pour ce vol.

G: Ich bedauere es außerordentlich, aber ich kann mich nur nach der Waage und dem Gepäck, das Sie für diesen Flug haben, richten.

I: Signore, mi dispiace molto, ma io posso solo giudicare dalla bilancia e dal bagaglio che Lei ha per questo volo.

P: Lamento imenso, mas só posso ajuizar pela balança e pela bagagem que tem para este vôo.

S: Lo siento mucho, Señor, pero tengo que regirme por la báscula (OR balanza) y por el equipaje que lleva en este vuelo.

125. You have to pay ———.

F: Vous devez payer ———.

G: Sie haben ——— zu zahlen.

I: Lei deve pagare ———.

P: Tem que pagar ———.

S: Ud. debe pagar ———.

126. I would like to help you, but these are the rules.

F: Je voudrais vous aider mais c'est le règlement.

G: Ich würde Ihnen gerne helfen, aber so sind die Bestimmungen.

I: Vorrei poterLa aiutare ma questi sono i regolamenti.

P: Gostaria de ajudá-lo mas estes são os regulamentos.

S: Me agradaría poder ayudarle pero estas son las normas.

127. Excuse me. Now I have these other passengers to process.

F: Excusez-moi, maintenant je dois m'occuper de ces autres passagers.

G: Entschuldigen Sie mich jetzt bitte, ich habe noch alle diese Passagiere abzufertigen.

I: Scusi, ora devo occuparmi di questi altri passeggeri.

P: Desculpe-me, mas tenho agora que despachar estes outros passageiros.

S: Perdóneme (OR Discúlpeme, Dispénseme), debo atender ahora a estos otros pasajeros.

128. **I am sorry, but you may not take that bag as hand luggage.**
   F: Je suis désolé (FEM. désolée), mais vous ne pouvez pas garder ce bagage à bord.
   G: Es tut mir leid, aber Sie können diesen Koffer nicht als Handgepäck mitnehmen.
   I: Mi dispiace, ma Lei non può portare questa valigia a mano.
   P: Lamento, mas não pode levar essa mala como bagagem de mão.
   S: Lo siento, pero no puede llevar esa maleta como equipaje de mano.

129. **It is too big [too heavy].**
   F: Il est trop grand [trop lourd].
   G: Es ist zu groß [zu schwer].
   I: È troppo grande [troppo pesante].
   P: É muito grande [muito pesada].
   S: Es demasiado grande [demasiado pesada].

130. **The size, weight and amount of baggage carried by hand onto the airplane are limited by international regulations.**
   F: La taille, le poids et le nombre des bagages à main en cabine sont limités par des règlements internationaux.
   G: Die Größe, das Gewicht und die Anzahl der Gepäckstücke, die Sie als Handgepäck mit auf die Maschine nehmen dürfen, sind durch internationale Regeln festgesetzt.
   I: La grandezza, il peso, e il numero dei bagagli che si possono portare a mano a bordo è limitato da regolamenti internazionali.
   P: O tamanho, o peso e a quantidade de bagagem de mão na cabina está limitado por regulamentos internacionais.
   S: El tamaño, el peso y la cantidad de equipaje de mano que se puede llevar en el avión se limita por las normas internacionales.

131. In what part of the plane would you like to be seated?
F: Où désirez-vous vous asseoir dans l'avion?
G: In welchem Teil der Kabine möchten Sie sitzen?
I: In quale parte dell'aereo vuole avere il Suo posto?
P: Em que parte do avião gostaria de ter o seu lugar?
S: ¿En qué parte del avión le gustaría sentarse?

132. I would like to be seated in the front [in the middle; in the rear].
F: Je voudrais avoir mon siège en avant [au milieu; en arrière].
G: Ich möchte vorn [in der Mitte; hinten] sitzen.
I: Vorrei avere il mio posto avanti [in mezzo; dietro].
P: Gostaria tê-lo na frente [no meio; na rectaguarda].
S: Me gustaría sentarme en la parte delantera [en el medio; en la parte posterior] del avión.

133. I shall do my best to get a seat for you [beside the aisle].
F: Je vais faire mon possible pour vous obtenir un siège [sur le couloir].
G: Ich werde mein Möglichstes tun, Ihnen einen Sitz [am Gang] zu reservieren.
I: Farò del mio meglio per ottenere un posto per Lei [accanto al corridoio].
P: Farei o possível para arranjar-lhe um lugar [na coxia*].
S: Haré quanto pueda por conseguirle un asiento [al lado del pasillo].

134. I prefer a seat in the center [over the wing; beside the window].
F: Je préfère un siège au milieu [sur les ailes; à côté de la fenêtre (OR à côté du hublot)].
G: Ich bevorzuge einen Sitz in der Mitte [über der Tragfläche; am Fenster].

* In Brazil this would be *no corredor*.

I: Preferisco un posto al centro [sopra le ali; accanto al finestrino].

P: Prefiro um lugar ao meio [sobre a asa; perto da janela].

S: Prefiero un asiento en el medio [sobre las alas; al lado de la ventanilla].

135. Here is your ticket with the baggage checks for [Washington].

F: Voici votre billet avec vos reçus de bagage pour [Washington].

G: Hier ist Ihr Flugschein mit Ihrem Gepäckschein für [Washington].

I: Ecco il Suo biglietto con gli scontrini del bagaglio per [Washington].

P: Aqui tem o seu bilhete com as etiquetas de bagagem para [Washington].

S: Aquí tiene su billete (OR boleto, pasaje) con los comprobantes de su equipaje para [Washington].

136. The boarding of your flight, Number ——, is scheduled for —— minutes past —— o'clock at gate Number ——.

F: L'embarquement de votre vol, numéro ——, est prévu à —— heures, —— minutes, porte numéro ——.

G: Wir rufen den Flug Nummer —— um —— Uhr und —— Minuten auf, Ausgang Nummer ——.

I: L'imbarco del Suo volo, numero ——, è previsto per le —— ore e minuti—— all'uscita numero ——.

P: O embarque de seu vôo, número ——, está marcado para —— horas, —— minutos, pela porta número ——.

S: De acuerdo con el plan de vuelo, su embarque se efectuará a las —— horas, —— minutos, por la puerta número ——.

137. On boarding, please present this envelope.

F: En embarquant présentez, s'il vous plaît, cette enveloppe.

G: Beim Einsteigen zeigen Sie bitte diesen Umschlag.
I: All'imbarco, per favore, mostri questa busta.
P: Ao embarque mostre este envelope, por favor.
S: Presente este sobre al embarcar, por favor.

138. Goodbye. Thank you. Have a nice trip!
F: Au revoir. Merci beaucoup. Je vous souhaite un bon
 voyage!
G: Vielen Dank und auf Wiedersehen! Wir wünschen
 Ihnen einen angenehmen Flug!
I: ArrivederLa. Grazie. Buon viaggio!
P: Adeus. Obrigado (FEM. Obrigada). Boa viagem!
S: Adiós. Muchas gracias. ¡Buen viaje!

Before Boarding (In the Passenger Lounge)

F: AVANT L'EMBARQUEMENT (*Dans la salle
 d'attente*)
G: VOR DEM EINSTEIGEN (*Im Warteraum*)
I: PRIMA DELL'IMBARCO (*Nella sala d'aspetto*)
P: ANTES DO EMBARQUE (*Na sala de espera*)
S: ANTES DE EMBARCAR (*En la sala de espera*)

**139. Are you one of our passengers on Flight Number ———
 to ———?**
F: Êtes-vous un de nos passagers du vol numéro ———
 pour ———?
G: Sind Sie Passagier für Flug Nummer ——— nach
 ———?
I: Lei è in partenza con il volo numero ——— per
 ———?
P: É o senhor nosso passageiro (TO FEM. É a senhora nossa
 passageira) no vôo número ——— para ———?
S: ¿Es Ud. pasajero del vuelo número ———para———?

140. *To the children:* **Are you going to fly with us today?**
- F: *Aux enfants:* Allez-vous voler avec nous aujourd'hui?
- G: *Zu den Kindern:* Fliegt ihr heute mit uns?
- I: *Ai bambini:* Volate con noi oggi?
- P: *Aos meninos:* Vôam connosco* hoje?
- S: *A los niños:* ¿Vais a volar con nosotros hoy?

141. *To a mother:* **Let me assist you!**
- F: *À une mère:* Laissez-moi vous aider!
- G: *Zu einer Mutter:* Darf ich Ihnen behilflich sein?
- I: *A una madre:* L'aiuto io?
- P: *A uma mãe:* Deixe-me ajudá-la!
- S: *A una madre:* ¡Permítame ayudarle!

142. **Do you mind waiting for a moment?**
- F: Verriez-vous un inconvénient à attendre un instant?
- G: Darf ich Sie bitten, einen Augenblick zu warten?
- I: Le dispiace di aspettare un momento?
- P: Não se importa de esperar um momento?
- S: Por favor, espere un momento.

143. **I will contact the ground personnel; they will answer your question.**
- F: Je vais contacter le personnel au sol; ils répondront à votre question.
- G: Ich werde mich mit dem Bodenpersonal in Verbindung setzen. Das Bodenpersonal wird Ihre Frage beantworten können.
- I: Chiamerò il personale di terra che risponderà alle Sue domande.
- P: Vou chamar o pessoal de terra† para responder à sua pergunta.
- S: Hablaré con el personal de tierra que contestará a su pregunta.

---

* In Brazil *conosco.*
† In Brazil *os funcionarios de terra.*

144. Please stay here until your flight is announced.

F: Veuillez, s'il vous plaît, rester ici jusqu'à l'appel de votre vol.

G: Ritte, bleiben Sie hier, bis Ihr Flug ausgerufen wird.

I: Per favore, stia qui fino all'annuncio del Suo volo.

P: Por favor, fique aqui até o seu vôo ser anunciado.

S: Por favor, quédese aquí hasta que anuncien el vuelo.

145. Your flight has not yet been announced.

F: Votre vol n'a pas encore été annoncé.

G: Bis jetzt ist Ihr Flug noch nicht ausgerufen.

I: Il Suo volo non è stato ancora annunciato.

P: O seu vôo não foi ainda anunciado.

S: Su vuelo no ha sido anunciado todavía.

146. Your flight is ——— hours [minutes] late.

F: Votre vol est en retard de ——— heures [minutes].

G: Ihr Flug hat ——— Stunden [Minuten] Verspätung.

I: Il Suo volo è ——— ore [minuti] in ritardo.

P: O seu vôo está atrazado ——— horas [minutos].

S: Su vuelo lleva ——— horas [minutos] de retraso (OR atraso).

147. Tell me, please, at which gate do I have to board the plane?

F: Dites-moi, s'il vous plaît, quelle est la porte d'embarquement?

G: Sagen Sie mir bitte, durch welchen Ausgang komme ich zu meinem Flugzeug?

I: Mi dice, per favore, da quale uscita si va a bordo?

P: Diga-me, por favor, qual é a porta por que devo embarcar?

S: Dígame, por favor, ¿por cuál puerta debo salir para embarcar?

148. At Gate Number ———.

F: Par la porte numéro ———.

G: Zum Ausgang Nummer ———.

I: Dall'uscita numero ———.
P: Pela porta número ———.
S: Por la puerta número ———.

149. **May I see your boarding card?**
   F: Puis-je voir votre carte d'embarquement?
   G: Darf ich um Ihre Bordkarte bitten?
   I: Posso vedere la Sua carta d'imbarco?
   P: Posso ver o seu cartão de embarque?
   S: ¿Puedo ver su tarjeta de embarque?

150. **Do not forget that your flight leaves from Gate Number ———.**
   F: N'oubliez pas que votre vol part de la porte numéro ———.
   G: Bitte vergessen Sie nicht, daß Ihr Flug am Ausgang Nummer ——— aufgerufen wird.
   I: Non dimentichi che il Suo volo parte dall'uscita numero ———.
   P: Favor não esquecer que o seu vôo parte da porta número ———.
   S: No se olvide de que debe embarcar por la puerta número ———.

151. **Do you serve a meal immediately after take-off?**
   F: Servez-vous le repas immédiatement après le décollage?
   G: Gibt es gleich nach dem Start etwas zu essen?
   I: Il pranzo sarà servito subito dopo il decollo?
   P: Servem uma refeição imediatamente após a partida?
   S: ¿Sirven comidas inmediatamente después del despegue?

152. **There is a meal service scheduled about an hour after take-off.**
   F: Il y a un repas prévu pour une heure environ après le décollage.
   G: Ungefähr eine Stunde nach dem Start wird das Essen serviert.

I: Il pranzo sarà servito a un'ora circa dopo il decollo.
P: Há uma refeição marcada cerca de uma hora após a partida.
S: Se sirve una comida alrededor de una hora después del despegue.

153. Is there liquor available on this flight?

F: Peut-on obtenir des liqueurs sur ce vol?
G: Gibt es alkoholische Getränke auf dem Flug?
I: Servono liquori a bordo?
P: Haverá bebidas neste vôo?
S: ¿Se sirven bebidas en este vuelo?

154. There are complimentary drinks in First Class.

F: Les liqueurs sont gratuites en Première Classe.
G: In der Ersten Klasse sind die Getränke frei.
I: Saranno offerti liquori in Prima Classe.
P: Há bebidas gratuitas na Primeira Classe.
S: Se sirven bebidas gratuitas en Primera Clase.

155. In the Economy Section drinks are available at a nominal charge.

F: En Classe Économique on peut obtenir les liqueurs au prix coûtant.
G: In der Touristenklasse können Sie für wenig Geld Getränke erhalten.
I: In Classe Economica i liquori sono in vendita al prezzo di costo.
P: Na Classe Económica há bebidas a venda a um custo nominal.
S: En Clase Económica se venden bebidas a precio de costo.

156. Are the flights rough at the altitudes at which you fly?

F: Les vols sont-ils mouvementés à l'altitude où vous volez?
G: Ist der Flug sehr unruhig in der Höhe, in der Sie fliegen?

I: È scomodo il volo all'altezza che volate?
P: É inconfortável às altitudes que vôam?
S: ¿Es molesto viajar a la altura que vuelan?

157. According to the captain we expect a smooth flight this evening.
F: D'après le capitaine nous aurons un vol tranquille ce soir.
G: Nach der Ansicht unseres Kapitäns werden wir heute abend einen sehr ruhigen Flug haben.
I: Il Capitano ci informa che questa sera avremo un volo tranquillo.
P: De acordo com o capitão esperamos um vôo suave (OR calmo) esta noite.
S: Según el capitán (OR comandante) esperamos un vuelo tranquilo para esta tarde.

158. What is the cruising altitude?
F: Quelle est l'altitude de croisière?
G: In welcher Höhe fliegen Sie?
I: Qual'è l'altezza di crociera?
P: Qual é a altitude de cruzeiro?
S: ¿Cuál es la altura de crucero?

159. About ——— feet, approximately ——— meters.
F: Environ ——— pieds, approximativement ——— mètres.
G: In ungefähr ——— Fuß, um ——— Meter.
I: Circa ——— piedi, cioè circa ——— metri.
P: Cerca de ——— pés, aproximadamente ——— metros.
S: Alrededor de ——— pies, es decir unos ——— metros.

160. I was promised a bassinet. Do you think it will be available?
F: On m'avait promis une bassinette (OR un berceau). Pensez-vous qu'elle (OR il) sera disponible?

G: Mir wurde ein Babybettchen versprochen. Glauben
Sie, daß ich es bekommen kann?

I: Mi hanno promesso una culla. Crede che potrò
averla?

P: Prometeram-me um berço. Pensa que haverá?

S: Me prometieron una cunita. ¿Cree Ud. que me la
facilitarán?

161. May I see your ticket (with the envelope)?

F: Puis-je voir votre billet (avec l'enveloppe)?

G: Darf ich bitte Ihren Flugschein (mit dem Kuvert—
OR Umschlag) sehen?

I: Posso vedere il Suo biglietto (con la busta)?

P: Posso ver o seu bilhete (com o envelope)?

S: ¿Puedo ver su pasaje (con el sobre)?

**162. Your seat is facing the bulkhead, where the bassinet
will be located.**

F: Votre siège est au premier rang, où sera la bassinette
(OR le berceau).

G: Ihr Sitz befindet sich direkt hinter der Trennwand.
Dort ist das Babybettchen.

I: Il Suo posto è di fronte alla partizione, dove sarà posta
la culla.

P: O seu lugar é ao pé da divisão, onde o berço será
colocado.

S: Su asiento queda en frente de la separación, donde irá
colocada la cunita.

**163. I will check with the purser to see if we can put you in
a three-seat row.**

F: Je vais vérifier avec le commissaire de bord si nous
pouvons vous donner trois sièges sur le même rang.

G: Ich werde mich mit dem Chefsteward in Verbindung
setzen und versuchen, für Sie drei Sitze nebeneinander
zu bekommen.

I: Controllerò con il commissario di bordo se possiamo farLa sedere in una fila di tre posti.

P: Verificarei com o comissário se poderemos dar-lhe uma fila de três lugares.

S: Voy a consultar con el comisario de abordo si pueden ocupar una fila de tres asientos.

164. I will remove the arm rests and then I will make a little bassinet for the child.

F: Je vais enlever les accoudoirs et puis je vais préparer un petit berceau pour l'enfant.

G: Ich werde die Armlehnen herausnehmen und dann werde ich ein Bettchen für das Kind machen.

I: Toglierò i braccioli e poi farò una piccola culla per il bambino.

P: Retirarei os apoios dos braços e em seguida prepararei um berço para a criança.

S: Quitaré los brazos de los asientos y luego prepararé una cunita para el niño.

165. *To an aged or incapacitated passenger in a wheelchair or to a mother with children:* Please remain calm. When your flight is announced I will come back to assist you aboard myself.

F: *À un passager âgé ou infirme dans une chaise roulante ou à une mère avec enfants:* S'il vous plaît, restez tranquille. Quand votre vol sera annoncé je viendrai moi-même vous aider à embarquer.

G: *Zu einem älteren oder behinderten Passagier mit Rollstuhl oder zu einer Mutter mit Kindern:* Bitte bleiben Sie ruhig. Wenn Ihr Flug ausgerufen wird, werde ich selber Sie abholen und in die Maschine bringen.

I: *A un passeggero anziano o a un invalido sulla sedia a rotelle o a una madre con bambini:* Prego di rimanere tranquillo (TO FEM. tranquilla). Io ritornerò quando sarà chiamato il Suo volo per assisterLa all'imbarco.

P: *A um passageiro* (FEM. *uma passageira*) *de idade o incapacitado* (FEM. *incapacitada*) *em cadeira de rodas ou a uma mãe com crianças:* Por favor, conserve-se tranquilo (TO FEM. tranquila). Quando o seu vôo for anunciado voltarei para assistir o seu embarque.

S: *A un pasajero de edad avanzada o incapacitado en silla de ruedas o a una madre con niños:* Por favor, permanezca tranquilo (TO FEM. tranquila). Cuando su vuelo se anuncie volveré para acompañarle abordo.

166. When do we take off?
F: Quand décollons-nous?
G: Wann fliegen wir ab?
I: Quando decolliamo?
P: Quando descolamos?*
S: ¿Cuándo despegamos?

167. As soon as everything is perfectly all right.
F: Dès que tout sera en ordre.
G: Sobald alles in Ordnung ist.
I: Appena tutto sarà pronto.
P: Tão cedo tudo esteja pronto.
S: Tan pronto como todo esté en regla (OR en orden).

168. What is the reason for the delay?
F: Quelle est la raison du délai?
G: Was ist der Grund für die Verspätung?
I: Qual'è la ragione del ritardo?
P: Qual é a razão para o atrazo?
S: ¿Cuál es el motivo del retraso (OR del atraso, de la demora)?

169. The air traffic is unusually heavy this evening.
F: Le trafic aérien est anormalement intense ce soir.
G: Wir haben ungewöhnlich starken Flugverkehr heute abend.

* In Brazil *decolamos.*

I: Questa sera il traffico aereo è particolarmente intenso.
P: O tráfego aéreo é muito intenso esta noite.
S: El tráfico aéreo es demasiado intenso esta tarde.

170. **We have to wait until the storm is over [until the rain stops; until the fog lifts].**
F: Nous devons attendre jusqu'à ce que l'orage soit fini [jusqu'à ce que la pluie s'arrête; jusqu'à ce que le brouillard se dissipe].
G: Wir müssen warten bis sich der Sturm gelegt hat [bis der Regen aufgehört hat; bis der Nebel sich gehoben hat].
I: Si deve aspettare finchè cessi il temporale [finchè cessi la pioggia; finchè la nebbia si diradi].
P: Temos que esperar que a tempestade pare [que a chuva pare; que o nevoeiro levante].
S: Tendremos que esperar hasta que la tormenta pare [hasta que la lluvia pare; hasta que se levante la niebla*].

171. **We are waiting for an improvement in weather conditions.**
F: Nous attendons une amélioration des conditions météorologiques.
G: Wir warten auf Wetterbesserung.
I: Si aspetta un miglioramento delle condizioni atmosferiche.
P: Estamos a espera duma melhoria das condições atmosféricas.
S: Esperamos que el tiempo mejore.

172. **Can I send a telegram?**
F: Puis-je envoyer un télégramne?
G: Besteht die Möglichkeit, ein Telegramm abzuschicken?
I: Posso mandare (OR spedire) un telegramma?
P: Posso enviar um telegrama?
S: ¿Puedo enviar un telegrama?

* *La neblina* in South America.

173. Here is a telegram form for you.

F: Voici un formulaire de télégramme pour vous.
G: Hier haben Sie ein Telegrammformular.
I: Ecco un modulo per telegramma.
P: Aqui tem um impresso de telegrama.
S: Aqui tiene un formulario (OR impreso) de telegrama.

174. I want to change my hotel reservation.

F: Je veux changer ma réservation d'hôtel.
G: Ich möchte meine Buchung für das Hotel ändern.
I: Vorrei cambiare la mia prenotazione d'albergo.
P: Quero alterar a minha reserva de hotel.
S: Deseo cambiar la reservación (OR reserva) de mi hotel.

175. Am I going to miss my connecting flight?

F: Est-ce que je vais manquer ma correspondance?
G: Werde ich meinen Anschlußflug verpassen?
I: Perderò la coincidenza (OR il mio volo in coincidenza)?
P: Perderei o meu vôo em ligação?
S: ¿Voy a perder mi vuelo de conexión?

176. I do not think so.

F: Je ne le pense pas.
G: Ich glaube nicht.
I: Non credo.
P: Penso que não.
S: No lo creo.

Boarding; Flight; Arrival

F: EMBARQUEMENT; VOL; ARRIVÉE
G: EINSTEIGEN; FLUG; ANKUNFT
I: IMBARCO; VOLO; ARRIVO
P: EMBARQUE; VÔO; CHEGADA
S: EMBARQUE; VUELO; LLEGADA

Seating of Passengers

F: EMPLACEMENT DES PASSAGERS
G: SETZEN DER PASSAGIERE
I: ACCOMODAMENTO DEI PASSEGGERI
P: ACOMODAÇÃO DOS PASSAGEIROS
S: ACOMODACIÓN DE LOS PASAJEROS

177. May I see your ticket?
F: Puis-je voir votre billet?
G: Darf ich um Ihren Flugschein bitten?
I: Posso vedere il Suo biglietto?
P: Posso ver o seu bilhete?
S: ¿Puedo ver su billete (OR boleto, pasaje)?

178. Your seat is behind the partition.
F: Votre siège est derrière la partition.
G: Ihr Sitz is hinter der Trennwand.
I: Il Suo posto è dietro la partizione.
P: O seu lugar (OR assento) è atrás da divisão.
S: Su asiento está situado trás la separación.

179. Walk straight ahead and to the rear.
F: Dirigez-vous tout droit vers l'arrière de l'appareil.
G: Gehen Sie bitte geradeaus in den hinteren Teil der Kabine.
I: Vada diritto in fondo.
P: Dirija-se para a rectaguarda.
S: Camine adelante dirigiéndose hacia el fondo.

180. The stewardess there will show you where your seat is.

F: L'hôtesse là-bas vous indiquera votre siège.

G: Dort wird Ihnen die Stewardeß Ihren Sitz zeigen.

I: La hostess Le farà vedere lì il Suo posto.

P: A hospedeira* lá indicar-lhe-á onde é o seu lugar.

S: La stewardess† ahí le indicará su asiento.

181. Would you mind proceeding to the rear [to the front], where your seat is located?

F: Voulez-vous, s'il vous plaît, vous diriger vers l'arrière [vers l'avant], où se trouve votre siège?

G: Würden Sie sich bitte nach hinten [nach vorne] bemühen, wo sich Ihr Sitz befindet?

I: Le dispiace proseguire verso il fondo [davanti], dove si trova il Suo posto?

P: Por favor, dirija-se para a rectaguarda [para a frente], onde é o seu lugar.

S: Por favor, diríjase hacia el fondo [al frente], donde se halla su asiento.

182. You have Seat Number ———— right here [beside the aisle; in the center].

F: Vous avez le siège numéro ———— juste ici [sur le couloir; au milieu].

G: Ihr Sitz ist Nummer ————, gerade hier [am Gang; in der Mitte].

I: Il Suo posto è numero ———— proprio qui [accanto al corridoio; al centro].

P: Tem o lugar número ————, aqui mesmo [na coxia;‡ ao meio].

S: Ud. tiene el asiento número ———— justo aquí [al lado del pasillo; en el centro].

---

* In Brazil *aeromoça*.

† Also; in Spain *azafata*; in South America *aeromoza, cabinera, auxiliar* (OR *asistente*) *de vuelo*.

‡ In Brazil *no corredor*.

183. Your seat is beside the window [——— rows to the rear; ——— rows ahead].

F: Votre siège est à côté de la fenêtre [——— rangs à l'arrière; ——— rangs à l'avant].

G: Ihr Sitz ist am Fenster [——— Reihen nach hinten; ——— Reihen nach vorne].

I: Il Suo posto è accanto al finestrino [——— file dietro; ——— file avanti].

P: O seu lugar é à janela [——— filas para a rectaguarda; ——— filas para a frente].

S: Su asiento está al lado de la ventanilla [——— filas hacia atrás; ——— filas hacia delante].

184. We were told we would be seated all together!

F: On nous avait dit que nous serions assis tous (FEM. assises toutes) ensemble!

G: Uns wurde versprochen, daß wir zusammen sitzen können!

I: Ci hanno detto che avremmo avuto i posti vicini!

P: Disseram-nos que ficávamos sentados juntos (FEM. sentadas juntas)!

S: Nos dijeron que estaríamos sentados todos juntos (FEM. sentadas todas juntas).

185. What can you do about it?

F: Que pouvez-vous faire pour arranger cela?

G: Können Sie da etwas tun?

I: Come ci può sistemare (OR accomodare)?

P: O que é que pode fazer?

S: ¿Qué puede hacer acerca de esto?

186. Would you please take the seat assigned to you for the time being?

F: Pouvez-vous, s'il vous plaît, garder pour le moment le siège qui vous à été donné (OR assigné)?

G: Bitte behalten Sie im Augenblick noch den Platz, der Ihnen zugewiesen wurde.

I: Per il momento voglia accomodarsi al posto che Le
hanno assegnato.

P: Se não se importa, use temporàriamente o assento que
lhe foi marcado.

S: ¿Quiere tomar por ahora el asiento que le ha sido
asignado?

187. I am very sorry that this happened.

F: Je suis désolé (FEM. désolée) que ceci soit arrivé.

G: Ich bedauere sehr, daß so etwas passierte.

I: Sono spiacente dell'accaduto.

P: Lamento imenso que isto tivesse acontecido.

S: Siento lo sucedido.

188. After the take-off I will come back.

F: Je reviendrai après le décollage.

G: Nach dem Start werde ich zu Ihnen kommen.

I: Dopo il decollo tornerò.

P: Após a descolagem eu voltarei.

S: Después de despegar volveré.

189. I will do my best to seat you together.

F: Je vais faire mon possible pour vous asseoir ensemble.

G: Ich werde mein Möglichstes tun, um Sie zusammen zu
setzen.

I: Farò il possibile per farVi sedere vicino (OR insieme).

P: Farei o possível para sentá-los juntos (TO FEM. sentá-
las juntas).

S: Haré todo lo que pueda para acomodarles juntos (TO
FEM. juntas).

**190. I will see if those passengers would not mind moving
to other seats.**

F: Je vais demander si ces passagers-là ne voient pas
d'inconvénient à changer de sièges.

G: Vielleicht haben diese Passagiere nichts dagegen,
andere Plätze einzunehmen.

I: Vedrò se a questi passeggeri non dispiace spostarsi ad un altro posto.

P: Vou ver se aqueles passageiros não se importam de mudar de lugares.

S: Veré si a esos pasajeros no les importa cambiar de asientos.

191. Would you be so kind as to move to your seat, Number ———? It's over there on the left.

F: Ayez l'obligeance d'aller occuper votre siège, numéro ———. C'est là-bas, à gauche.

G: Wären Sie bitte so freundlich und würden Sie sich zu Ihrem Platz, Nummer ———, begeben? Er ist dort drüben, links.

I: Le spiacerebbe sedersi al Suo posto, numero ———, là sulla sinistra?

P: Tenha a amabilidade de ir para o seu lugar, número ———, que é ali à esquerda.

S: ¿Tendría la bondad de ocupar su asiento, número ———? Está ahí, a la izquierda.

192. This seat is occupied, but that one on the right is free.

F: Ce siège est occupé, mais celui-là à droite est libre.

G: Dieser Sitz ist besetzt, aber der auf der rechten Seite ist frei.

I: Questo posto è occupato ma quello sulla destra è libero.

P: Este lugar está ocupado mas aquele à direita está livre.

S: Este asiento está ocupado pero el a la derecha está libre.

193. I was promised a seat over the wing.

F: On m'avait promis un siège sur les ailes.

G: Mir wurde ein Sitz über den Flügeln versprochen.

I: Mi avevano promesso un posto sopra le ali.

P: Prometeram-me um lugar sobre a asa.

S: Me prometieron un asiento sobre las alas.

194. When I made my reservation I requested a special seat.

F: Quand j'ai fait ma réservation, j'ai demandé un siège déterminé.

G: Als ich meine Buchung machte, bat ich um einen besonderen Sitz.

I: Quando ho fatto la prenotazione ho richiesto un posto particolare.

P: Quando fiz a minha reserva pedi um lugar especial.

S: Cuando hice mi reservación pedí un asiento (OR una plaza) especial.

195. I will check on this right away. Excuse me!

F: Je vais vérifier cela immédiatement. Excusez-moi!

G: Ich werde es sofort überprüfen. Entschuldigen Sie mich bitte!

I: Vado a controllare subito. Mi scusi!

P: Vou verificar imediatamente. Desculpe-me!

S: Lo comprobaré (OR verificaré) inmediatamente. ¡Discúlpeme!

196. I am very sorry, Sir, but we have no record of your request.

F: Je suis désolé (FEM. désolée), Monsieur, mais nous n'avons pas trace de votre demande.

G: Es tut mir außerordentlich leid, aber wir haben keine Unterlagen über Ihre Platzbestellung.

I: Sono spiacente, Signore, ma la Sua richiesta non è stata segnalata.

P: Lamento sinceramente, mas não temos registo do seu pedido.

S: Lo lamento, Señor, pero no tenemos nota de su petición (OR pedido).

197. However, I will try to make some arrangement to obtain that seat for you.

F: Néanmoins je vais essayer de vous obtenir ce siège.

G: Trotzdem werde ich mein Möglichstes tun, damit Sie diesen Platz behalten.

I: In ogni modo farò del mio meglio per ottenere il posto che Lei desidera.

P: Contudo tentarei fazer por obter aquele lugar para si.

S: Sin embargo haré todo lo posible para conseguirle ese asiento.

198. I can understand your disappointment.

F: Je comprends votre mécontentement.

G: Selbstverständlich verstehe ich Ihre Unzufriedenheit.

I: Capisco il disappunto.

P: Compreendo o seu desapontamento.

S: Comprendo perfectamente su contrariedad.

199. I assume there was a misunderstanding.

F: Je suppose qu'il y ait eu un malentendu.

G: Ich nehme an, daß es sich um ein Mißverständnis handelt.

I: Presumo ci sia stato un errore.

P: Suponho que houve um malentendido.

S: Supongo que hubo un malentendido (or malentendimiento).

200. We have a center seat available as an alternate.

F: Nous avons disponible comme alternative un siège au milieu.

G: Statt dessen könnten wir Ihnen einen Mittelsitz anbieten.

I: Saremo felici di offrirLe invece un posto di centro che è libero.

P: Como alternativa temos um lugar disponível no centro.

S: Podemos ofrecerle un asiento en el medio como alternativa.

201. We would be happy to let you sit there.

F: Nous serions heureux que vous l'occupiez.

G: Es würde uns freuen, wenn Sie diesen Sitz annehmen würden.

I: Saremmo felici se volesse accomodarsi lì.

P: Ficaremos contentes se quer ocupá-lo.

S: Nos agradará que lo ocupe.

202. We are sorry, but we have to request you to return to your original seat at the next stop.

F: Nous regrettons, mais vous devrez reprendre votre propre siège à la prochaine escale.

G: Es tut uns leid, aber wir müssen Sie bitten, bei der nächsten Zwischenlandung Ihren ursprünglichen Sitz wieder einzunehmen.

I: Ci dispiace, ma a un prossimo scalo La preghiamo di ritornare al posto originalmente assegnatoLe.

P: Lamento, mas devemos pedi-lhe que regresse ao seu lugar original na próxima paragem (OR estação, escala).

S: Lo siento, pero le debemos rogar que vuelva a su asiento original en la próxima escala.

203. I would like to have your name and address and the approximate date and place of your reservation.

F: Voulez-vous, s'il vous plaît, me donner votre nom et votre adresse, ainsi que la date approximative et le lieu de votre réservation?

G: Darf ich Sie um Ihren Namen und Ihre Adresse, sowie um das ungefähre Datum und den Ort Ihrer Reservierung (OR Buchung) bitten?

I: Vorrei avere il Suo nome e indirizzo, e approssimativamente la data e luogo della Sua prenotazione.

P: Gostaríamos de ter o seu nome e endereço (OR morada) e a data aproximada e o local da sua reserva.

S: Déme su nombre y dirección por favor, y también la fecha aproximada y el lugar de su reservación.

204. We shall report this discrepancy to our superiors.

F: Nous allons rapporter cet incident à nos supérieurs.

G: Wir werden dieses Vorkommnis unserer zuständigen Stelle melden.

I: Riporteremo questo inconveniente alla nostra direzione.

P: Informaremos os nossos superiores desta irregularidade.

S: Informaremos de este incidente a nuestros superiores.

205. I will try to reserve an aisle seat for you on our departure from ———.

F: Je vais essayer de vous réserver un siège-couloir quand nous partirons de ———.

G: Ich werde versuchen, Ihnen einen Sitz am Gang zu reservieren, wenn wir von ——— abfliegen.

I: Alla partenza da ——— cercherò di riservarLe un posto di corridoio.

P: Tentarei reservar-lhe um lugar de coxia* quando partiremos de ———.

S: Intentaré reservarle un asiento junto al pasillo cuando partamos de ———.

206. Perhaps at another stop there will be a window seat available.

F: Il y aura peut-être un siège-fenêtre disponible à une autre escale.

G: Vielleicht wird ein Fenstersitz bei einer anderen Zwischenlandung frei.

I: Potrebbe darsi che ad un altro scalo ci sia un posto al finestrino libero.

P: Talvez noutra estação exista um lugar de janela vago.

S: Quizás en otra escala haya un asiento de ventanilla vacante.

207. Is it possible to get more fresh air?

F: Est-il possible d'obtenir plus d'air frais?

G: Ist es möglich, etwas mehr frische Luft zu bekommen?

I: È possibile avere più aria?

P: É possível aumentar o ar fresco?

S: ¿Podríamos tener más aire fresco?

* In Brazil *de corredor*.

208. **I am sorry, the air conditioning does not work until we are aloft.**

F: Je suis désolé (FEM. désolée), mais le système d'air conditionné ne fonctionne qu'en vol.

G: Es tut mir leid, aber das Luftkühlungssystem funktioniert erst nach dem Start.

I: Sono spiacente, ma l'aria condizionata non funziona mentre non siamo in volo.

P: Tenho pena, mas o ar condicionado não trabalha emquanto não subirmos.

S: Lo siento, el aire acondicionado no funciona hasta que estemos en vuelo.

209. **Would you like a wet towel and a cold drink?**

F: Désirez-vous une serviette humide et des rafraîchissements?

G: Möchten Sie ein feuchtes Tuch und Erfrischungsgetränke haben?

I: Desidera avere una salvietta umida per rinfrescarsi e qualcosa di fresco da bere?

P: Gostaria de ter uma toalha húmida e uma bebida fresca?

S: ¿Quiere una toalla húmeda y alguna bebida fresca?

210. **Tell me, please, has all my luggage been loaded on the airplane?**

F: Dites-moi, s'il vous plaît, mes bagages ont-ils bien été mis à bord?

G: Bitte sagen Sie mir, ob mein ganzes Gepäck ins Flugzeug verladen ist.

I: Mi dica, per favore, se tutti i miei bagagli sono stati messi (OR caricati) a bordo.

P: Diga-me, por favor, foi toda a minha bagagem carregada no avião?

S: Dígame, por favor, si han cargado todo mi equipaje en el avión.

211. Let me install the bassinet for your baby.

F: Laissez-moi installer le berceau (OR la bassinette) pour votre bébé.

G: Gestatten Sie, daß ich das Bettchen für Ihr Baby installiere.

I: Mi permetta di mettere la culla per il Suo bebe.

P: Deixe-me instalar o berço para o seu bébé.

S: Permítame instalarle la cunita para el niño.

212. Is this bassinet safe on take-off, on landing and during turbulence?

F: Ce berceau est-il sûr (OR en sécurité) pendant le décollage, pendant l'atterrissage et en cas de mauvais temps?

G: Ist das Bettchen sicher genug beim Start, beim Landen und bei unruhigem Wetter?

I: La culla è stabile durante il decollo, durante l'atterraggio e con delle turbulenze (OR con dei vuoti d'aria)?

P: É este berço de segurança na descolagem, na aterragem e durante a turbulência?

S: ¿Va segura la cunita durante el despegue, al aterrizar y durante tiempo tormentoso?

213. Would you please put your handbag [your camera (*if it is big*)] underneath your seat?

F: Voulez-vous, s'il vous plaît, mettre votre sac à main [votre appareil photographique (*si c'est grand*)] sous votre siège?

G: Würden Sie bitte Ihre Handtasche [Ihren Photo-apparat (*falls er groß ist*)] unter Ihren Sitz legen?

I: La prego di mettere la Sua borsa [la macchina foto-grafica (*se è grande*)] sotto il Suo sedile.

P: Poderia pôr a sua mala de mão [a sua câmara (*se é grande*)] por baixo do seu assento?

S: ¿Quiere poner por favor su bolsa [su cámara (*si es grande*)] bajo su asiento?

214. Please put your camera (*if it is small*) into the seat pocket.

F: Mettez, s'il vous plaît, votre appareil photographique (*si c'est petit*) dans la pochette du fauteuil.

G: Stecken Sie bitte Ihre Kamera (*falls sie klein ist*) in die Sitztasche.

I: La prego di mettere la macchina fotografica (*se è piccola*) nella tasca del sedile.

P: Por favor, ponha a sua câmara (*se é pequena*) na bolsa da cadeira.

S: Ponga por favor su cámara (*si es pequeña*) en el bolsillo del asiento.

215. I am sorry, but you must not put any heavy object on the hat rack that might fall on the heads of the passengers in case of turbulence.

F: Je suis désolé (FEM. désolée), mais vous ne devez mettre dans le filet aucun objet lourd pouvant tomber sur la tête des passagers en cas de mauvais temps.

G: Es tut mir leid, aber Sie dürfen keine schweren Gegenstände in das Gepäcknetz legen. Sie könnten bei unruhigem Wetter den Passagieren auf den Kopf fallen!

I: Sono spiacente, ma non si può mettere nessun oggetto pesante sopra la rete (OR reticella). Potrebbe cadere sulla testa dei passeggeri in caso di turbulenza.

P: Lamento, mas não pode colocar qualquer objeto pesado na rede que pode cair na cabeça dos passageiros em caso de turbulência.

S: Lo siento, pero no puede colocar (OR poner) ningún objeto pesado en la rejilla (OR en el portaequipaje), ya que puede caer en la cabeza de los pasajeros en caso de tiempo tormentoso.

216. Will you please put your coat [hat] on the overhead rack?

F: Veuillez mettre votre pardessus [chapeau] dans le filet.

G: Würden Sie bitte Ihren Mantel [Hut] in das Gepäcknetz legen?

I: La prego di mettere il Suo cappotto [cappello] sopra
   la rete (OR reticella).

P: Por favor, ponha o seu casaco [chapéu] na rede.

S: ¿Quiere poner su abrigo [sombrero] en la rejilla?

**217. Would you mind holding your coat until all passengers
are seated?**

F: Pouvez-vous garder votre manteau jusqu'à ce que
   tous les passagers soient assis?

G: Würden Sie bitte Ihren Mantel halten, bis alle
   Passagiere sitzen?

I: Le dispiace tenere il Suo cappotto finchè tutti i
   passeggeri siano seduti?

P: Não se importaria de conservar o seu casaco até todos
   os passageiros estarem sentados?

S: ¿Le importaría guardar su abrigo hasta que todos los
   pasajeros estén sentados?

218. I shall be right back to pick it up.

F: Je vais venir le prendre dans quelques moments.

G: Ich werde sofort zurückkommen, um ihn dann
   mitzunehmen.

I: Verrò a prenderlo subito.

P: Voltarei dentro de momentos para levá-lo.

S: Volveré a recogerlo más tarde.

**219. I shall take care of you in just a moment, as soon as all
passengers have been seated.**

F: Je m'occuperai de vous dans un petit instant, dès que
   tous les passagers seront assis.

G: Ich werde mich sofort um Sie kümmern, sobald alle
   Passagiere sitzen.

I: Mi occuperò di Lei fra qualche minuto, appena tutti i
   passeggeri saranno seduti.

P: Atendê-lo-ei dentro de momentos, logo que todos os passageiros estejam sentados.

S: Me ocuparé de Ud. en un instante, tan pronto como todos los pasajeros se hayan sentado.

220. May I relieve you of your ———?
F: Puis-je vous débarrasser de votre ———?
G: Darf ich Ihren (Ihre, Ihr) ——— nehmen?
I: Posso togliere (OR prendere) il Suo (la Sua) ———?
P: Posso levar o seu (a sua) ———?
S: ¿Puedo llevar su ———?

221. May I put your ——— on one side?
F: Puis-je mettre de côté votre ———?
G: Darf ich Ihnen den (die, das) ——— abnehmen?
I: Posso mettere da parte il Suo (la Sua) ———?
P: Posso aliviá-lo (TO FEM. aliviá-la) do seu (da sua) ———?
S: ¿Puedo poner al lado su ———?

Cabin Facilities

F: DISPOSITIFS DE LA CABINE
G: KABINENEINRICHTUNGEN
I: ATTREZZATURE DI CABINA
P: INSTALAÇÕES DA CABINA
S: INSTALACIONES DE LA CABINA

222. Here is your reading light switch [your fresh air inlet].
F: Voici l'interrupteur de l'éclairage individuel [une buse d'air individuelle].
G: Das ist der Knopf für Ihre Leselampe [Ihr Frischluftventil].
I: Questo è l'interruttore della luce per leggere [l'interruttore per l'aria fresca].

P: Aqui está o interruptor da luz de leitura [o renovador de ar].

S: Aquí está su interruptor de luz [su toma de aire fresco].

223. This is your call button.
F: Voici votre bouton d'appel.
G: Hier ist Ihr Klingelknopf.
I: Questo è il Suo campanello.
P: Isto é o seu botão de chamada.
S: Este es el timbre de llamada.

224. If you need something, press this button.
F: Si vous avez besoin de quelque chose, appuyez sur ce bouton.
G: Wenn Sie etwas brauchen, drücken Sie bitte auf diesen Knopf.
I: Se ha bisogno di qualcosa spinga il bottone.
P: Se precisar de alguma coisa, carregue neste botão.*
S: Si necesita algo, toque este timbre.

225. The lavatory (OR toilet) is in the rear [in front].
F: Le lavabo (OR La toilette) se trouve (OR est) à l'arrière [à l'avant].
G: Die Toilette ist hinten [vorne].
I: C'è una toletta dietro [davanti].
P: O lavabo é à rectaguarda [à frente].
S: El lavabo está atrás (OR en el fondo) [en frente].

226. The ashtray is in the arm rest.
F: Le cendrier se trouve dans l'accoudoir.
G: Der Aschenbecher ist in der Armlehne.
I: Il portacenere è nel bracciolo.
P: O cinzeiro está no apoio do braço.
S: El cenicero está en el brazo del asiento.

* In Brazil *prema este botão.*

227. This is your tray-table.

F: Voici votre guide-tablette.

G: Das ist der Klapptisch für Ihr Tablett.

I: Questo è il Suo vassoio.

P: Isto é o seu tabuleiro.

S: Esta es su mesa-bandeja.

227a. This is your seat belt!

F: Voici votre ceinture de sécurité (OR sûreté)!

G: Das ist Ihr Sitzgurt!

I: Questo è la sua cintura di sicurezza!

P. Isto é o seu cinto de segurança!

S: ¡Esto es su cinturón de seguridad!

228. May I show you how to adjust your seat?

F: Puis-je vous montrer comment ajuster votre siège?

G: Darf ich Ihnen zeigen, wie Ihr Sitz verstellt wird?

I: Posso dimostrarLe (OR farLe vedere) come sistemare il Suo sedile?

P: Posso mostrar-lhe como se regula a sua cadeira?

S: ¿Puedo mostrarle cómo ajustar su asiento?

229. Now you can recline your seat. You will be more comfortable.

F: Maintenant vous pouvez incliner votre siège. C'est plus confortable pour vous.

G: Jetzt können Sie sich zurücklehnen. Das ist bequemer für Sie.

I: Adesso può reclinare il sedile. Starà più comodo.

P: Agora pode reclinar a sua cadeira. Fica mais confortável.

S: Ahora Ud. puede reclinar el asiento. Es más cómodo para Ud.

230. Push the recline control on your arm rest and lean back.

F: Appuyez sur le bouton de réglage de votre accoudoir et renversez-vous.

G: Drücken Sie auf den Knopf in der Armlehne und lehnen Sie sich zurück.

I: Prema il pulsante del bracciolo e si appoggi in dietro.
P: Carregue no botão* no apoio do braço e incline-se para trás.
S: Apriete (OR Empuje) el control en el brazo de su asiento y reclínese hacia atrás.

231. Please straighten up your seat!
F: S'il vous plaît, redressez votre siège!
G: Bitte stellen Sie Ihren Sitz nach vorne!
I: Raddrizzi il Suo sedile, per favore!
P: Por favor, endireite a sua cadeira!
S: ¡Por favor, enderezca su asiento!

232. There are water dispensers in both galley areas.
F: Il y a de l'eau potable à votre disposition dans les deux offices de la cabine.
G: Trinkwasser können Sie in beiden Bordküchen bekommen.
I: L'acqua da bere è disponibile nelle due cucinette.
P: Há água para beber em ambas cozinhas.
S: Hay agua para beber en el área de ambas cocinas de abordo.

233. Would you like to have a magazine [a newspaper; a route map; a timetable]?
F: Désirez-vous un magazine [un journal; une carte routière; un horaire]?
G: Möchten Sie eine Zeitschrift [eine Zeitung; eine Streckenkarte; einen Flugplan] haben?
I: Desidera una rivista [un giornale (OR quotidiano); una mappa della rotta; un orario]?
P: Gostaria de ter uma revista [um jornal; um mapa de rota; um horário]?
S: ¿Desea Ud. una revista [un periódico; un mapa de rutas; un horario]?

* In Brazil *Prema o botão.*

234. **Your cabin attendant will demonstrate the use of some equipment for your comfort.**
    F: Votre hôtesse vous expliquera le fonctionnement de certains dispositifs étudiés pour votre confort.
    G: Die Stewardeß wird Ihnen den Gebrauch einiger Geräte für Ihre Bequemlichkeit vorführen.
    I: La hostess vi mostrerà come usare alcuni accessori per il Vostro conforto (OR per la Vostra comodità).
    P: A sua assistente de bordo demonstrará o uso de algum equipamento para o vosso conforto.
    S: Su stewardess le enseñará el empleo de algún equipo para su comodidad.

235. **In the seat pocket you will find a folder with useful information written in several languages.**
    F: Dans la poche du fauteuil vous trouverez un dépliant en plusieurs langues contenant des renseignements utiles.
    G: In der Sitztasche finden Sie eine mehrsprachige Broschüre mit nützlichen Informationen.
    I: Nella tasca del Vostro sedile troverete una guida in diverse lingue con informazioni utili.
    P: No bolso de cadeira encontrará uma brochura escrita em várias línguas com úteis informações.
    S: En la bolsa del asiento hallará Ud. un folleto escrito en varios idiomas con informaciones útiles.

236. **If you read it you will be able to follow the demonstration of some of the equipment in your cabin.**
    F: En le lisant vous pourrez suivre la démonstration du fonctionnement de quelques dispositifs de votre cabine.
    G: Mit Hilfe dieser Broschüre werden Sie der Vorführung einiger Geräte in der Kabine folgen können.
    I: Leggendola potrete seguire la dimostrazione di alcuni accessori di cabina.

P: Pela sua leitura pode acompanhar a demonstração de algum equipamento da sua cabina.

S: Leyéndolo Ud. podrá seguir la demostración de algunos equipos de la cabina.

237. **The life jacket is located underneath your seat.**
F: Le gilet de sauvetage est sous votre siège.
G: Ihre Schwimmveste befindet sich unter Ihrem Sitz.
I: Il salvagente è situato sotto il Vostro sedile.
P: O cinto de salvação está por baixo do seu assento.
S: El chaleco (OR La chaqueta) salvavidas está colocado (colocada) debajo de su asiento.

238. **Do not inflate it inside the aircraft.**
F: Ne le gonflez pas à l'intérieur de l'appareil.
G: Blasen Sie die Schwimmveste nicht in der Kabine auf.
I: Non gonfiatelo nell'apparecchio.
P: Não o encham dentro do avião.
S: No lo (la) inflen dentro del avión.

239. **Life rafts are located in the ceiling of the cabin.**
F: Les radeaux (OR canots) de sauvetage se trouvent dans le plafond de la cabine.
G: Schlauchboote sind an der Decke der Kabine vorhanden (OR untergebracht).
I: I canotti di salvataggio sono situati nel tetto (OR nel soffitto) della cabina.
P: Barcos salva-vidas são localizados no teto da cabina.
S: Las balsas salvavidas están colocadas en el techo de la cabina.

240. **Hold the oxygen mask over your face.**
F: Tenez le masque à oxygène sur votre visage.
G: Ziehen Sie sich die Sauerstoffmaske über das Gesicht.
I: Mettete la maschera d'ossigeno davanti alla Vostra faccia.

P: Coloquem a máscara de oxigénio na sua cara.
S: Pónganse la máscara de oxígeno sobre la cara.

241. Cover your nose and mouth. Breathe normally.
F: Couvrez le nez et la bouche. Respirez normalement.
G: Halten Sie die Maske über Nase und Mund. Atmen Sie ganz normal.
I: Coprite il naso e la bocca. Respirate normalmente.
P: Por favor, cubram o nariz e a boca. Respirem normalmente.
S: Por favor, cúbranse la nariz y la boca. Respiren normalmente.

242. The emergency exits are here [there].
F: Les sorties de secours sont ici [là-bas].
G: Hier [Dort] sind die Notausgänge.
I: Le uscite d'emergenza sono qui [là].
P: As saídas de emergência são aqui [acolá].
S: Las salidas de emergencia están aquí [allí].

243. Here are the airsickness bags.
F: Ici se trouvent les sacs vomitoires.
G: Hier sind die Tüten für den Fall von Luftkrankheit.*
I: Ecco le borsette in caso di mal d'aria.
P: Aqui estão os sacos de enjôo.
S: Aquí están las bolsas en caso de mareo.

244. Here is a folder with the emergency instructions.
F: Voici un dépliant avec les consignes en cas d'urgence.
G: Hier ist eine Broschüre mit den Anweisungen im Notfall.
I: EccoLe un opuscolo con le istruzioni di emergenza.
P: Aqui está um folheto com as instrucções de emergência.
S: Aquí está un folleto con las instrucciones de emergencia.

* Or, more colloquially, *Hier sind die Spucktüten.*

In-Flight Conversation

F: CONVERSATIONS PENDANT LE VOL
G: GESPRÄCHE WÄHREND DES FLUGES
I: CONVERSAZIONI DURANTE IL VOLO
P: CONVERSAÇÕES DURANTE O VÔO
S: CONVERSACIONES DURANTE EL VUELO

245. We are going to take off [land] in a few minutes.
F: Nous allons décoller [atterrir] dans quelques moments.
G: Wir werden in wenigen Minuten starten [landen].
I: Stiamo per decollare [atterrare] fra qualche minuto.
P: Dentro de minutos descolaremos [aterraremos].*
S: Vamos a despegar [aterrizar] dentro de unos minutos.

246. We are waiting for our clearance from the control tower.
F: Nous attendons de la tour de contrôle la permission de rouler.
G: Wir warten auf Genehmigung vom Kontrollturm.
I: Attendiamo l'autorizzazione della torre.
P: Estamos a espera de autorização da torre de control.
S: Esperamos que la torre de control nos dé la señal de partida.

247. Please note the "No Smoking" sign!
F: S'il vous plaît, observez l'avis: "Défense de fumer."
G: Bitte beachten Sie das Zeichen: "Nicht rauchen."
I: Prego osservare il segnale di non fumare.
P: Favor notar o sinal de "Não fumar!"
S: Por favor, tomen nota del aviso de: "No fumar!"

248. Fasten your seat belt, please!
F: Attachez (OR Bouclez) votre ceinture, s'il vous plaît!
G: Bitte schnallen Sie sich an!

* In Brazil *decolaremos* [*aterrissaremos*].

I: Prego allacciare la cintura di sicurezza!
P: Por favor, apertem os vossos cintos de segurança!
S: ¡Ajuste* su cinturón de seguridad, por favor!

249. Do you know how to unfasten your seat belt?
    F: Savez-vous comment détacher votre ceinture?
    G: Können Sie Ihren Sitzgurt lösen?
    I: Sapete come slacciare la Sua cintura di sicurezza?
    P: Sabe como desapertar o seu cinto de segurança?
    S: ¿Sabe Ud. desabrochar (OR zafar) su cinturón de seguridad?

250. May I show you how to do it?
    F: Puis-je vous montrer comment le faire?
    G: Darf ich Ihnen zeigen, wie es gemacht wird?
    I: Posso mostrarLe come fare?
    P: Deixe-me mostrar-lhe como deve fazer.
    S: ¿Puedo mostrarle cómo sin hacerlo?

251. Is this a non-stop flight?
    F: Ce vol est-il direct (OR sans escale)?
    G: Ist das ein durchgehender Flug (OR ein Flug ohne Zwischenlandung)?
    I: È un volo senza scalo?
    P: É este um vôo direito (OR direto)?
    S: ¿Es este un vuelo sin escalas?

252. Do we stop at ———?
    F: Faisons-nous escale à ———?
    G: Machen wir eine Zwischenlandung in ———?
    I: Faremo scalo a ———?
    P: Paramos em ———?
    S: ¿Hacemos escala en ———?

253. What will be the transit time?
    F: Quelle sera la durée du transit?
    G: Wie lange wird die Aufenthaltszeit dauern?

* In South America *Abroche.*

I: Quanto sarà il tempo di (OR la durata del) transito?
P: Qual será o tempo de trânsito?
S: ¿Cuánto será el tiempo del tránsito?

254. How many stopovers are we going to have?
F: Combien d'escales ferons-nous?
G: Wieviele Zwischenlandungen werden wir machen?
I: Quanti scali faremo?
P: Quantas paragens vamos ter?
S: ¿Cuántas escalas haremos?

255. At what time will we arrive at our destination?
F: À quelle heure arriverons-nous à notre destination?
G: Wann werden wir an unserem Bestimmungsort (OR Zielort) sein?
I: A che ora arriveremo a destinazione?
P: A que horas chegaremos ao nosso destino?
S: ¿A qué hora llegaremos a nuestro destino (OR a nuestra destinación)?

256. At about ——— o'clock in the morning [afternoon; evening].
F: À ——— heures du matin [de l'après-midi; du soir] environ.
G: Ungefähr um ——— Uhr morgens [nachmittags; abends].
I: Verso le ore ——— di mattina [del pomeriggio; di sera].
P: Cerca das ——— horas de manhã [de tarde; de noite].
S: Alrededor de las ——— de la mañana [de la tarde; de la noche].

257. At noon; before [after] midnight.
F: À midi; avant [après] minuit.
G: Mittags; vor [nach] Mitternacht.
I: A mezzogiorno; prima della [dopo la] mezzanotte.
P: Ao meio-dia; antes [depois] de meia-noite.
S: Al mediodía; antes [después] de medianoche.

258. What is our actual flying time?
F: Quelle est la durée du vol?
G: Wie lange dauert die Flugzeit?
I: Quanto sarà il tempo di volo?
P: Qual é o tempo de vôo?
S: ¿Cuál es la duración total del vuelo?

259. Approximately —— hours and —— minutes.
F: Approximativement —— heures et —— minutes.
G: Ungefähr —— Stunden und —— Minuten.
I: Circa —— ore e —— minuti.
P: Aproximadamente —— horas e —— minutos.
S: Aproximadamente —— horas y —— minutos.

260. How far is the city from the airport?
F: Quelle est la distance entre la ville et l'aéroport?
G: Wie weit ist die Stadt vom Flughafen entfernt?
I: Quanto dista la città dall'aeroporto?
P: A que distância fica a cidade do aeroporto?
S: ¿A qué distancia está la ciudad del aeropuerto?

261. Is there a regular bus service between the airport and the city?
F: Y a-t-il un service de cars entre l'aéroport et la ville?
G: Gibt es einen regulären Busverkehr zwischen dem Flughafen und der Stadt?
I: C'è un servizio regolare di autobus fra l'aeroporto e la città?
P: Existe (OR Há) um serviço regular de autocarro entre o aeroporto e a cidade?
S: ¿Hay servicio regular de autobuses entre el aeropuerto y la ciudad?

262. How much does the trip cost?
F: Quel est le prix du trajet?
G: Wieviel kostet die Busfahrt?
I: Qual'è la tariffa del viaggio?
P: Quanto custa a passagem?
S: ¿Cuánto cuesta el viaje?

263. **How long does it take from the airport to the city?**
   F: Combien de temps faut-il pour aller de l'aéroport à la ville?
   G: Wie lange dauert die Fahrt vom Flughafen in die Stadt?
   I: Quanto tempo ci vuole dall'aeroporto alla città?
   P: Quanto tempo leva do aeroporto à cidade?
   S: ¿Cuánto tiempo dura el trayecto desde el aeropuerto a la ciudad?

264. **Please bring me a timetable.**
   F: S'il vous plaît, apportez-moi un horaire.
   G: Bitte bringen Sie mir einen Flugplan!
   I: Per cortesia, mi porti un orario.
   P: Por favor, traga-me um horário.
   S: Por favor, traígame un horario.

265. **Will you please check to see if there is a connecting flight tomorrow to ———?**
   F: Veuillez vérifier, s'il vous plaît, s'il y a demain un vol en correspondance pour ———.
   G: Würden Sie bitte nachsehen, ob es morgen einen Anschlußflug nach ——— gibt?
   I: Per cortesia, mi controlli se domani c'è un volo in coincidenza per ———.
   P: Favor verificar se há (OR existe) um vôo de ligação amanhã para ———.
   S: ¿Quiere comprobar, por favor, si hay algún vuelo de conexión a ——— para mañana?

266. **What is the flight number?**
   F: Quel est le numéro du vol?
   G: Wie ist die Flugnummer?
   I: Qual'è il numero del volo?
   P: Qual é o número do vôo?
   S: ¿Cuál es el número de vuelo?

267. What is the check-in time for that flight?
F: À quelle heure doit-on enregistrer pour ce vol?
G: Um wieviel Uhr muß ich mich für diesen Flug melden?
I: A che ora debbo (OR devo) presentarmi per il volo?
P: Qual é a hora de apresentação para esse vôo?
S: ¿Cuál es la hora de presentación para ese vuelo?

268. You will have to be at the airport an hour and a half before departure.
F: Vous devrez être à l'aéroport une heure et demie avant le départ.
G: Sie müssen anderthalb Stunden vor Abflug am Flughafen sein.
I: Deve presentarsi in aeroporto un'ora e mezza prima della partenza.
P: Terá que estar no aeroporto hora e meia antes da partida.
S: Ud. tendrá que estar en el aeropuerto una hora y media antes de la salida.

269. I want to take a connecting flight in the afternoon.
F: Je veux prendre un vol en correspondance dans l'après-midi.
G: Ich möchte einen Anschlußflug am Nachmittag nehmen.
I: Desidero prendere una coincidenza nel pomeriggio.
P: Eu desejo tomar um vôo de ligação de tarde.
S: Quiero tomar un vuelo de conexión por la tarde.

270. The next plane for ——— leaves Friday evening.
F: Le prochain avion pour ——— part vendredi soir.
G: Das nächste Flugzeug nach ——— geht Freitag abend.
I: Il prossimo volo per ——— parte venerdì sera.
P: O próximo avião para ——— parte sexta-feira à tarde.
S: El próximo avión para ——— sale el viernes por la tarde.

271. **If you wish you could spend nearly two days at ———.**
  F: Si vous le désirez, vous pouvez passer presque deux jours à ———.
  G: Wenn Sie möchten, könnten Sie fast zwei Tage in ——— verbringen.
  I: Se Lei lo desidera, potrebbe stare quasi due giorni a ———.
  P: Se desejar, pode passar quase dois dias em ———.
  S: Si lo desea, podría pasar casi dos días en ———.

272. **That is an excellent idea.**
  F: C'est une idée excellente.
  G: Das ist eine ausgezeichnete Idee.
  I: È un'idea eccellente, grazie.
  P: Essa é uma ideia excelente.
  S: Es una excelente idea.

273. **Then I will be able to take a sightseeing tour.**
  F: De cette façon je pourrai faire le tour de la ville.
  G: Dann kann ich eine (Stadt-)Rundfahrt machen.
  I: In questo caso posso fare un giro per la città.
  P: Então poderei fazer uma volta pela cidade.
  S: Entonces podré dar un vistazo a la ciudad.

274. **What city are we flying over now?**
  F: Quelle ville survolons-nous maintenant?
  G: Welche Stadt überfliegen wir jetzt?
  I: Su quale città stiamo volando ora?
  P: Qual é a cidade que estamos sobrevoando?
  S: ¿Sobre qué ciudad estamos volando ahora?

275. **At what altitude are we flying?**
  F: À quelle altitude volons-nous?
  G: In welcher Höhe fliegen wir?
  I: A quale altezza stiamo volando?
  P: A que altitude estamos voando?
  S: ¿A qué altura volamos?

276. At about ——— feet, that is, about ——— meters.
  F: À ——— pieds, c'est-à-dire ——— mètres environ.
  G: In ungefähr ——— Fuß, das heißt ——— Meter.
  I: A circa ——— piedi, cioè circa ——— metri.
  P: Cerca de ——— pés, isto é aproximadamente ———
    metros.
  S: A unos ——— pies, es decir unos ——— metros.

277. What is the speed of our plane?
  F: Quelle est la vitesse de notre avion?
  G: Wie hoch ist die Geschwindigkeit unserer Maschine?
  I: Qual'è la velocità di questo aereo?
  P: Qual é a velocidade do nosso avião?
  S: ¿Cuál es la velocidad de nuestro avión?

**278. About ——— miles, that is, about ——— kilometers,
per hour.**
  F: À peu près ——— milles, c'est-à-dire à peu près
    ——— kilomètres, par heure.
  G: Ungefähr ——— Meilen, das sind ——— Kilometer,
    in der Stunde.
  I: Circa ——— miglia, cioè ——— chilometri, all'ora.
  P: Cerca de ——— milhas, isto é aproximadamente
    ——— quilómetros, por hora.
  S: Unas ——— millas, es decir ——— kilómetros, por
    hora.

**279. Do not worry, you will not miss your connecting flight,
since we are on time.**
  F: Ne vous inquiétez pas, vous ne manquerez pas la
    correspondance puisque nous sommes à l'heure.
  G: Seien Sie unbesorgt, Sie werden Ihren Anschlußflug
    nicht versäumen, da wir keine Verspätung haben.
  I: Non si preoccupi, non perderà la Sua coincidenza dato
    che siamo in orario.

P: Não se preocupe, não perderá a sua ligação porque vamos dentro do horário.

S: No se preocupe, no perderá su vuelo de conexión ya que no llevamos retraso.

280. **We are ——— minutes [hours] behind schedule because of strong headwinds.**

F: Nous sommes en retard de ——— minutes [heures] à cause de violents contrevents.

G: Wir haben eine Verspätung von ——— Minuten [Stunden] wegen starkem Gegenwind.

I: Abbiamo un ritardo di ——— minuti [ore], causa forti venti contrari.

P: Nós temos um atrazo de ——— minutos [horas] devido a forte vento contrário.

S: Llevamos un retraso de ——— minutos [horas] a causa de los fuertes vientos.

281. **Do you think we could make up the lost time?**

F: Pensez-vous que nous pourrions rattraper le temps perdu?

G: Glauben Sie, daß wir den Zeitverlust wieder einholen können? ‹

I: Crede che recupereremo del tempo?

P: Pensa que poderemos recuperar o tempo perdido?

S: ¿Cree que podremos recuperar el tiempo perdido?

282. **I do not know, I am going to ask our commander (OR captain).**

F: Je ne sais pas, je vais le demander au commandant (OR capitaine).

G: Ich weiß es nicht, ich werde unseren Kapitän fragen.

I: Non saprei, vado a domandare al comandante.

P: Não sei, mas vou perguntar ao nosso capitão (OR comandante).

S: No lo sé, le preguntaré a nuestro capitán (OR comandante).

283. **I will let you know as soon as possible.**
F: Je vous le ferai savoir dès que possible.
G: Ich werde Ihnen sobald wie möglich Bescheid geben.
I: Glielo farò sapere appena possibile.
P: Dir-lhe-ei logo que seja possível.
S: Se lo comunicaré tan pronto como sea posible.

284. **What will the weather be like when we arrive at** ———?
F: Quel temps fera-t-il lorsque nous arriverons à ———?
G: Wie wird das Wetter bei der Ankunft in ——— sein?
I: Come sarà il tempo all'arrivo a ———?
P: Como estará o tempo na nossa chegada a ———?
S: ¿Qué tiempo hará cuando lleguemos a ———?

285. **According to the last weather forecast at ——— it is now cold [warm].**
F: D'après les dernières prévisions météorologiques à ——— il fait froid [chaud] maintenant.
G: Nach der letzten Wettermeldung es ist kalt [warm] in ———.
I: Secondo l'ultimo bollettino meteorologico a ——— adesso fa (OR è) freddo [caldo].
P: De acordo com a última previsão de tempo em ——— faz frio [calor] agora.
S: Según el último parte (OR boletín) meteorológico, hace frío [calor] en ———.

286. **It is sunny [it is cloudy; it is windy; it is foggy; it is humid; it is muggy].**
F: Il fait du soleil [il y a des nuages; il fait du vent; il y a du brouillard; il y a de l'humidité; il y a beaucoup d'humidité].
G: Es ist sonnig [es ist bewölkt; es ist windig; es ist nebelig; es ist feucht; es ist schwül].
I: C'è sole [è nuvoloso; c'è vento; c'è nebbia; fa umido; fa molto umido].

P: Está sol [está enevoado; está ventoso; está nevoeiro;
está húmido; está sufocante].

S: Hay sol [está nublado; hay viento; hay niebla (OR
neblina); hay humedad; hay mucha humedad].

287. It is raining [it is snowing; it is drizzling].

F: Il pleut [il neige; il y a une pluie fine].

G: Es regnet [es schneit; es nieselt].

I: Piove [nevica; pioviggina].

P: Está chovendo [está nevando; está chuviscando].

S: Está lloviendo [está nevando; está lloviznando].

288. You will need a raincoat [an umbrella; an overcoat].

F: Vous aurez besoin d'un imperméable [d'un parapluie;
d'un pardessus].

G: Sie werden einen Regenmantel [einen Regenschirm;
einen Mantel] brauchen.

I: Avrà bisogno di un impermeabile [di un ombrello;
di un soprabito].

P: Precisará dum impermeável [dum guarda-chuva;
dum sobretudo].

S: Necesitará un impermeable [un paraguas; un abrigo].

289. The temperature is ——— degrees F [C].

F: La température est de ——— degrés F [C].

G: Die Temperatur beträgt ——— Grad F [C].

I: La temperatura è di ——— gradi F [C].

P: A temperatura é ——— graus F [C].

S: La temperatura es de ——— grados F [C].

290. Because of bad weather the flight has been diverted.

F: Notre vol a été dérouté à cause du mauvais temps.

G: Infolge schlechten Wetters ist unser Flug umgeleitet
worden.

I: A causa del cattivo tempo l'aereo sarà dirottato.

P: Por causa do mau tempo o nosso vôo divergiu.

S: A causa del mal tiempo nuestro vuelo ha sido desviado.

291. Now we are going to land at ——— instead of ———.
F: Maintenant nous allons atterrir à ——— au lieu
de ———.
G: Wir werden jetzt in ——— statt in ——— landen.
I: Adesso atterreremo a ——— invece di ———.
P: Agora nós vamos aterrar* em ——— em vez
de ———.
S: Ahora vamos a aterrizar en ——— en lugar de ———.

292. Are you comfortable?
F: Vous sentez-vous à votre aise?
G: Fühlen Sie sich wohl?
I: Sta comodo?
P: Está confortável?
S: ¿Se encuentra bien (OR ¿Se siente cómodo)?

293. May I help you?
F: Puis-je vous aider?
G: Kann ich Ihnen behilflich sein?
I: Posso aiutarLa?
P: Posso ajudá-lo (TO FEM. ajudá-la)?
S: ¿Le puedo ayudar?

294. May I show you ———?
F: Puis-je vous montrer ———?
G: Darf ich Ihnen ——— zeigen?
I: Posso mostrarLe ———?
P: Posso mostrar-lhe ———?
S: ¿Me permite enseñarle ———?

295. May I bother (OR trouble) you for a moment?
F: Puis-je vous déranger pour un instant?
G: Darf ich Sie einen Moment stören?
I: Posso disturbarLa per un momento?
P: Posso importuná-lo (TO FEM. importuná-la) por um
momento?
S: ¿Me disculpa (OR ¿Puedo molestarle) un momento?

* In Brazil *aterrissar.*

296. Would you like to have a cigarette?

F: Voudriez-vous une cigarette?

G: Darf ich Ihnen eine Zigarette anbieten?

I: Desidera una sigaretta?

P: Gostaria de fumar um cigarro?

S: ¿Quiere un cigarillo?

297. Thanks, but I am not permitted to smoke while on duty.

F: Je vous en remercie, mais je ne dois pas fumer pendant mon travail.

G: Danke, aber ich darf im Dienst nicht rauchen.

I: Grazie, ma non mi è permesso fumare durante il servizio.

P: Muito obrigado (FEM. obrigada), mas não é permitido fumar durante o serviço.

S: Gracias, no puedo fumar durante mi trabajo.

298. Where is the coatroom (OR cloakroom)?

F: Où est le vestiaire?

G: Wo ist die Garderobe?

I: Dov'è la guardaroba?

P: Onde é o guarda-fato (OR vestiário)?

S: ¿Dónde está el vestuario (OR guardarropa)?

299. Do you have an electric razor?

F: Avez-vous un rasoir électrique?

G: Haben Sie einen elektrischen Rasierapparat?

I: Avete un rasoio elettrico?

P: Tem uma máquina de barbear eléctrica?

S: ¿Tiene una máquina (OR maquinilla) de afeitar eléctrica?

300. Yes, I am going to bring you one.

F: Oui, je vais vous l'apporter.

G: Ja, ich werde Ihnen einen bringen.

I: Sì, Le porterò uno.

P: Sim, vou-lhe trazer uma.

S: Sí, le traeré una.

301. You may use it whenever you wish.
F: Vous pouvez vous en servir quand vous voudrez.
G: Sie können ihn jederzeit benutzen.
I: Può usarlo quando vuole.
P: Pode usá-la quando o desejar.
S: Ud. puede usarla cuando quiera.

302. In the washroom you will find the electrical outlets.
F: Dans le lavabo vous trouverez une prise de courant.
G: Den Stecker finden Sie in den Toiletten.
I: Al gabinetto troverà le prese elettriche.
P: Nos lavabos encontrará a tomada de corrente.
S: En el lavabo Ud. hallará los enchufes eléctricos.

303. How many passengers are on board?
F: Combien de passagers y a-t-il à bord?
G: Wieviel Passagiere sind an Bord?
I: Quanti passeggeri sono a bordo?
P: Quantos passageiros estão a bordo?
S: ¿Cuántos pasajeros hay a bordo?

304. In First Class [Economy Class] we have a total of ———.
F: En Première Classe [Classe Économique] nous avons un total de ———.
G: In der Ersten Klasse [Touristenklasse] haben wir insgesamt ——— Passagiere.
I: In Prima Classe [Classe Economica] abbiamo un totale di ———.
P: Em Primeira Classe [Classe Económica] temos um total de ——— passageiros.
S: En Primera Clase [Clase Económica] tenemos un total de ——— pasajeros.

305. Excuse me, somebody is calling me.
F: Excusez-moi, quelqu'un m'appelle.
G: Entschuldigen Sie bitte, jemand ruft mich.
I: Scusi, qualcuno mi sta chiamando.

P: Desculpe-me, alguém está a chamar-me.*
S: Perdóneme, alguien me llama.

306. Have you any newspapers or magazines?
F: Avez-vous des journaux ou des magazines?
G: Haben Sie Zeitungen oder Zeitschriften?
I: Ha dei giornali o riviste?
P: Tem alguns jornais ou revistas?
S: ¿Tiene Ud. algunos periódicos o revistas?

307. In what languages?
F: En quelles langues?
G: In welchen Sprachen?
I: In che lingue?
P: Em que línguas?
S: ¿En qué idiomas?

308. In English [French, German, Italian, Portuguese, Spanish, Russian, Japanese].
F: En anglais [français, allemand, italien, portuguais, espagnol, russe, japonais].
G: Auf englisch [französisch, deutsch, italienisch, portugiesisch, spanisch, russisch, japanisch].
I: In inglese [francese, tedesco, italiano, portoghese, spagnolo, russo, giapponese].
P: Em inglês [francês, alemão, italiano, português, espanhol, russo, japonês].
S: En inglés [francés, alemán, italiano, portugués, español, ruso, japonés].

309. I cannot close the curtain.
F: Je ne peux pas fermer le rideau.
G: Ich kann den Vorhang nicht zumachen (OR zuziehen, schließen).

---

* In Brazil *alguém me está chamando.*

I: Non posso chiudere la tendina.
P: Não consigo fechar a cortina.
S: No puedo cerrar la cortina.

310. Could you help me?
F: Pouvez-vous m'aider?
G: Können Sie mir helfen?
I: Mi può aiutare?
P: Pode ajudar-me?
S: ¿Puede Ud. ayudarme?

311. Certainly! I will be with you in a moment.
F: Certainement! Je serai à vous dans un instant.
G: Ja, gewiß! Ich komme in einem Augenblick zurück.
I: Senz'altro! Sarò da Lei in un minuto!
P: Certamente! Estarei consigo dentro de momentos.
S: ¡Cómo no! Estaré con Ud. dentro de un momento.

312. Do you travel frequently?
F: Voyagez-vous souvent?
G: Reisen Sie oft (OR häufig)?
I: Viaggia spesso?
P: Viaja frequentemente?
S: ¿Viaja Ud. frecuentemente?

313. I have made many trips this year.
F: J'ai fait plusieurs voyages cette année.
G: In diesem Jahre bin ich viel gereist.
I: Ho fatto molti viaggi quest'anno.
P: Já fiz várias viajens este ano.
S: He viajado mucho este año.

314. Have you ever visited ———?
F: Avez-vous déjà visité ———?
G: Waren Sie schon einmal in ———?
I: È mai stato (TO FEM. stata) a ———?
P: Já visitou ———?
S: ¿Ha estado alguna vez en ———?

315. How was the weather during your last flight to ———?

    F: Quel temps a-t-il fait pendant votre dernier vol à ———?

    G: Wie war das Wetter auf Ihrem letzten Flug nach ———?

    I: Come era il tempo durante il Suo ultimo volo per ———?

    P: Como estava o tempo no seu último vôo para ———?

    S: ¿Qué tiempo hizo durante su último vuelo para ———?

316. Do you speak ———?

    F: Parlez-vous ———?

    G: Sprechen Sie ———?

    I: Parla ———?

    P: Fala ———?

    S: ¿Habla Ud. ———?

317. I speak a little English [French; German].

    F: Je parle un peu l'anglais [le francais; l'allemand].

    G: Ich spreche etwas Englisch [Französisch; Deutsch].

    I: Parlo un pochino d'inglese [di francese; di tedesco].

    P: Eu falo um pouco de inglês [de francês; de alemão].

    S: Hablo un poco de inglés [francés; alemán].

318. I do not speak it correctly.

    F: Je ne le parle pas correctement.

    G: Ich spreche es fehlerhaft.

    I: Non lo parlo correttamente.

    P: Eu não o falo correctamente.

    S: No lo hablo correctamente.

319. I speak well enough to make myself understood.

    F: Je parle assez bien pour me faire comprendre.

    G: Ich spreche gut genug, um mich verständlich zu machen.

I: Parlo abbastanza bene da farmi capire.

P: Eu falo-o suficiente para me fazer compreender.

S: Hablo lo suficiente para que me entiendan.

320. Where are you from?

F: D'où êtes-vous?

G: Wo sind Sie her?

I: Di dov'è Lei?

P: Donde é Vossa Excelência (OR o Senhor, Você)?

S: De dónde es Ud.?

321. I am from ———.

F: Je suis de ———.

G: Ich komme aus ———.

I: Sono di ———.

P: Eu sou de ———.

S: Soy de ———.

322. May I introduce Mister [Mrs.; Miss] ———?

F: Permettez-moi de vous présenter Monsieur [Madame; Mademoiselle] ———.

G: Darf ich Ihnen Herrn [Frau; Fräulein] ——— vorstellen?

I: Permetta che Le presenti il Signor [la Signora; la Signorina] ———.

P: Permita-me que apresente o Senhor [a Senhora Dona*] ———.

S: Permítame que le presente al Señor [a la Señora; a la Señorita] ———.

323. How do you do?

F: Enchanté (FEM. Enchantée).

G: Es freut mich sehr.

I: Piacere di fare la Sua conoscenza.

P: Tenho muito prazer (OR gosto).

S: Mucho gusto en conocerle.

* In Brazil there is a separate word for "Miss": *a Senhorita.*

324. Who is the gentleman in uniform?

F: Qui est ce monsieur en uniforme?

G: Wer ist der Herr in Uniform?

I: Chi è il Signore in uniforme?

P: Quem é o cavalheiro em uniform?

S: ¿Quién es ese señor en uniforme?

325. He is our commander (OR captain) [one of our officers; our purser].

F: Il est notre commandant (OR capitaine) [un de nos officiers; notre commissaire de bord].

G: Das ist unser Kapitän [einer unserer Offiziere; unser Chefsteward].

I: È il nostro comandante (OR capitano) [uno dei nostri ufficiali; il nostro commissario di bordo].

P: É o nosso capitão (OR comandante) [um de nossos oficiais; o nosso comissário].

S: Es nuestro capitán (OR comandante) [uno de nuestros oficiales; nuestro comisario de abordo (OR nuestro sobrecargo)].

326. How many people does the crew consist of?

F: De combien de personnes se compose l'équipage?

G: Aus wieviel Personen besteht die Besatzung?

I: Di quante persone è composto l'equipaggio?

P: Quantas pessoas tem a tripulação?

S: ¿De cuántas personas se compone la tripulación?

327. I would like to see the cockpit.

F: Je voudrais voir le poste de pilotage.

G: Ich möchte gern die Kanzel besichtigen.

I: Vorrei vedere la cabina di comando.

P: Eu gostaria de ver a cabina de comando (OR o cockpit).

S: Me gustaría ver la cabina de mando.

328. I am sorry, it is not permitted while we are aloft.

F: Je regrette, ce n'est pas permis en vol.

G: Ich bedauere, aber während des Fluges ist das verboten.

I: Mi dispiace, ma non è permesso mentre siamo in volo.

P: Lamento, mas não é permitido durante o vôo.

S: Lo siento, pero no es permitido mientras estamos en vuelo.

329. You may see it during our next stop.

F: Vous pourrez le visiter pendant notre prochaine escale.

G: Bei der nächsten Zwischenlandung werden Sie sie besichtigen können.

I: Potrà vederla durante la prossima fermata.

P: Pode vê-la (vê-lo) durante a nossa próxima paragem.

S: Ud. podrá verla durante nuestra próxima escala.

330. When did you leave ———?

F: Quand avez-vous quitté ———?

G: Wann haben Sie ——— verlassen?

I: Quando è partito (TO FEM. partita) da ———?

P: Quando saiu de ———?

S: ¿Cuándo partió Ud. de ———?

331. I left ——— last Wednesday [last week; last month; ——— days ago].

F: Je suis parti (FEM. partie) de ——— mercredi dernier [la semaine dernière; le mois dernier; il y a ——— jours].

G: Ich habe ——— am vorigen Mittwoch [vorige Woche; im vorigen (OR vergangenen) Monat; vor ——— Tagen] verlassen.

I: Sono partito (FEM. partita) da ——— mercoledì scorso [la settimana scorsa; il mese scorso; ——— giorni fa].

P: Saí (OR Parti) de ——— na última quarta-feira [na última semana; no último mês; ——— dias atrás].

S: Partí de ——— el miércoles pasado [la semana pasada; el mes pasado; hace ——— días].

332. You speak English fluently [very well; quite well].

F: Vous parlez couramment [très bien; assez bien] l'anglais.

G: Sie sprechen Englisch fließend [sehr gut; ziemlich gut].

I: Lei parla inglese correntemente [molto bene; piuttosto bene].

P: O Senhor (TO FEM. A Senhora) fala inglês correntemente [muito bem; bastante bem].

S: Ud. habla el inglés corrientemente (OR de corrido) [muy bien; bastante bien].

333. How long have you been studying French?

F: Depuis combien de temps étudiez-vous le français?

G: Seit wann lernen Sie Französisch?

I: Per quanto tempo ha studiato il francese?

P: Há quanto tempo estuda o francês?

S: ¿Durante cuánto tiempo ha estudiado Ud. el francés?

334. Not very long.

F: Il n'y a pas très longtemps.

G: Noch nicht sehr lange.

I: Non molto.

P: Há pouco tempo.

S: Durante un corto período.

335. What is your native language?

F: Quelle est votre langue maternelle?

G: Was ist Ihre Muttersprache?

I: Qual'è la Sua madre lingua?

P: Qual é a sua língua nativa?

S: ¿Cuál es su idioma materno?

336. Where did you learn German?

F: Où avez-vous appris l'allemand?

G: Wo haben Sie Deutsch gelernt?

I: Dove ha imparato il tedesco?

P: Onde aprendeu o alemão?

S: ¿Dónde aprendió Ud. el alemán?

337. In (grammar) school [in high school; at college].

F: À l'école [au lycée; à l'université].

G: In der Schule [im Gymnasium; an der Universität].

I: A scuola [al liceo; all'università].

P: Na escola [no liceu; na universidade].

S: En la escuela [en el colegio; en la Universidad].

338. In a language laboratory, with the help of tape recorders and records.

F: Au laboratoire de langues, à l'aide des magnétophones et des disques.

G: In dem Sprachlaboratorium, mit Hilfe von Tonbandgeräten und Schallplatten.

I: Nel laboratorio di lingue, con l'aiuto di registratori a nastro e di dischi.

P: No laboratório de línguas, com ajuda de fitas gravadas e discos.

S: En el laboratorio de idiomas, con ayuda de cintas magnetofónicas y discos.

339. I spent several months in ———.

F: J'ai passé plusieurs mois en (à, au, aux) ———.

G: Ich habe einige Monate in ——— verbracht.

I: Sono stato (FEM. stata) parecchi mesi in ———.

P: Passei vários meses em ———.

S: Pasé varios meses en ———.

340. I learned Italian at home from my parents.

F: Mes parents m'ont enseigné l'italien chez moi.

G: Ich habe Italienisch zu Hause von meinen Eltern gelernt.

I: Ho imparato l'italiano a casa dai miei genitori.

P: Aprendi o italiano em casa com os meus pais.

S: Aprendí el italiano en casa de mis padres.

341. I had a private teacher.
F: J'ai eu un professeur privé.
G: Ich hatte einen Privatlehrer.
I: Ho avuto un maestro privato.
P: Tive um professor particular.
S: Tuve un professor privado.

342. How do you say ⸺ in Portuguese?
F: Comment dit-on ⸺ en portugais?
G: Wie sagt man ⸺ auf portugiesisch?
I: Come si dice ⸺ in portoghese?
P: Como diz-se ⸺ em português?
S: ¿Cómo se dice ⸺ en portugués?

343. Excuse me, I did not understand you completely.
F: Excusez-moi, je ne vous ai pas compris parfaitement.
G: Verzeihung, ich habe Sie nicht richtig verstanden.
I: Mi scusi, non ho capito bene.
P: Desculpe-me, mas não percebi completamente.
S: Perdón, no le he comprendido del todo.

344. You speak too fast for me. Please speak more slowly.
F: Vous parlez trop vite pour moi. Parlez plus lentement, s'il vous plaît.
G: Sie sprechen zu schnell für mich. Sprechen Sie bitte etwas langsamer!
I: Lei parla troppo velocemente per me. Per favore, parli più lentamente (OR adagio).
P: Fala muito depressa para mim. Por favor, fale mais devagar!
S: Ud. habla demasiado rápido (OR de prisa) para mí. ¡Por favor, hable más despacio!

345. I know that I have to improve my pronunciation.
F: Je sais que je dois perfectionner ma prononciation.
G: Ich weiß, daß ich meine Aussprache noch verbessern muß.
I: So che devo migliorare la mia pronuncia.

P: Eu sei que tenho de melhorar a minha pronúncia.
S: Sé que debo mejorar mi pronunciación.

346. I will have to increase my vocabulary.
F: Il faut que j'augmente mon vocabulaire.
G: Ich muß meinen Wortschatz noch erweitern.
I: Devo arricchire il mio vocabolario.
P: Terei que aumentar o meu vocabulário.
S: Tendré que aumentar mi vocabulario.

347. I always try to speak in Spanish.
F: Je tâche toujours de parler en espagnol.
G: Ich versuche immer, Spanisch zu sprechen.
I: Cerco sempre di parlare in spagnolo.
P: Eu tento sempre falar espanhol.
S: Siempre intento hablar español.

**348. I take advantage of every opportunity to speak French
[read French books; see French films; listen to French
records and tapes].**
F: Je profite de toutes les occasions de parler français
[lire des livres en français; voir des films en français;
écouter des disques et des bandes magnétiques en
français].
G: Ich benütze jede Gelegenheit, um Französisch zu
sprechen [französische Bücher zu lesen; französische
Filme zu sehen; französische Schallplatten und Ton-
bandaufnahmen zu hören].
I: Approfitto di ogni opportunità per parlare francese
[leggere libri francesi; vedere dei film in francese;
ascoltare dischi e registrazioni in francese].
P: Eu aproveito todas as oportunidades para falar francês
[ler livros franceses; ver filmes franceses; ouvir discos
e gravações em francês].
S: Siempre aprovecho cada oportunidad para hablar
francés [leer libros en francés; ver películas (OR cintas)
en francés; escuchar discos y cintas (magnéticas)
grabadas en francés].

349. Did you understand what I was saying?
F: Avez-vous compris ce que j'ai dit?
G: Haben Sie verstanden, was ich gesagt habe?
I: Ha capito quello che ho detto?
P: Compreendeu (OR Percebeu) o que eu disse?
S: ¿Ha entendido (OR comprendido) Ud. lo que he dicho?

350. Do you understand what you are reading?
F: Comprenez-vous ce que vous lisez?
G: Verstehen Sie, was Sie lesen?
I: Capisce quello che sta leggendo?
P: Compreende o que está a ler?*
S: ¿Entiende (OR Comprende) Ud. lo que está leyendo?

351. I do not understand this sentence [this word; the question; the answer].
F: Je ne comprends pas cette phrase [ce mot; la question; la réponse].
G: Diesen Satz [dieses Wort; die Frage; die Antwort] verstehe ich nicht.
I: Non capisco questa frase [questa parola; la domanda; la risposta].
P: Eu não compreendo (OR percebo) esta frase [esta palavra; a pergunta; a resposta].
S: No comprendo esta frase [esta palabra; la pregunta; la respuesta].

352. Can you explain this to me?
F: Pouvez-vous m'expliquer ceci?
G: Können Sie mir das erklären?
I: Può spiegarmi questo?
P: Pode-me explicar isto?
S: ¿Me puede explicar esto?

353. I will try to translate this for you.
F: Je vais essayer de vous traduire ceci.
G: Ich werde versuchen, das für Sie zu übersetzen.

* In Brazil *está lendo.*

I: Cercherò di tradurLe questo.
P: Tentarei traduzir-lhe isto.
S: Trataré de traducirle esto a Ud.

354. Have you a dictionary by any chance?

F: Avez-vous par hasard un dictionnaire?
G: Haben Sie zufällig ein Wörterbuch?
I: Ha per caso un dizionario?
P: Tem por acaso um dicionário?
S: ¿Tiene Ud. por casualidad un diccionario?

355. Does anyone here speak English?

F: Y a-t-il quelqu'un qui parle anglais?
G: Spricht hier irgendjemand Englisch?
I: C'è qualcuno qui che parla inglese?
P: Há alguém aqui que fale inglês?
S: ¿Hay alguien aquí que hable inglés?

356. I speak it a little.

F: Je le parle un peu.
G: Ich kann es ein wenig.
I: Io lo parlo un pochino.
P: Eu falo um pouco.
S: Yo lo hablo un poco.

357. I can understand everything, but I cannot speak it.

F: Je peux tout comprendre, mais je ne le parle pas.
G: Ich kann alles verstehen, aber ich spreche es nicht.
I: Capisco tutto, ma non posso parlare.
P: Eu compreendo tudo, mas não posso falar.
S: Puedo entenderlo todo, pero no puedo hablarlo.

358. I have forgotten that word.

F: J'ai oublié ce mot.
G: Ich habe das Wort vergessen.
I: Ho dimenticato questa parola.
P: Eu esqueci-me dessa palavra.
S: He olvidado esta palabra.

359. I do not remember.
F: Je ne me souviens pas (OR Je ne me rappelle pas).
G: Ich kann mich nicht erinnern.
I: Non mi ricordo.
P: Eu não me lembro.
S: No lo recuerdo.

360. I am going to ask the other stewardess.
F: Je vais le demander à l'autre hôtesse.
G: Ich werde die andere Stewardeß fragen.
I: Lo domando all'altra hostess.
P: Vou perguntar à outra hospedeira.*
S: Voy a preguntar a la otra stewardess.

361. Do you have much trouble understanding me?
F: Avez-vous beaucoup de difficulté à me comprendre?
G: Haben Sie Schwierigkeiten, mich zu verstehen?
I: È molto difficile per Lei capirmi?
P: É-lhe muito difícil perceber-me?
S: ¿Le es muy difícil a Ud. el entenderme?

362. No, on the contrary, it is very easy.
F: Non, au contraire, c'est très facile.
G: Nein, im Gegenteil, es geht sehr gut.
I: No, al contrario, è molto facile.
P: Não, pelo contrário, é muito fácil.
S: No, al contrario, es muy fácil.

363. I am not feeling well.
F: Je ne me sens pas bien.
G: Ich fühle mich nicht wohl.
I: Non mi sento bene.
P: Eu não me sinto bem.
S: No me siento bien.

* In Brazil *aeromoça.*

364. Do you have some tablets for airsickness?
 F: Avez-vous des pilules contre le mal d'avion?
 G: Haben Sie Tabletten gegen Luftkrankheit?
 I: Ha delle pillole per il mal d'aria?
 P: Tem algum comprimido para o enjôo?
 S: ¿Tiene Ud. algunas tabletas (OR píldoras, pastillas) contra el mal de vuelo?

365. I have a headache.
 F: J'ai mal à la tête.
 G: Ich habe Kopfschmerzen.
 I: Ho mal di testa.
 P: Eu tenho dor de cabeça.
 S: Tengo dolor de cabeza.

366. I have a buzzing in my ears.
 F: Mes oreilles bourdonnent.
 G: Ich habe Ohrensausen.
 I: Ho un ronzio nelle orecchie.
 P: Eu tenho um zumbido nos meus ouvidos.
 S: Tengo zumbidos en los oídos.

367. I am very tired. I want to sleep.
 F: Je suis très fatigué (FEM. fatiguée). Je veux dormir.
 G: Ich bin sehr müde. Ich möchte schlafen.
 I: Sono molto stanco (FEM. stanca). Vorrei dormire.
 P: Estou muito cansado (FEM. cansada). Gostava de dormir.
 S: Estoy muy cansado (FEM. cansada). Deseo dormir.

368. Here is a pillow [a blanket] for you.
 F: Voici un oreiller [une couverture] pour vous.
 G: Hier ist ein Kissen [eine Decke] für Sie!
 I: Ecco un cuscino [una coperta] per Lei!
 P: Aqui tem uma almofada [um cobertor] para si!
 S: Aquí hay una almohada [una manta (OR frazada)] para Ud.

369. **Would you please turn off the light?**
F: Voulez-vous, s'il vous plaît, éteindre la lumière?
G: Würden Sie bitte das Licht ausmachen (OR ausschalten)?
I: Per favore, spenga la luce!
P: Fazia o favor de apagar a luz?
S: ¡Por favor, apague la luz!

370. **Please wake me up at ——— o'clock.**
F: Veuillez me réveiller à ——— heures.
G: Wecken Sie mich bitte um ——— Uhr!
I: Per favore, mi svegli alle ———.
P: Por favor, acorde-me às ——— horas!
S: ¡Por favor, despiérteme a las ———!

371. **I shall not forget to wake you up at ———.**
F: Je n'oublierai pas de vous réveiller à ——— heures.
G: Ich werde nicht vergessen, Sie um ——— Uhr zu wecken.
I: Non dimenticherò di svegliarLa alle ———.
P: Não me esquecerei de o (TO FEM. a) acordar às ——— horas.
S: No me olvidaré despertarle a las ———.

372. **Did you sleep well?**
F: Avez-vous bien dormi?
G: Haben Sie gut geschlafen?
I: Ha dormito bene?
P: Dormiu bem?
S: ¿Durmió bien?

373. **Unfortunately I could not sleep.**
F: Malheureusement je n'ai pas pu dormir.
G: Leider konnte ich nicht schlafen.
I: Purtroppo non ho potuto dormire.
P: Infelizmente não consegui (OR pude) dormir.
S: Desgraciadamente no pude dormir.

374. What is the date today?
F: Quelle est la date aujourd'hui?
G: Den wievielten haben wir heute?
I: Quanti ne abbiamo oggi?
P: A quantos estamos hoje?
S: ¿Qué fecha es hoy?

375. March nineteenth. April first.
F: Le dix-neuf mars. Le premier avril.
G: Den neunzehnten März. Den ersten April.
I: Il diciannove marzo. Il primo aprile.
P: O dezenove de março. O primeiro de abril.
S: El diez y nueve de marzo. El primero de abril.

376. What day of the week is it?
F: Quel jour sommes-nous?
G: Welcher Tage ist heute?
I: Che giorno è oggi?
P: Que dia é hoje?
S: ¿Qué día de la semana es hoy?

377. Today is Wednesday.
F: C'est aujourd'hui mercredi.
G: Heute ist Mittwoch.
I: Oggi è mercoledì.
P: Hoje é quarta-feira.
S: Hoy es miércoles.

378. This week; next month; last year.
F: Cette semaine; le mois prochain; l'année dernière.
G: Diese Woche; nächsten Monat; voriges Jahr.
I: Questa settimana; il mese prossimo; l'anno scorso
(OR passato).
P: Esta semana; o próximo mês (OR o mês seguinte); o
ano passado.
S: Esta semana; el próximo mes; el año pasado.

379. **In spring; in summer; in the fall** (OR **autumn**); **in winter.**
    F: Au printemps; en été; en automne; en hiver.
    G: Im Frühling; im Sommer; im Herbst; im Winter.
    I: Durante la primavera; nell'estate; nell'autunno; nell'inverno.
    P: Na primavera; no verão; no outono; no inverno.
    S: En primavera; en verano; en otoño; en invierno.

380. **What is your favorite season?**
    F: Quelle est votre saison favorite (OR préférée)?
    G: Welche Jahreszeit haben Sie am liebsten?
    I: Quale stagione preferisce?
    P: Qual é a sua estação preferida?
    S: ¿Cuál es su estación favorita (OR preferida)?

381. **Do you like swimming [do you like ice skating; do you like skiing; do you like horseback riding?]**
    F: Aimez-vous nager [aimez-vous patiner; aimez-vous faire du ski; aimez-vous monter à cheval]?
    G: Schwimmen Sie gerne [laufen Sie gerne Schlittschuh; laufen Sie gerne Schi (OR Ski); reiten Sie gerne]?
    I: Le piace il nuoto [le piace il pattinaggio sul ghiaccio; le piace lo sci; le piace l'equitazione]?
    P: Gosta de nadar [gosta da patinagem no gelo; gosta de esquiar; gosta da equitação]?
    S: ¿Le gusta Ud. nadar [le gusta patinar sobre hielo; le gusta esquiar; le gusta montar a caballo]?

382. **I prefer playing tennis [golf].**
    F: Je préfère jouer au tennis [au golf].
    G: Ich spiele lieber Tennis [Golf].
    I: Preferisco giocare a tennis [a golf].
    P: Eu prefiro jogar ténis [golfe].
    S: Prefiero jugar al tenis [al golf].

383. **Tell me, please, where can I buy duty-free liquor?**
    F: Dites-moi, s'il vous plaît, où puis-je acheter des liqueurs détaxées?

G: Können Sie mir bitte sagen, wo ich zollfreie Getränke kaufen kann?

I: Mi dica, per favore, dove posso comprare liquori esenti da tasse doganali?

P: Diga-me, por favor, onde posso comprar bebidas isentas da taxa?

S: Dígame, por favor, ¿dónde puedo comprar bebidas libres (OR exentas) de impuesto?

384. Most airports have their own duty-free stores.

F: La plupart des aéroports ont leurs propres boutiques détaxées.

G: Die meisten Flughäfen haben ihre eigenen zollfreien Läden.

I: Quasi tutti gli aeroporti hanno un magazzino per merce esente da tasse doganali.

P: A maioria dos aeroportos tem os seus armazéns de isenção de taxas.

S: La mayoría de los aeropuertos tienen tiendas donde venden libre de impuestos.

385. *To an intoxicated passenger:* I am sorry, Sir, but we are not allowed to serve you any more drinks.

F: *À un passager enivré:* Je suis désolé (FEM. désolée), Monsieur, mais nous ne pouvons plus vous servir à boire.

G: *Zu einem betrunkenen Passagier:* Es tut mir leid, mein Herr, aber wir dürfen Ihnen keine Getränke mehr servieren.

I: *Ad un passeggero ubriaco:* Mi dispiace, Signore, ma non possiamo servirLe altri liquori.

P: *Para um passageiro embriagado:* Lamento, mas não nos é permitido servir-lhe mais bebidas.

S: *A un pasajero ebrio:* Lo siento, pero no podemos servirle más bebidas.

386. We have to take the bottle away from you.

F: Nous devons vous enlever cette bouteille.

G: Wir müssen Ihnen die Flasche wegnehmen.
I: Dobbiamo portare via la bottiglia.
P: Nós temos que retirar-lhe a garrafa.
S: Tenemos que retirarle la botella.

387. **To a passenger smoking a cigar: Would you be kind enough to refrain from smoking the cigar?**
    F: *À un passager fumant un cigare:* Ayez la bonté de cesser de fumer le cigare.
    G: *Zu einem zigarrerauchenden Passagier:* Würden Sie so freundlich sein, das Zigarrenrauchen einzustellen?
    I: *Ad un passaggero che fuma un sigaro:* Vuole essere così gentile di non fumare il sigaro?
    P: *Para um passageiro fumando charuto:* Agradeceríamos se não fumasse charuto.
    S: *A un pasajero fumando un cigarro* (OR *puro*): ¿Tendría la bondad de abstenerse de fumar el cigarro (OR puro)?

388. **You may go to the back and smoke just one.**
    F: Vous pouvez aller à l'arrière et en fumer un seulement.
    G: Sie können nach hinten gehen und *eine* Zigarre rauchen.
    I: Può andare dietro a fumarne uno soltanto.
    P: Pode ir para a rectaguarda e fumar sòmente um charuto.
    S: Puede ir al fondo y ahí puede fumar uno.

389. **The smoke in the air system can be nauseating to passengers who have a weak stomach.**
    F: La fumée du cigare avec le systeme d'air conditionné peut incommoder les passagers ayant un estomac délicat.
    G: Der Rauch in der Luft kann Übelkeit bei den Passagieren hervorrufen, die einen empfindlichen Magen haben.
    I: Il fumo nell'aria può nauseare i passeggeri che soffrono di stomaco.

P: O fumo no sistema de ventilação pode ser nausea-bundo para os passageiros com estômago sensível.

S: El humo en el aire puede causar malestar a otros pasajeros con estómago delicado.

390. Thanks very much for your cooperation, Sir.

F: Je vous remercie beaucoup de votre compréhension, Monsieur!

G: Vielen Dank für Ihr Verständnis.

I: Grazie per la Sua cooperazione, Signore.

P: Muito obrigado (FEM. obrigada) pela sua cooperação.

S: ¡Gracias por su comprensión, Señor!

391. I am very sorry, but pipe smoking is forbidden by the international regulations.

F: Je suis désolé (FEM. désolée), mais les règlements internationaux interdisent de fumer la pipe.

G: Es tut mir leid, aber das Pfeiferauchen ist nach den internationalen Vorschriften verboten.

I: Mi dispiace, ma il fumare la pipa è vietato da regola-menti internazionali.

P: Lamento imenso, mas os regulamentos internacionais proibem fumar cachimbo.

S: Lo siento, pero el fumar en pipa está prohibido por reglamentos internacionales.

392. Sit here and chat with me!

F: Asseyez-vous ici et bavardez un peu avec moi!

G: Setzen Sie sich bitte hierher und unterhalten Sie sich ein bißchen mit mir!

I: Perchè non si siede qui e chiacchera con me?

P: Porque não se senta aqui e conversa um pouco comigo?

S: Siéntase por favor y charle conmigo.

393. I would like to, but I have a few more things to do.

F: Je le voudrais bien, mais j'ai encore quelque chose à faire.

G: Ich würde es gern tun, aber ich muß noch einige Sachen erledigen.

I: Mi piacerebbe, ma ho ancora da fare.

P: Eu gostaria, mas tenho algumas coisas mais para fazer.

S: Me gustaría hacerlo, pero tengo unas otras cosas que hacer.

394. Is this your first flight with us?

F: Est-ce votre premier vol avec nous?

G: Ist dies Ihr erster Flug mit uns?

I: È questo il Suo primo volo con noi?

P: É este o seu primeiro vôo connosco?*

S: ¿Es la primera vez que vuela con nosotros?

395. I hope you have enjoyed this flight so far.

F: J'espère que vous soyez satisfait (TO FEM. satisfaite) de ce vol jusqu'à présent.

G: Ich hoffe, daß dieser Flug Ihnen bis jetzt gefallen hat.

I: Spero che fino ad ora Le sia piacuto il volo.

P: Espero que o vôo até agora lhe tenha sido agradável.

S: Espero que esté disfrutando su viaje.

396. Certainly, I have enjoyed it, except that I feel so nervous because this plane is shaking.

F: Certainement, je suis satisfait (FEM. satisfaite), bien que les secousses de l'appareil m'inquiètent.

G: Es hat mir schon gefallen, nur bin ich so nervös, weil diese Maschine rüttelt.

I: Certamente mi è piacuto, eccetto che sono molto nervoso (FEM. nervosa) perchè l'aereo si agita.

P: Certamente que eu tenho gostado, contudo sinto-me muito nervoso (FEM. nervosa) porque este avião tem abanado.

S: Ciertamente lo estoy disfrutando, salvo que estoy siempre nervioso (FEM. nerviosa) porque el avión se sacude.

* In Brazil *conosco*.

397. I would not worry about that. It is just a mild turbulence.
F: Cela ne m'inquièterait pas, ce sont des secousses normales.
G: Ich würde mich darüber nicht aufregen, es ist nur eine leichte Turbulenz.
I: Non si preoccupi per questo, è solo una leggera turbolenza.
P: Eu não me preocuparia porque é sòmente uma turbulência ligeira.
S: No me preocuparía, ya que es una pequeña turbulencia en el aire.

398. It is very much like rough weather on the ocean, except that we cannot see the waves.
F: C'est à peu près comme du mauvais temps sur l'océan, sauf que nous ne voyons pas les vagues.
G: Es ist ungefähr so wie bei stürmischem Wetter auf dem Meer, nur daß wir die Wellen nicht sehen können.
I: È simile al cattivo tempo sull'oceano, eccetto che non possiamo vedere le onde.
P: É muito parecido com o mau tempo no oceano, excepto que não podemos ver as ondas.
S: Este fenómeno es parecido al oleaje en el océano, salvo que no vemos las olas.

399. *To an elderly passenger:* Are you going to visit your family?
F: *À un passager âgé:* Allez-vous visiter votre famille?
G: *Zu einem älteren Fluggast:* Wollen Sie Ihre Familie besuchen?
I: *Ad un passeggero anziano:* Va visitare la famiglia?
P: *Para um passageiro de idade:* Vai visitar a sua família?
S: *A una persona de edad:* ¿Va Ud. a visitar a sus familiares?

400. How long has it been since you have seen your family?
F: Depuis combien de temps n'avez-vous pas vu votre famille?
G: Wie lange ist es her, daß Sie Ihre Familie nicht mehr gesehen haben?
I: Quant'è che non vede la Sua famiglia?
P: Há quanto tempo não vê a sua família?
S: ¿Cuánto tiempo hace que no ha visto a sus familiares?

401. The last time I saw them was ten years ago.
F: Je les ai vus la dernière fois il y a dix ans.
G: Ich habe sie vor zehn Jahren zum letzten Mal gesehen.
I: L'ultima volta che ho visto i miei familiari è stato dieci anni fa.
P: A última vez que os vi foi há dez anos.
S: Los ví por última vez hace diez años.

402. Do they speak German?
F: Parlent-ils allemand?
G: Sprechen sie Deutsch?
I: Parlano tedesco?
P: Falam eles alemão?
S: ¿Hablan ellos alemán?

403. Yes, quite well.
F: Oui, assez bien.
G: Ja, ganz gut.
I: Sì, piuttosto bene.
P: Sim, bastante bem.
S: Sí, bastante bien.

404. Are you going to visit New York [Paris]?
F: Allez-vous visiter New York [Paris]?
G: Werden Sie New York [Paris] besichtigen?
I: Visiterà Nuova York [Parigi]?
P: Vai visitar Nova Iorque [Paris]?
S: ¿Va Ud. a visitar Nueva York [París]?

405. I am going to ———, then continuing to ——— and then returning by way of ———.

F: Je vais aller à ———, puis continuer vers ——— et ensuite retourner par ———.

G: Ich gehe nach ———, dann weiter nach ——— und dann zurück über ———.

I: Vado a ———, poi continuo per ——— e ritorno via ———.

P: Eu vou para ———, depois continuo para ——— e por fim regresso via ———.

S: Voy a ———, luego continuaré a ———, regresando vía (OR por) ———.

406. What days do you work and what days are you off?

F: Quels jours travaillez-vous et quels jours vous reposez-vous?

G: An welchen Tagen arbeiten Sie und welche Tage haben Sie frei?

I: In quali giorni lavora e in quali giorni riposa?

P: Em que dias trabalha e em que dias descansa?

S: ¿En qué días trabaja Ud. y en qué días descansa Ud.?

407. That depends on our monthly schedule.

F: Cela dépend de notre horaire mensuel.

G: Das hängt von unserem monatlichen Flugplan ab.

I: Dipende dal nostro orario mensile.

P: Isso depende do nosso horário mensal.

S: Eso depende de nuestro plan mensual de vuelo.

408. How many hours do you work on a flight?

F: Combien d'heures travaillez-vous en vol?

G: Wieviele Stunden arbeiten Sie auf einem Flug?

I: Quante ore lavora per volo?

P: Quantas horas trabalha num vôo?

S: ¿Cuántas horas trabaja Ud. en un vuelo?

409. We are always at the disposal of our passengers.
F: Nous sommes toujours à la disposition de nos passagers.
G: Wir stehen unseren Passagieren immer zur Verfügung.
I: Siamo sempre a disposizione dei nostri passeggeri.
P: Estamos sempre à disposição dos nossos passageiros.
S: Siempre estamos a la disposición de nuestros pasajeros.

410. We never leave them completely unattended.
F: Nous ne les laissons jamais seuls.
G: Wir lassen sie nie ganz alleine.
I: Non li lasciamo mai completamente soli.
P: Nós nunca os deixamos completamente sós.
S: Nunca les dejamos completamente solos.

411. Consequently, we take turns eating.
F: En conséquence nous mangeons à tour de rôle.
G: Demzufolge wechseln wir uns im Essen ab.
I: Di conseguenza, mangiamo a turno.
P: Em consequência, nós comemos por turnos.
S: Por lo tanto, turnamos para comer.

412. Because of turbulence we are compelled to put on the seat belt sign.
F: À cause de la turbulence nous sommes obligés d'allumer le signal d'attacher vos ceintures.
G: Wegen Turbulenz müssen wir das Zeichen zum Anschnallen einschalten.
I: A causa della turbolenza dobbiamo accendere il segnale per allacciare le cinture di sicurezza.
P: Em resultado de turbulência somos forçados a iluminar o sinal de pôr os cintos de segurança.
S: A causa del temporal (OR de la turbulencia) debemos encender* la señal de abrochar sus cinturones de seguridad.

* In South America *poner*.

413. You should not be afraid.
F: Vous ne devez pas vous inquiéter.
G: Sie brauchen keine Angst zu haben.
I: Non deve avere paura.
P: Não deve ter medo.
S: ¡No tema (OR ¡No tenga miedo)!

414. You will not fall out of the seat, because you have the seat belt on.
F: Votre ceinture de sécurité vous empêchera de tomber de votre siège.
G: Sie werden nicht aus dem Sitz fallen, da Sie den Sitzgurt anhaben.
I: Non cadrà dal posto perchè ha la cintura di sicurezza.
P: Não cairá do assento porque tem o cinto de segurança posto.
S: No se caerá del asiento porque tiene puesto el cinturón de seguridad.

415. Any noises that you hear are routine.
F: Tous les bruits que vous entendez sont normaux.
G: Irgendwelche Geräusche, die Sie hören, sind normal.
I: I rumori che sente sono normali.
P: Qualquer barulho que ouça é normal.
S: Los ruidos que oye son de rutina.

416. What is wrong? Is anything going to happen?
F: Que se passe-t-il? Va-t-il arriver quelque chose?
G: Was ist los? Wird etwas passieren?
I: Cosa c'è? Succederà qualcosa?
P: O que é que está mal? Vai suceder alguma coisa?
S: ¿Qué ocurre (OR ¿Qué pasa)? ¿Va a suceder algo?

417. There is nothing to worry about.
F: Il n'y a pas lieu de s'inquiéter.
G: Sie brauchen sich keine Sorgen zu machen.

I: Non c'è da preoccuparsi.
P: Não há nada que se preocupar.
S: No hay por qué preocuparse.

418. We are going through clear-air turbulence; therefore you do not see any clouds.

F: Nous passons une turbulence de clair air; c'est pourquoi vous ne voyez aucun nuage.
G: Wir fliegen durch Turbulenz in klarer Luft, darum sehen Sie keine Wolken.
I: Attraversiamo turbolenza in cielo sereno, quindi non si vedono nubi.
P: Nos vamos através de turbulência em céu limpo, por tanto não vê qualquer nuvem.
S: Atravesamos un ligero temporal pese al cielo despejado, por eso no ve ninguna nube.

419. I see the wings moving. Are they going to fall off?

F: Je vois les ailes qui bougent. Vont-elles tomber?
G: Ich sehe, daß sich die Tragflächen bewegen. Werden sie abfallen?
I: Vedo le ali muoversi. Cadranno?
P: Eu vejo as asas moverem-se. Irão cair?
S: Veo que se mueven las alas. ¿Se van a caer?

420. The wings of an aircraft are designed to be flexible.

F: Les ailes d'un avion sont prévues flexibles.
G: Die Maschine hat bewegliche Tragflächen.
I: Le ali degli aerei sono flessibili.
P: As asas de um avião são disenhadas para serem flexíveis.
S: Las alas del avión han sido diseñadas para que sean flexibles.

421. Please have no fear. The pilots have everything under control.

F: Ne vous inquiétez pas, s'il vous plaît. L'équipage a le contrôle absolu de l'appareil.

G: Bitte haben Sie keine Angst. Die Piloten haben alles unter Kontrolle.

I: Non abbia paura. I piloti hanno tutto sotto controllo.

P: Por favor, não tenha receio. Os pilotos têm tudo controlado.

S: Por favor, no tema, ya que los pilotos tienen todo bajo control.

422. I want to change my seat.

F: Je veux changer de siège.

G: Ich möchte meinen Platz wechseln.

I: Voglio cambiare il posto.

P: Eu quero mudar de lugar.

S: Deseo cambiar de asiento.

423. The passenger behind me is constantly singing.

F: Le passager derrière moi chante sans interruption.

G: Der Passagier hinter mir singt unaufhörlich.

I: Il passaggero dietro di me canta continuamente.

P: O passageiro atrás de mim canta constantemente.

S: El pasajero detrás mí canta continuamente.

424. I have been traveling a lot the last few days and I am very tired.

F: J'ai beaucoup voyagé ces derniers jours et je suis très fatigué (FEM. fatiguée).

G: Ich bin in den letzten Tagen ständig unterwegs gewesen und ich bin sehr müde.

I: Ho viaggiato molto in questi giorni e sono molto stanco (FEM. stanca).

P: Tenho viajado muito estes dias e estou muito cansado (FEM. cansada).

S: He viajado mucho durante estos días y estoy muy cansado (FEM. cansada).

425. Sir, could you kindly refrain from singing so loudly?

F: Monsieur, pourriez-vous, s'il vous plaît, vous abstenir de chanter si fort?

G: Mein Herr, würden Sie so freundlich sein und auf-
hören, so laut zu singen?

I: Signore, può farmi il piacere di non cantare così
forte?

P: Podia deixar de cantar tão alto?

S: Señor, ¿tendría la gentileza de dejar de cantar en voz
alta?

426. A few passengers have already complained.
F: Quelques passagers se sont déja plaints.
G: Ein paar Passagiere haben sich schon beschwert.
I: Qualche passeggero ha già reclamato.
P: Alguns passageiros já se queixaram.
S: Algunos de los pasajeros ya se han quejado.

427. Please turn off the lights.
F: S'il vous plaît, éteignez la lumière.
G: Machen Sie das Licht aus, bitte!
I: Spenga le luci, per favore.
P: Por favor, apague as luzes.
S: Por favor, apague la luz.

428. Have a good rest. Good night.
F: Reposez-vous bien. Bonne nuit.
G: Ruhen Sie sich gut aus! Gute Nacht.
I: Buon riposo. Buona notte.
P: Tenha um bom descanso. Boa noite.
S: ¡Qué Ud. descanse bien! ¡Buenas noches!

429. If you need anything, just call me.
F: Si vous avez besoin de quelque chose, appelez-moi!
G: Wenn Sie irgendetwas brauchen, rufen Sie mich!
I: Se ha bisogno di qualcosa, mi chiami.
P: Se precisar de alguma coisa, basta chamar-me.
S: Si necesita algo, llámeme.

Eating and Drinking

F: REPAS ET BOISSONS
G: ESSEN UND TRINKEN
I: MANGIARE E BERE
P: REFEIÇÕES E BEBIDAS
S: COMIDAS Y BEBIDAS

430. At what time do you serve breakfast [lunch; dinner]?
F: À quelle heure servez-vous le petit déjeuner [le déjeuner; le dîner]?
G: Um wieviel Uhr werden Sie Frühstück [Mittagessen; Abendessen] servieren?
I: A che ora servite la prima colazione [il pranzo; la cena]?
P: A que horas servem o pequeno almoço* [o almoço; o jantar]?
S: ¿A qué hora sirven el desayuno [el almuerzo; la cena]?

431. Generally at ——— o'clock; in an hour; in a half hour.
F: Généralement à ——— heures; dans une heure; dans une demi-heure.
G: Im allgemeinen um ——— Uhr; in einer Stunde; in einer halben Stunde.
I: Generalmente alle ———; fra un'ora; fra mezz'ora.
P: Normalmente às ——— horas; dentro de uma hora; dentro de hora e meia.
S: Generalmente a las ———; dentro de una hora; dentro de media hora.

432. ——— hours after take-off; ——— hours prior to arrival.
F: ——— heures après le décollage; ——— heures avant l'arrivée.

* In Brazil, "breakfast" is *o café da manhã*.